Challenges in natural language processing

Studies in Natural Language Processing
Branimir K. Boguraev, *Editor*

This series publishes monographs, texts, and edited volumes within the inter-disciplinary field of computational linguistics. It represents the range of topics of concern to the scholars working in this increasingly important field, whether their background is in formal linguistics, psycholinguistics, cognitive psychology, or artificial intelligence.

Also in this series:

Memory and context for language interpretation by Hiyan Alshawi
The linguistic basis of text generation by Laurence Danlos
Natural language parsing edited by David R. Dowty, Lauri Karttunen, and Arnold Zwicky
Relational models of the lexicon by Martha Walton Evens
Computational linguistics by Ralph Grishman
Semantic interpretation and the resolution of ambiguity by Graeme Hirst
Reference and computation by Amichai Kronfeld
Machine translation edited by Sergei Nirenburg
Semantic processing for finite domains by Martha Stone Palmer
Systemic text generation as problem solving by Terry Patten

Challenges in
natural language processing

Edited by
MADELEINE BATES
and
RALPH M. WEISCHEDEL

BBN Systems and Technologies
Cambridge, MA

CAMBRIDGE
UNIVERSITY PRESS

Published by the Press Syndicate of the University of Cambridge
The Pitt Building, Trumpington Street, Cambridge CB2 1RP
40 West 20th Street, New York, NY 10011–4211, USA
10 Stamford Road, Oakleigh, Victoria 3166, Australia

First published 1993

Printed in the United States of America

Library of Congress Cataloging-in-Publication Data
Challenges in natural language processing / edited by Madeleine Bates.
Ralph M. Weischedel.
   p.   cm. — (Studies in natural language processing)
Chiefly papers presented at a symposium held in Cambridge, Mass.
from Nov. 29, 1989 to Dec. 1, 1989 and sponsored by the Science
Development Program of Bolt, Beranek, and Newman, Inc.
Includes index.
ISBN 0–521–41015–0 (hardback)
1. Computational linguistics – Congresses.   I. Bates, Madeleine.
II. Weischedel, Ralph M.   III. Series.
P98.C45   1992
410'.285–dc20   91–45913
                                                          CIP

A catalog record for this book is available from the British Library.

ISBN 0–521–41015–0 hardback

Contents

Part VI. Conclusion

Preface

Throughout most of the 1960s, 1970s, and 1980s, computational linguistics enjoyed an excellent reputation. A sense of the promise of the work to society was prevalent, and high expectations were justified by solid, steady progress in research.

Nevertheless, by the close of the 1980s, many people openly expressed doubt about progress in the field. Are the problems of human language too hard to be solved even in the next eighty years? What measure(s) (other than the number of papers published) show significant progress in the last ten years? Where is the technology successfully deployed in the military, with revolutionary impact? In what directions should the field move, to ensure progress and avoid stagnation?

The symposium

A symposium on Future Directions in Natural Language Processing was held at Bolt Beranek and Newman, Inc. (BBN), in Cambridge, Massachusetts, from November 29, 1989, to December 1, 1989.

The symposium, sponsored by BBN's Science Development Program, brought together top researchers in a variety of areas to discuss the most significant problems and challenges that will face the field of computational linguistics in the next two to ten years. Speakers were encouraged to present both recently completed and speculative work, and to focus on topics that will have the most impact on the field in the coming decade. They were asked to reconsider unsolved problems of long standing as well as to present new opportunities. The purpose was to contribute to long-range planning by funding agencies, research groups, academic institutions, graduate students, and others interested in computational linguistics.

The thirty-six symposium attendees, who are listed following this preface, were all invited participants. They included speakers, respondents to papers, and people from government, industry, and academia. Though varying greatly in age and in backgrounds, they all shared a strong interest in computational linguistics.

The format of the meeting provided for one-and-a-half-hour presentations, much longer than at most conferences, in order to give speakers sufficient time to present ideas completely. The schedule also allowed plenty of time for lively discussions. A brief review of the symposium was published by Mark Maybury in the Summer 1990 issue of *AI Magazine*.

The papers and the book

We have taken the liberty of arranging the chapters in this book in a slightly different order than they were presented at the symposium. This allows our own paper, "Critical Challenges for NLP," to come first, both to set the tone for the subsequent papers and to provide a number of definitions and examples that may be helpful to readers who are not fully familiar with this field.

The three "traditional" areas of NLP – syntax, semantics, and pragmatics – all focus on language that is made up of words (or entities very similar to words). It is curious that the study of words themselves has not traditionally been a major area of interest in computational linguistics. Perhaps this is because it has always been assumed that each NL system has its own, usually small (under 5,000 words) lexicon that has been developed by hand for the application under study.

One of the key insights of the BBN symposium is that more attention must be paid to the development of large, sharable lexicons that are produced specifically for use by NL systems. Traditional dictionaries have been produced for use in book form by humans, but this is completely inadequate for computational applications.

The three papers that form Part II, Building the lexicon, address these issues. Sue Atkins (Oxford University Press), whose talk was originally titled "Beware the lexicon" but appears here as "The contribution of lexicography," gives a lexicographer's view of a proposed structure for lexical entries. Beth Levin (Northwestern University) provides an analysis of verbs, specifically verbs of making sound, that allows for the handling of new uses of known words. Branimir Boguraev (IBM Yorktown Heights) discusses the use of machine-readable sources to construct thesauri and other knowledge bases.

The areas of semantics and knowledge representation remain closely coupled and of great import. Robert Moore (SRI International) presents a study of the adverb, a part of speech that has been largely ignored in the past. James Allen (University of Rochester) provides an excellent discussion of the use of ambiguity and a related concept, vagueness, in logical form.

The subject of discourse has been receiving increased attention in the past few years. Rebecca Passonneau (Paramax) addresses this important issue. Mark Steedman (University of Pennsylvania) originally titled his presentation "Prosody, parsing, and discourse," and thus it is included in the discourse section, although its title here is "Surface structure, intonation, and discourse meaning."

It has long been the goal of many researchers to integrate speech processing techniques (such as speech recognition) with natural language processing to produce systems capable of understanding spoken language. Janet Pierrehumbert

(Northwestern University) argues that a rich model of prosodic structure is necessary to understand how prosody and intonation convey information about attention and intention.

The book concludes with the results of a lengthy and lively discussion on the future of computational linguistics. This discussion attempted to enumerate some of the most important problems to be tackled in the next few years and to describe what will be needed to solve them.

The papers that were presented at the BBN symposium represent not only cutting-edge research on familiar topics but also new directions for the field. This is indicated by the presence of such topics as the lexicon and speech (and the absence of such topics as parsers and grammars), which would not have been the case in a similar meeting held even five years ago.

The purpose of this volume is to convey that excitement, to suggest concrete ideas that the contributing authors think most promising for future research, and to encourage the readers to pursue ideas for a new generation of NLP technology.

Madeleine Bates
Ralph M. Weischedel

Symposium participants

JAMES F. ALLEN
University of Rochester (s) (r)

B. T. SUE ATKINS
Oxford University Press (s)

MADELEINE BATES
BBN Systems & Technologies (s)

ROBERT J. BOBROW
BBN Systems & Technologies (s) (r)

BRANIMIR K. BOGURAEV
IBM Research (s)

YEN-LU CHOW
BBN Systems & Technologies

STEPHEN DENNIS
Department of Defense

JOYCE FRIEDMAN
Boston University

JANE GRIMSHAW
Brandeis University

HENRY HAMBURGER
George Mason University

ROBERT J. P. INGRIA
BBN Systems & Technologies

BORIS KATZ
MIT AI Laboratory

BETH LEVIN
Northwestern University

MARK MAYBURY
RADC

ROBERT MERCER
IBM Research (r)

CHRISTENE MONTGOMERY
LIS (r)

ROBERT C. MOORE
SRI International (s)

REBECCA J. PASSONNEAU
Paramax (s)

JANET PIERREHUMBERT
Northwestern University (s)

JAMES PUSTEJOVSKY
Brandeis University (r)

RICHARD SCHWARTZ
BBN Systems & Technologies (s)

STEPHANIE SENEFF
MIT

VARDA SHAKED
BBN Systems & Technologies

CANDY SIDNER
Digital Equipment Corporation (r)

NORM SONDHEIMER
GE Research (r)

MARK STEEDMAN
University of Pennsylvania (s)

MIKE THOMAS
KSC, Inc.

DONALD WALKER
Bellcore (r)

(s) indicates a speaker.

(r) indicates a respondent.

x

SHARON WALTER
RADC

RAND WALTZMAN
DARPA/ISTO

CHARLES L. WAYNE
DARPA/ISTO

BONNIE LYNN WEBBER
University of Pennsylvania

RALPH M. WEISCHEDEL
BBN Systems & Technologies (s)

DOUGLAS WHITE
RADC

COLIN WIGHTMAN
Boston University

WILLIAM WOODS
Harvard Univesity (r)

PART I

Challenging problems

1   Critical challenges for natural language processing

MADELEINE BATES, ROBERT J. BOBROW,
AND RALPH M. WEISCHEDEL

1.1   Introduction

Although natural language processing (NLP) has come very far in the last twenty years, the technology has not yet achieved a revolutionary impact on society. Is this because of some fundamental limitation that can never be overcome? Is it because there has not been enough time to refine and apply theoretical work that has already been done?

We believe it is neither. We believe that several critical issues have never been adequately addressed in either theoretical or applied work, and that, because of a number of recent advances that we will discuss, the time is due for great leaps forward in the generality and utility of NLP systems. This paper focuses on roadblocks that seem surmountable within the next ten years.

Rather than presenting new results, this paper identifies the problems that we believe must block widespread use of computational linguistics, and that can be solved within five to ten years. These are the problems that most need additional research and most deserve the talents and attention of Ph.D. students. We focus on the following areas, which will have maximum impact when combined in software systems:

1. *Knowledge acquisition* from natural language (NL) texts of various kinds, from interactions with human beings, and from other sources. Language processing requires lexical, grammatical, semantic, and pragmatic knowledge. Current knowledge acquisition techniques are too slow and too difficult to use on a wide scale or on large problems. Knowledge bases should be many times the size of current ones.
2. *Interaction with multiple underlying systems* to give NL systems the utility and flexibility demanded by people using them. Single application systems are limited in both usefulness and the language that is necessary to communicate with them.

Some of the work reported here was supported by the Advanced Research Projects Agency under Contracts No. N00014-85-C-0016 and N00014-89-C-008, monitored by the Office of Naval Research. The views and conclusions contained in this document are those of the authors and should not be interpreted as necessarily representing the official policies, either expressed or implied, of the Defense Advanced Research Projects Agency of the United States Government.

3

3. *Partial understanding* gleaned from multi-sentence language, or from fragments of language. Approaches to language understanding that require perfect input or that try to produce perfect output seem doomed to failure because novel language, incomplete language, and errorful language are the norm, not the exception.

In the following sections, we first present a brief overview of the state of the art in the traditional areas of syntax, semantics, and pragmatics. Then each of the three critical challenge topics is discussed in a separate section, beginning with an explanation of the problem and its importance, and continuing through with an explanation of the techniques that we believe are now ready to be applied to those problems. Each section concludes with a summary of the challenges and the suggested new approaches.

1.2   State of the art

The most visible results in NLP in the last five years are several commercially available systems for database question-answering. These systems, the result of transferring technology developed in the 1970s and early 1980s, have been successfully used to improve productivity by replacing fourth-generation database query languages. The following case study (Bates, 1989) illustrates their capabilities: with 8-person-weeks, the Parlance™ system[1] was ported to a Navy relational database of 666 fields (from 75 relations) with a vocabulary of over 6,000 (root) words. Queries from a new user of one of these systems succeed 60–80% of the time; with use of the system, users naturally and automatically adjust to what data is in the database and to the limits of the language understood by the system, giving a success rate of 80–95% depending on the individual.

The success of these systems has depended on the fact that sufficient coverage of the language is possible with relatively simple semantic and discourse models. The semantics are bounded by the semantics of the relations used in databases and by the fact that words have a restricted number of meanings in one domain. The discourse model for a query is usually limited to the previous answer (usually numeric, simple strings, or a table) and the noun phrases mentioned in the last few queries.

The limitations of today's practical language processing technology have been summarized (Weischedel et al., 1990) as follows:

1. Domains must be narrow enough so that the constraints on the relevant semantic concepts and relations can be expressed using current knowledge representation techniques, i.e., primarily in terms of types and sorts. Processing may be viewed abstractly as the application of recur-

---

[1]Parlance is a trademark of BBN Systems and Technologies.

sive tree rewriting rules, including filtering out trees not matching a certain pattern.

2. Handcrafting is necessary, particularly in the grammatical components of systems (the component technology that exhibits least dependence on the application domain). Lexicons and axiomatizations of critical facts must be developed for each domain, and these remain time-consuming tasks.

3. The user must still adapt to the machine, but, as the products testify, the user can do so effectively.

4. Current systems have limited discourse capabilities that are almost exclusively handcrafted. Thus current systems are limited to viewing interaction, translation, and writing and reading text as processing a sequence of either isolated sentences or loosely related paragraphs. Consequently, the user must adapt to such limited discourse.

It is traditional to divide natural language phenomena (and components of systems designed to deal with them) into three classes:

1. Syntactic phenomena – those that pertain to the *structure* of a sentence and the order of words in the sentence, based on the grammatical classes of words rather than their meaning.

2. Semantic phenomena – those that pertain to the *meaning* of a sentence relatively independent of the context in which that language occurs.

3. Pragmatic phenomena – those that relate the meaning of a sentence to the *context* in which it occurs. This context can be linguistic (such as the previous text or dialogue), or nonlinguistic (such as knowledge about the person who produced the language, about the goals of the communication, about the objects in the current visual field, etc.).

1.2.1 Syntax

Syntax is without doubt the most mature field of study in both computational linguistics and the closely related field of linguistics. The most thorough computational accounts of natural language phenomena exist for syntax; and grammars with very large coverage of English have existed since the early 1980s. Formalisms for describing syntactic phenomena, mathematical analyses of the expressive power of those formalisms, and computational properties of processors for those formalisms have existed for more than twenty-five years, since the definition of the Chomsky hierarchy (finite state languages, context-free languages, context-sensitive languages, and the recursively enumerable languages).

During the 1970s and most of the 1980s, the dominant NLP formalism for writing grammars of natural language was the augmented transmission network (ATN) (Woods, 1970), a procedural language that allowed compact statements of not only the context-free aspects of language but also the apparently context-sensitive aspects as well. In the late 1980s, a shift began from the ATN and its procedural aspects toward a declarative formalism. What the new dominant formalism will be is not yet clear, but a likely candidate is a class of grammar formalisms (Shieber, 1986) that combine context-free rules with unification as a way of compactly capturing both context-free and context-sensitive aspects of language. The declarative formalisms offer the promise of exploring alternative parsing algorithms and pose minimum constraints on parallel algorithms for parsing. This shift in the research community from procedural specifications of syntax, such as ATN grammars, to declarative specifications, such as unification grammars, parallels the similar shift in interest in programming language research away from procedural languages and toward newer functional programming languages and declarative representations.

Because syntax is by far the most mature area in natural language processing, it is difficult to foresee that further developments in syntax will have as great an impact on utility as would emphasis on research and development on other, less developed areas of technology.

1.2.2   Semantics

In semantics, much recent progress has been made by focusing on limited application domains. For database access, the semantics of the system can be confined to that of the individual entities, classes of entities, relationships among the entities, attributes of the entities, and the typical operations that are performed in database retrieval. This simplifies the problem of semantics in at least the following ways: first, the meaning of individual words and of the phrases they compose can be restricted to the domain-specific meanings actually modeled in the database. Instead of needing to come up with a very general semantics for each word, a very literal semantics providing the mapping from the words to the entities modeled in the database is all that is required, for the database could not provide additional information even if a more general semantics were available. Second, problems of semantic ambiguity regarding alternative senses for a word are reduced, for only those word senses corresponding to entities in the database will contribute to the search space of possible alternatives.

For the task of database updating from messages, a key simplifying condition is that the information sought can be characterized ahead of time. Suppose the goal is to update automatically a database regarding takeover bids. Suppose further that the information desired is the date of the bid, the bidder, the target, the percentage of stock sought, the value of the offer, and whether it is a friendly or hostile bid. A first approximation is that the remaining information in the article can be ignored. The assumption is that although other concepts may be mentioned in the message or news wire item, they normally do not impact the values of the fields to be updated in the database. If that assumption applies in the proposed message processing application, then one can model the literal semantics of those words and phrases that have a correlate in the data being sought. For cases where the proposed update would be in error because the unanalyzed text does impact the update, human review of the proposed update can minimize erroneous entries into the database. Semi-automatic update with a human in the loop may be more cost effective and timely than fully manual update and may be more desirable than not having the data at all.

No uniform semantics representation language has emerged, although three general classes of semantic representations are employed: those that allow one to state anything that arises in a propositional logic, those that allow expressions equivalent to a first-order logic, and those that allow expressions not representable in a first-order logic. Most framed-base representations are equivalent to a propositional logic, since they do not allow expression of quantifiers. Most systems for database retrieval use a first-order logic. Many research systems employ extensions beyond first-order logic, such as the modal intensional logic defined by Montague (1970). Encoding the semantics of all the words and phrases for a particular application domain is one of the most significant costs in bringing up a natural language system in a new application domain. Knowledge acquisition procedures that would reduce this cost would therefore have great impact on the applicability of the technology.

1.2.3   *Pragmatics*

The modeling of context and using context in understanding language is the most difficult, and therefore the least well-understood, area of natural language processing. Unlike programming languages where one can define contextual influence in a limited and controlled way, context is all-pervasive and very powerful in natural language communication.

Context is fundamental to communicating substantial information with few words. For instance, if one says, *How about Evans?*, those three words may suggest a lot. If the context had been that the immediately previous request was *List the salary, highest degree, race, and marital status of Jones*, then *How about Evans?* means *List the salary, highest degree, race, and marital status of Evans*. If the context has been your boss saying *I need someone to go to Phoenix next week without jeopardizing meeting the XYZ deadline*, then *How about Evans?* means *Consider Evans for going to Phoenix next week without jeopardizing meeting the XYZ deadline*.

The single phenomenon that has received the most attention in pragmatics is pronominal or other referring expressions. Progress has been substantial enough that pronouns *it, they, those*, etc.) and definite reference (*those submarines, the first three men*, etc.) can be used rather freely in today's systems.

1.3   Knowledge acquisition for language processing

It goes without saying that any NLP system must know a fair amount about words, language, and some subject area before being able to understand language. Currently, virtually all NLP systems operate using fairly laboriously hand-built knowledge bases. The knowledge bases may include both linguistic knowledge (morphological, lexical, syntactic, semantic, and discourse) and nonlinguistic knowledge (semantic world knowledge, pragmatic, planning, inference), and the knowledge in them may be absolute or probabilistic. (Not all of these knowledge bases are necessary for every NLP system.)

1.3.1   Types of knowledge

Typically, porting a NLP system to a new domain requires acquiring knowledge for the domain-dependent modules, which often include:

> *Domain model.* The major classes of entities in the domain and the relations among them must be specified. In a Navy command and control domain, example concepts are Naval unit, vessel, surface vessel, submarine, carrier, combat readiness ratings, and equipment classes. Class–subclass relationships must be specified, e.g., every carrier is a surface vessel, and every surface vessel is a vessel and a Naval unit. Other important relationships among concepts must be specified. For instance, each vessel has a single overall combat readiness rating, and each Navy unit has an equipment loadout (a list of equipment classes).
>
> *Lexical syntax.* Syntactic information about each word of the domain includes its part of speech (e.g., noun, verb, adjective, adverb, proper noun), its related forms (e.g., the plural of *ship* is regular *ships,* but the plural of *sheep* and *child* are irregular *sheep* and *children*), and its grammatical properties (e.g., the verb *sleep* is intransitive).
>
> *Lexical semantics.* For each word, its semantics must be specified as a concept in the domain model, a relation in the domain model, or some formula made up of concepts and relations of the domain model.
>
> *Mappings to the target application.* Transformations specify how to map each concept or relation of the domain model into an appropriate piece of code for the underlying application system. For example, to find out whether a given vessel is equipped with helicopters, one might have to check whether there is a "Y" in the HELO field of the VES table of the database.

Currently, domain-independent knowledge is usually hand-built and is not reacquired when moving to a new domain, although it may be necessary to "tweek" rules and extend this knowledge, again, often by hand. It includes:

> *Grammar rules.* Most rules of English grammar are domain independent, but almost every domain encountered in practice either turns up instances

of general rules that had not been encountered in previous domains, or requires that some domain-specific additions be made to the grammar. *General semantic interpretation rules.* Some semantic rules may be considered to be domain independent, such as the general entity/property relationship that is often expressed with the general verb "have" or the general preposition "of." To the extent that such general rules can be found and embedded in a system, they do not have to be redone for every new domain.

The success of all current NLP systems depends on what we call the Limited Domain Assumption, which may be stated as follows: one does not have to acquire domain-dependent information about words that do not denote some concept or relation in the domain. Another way of looking at this assumption is that it says understanding can be confined to a limited domain. The Limited Domain Assumption simplifies the problem of NLP in three ways: (1) formal modeling of the concepts and relationships of the domain is feasible, (2) enumeration of critical nonlinguistic knowledge is possible, and (3) both lexical and semantic ambiguity are limited. Reducing lexical ambiguity reduces the search space and improves effectiveness of most NL systems.

Those three facts have the combined effect of making it more tractable to determine what the user meant by a given input, among a welter of possibilities. But whether one tries to loosen the domain restrictions or is willing to live within them, it seems obvious (although we will examine this assumption later) that the more knowledge that is available to the system, the better its chances of understanding its input.

1.3.2   Types of knowledge acquisition

Just as there are many kinds of knowledge, there are a number of different ways of acquiring that knowledge:

> *Knowing by being pre-programmed* – this includes such things as handbuilt grammars and semantic interpretation rules.
>
> *Knowing by being told* – this includes things that a human can "tell" the system using various user-interface tools, such as semantic interpretation rules that can be automatically built from examples, selectional restrictions, and various lexical and morphological features.
>
> *Knowing by looking it up* – this means using references such as an online dictionary, where one can find exactly the information that is being sought.
>
> *Knowing by using source material* – this means using references such as an encyclopedia or a corpus of domain-relevant material, from which one might be able to find or infer the information being sought; it may also mean using large volumes of material as the source of probabilistic

Knowledge Type	Pre-Program	Being Told	Look It Up	From Sources	Figure It Out	Combined
Lexical (morph, etc)	o	o	X	X	X	X
Grammar rules	o					
Select. restrict.	o	o		X		
Domain semantics	o	o	X	X	X	
Real world semantics	o	o	X	X		
Plans	o	o				
Inference	o					

Figure 1.1. How natural language systems acquire knowledge, today (o) and in the near future (X).

knowledge (e.g., "bank" is more likely to mean a financial institution than the side of a river).

Knowing by figuring it out – this means using heuristics and the input itself (such as the part of speech of words surrounding an unknown word).

Knowing by using a combination of the above techniques – this may or may not involve human intervention.

Figure 1.1 shows, for a typical NLP system of the 1980s, which knowledge bases are derived from which processes, and where we expect significant changes in the near future. Notice that the ways of learning do not necessarily correspond to the types of knowledge in any direct way. Certainly all of the types of knowledge can be pre-programmed into an NLP system; indeed that is how most of the current systems were created. It is a fairly simple step from that to learning by being told – usually all that is needed is a nice user interface for creating the same structures that can be pre-programmed. It is not until we reach the level of knowing by looking it up that it seems right to use the word "learning" to describe what is going on.

The two areas of particular interest here are learning from sources, and learning by figuring it out, or some combination of these with learning by being told by a human being reserved for situations that cannot be covered by the other means.

Learning by looking it up

It is hard to learn by looking it up or from sources, but it is going to get easier.

On-line dictionaries and other reference books have been available for many years, as have bodies of text such as news wires and technical abstracts, but they have not enjoyed wide usage. Why not? It is not entirely a matter of cost, or speed of access. We believe there are four fundamental reasons why computational linguists have been avoiding these sources:

1. The required information is often not there.
2. Information is hard to extract from the sources.
3. Once extracted, the information is hard to use.
4. The information is often incomplete and/or incorrect.

Most domains use common English words with specialized meanings. For example, most dictionaries contain definitions of the words "virus" and "worm," but not with the meanings that are current in the computer industry. Even if a word is found with its appropriate meaning, the dictionary entry may lack information that is critical to the NL system (e.g., selectional restrictions). And if the word is found in a corpus of source material, how is the meaning to be inferred? As a larger volume of domain-specific material becomes available for many domains, this problem may be reduced, but it will always be with us.

Extracting detailed information about words or concepts from the kind of text found in dictionaries and encyclopedias is an enticing prospect, but it presents a chicken-and-egg problem. A system cannot read a dictionary or encyclopedia entry unless it knows all the words in the definition (and usually a great deal more). Since language of this type is often beyond the capabilities of NL systems (particularly those built on the premise that the input and output must be complete), NLP systems typically cannot read the reference material. One solution to this problem is to pre-process the reference material, as is being done by Mitch Marcus at the University of Pennsylvania in an effort to produce text roughly annotated with part of speech and syntactic structure.

Another solution is to relax the constraints on input and output of NLP systems, and to develop partial understanders that can glean some information from sources and, using that information, can re-read the sources to increase their understanding by bootstrapping. Recent work by Will Crowther (1989) has taken this approach quite successfully.

Learning from sources

Does knowing more mean that understanding is easier, or harder?

Suppose we solve the problem of extracting information about words and other things from reference books. Will that automatically mean that our NLP systems will perform better? There is strong evidence that this is not the case – because the increased lexical, syntactic, and semantic alternatives that are introduced by knowing, for example, all the parts of speech and all the possible meanings of all the words in a sentence can easily swamp a NL processor with an explosion of possible alternatives to explore, and unresolvable ambiguities may arise when exploring even just a few!

The last major reason for avoiding source material is that such sources, massive as they are, are inevitably incomplete and incorrect. Nearly all NLP systems deal with specific limited domains, generally rather technical domains (weather forecasts, Navy messages, banking, etc.) in which ordinary English words are given special or restricted meanings. Thus general sources such as dictionaries give meanings that are misleading or actually wrong, but the NLP system has no way of knowing this. It would be far better for the sources to have no information than to have the wrong information, but that is not realistic or even remotely possible.

Our conclusion is that dictionary and other source information will not be useful unless we learn how to focus NL processing, order meanings and partially understood phrases, and interact with other knowledge sources (including humans) when necessary. Fortunately, there are several ways of achieving these goals, including:

1. Representing ambiguity at many levels of processing in a computationally tractable way.
2. Using statistical probabilities at many levels to order choices and cut off low likelihood paths.

Learning by being told

Some situations will always call for learning by being told. To illustrate this, consider the following sentence:

Sebastian compensated his Glock.

Do you know what that means? What can you figure out, and how? Presumably you know that Sebastian is a male's name, although if you did not know that, you might find it out by consulting a good dictionary with a list of names. You already know the verb "compensate" (or can look it up), with meanings roughly comparable to "pay" and "make up for"; the latter meaning is unlikely since it requires a for-clause. The word "Glock" is a stumper. You are unlikely to find it in any dictionary or encyclopedia you have handy. It seems to be a proper noun, judging from the capitalization. You might guess that it is a person's name, although the use of the possessive pronoun with a proper name is quite unusual, and would probably carry some special meaning that cannot be figured out from the sentence itself. Perhaps you have some other hypothesis about the word "Glock". The point is, without help from a human being knowledgeable about the subject area (or an extremely specialized dictionary), you are unlikely to figure out what that sentence means, even with considerable effort.

Adding context is not necessarily a help! Suppose the sentence had come to you as part of a message which said, in its entirety:

Henry and Sebastian were rivals, each preparing for the upcoming competition in his own way. In order to improve his chances, Henry practiced hard. Sebastian compensated his

Glock. Lyn didn't think this would help, and advocated more practice instead, but Sebastian pursued his plan single-mindedly.

There is quite a lot of information in that paragraph, but nothing that is very helpful in figuring out about compensating Glocks.

But if you are told that Glock is a firearms manufacturer (and therefore can be used to refer generically to any firearm they produce, as is the case with Colt), and that certain guns can have a device called a compensator installed to reduce the recoil when they are fired, then you can probably figure out that *Sebastian compensated his Glock* means that Sebastian had a compensator added to his Glock pistol. There is no good alternative to being told this information.

The hard part is not developing rules to infer the meaning of XXXed from XXXor; such rules have been known for a long time. The hard part is to know when to apply those rules, and how to keep hundreds of those rules from interacting to produce more fog than clarity.

1.3.3   New approaches to knowledge acquisition

A breakthrough in the effectiveness and applicability of knowledge acquisition procedures may be possible within the next five years. In this section the following two research approaches are identified:

1. Employing large, growing knowledge bases acquired from reference texts such as dictionaries. This contributes to robustness by facilitating acquisition of knowledge for semantic and pragmatic components.
2. Acquisition of syntactic, semantic, and discourse facts from annotated bodies of language. This contributes to robustness of syntactic, semantic, and discourse components and allows semi-automatic learning of syntactic and semantic knowledge.

Knowledge from text

Recently a handful of efforts have focused on creating large knowledge bases of common facts. The CYC project at MCC is employing ten to twenty programmers to handcraft a knowledge base based on a selection of encyclopedia articles (Lenat et al., 1986). At IBM Yorktown Heights (Chodorow, Ravin, and Sachar, 1988; Jensen and Binot, 1988; Neff and Boguraev, 1989) and Bell Communications Research, efforts are underway to derive automatically synonym sets, lexical syntax, and other information from on-line dictionaries. One effort underway at BBN is the Common Facts Data Base (CFDB) (Crowther, 1989), which has been used to derive common facts from dictionaries and is being applied experimentally to other reference material.

In this section we illustrate two of the many ways such automatically derivable databases can increase robustness compared to today's systems. A long-standing problem is the interpretation of nominal compounds, sequences of nouns such as *carrier task force*. Heretofore one had to handcraft a definition for each example or small class of examples. Some informal definitions are provided directly in dictionaries for frequently occurring, well-known expressions, e.g., *fire engine*. These may be automatically derivable by analyzing a dictionary. Others follow regular patterns (Ayuso, 1985; Finin, 1980), such as part-whole relations, which require common facts in order to be interpreted. For example, if the NLP system encounters *helicopter rotor* for the first time, it could be understood if the knowledge base contains the information that a rotor is part of a helicopter.

Another long-standing problem is interpreting definite references. The use of syntactic information to constrain and rank what an anaphoric expression can refer to is rather well understood. References involving the same terminology are also rather well understood, e.g., using *those ships* as a short form after mentioning *all C1 surface ships in the Indian Ocean*. However, the class of references that illustrates non-robustness in current discourse components are those that require a "bridge" (Clark, 1975) between what is mentioned, e.g., a connection between the expression *the flight deck,* and the expression that implies its existence, e.g., *the carrier Midway*. One hypothesis is that bridges fall into one of potentially a few dozen patterns, in this case, referring to a part after mentioning the whole. The common fact needed is that aircraft carriers have a flight deck. Such bridges require large volumes of common, mundane facts, such as those that might be derived from a dictionary, glossary, or parts manual.

Both nominal compounds and discourse anaphora seem to fall into a few dozen semantic patterns, each of which assumes a large set of common facts. It has been easy to implement such semantic patterns for some time; what has been lacking is a way to derive automatically the large set of common facts assumed.

Linguistic analysis of large bodies of text

NLP research has been hampered by a lack of sufficient linguistic data to derive statistically significant patterns. Volumes of text are available on-line; the problem has been how to derive linguistic facts from unanalyzed text. However, through a DARPA-funded effort at the University of Pennsylvania, corpora of annotated text will be available to other research sites. The annotations will include parts of speech and phrasal structure, e.g., syntactic structure. This syntactically annotated corpus should make two new developments feasible:

1. Development of acquisition procedures to learn new grammar rules for expressions never seen before by the NLP.
2. Collection of statistics regarding constructions and their probability of occurrence in context.

Automatic acquisition will reduce the need for handcrafting of both grammars and lexicons (the formal model of dictionary information for an NLP).

Original text:

> *Collection of statistics regarding constructions and their probability of occurrence in context.*

Part of Speech Tagging:

Collection **Noun** of **Prep** statistics **Noun** regarding **Prep** constructions **Noun** and **Conjunction** their **Pro** probability **Noun** of **Prep** occurrence **Noun** in **Prep** context **Noun**

Structure Tagging:

[Collection [of [statistics [regarding [[constructions]**NP** and [their probability [of [occurrence [in [context]**NP**]**PP**]**NP**]**PP**]**NP**]**NP**]**PP**]**NP**]**PP**]**NP**

Figure 1.2. Examples of two types of tagging.

Example annotations of the type of syntactic information that might be useful appear in Figure 1.2.

Any rules implicit in the annotation but not present in the current grammar are candidates to be automatically added to the grammar.

The annotations also allow acquisition of lexical information; for words not in the system dictionary, the annotations state part of speech and the syntactic context in which they occur. Suppose *regarding* were not known to the system before it encountered the annotated example above; this word could be added to the system lexicon as a preposition through processing the annotated example. Thus, annotations provide data that can be used to create systems that adapt by acquiring grammar rules and information about new words.

Summary

The challenge: To develop ways of acquiring knowledge in such a way as to permit focusing parsing and semantic interpretation without combinatorial explosion.

The new approach: Glean probabilistic information from bodies of text. Develop ways to combine automatically acquired knowledge with "being told" by humans. Use disjunctive processing, merging alternatives at all levels, guided by probabilistics and using cutoffs to reduce the number of alternatives considered. (Also use the understanding-by-fragments approach outlined in Section 1.5 of this chapter.)

1.4   Interfacing to multiple underlying systems

Most current NL systems, whether accepting spoken or typed input, are designed to interface to a single homogeneous underlying system; they have a component geared to producing code for that single class of application systems, such as a relational database (Stallard, 1987; *Parlance User Manual, Learner User Manual*). These systems take advantage of the simplicity of the semantics and the availability of a formal language (relational calculus and relational algebra) for the system's output.

The challenge is to recreate a systematic, tractable procedure to translate from the logical expression of the user's input to systems that are not fully relational, such as expert system functions, object-oriented and numerical simulation systems, calculation programs, and so on. Implicit in that challenge is the need to generate code for non-homogeneous software applications – those that have more than one application system.

The norm in the next generation of user environments will be distributed, networked applications. A seamless, multi-modal, NL interface will make use of a heterogeneous environment feasible for users and, if done well, transparent. Otherwise, the user will be limited by the complexity, idiosyncrasy, and diversity of the computing environment.

Such interfaces will be seamless in at least two senses:

1. The user can state information needs without specifying how to decompose those needs into a program calling the various underlying systems required to meet those needs. Therefore, no seams between the underlying systems will be visible.
2. The interface will use multiple input/output modalities (graphics, menus, tables, pointing, and natural language). Therefore, there should be no seams between input/output modalities.

In military uses, we expect that the need to access several heterogeneous application systems will arise as the norm in command and control, in logistics, and in contract management. Because of the need to include previously existing application software, each having its own assumptions regarding operating systems, heterogeneous software environments will arise. Because of the relative performance-cost trade-offs in workstations, mainframes, and parallel hardware, the hardware equipment will be heterogeneous as well.

For example, in DARPA's Fleet Command Center Battle Management Program (FCCBMP), several applications (call them underlying systems) are involved, including a relational database (IDB), two expert systems (CASES and FRESH), and a decision support system (OSGP). The hardware platforms include workstations, conventional time-sharing machines, and parallel mainframes. Suppose the user asks *Which of those submarines has the greatest probability of locating A within 10 hours?* Answering that question involves subproblems from several underlying applications: the display facility (to determine both what *those submarines* means and to display those which fulfill the user's request); FRESH to calculate how long it would take each submarine to get to the area *A;* CASES, for an intensive numerical calculation estimating the probabilities; and the display facility again, to present the response.

Although acoustic and linguistic processing can determine what the user wants, the problem of translating that desire into an effective program to achieve the user's objective is a challenging, but solvable problem.

In order to deal with multiple underlying systems, not only must our NL interface be able to represent the meaning of the user's request, but it must also be capable of organizing the various application programs at its disposal, choosing which combination of resources to use, and supervising the transfer of data among them. We call this the Multiple Underlying Systems (MUS) problem. BBN's approach and results on the MUS problem are part of the back end of the Janus natural language interface and are documented in Resnik (1989).

1.4.1 The scope of the problem

In our view of access to multiple underlying systems, the user's request, whatever its modality, is translated into an internal representation of the meaning of what the user needs. We initially explored a first-order logic for this purpose; however, in Janus (Weischedel, 1987) we have adopted an intensional logic (Hinrichs et al., 1987; Weischedel, 1989) to investigate whether intensional logic offers more appropriate representations for applications more complex than databases, e.g., simulations and other calculations in hypothetical situations. From the statement of what the user needs, we next derive a statement of how to fulfill that need – an executable plan composed of abstract commands. The executable plan is in essence an abstract data-flow program on a virtual machine that includes the capabilities of all of the application systems. At the level of that virtual machine, specific commands to specific underlying systems are dispatched, results from those application systems are composed, and decisions are made regarding the appropriate presentation of information to the user.

Thus, the Multiple Underlying Systems (MUS) problem is a mapping,

MUS: Semantic representation $\rightarrow$ Program

that is, a mapping from what the user wants to a program to fulfill those needs, using the heterogeneous application programs' functionality.

Although the statement of the problem as phrased above may at first suggest an extremely difficult and long-range program of research in automatic programming (e.g., see Rich and Waters, 1988), there are several ways one can narrow the scope of the problem to make utility achievable. Substantially restricting the input language is certainly one way to narrow the problem to one that is tractable.

In contrast, we allow a richer input language (an intensional logic), but assume that the output is a restricted class of programs – acyclic data-flow graphs. We assume that all primitives of the logic have a defined transformation from the level of the statement of the user's needs to the level of the executable plan. That definition will have been elicited from the application system experts (e.g., expert system builders, database administrators, and systems programming staff of other application systems).

A way to paraphrase the effect of assuming acyclic data-flow graphs as the output of the component is that the programs generated will be assumed to include

> Functions available in the underlying applications systems,
> Routines pre-programmed by the application system staff, and
> Operators on those elements such as: functional composition, if-then-else, operators from the relational algebra, and MAPCAR.

Therefore, the system need not derive programs for terms that it does not already know. Contrast that with the general automatic programming problem. Suppose that someone says to the system *Find the square root of the sum of the squares of the residuals,* so that the input can be correctly translated into a logical form, but that the underlying applications do not provide a square-root function. Then the interface will not be expected to derive a square-root program from arithmetic functions. Rather, this system will be expected to respond *I don't know how to compute square root.* Furthermore, if all the quantifiers are assumed to be restricted to finite sets with a generator function, then the quantifiers can be converted to simple loops over the elements of sets, such as the mapping operators of Lisp, rather than having to undertake synthesis of arbitrary program loops.

Even with these simplifying assumptions, there are interesting problems remaining, and the work offers highly desirable utility. The utility arises from two dimensions:

1. It frees the user from having to identify for each term (word) pieces of program that would carry out their meaning, for the application system programmers would do that for some appropriate set of terms.
2. It provides good software engineering of the interface, so that table input/output functionality, for instance, is insulated from the details of the underlying application or applications as they evolve.

1.4.2   Approach

The problem of multiple systems may be decomposed into the following sub-problems:

> *Representation.* It is necessary to represent underlying system capabilities in a uniform way, and to represent the user request in a form independent of any particular underlying system. The input/output constraints for each function of each underlying system must be specified, thus defining the services available.
> *Formulation.* One must choose a combination of underlying system services that satisfies the user request. Where more than one alternative

exists, it is preferable to select a solution with low execution costs and low passing of information between systems.

Execution. Actual calls to the underlying systems must be accomplished, information must be passed among the systems as required, and an appropriate response must be generated.

Representing the semantics of utterances

Since the meaning of an utterance in Janus is represented as an expression in WML (World Model Language [Hinrichs et al., 1987], an intensional logic, the input to the MUS component is in WML. The choice of WML was based on two grounds: first and foremost, although we found first-order representations adequate (and desirable) for NL interfaces to relational databases, we felt a richer semantic representation was important for future applications. The following classes of representation challenges motivated our choice: explicit representations of time and world, for instance, to support object-oriented simulation systems and expert systems involving hypothetical worlds; distributive/collective readings; generics, and mass terms; and propositional attitudes, such as statements of user preference and belief. Our second motivation for choosing intensional logic was our desire to capitalize on other advantages we perceived for applying intensional logic to natural language processing (NLP), such as the potential simplicity and compositionality of mapping from syntactic form to semantic representation and the many studies in linguistic semantics that assume some form of intensional logic.

For a sentence such as *Display the destroyers within 500 miles of Vinson*, the WML is as follows:

```
(bring-about
  ((intension
    (exists ?a display
      (object-of ?a
        (iota ?b (power destroyer)
          (exists ?c
            (lambda (?d) interval
              (& (starts-interval ?d VINSON)
                 (less-than
                   (iota ?e length-measure
                     (interval-length ?d ?e))
                   (iota ?f length-measure
                     (& (measure-unit ?f miles)
                        (measure-quantity ?f 500))))))
              (ends-interval ?c ?b))))))
   TIME WORLD))
```

Representing the functions of the applications

To represent the functional capabilities of underlying systems, we define services and servers. A server is a functional module typically corresponding to an underlying system or a major part of an underlying system. Each server offers a number of services: objects describing a particular piece of functionality provided by a server. Specifying a service in MUS provides for the mapping from fragments of logical form to fragments of underlying system code. For instance, the following is a list of services in a naval application. Each service has associated with it the server it is part of, the input variables, the output variables, the conjuncts computed, and an estimate of the relative cost in applying it.

```
Land-avoidance-distance:
    owner: Expert System 1
    inputs: (x y)
    locals: (z w)
    pattern:
        ((in-class x vessel)
         (in-class y vessel)
         (in-class z interval)
         (in-class w length-measure)
         (starts-interval z x)
         (ends-interval z y)
         (interval-length z w))
    outputs: (w)
    method: ((route-distance (location-of x) (location-of y)))
    cost: 5

Great-circle-distance:
    owner: Expert System 1
    inputs: (x y)
    locals: (z w)
    pattern:
        ((in-class x vessel)
         (in-class y vessel)
         (in-class z interval)
         (in-class w length-measure)
         (starts-interval z x)
         (ends-interval z y)
         (interval-length z w))
    outputs: (w)
    method: ((gc-distance (location-of x) (location-of y)))
    cost: 1
```

In the example above, there are two competing services for computing distance between two ships: Great-circle-distance, which simply computes a great circle route between two points, and Land-avoidance-distance, which computes the distance of an actual path avoiding land and sticking to shipping lanes.

Clause lists

Usually, the applicability of a service is contingent on several facts, and therefore several propositions must all be true for the service to apply. To facilitate matching the requirements of a given service against the needs expressed in an utterance, we convert expressions in WML to a disjunction normal form (DNF), i.e., a disjunction of conjunctions where quantifiers and higher level operators have been removed. We chose DNF because:

> In the simplest case, an expression in disjunctive normal form is simply a conjunction of clauses, a particularly easy logical form with which to cope.
> Even when there are disjuncts, each can be individually handled as a conjunction of clauses, and the results then combined together via union, and
> In a disjunctive normal form, each disjunct effectively carries all the information necessary for a distinct subquery.

For details of the algorithm for converting an intensional expression to DNF, see Resnik, (1989). For the sentence *Display the destroyers within 500 miles of Vinson,* whose WML representation was represented earlier, the clause list is as follows:

```
((in-class ?a display)
 (object-of ?a ?b)
 (in-class ?b destroyer)
 (in-class ?c interval)
 (in-class ?d interval)
 (equal ?c ?d)
 (starts-interval ?d VINSON)
 (in-class ?e length-measure)
 (interval-length ?d ?e)
 (in-class ?f length-measure)
 (measure-unit ?f miles)
 (measure-quantity ?f 500)
 (less-than ?e ?f)
 (ends-interval ?c ?b))
```

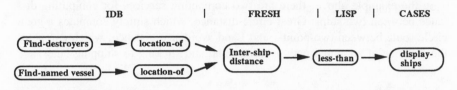

Figure 1.3. A data-flow graph.

Formulation

If one takes the input request to be a conjunction of requirements, finding the services to fulfill the request may be viewed as a form of covering problem: one seeks a plan of execution that satisfies all requirements at minimal cost.

A search is required both to find collections of services that fulfill the request, and to find a low cost solution. A beam search is used.

Inherent in the collection of services covering a DNF expression is the data flow that combines the services into a program to fulfill the DNF request. The next step in the formulation process is data-flow analysis to extract the data-flow graph corresponding to an abstract program fulfilling the request.

In Figure 1.3, the data-flow graph for *Display the destroyers within 500 miles of Vinson* is pictured.

Note that the integrated database (IDB) is called to identify the set of all destroyers, their locations, and the location of Vinson. An expert system FRESH is being called to calculate the distance between pairs of locations using land-avoidance routes. A LISP utility for comparing measures is called, followed by the display command in the CASES system.

Execution

The execution phase has two purposes:

1. Walk through the data-flow graph, calling operators in the underlying systems corresponding to the nodes of the graphs.
2. Supply functions for data combination not available in any of the underlying systems. In our example, a general function for comparing two measures, performing the appropriate unit conversions, was assumed.

Previous approaches to the multiple systems problem seem to have assumed that the data-flow model passes streams of values. This is not always adequate; in many cases, it is necessary to pass sets of tuples rather than sets of values, using a generalization of the join operation to combine data. The details of this are provided in Resnik (1989).

Most previous work dealt with simpler problems, e.g., access to a single relational database. Two pioneering efforts at Honeywell and at USC/Information Sciences Institute dealt with multiple systems but under a highly restrictive assumption: the user request had to be expressible as a conjunction of simple relations, equivalent to the select/project/join operations of a relational algebra. That restriction is removed in Janus. The class of formal expressions handled includes those involving negation of elementary predicates, existential and universal quantification, cardinality, and some common disjunctions, as well as queries that are simply conjunctions of clauses. Wh-questions (who, what, when where, etc.), commands, and yes/no queries are handled.

Experience in applying the system

The MUS component has been applied in the domain of the Fleet Command Center Battle Management Program (FCCBMP), using an internal version of the Integrated Database (IDB) – a relational database – as one underlying resource, and a set of LISP functions as another. The system includes more than 800 services.

An earlier version of the system described here was also applied to provide natural language access to data in Intellicorp's KEE knowledge-base system, to objects representing hypothetical world-states in an object-oriented simulation system, and to LISP functions capable of manipulating this data.

We have begun integrating the MUS component with BBN's Spoken Language System HARC (Hear And Respond to Continuous speech).

1.4.3   MUS conclusions

We have found the general approach depicted in Figure 1.3 quite flexible. The approach was developed in work on natural language processing; however, it seems to be valuable for other types of I/O modalities. Some preliminary work has suggested its utility for table input and output in managing database update, database retrieval, and a directly manipulable image of tabular data. Our prototype module generates forms in the intensional logic; then the components originally developed for the natural language processor provide the translation mechanism to and from intensional logic and underlying systems that actually store the data.

1.4.4   Summary

The challenge: To develop ways of easily interfacing NL systems to multiple instances of various types of underlying application systems.

The new approach: Define functional representations of the capabilities of underlying systems. Produce mappings to underlying systems based on this functionality. Represent the result of NL processing in this form. Use techniques from expert systems to formulate a process to satisfy the user's request or command.

1.5   Partial understanding of fragments, novel language, and errorful language

It is time to move away from dependence on the sentence as the fundamental unit of language. Historically, input to NL systems has often had to consist of complete, well-formed sentences. The systems would take those sentences one at a time and process them. But language does not always naturally occur in precise sentence-sized chunks. Multi-sentence input is the norm for many systems that must deal with newspaper articles or similar chunks of text. Subsentence fragments are often produced naturally in spoken language and may occur as the output of some text processing. Even when a sentence is complete, it may not be perfectly formed; errors of all kinds, and new words, occur with great frequency in all applications.

1.5.1   Multi-sentence input

Historically, computational linguistics has been conducted under the assumption that the input to a NL system is complete sentences (or, in the case of speech, full utterances) and that the output should be a complete representation of the meaning of the input. This means that NL systems have traditionally been unable to deal well with unknown words, natural speech, language containing noise or errors, very long sentences (say, over 100 words), and certain kinds of constructions such as complex conjunctions.

One of the problems is that advocates of local processing have tended to ignore syntactic and other constraints, while advocates of top down processing have tended to ignore coherent fragments unless they fit properly in the overall scheme.

The solution, we believe, is to move away from thinking that language comes in sentences and that the goal of understanding is a complete representation of meaning. We must move toward processing bits and pieces of language, whether the input to our NL systems comes that way or not, and toward creating structures that, like the fractals found in nature, have a kind of coherency that can be viewed at many levels.

Some semantic distinctions have no selectional import (e.g., quantifiers, and some adjuncts), while others have considerable selectional import.

One of the ideas whose time has passed is the notion of prepositional phrase attachment. Although in many cases it is not harmful to think of a PP attaching to a particular constituent, sometimes it is more useful to think of a single PP attaching simultaneously at several different points (for example, "I kicked the shell on the beach"), or relating two different constituents in a sentence (for example, "The average concentration of aluminum in breccias"). When fixed constituent structure pinches too much, language should not be forced into it.

What is the right representation for the meaning of multi-sentence language? The "right" representation for text may depend on the type of text and its purpose. For example, commands may be represented very differently from questions. It may also depend on the purpose of the user: for example, question answering versus controlling a process versus storing information for later retrieval.

Currently, most systems that attempt to understand multi-sentence text create a frame as output (or some other structure that is similar in function). Generally, the names of the slots of the frame consist of the type of information and relationships that were to be gleaned from the text, and the fillers describe the entities that were found. Thus it is difficult to represent unexpected information.

1.5.2 Errorful language, including new words

Handling novel, incomplete, or errorful forms is still an area of research. In current interactive systems, new words are often handled by simply asking the user to define them. However, novel phrases or novel syntactic/semantic constructions are also an area of research. Simple errors, such as spelling or typographical errors resulting in a form not in the dictionary, are handled in the state-of-the-art technology, but far more classes of errors require further research.

The state-of-the-art technology in message understanding systems is illustrative. It is impossible to build in all words and expressions ahead of time. As a consequence, approaches that try for full understanding appear brittle when encountering novel forms or errorful expressions.

The state of the art in spoken language understanding is similarly limited. New words, novel language, incomplete utterances, and errorful expressions are not generally handled. Including them poses a major roadblock, for they will decrease the constraint on the input set, increase the perplexity[2] of the language model, and therefore decrease reliability in speech recognition.

There is ample evidence that the ability to deal with novel, incomplete, or errorful forms is fundamental to improving the performance users can expect from NLP systems. Statistical studies for written database access (Eastman and McLean, 1981; Thompson, 1980) show that novel, errorful, or incomplete language comprises as much as 25–30% of type input; such phenomena (Fromkin, 1973) probably arise even more frequently in spoken language than in written language. In addition, we believe that interpreting incomplete input is particularly important for the following reasons:

1. Fragments occur frequently in military messages, such as Navy CAS-REPs, Navy OPREPs, Army SITREPs, and Army Operations Orders.

---

[2]Perplexity is a measure of the average number of words that may appear next at any point in the input.

2. Incomplete input arises in spoken language not only because we speak in fragments but also because acoustic processing at times can detect only fragments with high confidence.
3. Fragments result when processing an incomplete, novel, or errorful input, since a complete interpretation cannot be produced.

The problem

In current technology, almost all systems employ a search space of the possible ways of combining the meanings of words into meaningful phrases and a meaningful whole in context. In artificial intelligence terms, the search is a constraint satisfaction problem: find one or more interpretations such that no applicable constraint is violated. Formal models of grammar, semantics, and discourse state constraints on language in an all-or-nothing fashion, as if we always spoke and wrote in complete thoughts, saying exactly what we mean without vagueness, inaccuracy, error, or novelty in expression.

In constraint satisfaction problems, if a search fails to find a solution where all constraints are satisfied, many search alternatives will have been tried without leading to ultimate success. The problem is to come up with a partial solution (in the case of language processing, a partial interpretation), an explanation of why no solution is found (e.g., why no interpretation can be found), or a way to relax a constraint to produce with a complete solution (a complete interpretation). Which of the partial solutions, if any, is the most likely path to lead to success if a constraint is relaxed? Which partial path(s) in the search space is a good basis for explaining why no solution can be found?

All previous work suffers from this problem mentioned above, unless the application domain is very limited or the types of errorful/novel forms allowed are very few. This is because too many alternatives for what was meant are possible; an NLP system does not even have a foolproof way of knowing whether the user's input is errorful or whether the input represents a novel form. How to hypothesize the problem in an input and how to deal with it is understood for a large class of possible problems, e.g., see Carbonell and Hayes (1983); Jensen et al. (1983); Weischedel and Sondheimer (1983). What is not known is how to rank the many alternative interpretations that arise, as illustrated in the example above. The lack of a reliable scoring mechanism has been a technological roadblock.

Real language may be absolutely ill-formed (a native speaker would judge it to be something to be edited, an error, not what was intended, or otherwise "bad"), or relatively ill-formed (ill-formed with respect to a NL system's well-formedness constraints, even though a native speaker may judge it well-formed).

The following kinds of problems were enumerated by Weischedel (1987); others are readily available. Some examples of absolutely ill-formed language that are peculiar to written language are:

1. Typographical errors, e.g., *oter,* instead of *other.* Typos may also result in recognizable words, such as *an* instead of *and.*
2. Spelling errors, e.g., *Ralf* instead of *Ralph.*
3. Punctuation errors, e.g., inserting or omitting commas incorrectly, misplacement or omission of apostrophes in possessives, etc.
4. Homonym errors, e.g., *to* instead of *too,* or confusing *there, their,* and *they're.*

Similarly, there are classes of absolute ill-formedness peculiar to spoken language.

5. Mispronunciations, e.g., saying that word as if it were spelled *mispronounciations,* or stressing the wrong syllable. Fromkin (1973) has provided a taxonomy of human speech production errors that appear rule-based, as opposed to ungoverned or random occurrences.
6. Spoonerisms, e.g., saying *fauter waucet* instead of *water faucet.*

Each of the classes above are human performance errors, resulting in absolute ill-formedness. However, the overwhelming variety of ill-formedness problems arise in both the spoken and written modality; examples of absolute ill-formedness include:

1. Misreference, as in describing a purple object as *the blue one.*
2. Word order switching, as in saying *the terminal of the screen* when one meant *the screen of the terminal.* (Fromkin [1973] has recorded these errors.)
3. Negation errors, e.g., *All doors will not open* when the train conductor meant *Not all doors will open.*
4. Omitting words, as in *Send file printer* rather than the full form *Send the file to the printer.* (Although this may seem to occur only in typed language, we have heard such omissions in spoken language. Further, consider how many times, when struggling for the appropriate word, you start the utterance over, or someone supplies an appropriate word for you.)
5. Subject–verb disagreement, as in *A particularly important and challenging collection of problems are relatively ill-formed and arise in both spoken and written language* or in *One of the overwhelming number of troubles that befell them are . . .*
6. Resumptive pronouns and resumptive noun phrases, as in *The people that he told them about it,* where *them* is intended to be coreferential with *people.*
7. Run-together sentences, as if the person forgot how the sentence was started. An example is: *She couldn't expect to get a high standard salary and plus being so young.*

8. Restarted sentences, as in *Some people many try to improve society,* which was also collected in a written corpus.
9. Pronominal case errors, as in *between you and I.*
10. Word order errors, as non-native speakers can make, e.g., *I wonder where is the problem.*

Some particularly important and challenging problems are relatively ill-formed and arise in both spoken and written language.

1. Words unknown to the hearer or reader, but part of the language.
2. Novel or unknown word senses, although the word itself is known. For instance, Navy jargon includes phrases such as *What is Stark's readiness?* Although that sublanguage does not include *preparedness* as a synonym for readiness, it would be useful for a system to be able to infer what a user means by the input *What is Stark's preparedness?*
3. Novel (non-frozen) figures of speech, e.g., metaphor, metonymy, and synecdoche.
4. Novel nominal compounds, as in *window aisle seat,* which was used by a flight attendant on a wide-body jet.
5. Violated presuppositions, as in *Did John fail to go?* when John did not try to go.

The above lists are not intended to be exhaustive. More thorough taxonomies of ill-formedness exist. Statistical studies of frequency of occurrence for various classes of ill-formedness have been conducted for written database access; those studies suggest that as much as 25–30% of typed input may be absolutely or relatively ill-formed.

From the definitions and examples, it is clear that

1. Ill-formed input need not be ungrammatical; there may be no interpretation due to semantic or pragmatic problems.
2. The NL system will probably not know whether the input contains an error or whether its models are too limited to process the input.
3. Since there is no interpretation for the input, then one or more of the constraints of the NL system are violated; understanding ill-formed input therefore is a constraint satisfaction problem.
4. Since one or more of the constraints are violated, relaxing constraints in order to find an interpretation will mean opening up the search space for an interpretation substantially.

A suggestion

One new approach is to use probabilistic language models based on statistics derived from a chosen corpus, and utilizing those statistics together with the knowledge bases acquired from the corpus. The probabilistic model will rank partial interpretations for incomplete, errorful, or novel expressions. This will enable ranking of alternative interpretations when the input is complete, incomplete, or errorful.

The large annotated corpora described in the previous section will offer significant data to estimate such probabilities. For instance, the frequency of occurrence of types of phrases (e.g., NP and PP in the earlier annotated example) and statistics on relative frequency of grammar rules can be computed. Such statistics can be used to find the most predictive statistical language models for NLP systems.

The probabilistic language models in speech recognition are probably not directly applicable. Typically probabilities of two- or three-word sequences are computed from a corpus of utterances and are used in assigning weights to each alternative rendering of the speech wave into sequences of words. The limitation in those models is that only local information is used, whereas it is well known in linguistics that there are long distance dependencies well beyond three-word sequences.

Scoring techniques based on large annotated corpora may provide the missing link for progress in understanding fragmentary language, in processing errorful language, in determining what was meant in novel expressions, and in processing incomplete forms.

In the last ten years, it has often been suggested that ignoring constraints, or bottom-up parsing, or a semantics-first strategy might be used to deal with ill-formed input, but in each case, although particular examples could be made to work, the approach generated too many possibilities to be used in a truly general way. However, there seems to be a clear distinction between those classes of problems for which reasonably good syntactic and semantic strategies exist, and classes of ill-formedness that seem particularly intractable without a strong model of pragmatic knowledge for proper understanding. Examples of the latter include asias errors (spelling/typographical errors that result in a known word), run-together sentences, pragmatic overshoot, contextual ellipsis requiring considerable reasoning to resolve, and inferring the meaning of unknown words.

1.5.3   Summary

The challenge. To develop appropriate representations of fragmented, extended, errorful language, partially understood.

The new approach. Use local structure-finding processes that work primarily bottom-up, inserting local information into a global framework (not a standard parse tree or logical expression), and switching strategies to top-down when possible.

1.6   Additional research opportunities

We suggest the following as areas of opportunity for near-term research to make significant breakthroughs that will move NLP through the 1900s and beyond:

Acquisition of corpora, grammars, and lexicons. The development of useful systems requires observation of the behavior of potential users of interactive systems under realistic circumstances, and the collection of corpora of typical data for text analysis and machine translation systems. Although we believe it is unlikely that full grammars and lexicons can be induced completely automatically in the near future, useful results may be obtained soon from induction and acquisition techniques based on annotated corpora and machine-readable dictionaries. It is also likely that statistical measures useful for biasing algorithms can be extracted from a handcrafted grammar and a corpus. Approaches that appear promising are (1) the learning of grammatical structures where the input has already been annotated by part of speech and/or phrase structure, and (2) the learning of lexical syntax/semantics from examples and/or queries to the user given some pre-coded domain knowledge.

Increasing expressive power of semantic representation languages. Moving beyond database query systems will require increasing the expressive power of the languages used to express meaning, to include at least modal and higher-order constructs. Reasoning tools for modal logics and for second-order logics already exist, but appear intractable for language processing tasks. Approaches that seem promising include encoding modal constructs in first-order logic, hybrid approaches to representation and reasoning, and approaches to resource-limited and/or shallow reasoning, such as adding weights to formulae and sub-formulae.

Reasoning about plans. Recent work on plan recognition – the inference of the beliefs and intentions of agents in context – has provided formal definitions of the problem and some new algorithms. These have not yet been used as part of a discourse component to help resolve reference, quantification, and modification ambiguities or to formulate an appropriate response. The interaction between plans, discourse structure, and focus of attention must also be investigated. Promising approaches include incorporation of beliefs of the discourse participants, integrating existing models into discourse processing under simplifying conditions, and exploring prosodic/linguistic cues to dialogue.

Combination of partial information. The standard control structure by which various sources of information are combined in language interpretation seems to limit what NL systems can do. Several proposals for more flexible control structures have been made recently, each covering a subset of the knowledge sources available. More comprehensive schemes need to be developed. Two promising approaches are generalization of unification to NL architectures, and use of global, weighted control strategies, such as in evidential reasoning.

Improving robustness. Published studies suggest that as much as 25–30% of typed input contains errors, is incomplete, uses novel language, or otherwise involves challenging phenomena that are not well handled theoretically. The frequency of occurrence for these classes is even higher in spoken language than in written language. The text of some messages, such as Navy RAINFORM and CASREP messages and bank telexes, is highly telegraphic. It should be possible to develop a domain-independent theory that allows at least partial understanding of some of these novel and errorful uses, and test it in narrowly defined domains. Promising approaches are to employ unification strategies, plan recognition, and/or weighted control strategies to determine the most likely interpretation and the most appropriate response/action.

Relating interpretation and action. The problem of how to relate interpretations expressed in a meaning representation language and calls to application systems (databases, summarizing algorithms, etc.) has not been fully resolved, nor in fact precisely stated. This is crucial to the systematic separation of the natural language part of the system from the application part. Any approach should deal with applications beyond databases (beyond the semantics of tables) and should avoid the challenges of automatic programming.

Finding the relationship between prosody, syntactic ambiguity, and discourse structure. Syntactic and discourse boundaries are one of the main sources of interpretation ambiguity. Recently discovered evidence shows that prosodic information is a good indicator of these boundaries. Automatic extraction of prosodic information would revolutionize the interpretation of spoken language. Further, generation systems could add prosodic information to signal syntactic structure and discourse structure.

Measuring progress. The means of measuring progress is still an active area of discussion among NL scientists, as evidenced by workshops on Natural Language Evaluation held in December 1988 and June 1991 (Neal and Walter, 1991). Measures of correctness can be relatively simply stated for database query systems without dialogue capabilities (e.g., without sequence-related queries or clarifications), or for text analysis systems for database entry. They are much more difficult to state when stylistic matters need to be considered (as in machine translation systems) or when system responses affect subsequent user utterances. They probably cannot be usefully stated in a domain- or task-independent way. Measures of task difficulty, or of ambiguity of the language model, analogous to speech recognition's perplexity, are much more difficult to state. The recent DARPA program in spoken language understanding is developing formalisms for evaluating spoken language systems (Boisen et al., 1989; Bates et al., 1991).

Measurement of NL systems requires three distinct types of comparisons:

1. Longitudinal: It is critical to be able to measure the performance of a system over time, so that progress can be tracked.
2. Cross-System: It should be possible to compare the overall performance of two systems in explicit terms. This focus on whole-system performance will help localize the strengths and weaknesses of complete systems and will identify topics for research and development efforts.
3. Component: It should be possible to evaluate and compare parts of systems and evaluate coverage of unknown phenomena. This focus on components will help point out areas of relative strength in different systems and will provide priorities and goals for specific research.

Both the longitudinal and cross-system measures should include not merely the percentage of inputs banded correctly but also estimates of productivity improvements for the end user.

1.7   Conclusion

The list of hard, interesting problems on which to make progress in computational linguistics could go on and on. However, we feel that knowledge acquisition, interaction with multiple underlying systems, and techniques for partial understanding are the three solvable problems that will have the most impact on the utility of natural language processing. We encourage students to embark on these rewarding research areas, and look forward with eagerness to see what advances the next decade will bring.

References

Ayuso, D. (1985). *The Logical Interpretation of Noun Compounds.* Master's thesis, Massachusetts Institute of Technology.

Ayuso, D. M., Shaked, V., and Weischedel, R. M. (1987). "An Environment for Acquiring Semantic Information." In *Proceedings of the 25th Annual Meeting of the Association for Computational Linguistics,* pp. 32–40. ACL.

Bates, M. (1989). "Rapid Porting of the Parlance Natural Language Interface." In *Proceedings of the Speech and Natural Language Workshop,* pp. 83–88. Morgan Kaufmann Publishers Inc., San Mateo, CA.

Bates, M., Bobrow, R., Boisen, S., Ingria, R., and Stallard, D. (1991). "BBN ATIS System Progress Report – June 1990," *DARPA Speech and Natural Language Workshop,* Hidden Valley, PA, Morgan Kaufmann Publishers, pp. 125–126.

Bates, M., Boisen, S., and Makhoul, J. (1991). "Developing an Evaluation Methodology for Spoken Language Systems," *DARPA Speech and Natural Language Workshop,* Hidden Valley, PA, Morgan Kaufmann Publishers, pp. 102–108.

Bobrow, R., Ingria, R., and Stallard, D. (1991). "Syntactic and Semantic Knowledge in the DELPHI Unification Grammar," *DARPA Speech and Natural Language Workshop,* Hidden Valley, PA, Morgan Kaufmann Publishers, pp. 230–236.

Bobrow, R., and Ramshaw, L. (1991). "On Deftly Introducing Procedural Elements into

Unification Parsing," *DARPA Speech and Natural Language Workshop,* Hidden Valley, PA, Morgan Kaufmann Publishers, pp. 237–240.

Boisen, S., Ramshaw, L., Ayuso, D., and Bates, M. (1989). "A Proposal for SLS Evaluation," *DARPA Speech and Natural Language Workshop,* Cape Cod, MA, Morgan Kaufmann Publishers, pp. 135–146.

Brachman, R. J., and Schmolze, J. G. (1985). "An Overview of the KL-ONE Knowledge Representation System." *Cognitive Science,* 9(2).

Carbonell, J. G., and Hayes, P. J. (1983). "Recovery Strategies for Parsing Extragrammatical Language." *American Journal of Computational Linguistics,* 9(3–4):123–146.

Chodorow, M. S., Ravin, Y., and Sachar, H. E. (1988). "A Tool for Investigating the Synonymy Relation in a Sense Disambiguated Thesaurus." In *Proceedings of the Second Conference on Applied Natural Language Processing,* pp. 144–152. ACL.

Clark, H. H. (1975). "Bridging." In *Theoretical Issues in Natural Language Processing,* pp. 169–174. ACL.

Crowther, W. (1989). "A Common Facts Data Base." In *Speech and Natural Language,* pp. 89–93. Morgan Kaufmann Publishers Inc., San Mateo, CA.

Eastman, C. M., and McLean, D. S. (1981). "On the Need for Parsing Ill-Formed Input." *American Journal of Computational Linguistics,* 7(4):257.

Finin, T. W. (1980). "The Semantic Interpretation of Nominal Compounds." In *Proceedings of the First Annual National Conference on Artificial Intelligence,* pp. 310–312. The American Association for Artificial Intelligence.

Fromkin, V. A. (1973). *Janua Linguarum, Series maior 77: Speech Errors as Linguistic Evidence.* Mouton, The Hague.

Grosz, B., Appelt, D. E., Martin, P., and Pereira, F. (1985). "TEAM: An Experiment in the Design of Transportable Natural Language Interfaces." *Artificial Intelligence.*

Hinrichs, E. W., Ayuso, D. M., and Scha, R. (1987). "The Syntax and Semantics of the JANUS Semantic Interpretation Language." In *Research and Development in Natural Language Understanding as Part of the Strategic Computing Program,* Annual Technical Report December 1985–December 1986, pp. 27–31. BBN Laboratories, Report No. 6522.

Jensen, K., and Binot, J.-L. (1988). "Dictionary Text Entries as a Source of Knowledge for Syntactic and Other Disambiguations." In *Proceedings of the Second Conference on Applied Natural Language Processing,* pp. 152–159. ACL.

Jensen, K., Heidorn, G. E., Miller, L. A., and Ravin, Y. (1983). "Parse Filling and Prose Fixing: Getting a Hold on Ill-Formedness." *American Journal of Computational Linguistics,* 9(3–4):147–160.

Kaemmerer, W., and Larson, J. (1986). "A graph-oriented knowledge representation and unification technique for automatically selecting and invoking software functions." In *Proceedings AAAI-86 Fifth National Conference on Artificial Intelligence,* pp. 825–830. American Association for Artificial Intelligence, Morgan Kaufmann Publishers, Inc.

Learner User Manual, BBN Systems and Technologies.

Lenat, D., Prakash, M., and Shepherd, M. (1986). "CYC: Using Common Sense Knowledge to Overcome Brittleness and Knowledge Acquisition Bottlenecks." *AI Magazine,* 6(4):65–85.

Montague, R. (1970). "Pragmatics and Intensional Logic." *Synthese,* 22:68–94.

Montgomery, C. A., and Glover, B. A. (1986). "A Sublanguage for Reporting and Analysis of Space Events." *Analyzing Language in Restricted Domains: Sublanguage Description and Processing,* pp. 129–162. Lawrence Erlbaum Associates.

Neal, J., and Walter, S. (editors). (1991). *Natural Language Processing Systems Evaluation Workshop,* Rome Laboratory.

Neff, M. S., and Boguraev, B. K. (1989). "Dictionaries, Dictionary Grammars, and Dictionary Parsing." In *Proceedings of the 27th Annual Meeting of the Association for Computational Linguistics,* pp. 91–101. ACL.

Parlance User Manual, BBN Systems and Technologies.

Pavlin, J. and Bates, R. (1988). *SIMS: Single Interface to Multiple Systems.* Technical Report ISI/RR-88-200, University of Southern California Information Sciences Institute.

Resnik, P. (1989). *Access to Multiple Underlying Systems in Janus.* BBN Report 7142, Bolt, Beranek and Newman Inc.

Rich, C., and Waters, R. C. (1988). *Automatic Programming: Myths and Prospects.* MIT Press.

Schank, R., and Abelson, R. (1977). *Scripts, Plans, Goals, and Understanding.* Lawrence Erlbaum Associates.

Shieber, S. M. (1986). *An Introduction to Unification-Based Approaches to Grammars.* Center for the Study of Language and Information, Stanford, CA.

Stallard, David. (1987). "Answering Questions Posed in an Intensional Logic: A Multi-level Semantics Approach." In R. Weischedel, D. Ayuso, A. Haas, E. Hinrichs, R. Scha, V. Shaked, D. Stallard (editors), *Research and Development in Natural Language Understanding as Part of the Strategic Computing Program,* pp. 35–47. BBN Laboratories, Cambridge, Mass. Report No. 6522.

Thompson, B. H. (1980). "Linguistic Analysis of Natural Language Communication with Computers." In *Proceedings of the Eighth International Conference on Computational Linguistics,* pp. 190–201. International Committee on Computational Linguistics.

Weischedel, R. M., and Sondheimer, N. K. (1983). "Meta-rules as a Basis for Processing Ill-Formed Input." *American Journal of Computational Linguistics,* 9(3–4):161–177.

Weischedel, R., Ayuso, D., Haas, A., Hinrichs, E., Scha, R., Shaked, V., Stallard, D., (editors). (1987). *Research and Development in Natural Language Understanding as Part of the Strategic Computing Program.* Technical Report, BBN Laboratories, Cambridge, Mass. Report No. 6522.

Weischedel, R. M. (1987). "A View of Ill-Formed Input Processing." In *Research and Development in Natural Language Understanding as Part of the Strategic Computing Program.* Technical Report, BBN Laboratories, Cambridge, MA. Report No. 6463.

Weischedel, R. M., Bobrow, R., Ayuso, D. M., and Ramshaw, L. (1989). "Portability in the Janus Natural Language Interface." In *Speech and Natural Language,* pp. 112–117. Morgan Kaufmann Publishers Inc., San Mateo, CA.

Weischedel, R. M. (1989). "A Hybrid Approach to Representation in the Janus Natural Language Processor." In *Proceedings of the 27th Annual Meeting of the Association for Computational Linguistics,* pp. 193–202. ACL.

Weischedel, R. M., Carbonell, J., Grosz, B., Marcus, M., Perrault, R.; and Wilensky, R. (1990). *Natural Language Processing,* Annual Review of Computer Science, Vol. 4, pp. 435–452.

Woods, W. A. (1970). "Transition Network Grammars for Natural Language Analysis." *Communications of the Association for Computing Machinery,* 13(10):591–606.

PART II

Building a lexicon

2   The contribution of lexicography

B. T. SUE ATKINS

2.1   Introduction

One of the major resources in the task of building a large-scale lexicon for a natural-language system is the machine-readable dictionary. Serious flaws (for the user-computer) have already been documented in dictionaries being used as machine-readable dictionaries in natural language processing, including a lack of systematicity in the lexicographers' treatment of linguistic facts; recurrent omission of explicit statements of essential facts; and variations in lexicographical decisions which, together with ambiguities within entries, militate against successful mapping of one dictionary onto another and hence against optimal extraction of linguistic facts.

Large-scale electronic corpora now allow us to evaluate a dictionary entry realistically by comparing it with evidence of how the word is used in the real world. For various lexical items, an attempt is made to compare the view of word meaning that a corpus offers with the way in which this is presented in the definitions of five dictionaries at present available in machine-readable form and being used in natural language processing (NLP) research; corpus evidence is shown to support apparently incompatible semantic descriptions. Suggestions are offered for the construction of a lexical database entry to facilitate the mapping of such apparently incompatible dictionary entries and the consequent maximization of useful facts extracted from these.

2.2   How 'reliable' are dictionary definitions?

Writing a dictionary is a salutary and humbling experience. It makes you very aware of the extent of your ignorance in almost every field of human experience. It fills your working day with a series of monotonous, humdrum, fascinating, exasperating, frustrating, rewarding, and impossible tasks. It goes on for years and years longer than you ever thought it (or you) could. And when it is all over, the fruits of this labor are enshrined forever in a form that allows other people to take it (and you) apart, in print, publicly and permanently. Lexicographers should, therefore, be even more enthusiastic than the rest of the linguistic world

I am grateful to Beth Levin for her comments on an earlier version of the chapter, and, more generally, for all her help in bridging the gap between linguistic theory and lexicography.

at the prospect of large-scale lexicons for natural-language systems being built by semi-automatic means. Yet I approach this ambition of the world of computational linguistics with a deep reserve, which is focused on the central position of the machine-readable dictionary (MRD) in this process.

Machine-readable or not machine-readable, a dictionary is a dictionary is a dictionary. Most machine-readable dictionaries were person-readable dictionaries first. As every lexicographer will confirm, systematicity is high on our list of priorities: but higher still comes user-friendliness. If we had a choice between being completely consistent throughout a 2,000 page (18 million-character) dictionary – were it even possible – and making one line of one entry totally intelligible to the least motivated user, the user would win. Again, consider the time scale: such a dictionary will take at least five years, and can take fifteen to write. No lexicographical task is ever quite the same as the one just completed. There may be twenty, thirty, or forty (or more) lexicographers in the compiling team. However complex the editor's instructions and however conscientious the compilers, the entries in *A* and *B* will differ from those in *X, Y,* and *Z* by much more than their place in the alphabet. And this is, in human terms, just as it should be. A dictionary is a human artifact, designed to be used by human users. Until the advent of the computer, people took dictionaries in their stride. Their human brains compensated for a lack of systematicity throughout the work. They knew, albeit vaguely sometimes, more or less what words could – and did – do.

In the computer, however, we have the ultimate learner, and one with a terrifying capacity for homing in on inconsistencies invisible to the naked eye. Serious flaws (for the user-computer) have already been documented in 'hand-held' dictionaries – indeed, in the very dictionaries at present available and being used in machine-readable form. These include the omission of explicit statements of essential linguistic facts (Atkins, Kegl, & Levin, 1986); lack of systematicity in the compiling in one single dictionary, ambiguities within entries, and incompatible compiling across dictionaries (Atkins & Levin, 1991). However, these are in the main sins of omission rather than commission; they make it more difficult to extract information from the MRD but ultimately detract very little from the value of the information extracted.

The question at issue now is more fundamental: how much semantic information accurate enough to be useful in a computational lexicon is contained in a dictionary definition written for the human user, who often unconsciously supplements and corrects what is being read? Is it indeed possible to write dictionary definitions that encapsulate the essential facts about the senses of a word? Can the meaning of a word be divided into discrete senses without distorting it beyond reason? Large text corpora allow a detailed study of how a word is used, thus enabling us to evaluate the accuracy of dictionary entries much more objectively than before. Lexicographers who have worked with such corpora, and examined hundreds of individual citations minutely in an attempt to find objective evidence for the existence of dictionary senses, report that in many cases such objective evidence simply is not there (Moon, 1987, 1988; Stock, 1984; Atkins, 1987).

In this chapter I shall compare the view of word meaning that a corpus offers for a number of words (*admire, acknowledge, admit, safety, danger, reel*) with the way in which this is presented in the definitions of five dictionaries at present available in machine-readable form and used in NLP research, though not always in these precise editions. These are: *Collins English Dictionary* (1986) (CED); *Webster's New World Dictionary* (1988) (WNWD); *Oxford Advanced Learner's Dictionary* (1989) (OALD); *Longman Dictionary of Contemporary English* (1987) (LDOCE); and *Collins Cobuild English Language Dictionary* (1987) (CCELD).[1] I shall show how corpus citations may be found to support very diverging descriptions of the sense of the same lexical item, suggest some reasons for this, and make some proposals about how the 'ultimate' machine-readable entry could be structured to allow the reconciliation of anisomorphic sense differentiations in MRDs.

2.3   The problem of lumping versus splitting: the case of *safety*

An examination of the way in which meaning is handled in dictionaries immediately raises the specter of homonymy versus polysemy in the lexicographers' approach to word meaning. As Lyons (1969) points out, the choice of one polysemous entry or two or more homonymous entries (which may or may not themselves be polysemous) "is, the last resort, indeterminate and arbitrary . . . it rests upon the lexicographer's judgement . . . the arbitrariness of the distinction between homonymy and multiple meaning is reflected in the discrepancies in classification between different dictionaries". A glance at the entries for *reel* in the various dictionaries under consideration (see 29 below) confirms this: what is treated in a single entry in CCELD is given three entries in the other works. However, although homonymy versus polysemy is an eternal debating point in lexicography, it is really irrelevant to the business in hand, that of trying to evaluate sense assignment in MRDs and the concept of dictionary senses per se.

Is there any reason – other than tradition or pious optimism – to believe that a dictionary entry gives a true account of what a native speaker knows about the semantic properties of a word? The word meaning is often divided into discrete senses (and sometimes subsenses), which are then analyzed and recorded as though they had a life of their own, with little to link them except the coincidence of their being expressed by the same string of characters pronounced in the same

[1]CED and the WNWD are both collegiate dictionaries for native speakers, advertising 170,000 'references' (CED) or 'entries' (WNWD). The other three are learners' dictionaries advertising 67,100 'words and phrases' (OALD), 55,000 'words and phrases' (LDOCE), and 70,000 'references' (CCELD). One must assume that in this context 'references' 'entries,' and 'words and phrases' are probably synonymous.

way. One's own reactions to such distinctions often suggest that other interpretations are equally possible: but subjective evidence is rightly suspect. With the advent of electronic corpora it is at last possible to scrutinize enough examples of a word in normal use to allow a more objective evaluation of the accuracy of this approach.

Let us look first at the word *safety*. We find in the corpus[2] the following:

(1)   worries concerning the safety of your gas supply
        the Center for Auto Safety
        serious problems connected with nuclear safety

These citations suggest that one meaning of the word *safety* is (roughly speaking) 'the quality of not being dangerous'. However, we also find in the corpus:

(2)   he did something to jeopardize my safety
        to ensure the safety and well-being of mother and child
        it's for your own safety.

Since the 'safety of mother and child' clearly does not refer to potential damage that mother and child may wreak on an innocent bystander, we may propose a second meaning, namely 'the condition of not being in danger'. Thus we have the following initial sense differentiation for *safety:*

(3)   1.   the quality of not being dangerous.
        2.   the condition of not being in danger.

The word *safe* parallels these two senses: (1.) 'not dangerous' ("the gas supply is safe"), and (2.) 'not in danger' ("the child is safe"). In the CED entry for this word, four of its six senses are roughly paraphrasable by 'not dangerous': if we assume that meaning in the first definition of 3 below, we find that a semantic description corresponding to the corpus citations grouped in 1 and 2 is indeed to be found in the CED entry for *safety:*

(4)
CED   1.   the quality of being safe.
        2.   freedom from danger or risk of injury.

This agreement between corpus and dictionary suggests that by dividing the meaning of the word *safety* into two distinct senses, the entry records a verifiable truth about this word. So far so good. Doubt begins to creep in when another

[2]The citations in this chapter come from the Cobuild Corpus, held at the University of Birmingham, England, and jointly owned by that university, and by Collins Publishers Ltd. This corpus contains 7.3 million words (tokens) and includes approximately 3.1 m words of non-fiction, 2 m words of fiction, 1 m words of journalism, and 1.2 m words of spoken English (conversations, unscripted broadcasts, lectures); 5 m words are British English and 2 m are American English, the remaining 0.3 m coming from other regions.

dictionary (of virtually the same size and coverage) is consulted and its first definition is found to combine both the CED senses:

(5)

WNWD the quality or condition of being safe; freedom from danger, injury, or damage: security.

Both LDOCE and OALD show the same technique of 'lumping' the semantic description into one broad general sense rather than 'splitting' it into narrower senses:

(6)

LDOCE [U] the condition of being safe; freedom from danger, harm, or risk: . . . *the safety of the climbers . . . safety checks on industrial machinery . . . road safety.*

(7)

OALD being safe; not being dangerous or in danger: . . . *the safety of the children . . . the safety of the product . . . road safety.*

In the definitions in 5, 6, and 7, we again find the ambiguous *safe,* but here it allows the inclusion in one single definition of both CED 1 ('the safety of the product') and ED 2 ('the safety of the children'). It is tempting to conclude that this is simply a case of lexicographer error, as indeed it would be if it were true that the CED entry reflected a canonical truth about the meaning of the word. However, the same corpus that showed two distinct senses of *safety* also supports the single-sense view:

(8)   regulations on planning, safety, and public health; an energetic campaigner in the cause of road safety.

As regards the two senses of *safety* given in 3 above, 'road safety' might equally well be described in terms of 'road users not being in danger' (sense 2, i.e., their safety on the roads) or 'road users not being dangerous to others' (sense 1, i.e., the safety of the roads); indeed the meaning of *safety* in this context encompasses both senses. A similar dual interpretation is possible in the case of the first citation. Therefore, if we compare the citations grouped in 1, 2, and 8, we find the corpus evidence supporting two contradictory descriptions of the sense of *safety:* on the one hand, 'split' into two senses, and on the other, 'lumped' into one.

The last of the dictionaries, the CCELD, differs from both of these approaches:

(9)

CCELD 1.   Safety is . . .

1.1.   the state of being safe. E.g., *He was assured of his daughter's safety.*

1.2. *the possibility of your being harmed in a particular situation.*
   E.g., *many worried about the safety of their children.*

1.3. a place where you are safe from a particular danger.
   E.g., *They were busy helping survivors to safety . . . They swam to the safety of a small, rocky island.*

2.   if you are concerned about the safety of a product, a course of action, etc, you are concerned that it might be harmful or dangerous. E.g., *People worry about the safety of nuclear energy.*

3.   Safety features, safety measures, etc., are intended to make something less dangerous. E.g., *Every car will come with built-in safety features . . . Heating was by oil stoves without proper safety measures.*

In the case of 1.2 the presence in the context of 'worried' seems to have given rise to the interpretation of *safety* in terms of its opposite *harm*. This reflects the point made in Cruse (1986) that "the meaning of any word form is in some sense different in every distinct context in which it occurs"; but, as Cruse rightly adds, "that does not mean that the 'word-form-in context' is the appropriate unit for lexicological purposes." Setting aside 1.2, then, we find that the CCELD entry actually combines the contradictory approaches of the other dictionaries. CCELD's 1.1 ('his daughter's safety') parallels CED's 'freedom from danger' sense 2; CCELD's sense 2 ('safety of nuclear energy') matches CED's first sense; CCELD's sense 3, with its examples of *safety* used as a noun modifier, reflects the 'two sense in one' definitions of WNWD, LDOCE, and OALD.

However, sense 1.3 in CCELD introduces a new concept: in it, *safety* is defined as 'a *place* where you are safe from a particular danger'. Once again, corpus evidence may be found to support his interpretation, which is possible when the word is the object of certain prepositions such as *to* and *from:*[3]

(10)   the wounded could be dragged to safety
    only tens of miles from safety
    the bridge that led to safety.

Taking into account all these entries, the lexicographers' options in analyzing into dictionary senses the semantics of *safety* may be summarized thus:

(11)   NOT IN DANGER   'the safety of the children'
    NOT DANGEROUS   'the safety of the product'
    AMBIGUOUS   'road safety'
    PLACE   'jumped to safety'

The few dictionaries studied show three very different selections from these options in their descriptions of the meaning of the noun *safety,* as may be seen

---

[3]This is a feature of many lexical items denoting an emotion or condition, of 'fled from poverty', 'escaped to happiness', etc.

from the following table, where 'x' signifies the presence of the dictionary sense in question, and '—' its absence:

(12)		NOT IN DANGER	NOT DANGEROUS	AMBIGUOUS	PLACE
1.	CED	x	–	x	–
	WNWD	x	–	x	–
	LDOCE	x	–	x	–
2.	OALD	x	x	x	–
3.	CCELD	x	x	–	x

Corpus evidence seems to confirm each of these contradictory views in turn. It is appropriate to wonder whether this is an isolated phenomenon. Experience suggests that it is not.

2.4   Similar sense overlaps: *danger* and *risk*

Very similar sense-defining problems occur with *danger* and *risk,* two words with close semantic links with *safety*. The case of *danger* is documented in Atkins (1987), where out of 404 citations, 122 (30%) were noted as capable of being assigned to two of the three 'dictionary senses' identified for this word. In a study of 192 KWIC concordance lines for the noun *risk* from the Cobuild corpus (excluding the phrases 'take/run a risk'), 29 (15%) were ambiguous vis-à-vis two dictionary senses, and the word fared no better when sentence-length citations from another corpus were scrutinized (Fillmore & Atkins, in press: b).

It might, however, be argued that such fuzziness in sense boundaries is a function of the semantic content shared by the words *safety, danger,* and *risk*. I believe this to be a forlorn hope, in that very many other words – perhaps eventually the majority of the word stock of the language – show the same symptoms on close examination. Take, for example, the behavior of words that have in their semantics a 'communication' component.

2.5   Ambiguity of the communication component: *acknowledge, admit,* etc.

One set of words that systematically shows the same blurring of the sense boundaries is the group of verbs meaning (1.) 'accept the fact that . . .' and/or (2.) 'communicate one's acceptance of the fact that . . .', which for brevity's sake could be summarized as (1.) KNOW and (2.) COMMUNICATE. The presence or absence of the COMMUNICATE component is very often unclear in the way we use these words and in the way they are interpreted, as is shown by the fact that 'You'll never get him to acknowledge it' could equally well be followed by '. . . even to himself' (−COMMUNICATE) as by '. . . to his children'

(+COMMUNICATE). The same is true if *admit* or *recognize* (among others) is substituted for *acknowledge* in that sentence. The Cobuild corpus supplies many examples of such ambiguity:

(13)   It took me some time to acknowledge that ordinary daily events could be political.
He might be more interesting than we acknowledge.
Few of us are prepared to admit to being happy.
They had to admit that the Colonel knew his railways.

The words 'to myself' (or 'to ourselves' etc.) and 'to others' fit equally easily in any of the above. Sometimes, however, this aspect of the meaning is made explicit by the addition of such a phrase, as in the following citations, where the absence of the COMMUNICATE component is explicit (my emphasis in the following excerpts):

(14)   Mankind does not readily acknowledge even *to itself,* far less discuss . . .
She was candid enough to admit it *to herself.*
He does not want to admit it *to himself* even now.

As well as by the selection of explicit 'to' prepositional phrases, the absence of the COMMUNICATE component may be unambiguously signaled by the choice of lexical content:

(15)   There was a bond between them, *privately* acknowledged but unspoken.
I *consciously* acknowledge that for me sneering upper lips were . . .

Similarly the context may reveal an implicit +COMMUNICATE component:

(16)   He would not *publicly* acknowledge that he was finding . . .
They *came forward to* acknowledge their debts.
He was obliged to admit *officially* what had long been common gossip.
"Yes, I do," Calderwood *admitted.*

None of the dictionaries under review records this blurring of the sense boundaries in these verbs; indeed, none explicitly records the dimension of communication at all. The lack of clarity here is compounded by the use in definitions of other equally polysemous members of this set:

(17)   Definitions of *Acknowledge*
CCELD   If you acknowledge a fact or a situation, you *accept* or *admit* that it is true or that it exists . . .
CED   to *recognize* or *admit* the existence, truth, or reality of.
LDOCE   (as) to *accept* or *admit* (as); *recognize* the fact or existence (of) . . .

OALD   *accept* the truth of (sth); *admit* (sth) . . .
WNWD   to *admit* to be true or as stated; confess.

The defining options for lexicographers might be summarized thus:

(18)   KNOW   = accept that something is the case
       COMMUNICATE   = say that one accepts this
       KNOW+COMMUNICATE = use a polysemous genus term covering
                                 both

Despite this, the dictionaries all handle the word in the same way, all obscuring the distinctive options within its meaning:

(19)   KNOW +
                         COMMUNICATE   KNOW   COMMUNICATE

         CCELD   x   –   –
         CED   x   –   –
         LDOCE   x   –   –
         OALD   x   –   –
         WNWD   x   –   –

2.6   Polysemy in *admire*

The verbs belonging to the *admit–acknowledge* group have been shown to contain in their meaning the component 'know' together with the optional 'and communicate it'. Another word with an optional communication component is the verb *admire*, where the basic sense is a hyponym of *feel* rather than *know*. Here again, it is very often impossible to discern from the context whether the admiration is communicated or not, as in the following:

(20)   Everyone admires her.
       At the very moment when we were admiring the Monet . . .
       The more she is admired . . . the more . . .

Sometimes, however, the context makes it quite clear that the admiration is being communicated:

(21)   . . . the first price a Persian quotes to you when you admire a rug.
        Another child is more polite. He admires the baby for a couple of days
        without enthusiasm . . .

At other times it is equally clear that the admiration is felt but not spoken:

(22)   It must be her wit that our master admires – if indeed he does.
       He found himself admiring whiting, in a sneaky way.

However, the verb *admire* is doubly complex, for the basic 'feel' component operates with a second optional extra: that of 'look at something'. In the following citations, the '+LOOK' component is quite evident (it is for instance impossible to add 'with his/her/my eyes shut' after them):

(23)   He held the clothes to his body and admired himself.
        She supported her sketchbook on it the better to admire her drawing.
        I wandered round the dewy garden, admiring the velvety dark phlox.

Equally clear, in the next group of citations, is the absence of a LOOK component:

(24)   You have to admire his recuperative powers.
        I admire the sentiments of Marx.
        I came to admire the skepticism of the press.

In this instance, there are few ambiguous citations, principally because the presence of a concrete inanimate noun in object position tends to force a +LOOK reading, while an abstract noun forces a −LOOK interpretation. An animate noun leaves scope for ambiguity, it seems, as in:

(25)   She used to secretly admire the famous young actor.

However, in the full citation the context forces a +LOOK reading:

(26)   She used to secretly admire the famous young actor as he ate sundaes
        in . . .

Thus we have, for the verb *admire,* a basic sense of 'feel admiration for' which only in very rare cases indeed may be missing (there is no example of such an omission in the Cobuild corpus, but one might conceive of a situation where someone says, "don't forget to admire the baby, even if it's awful"). As well as this basic +FEEL sense there is sometimes an indisputable +COMMUNICATE component, and sometimes an equally indisputable +LOOK component. In this shadowy tangle of sense it is no surprise to find that the dictionaries do not agree in their description of the meaning of this word, and here again the selection by CED and OALD of a polysemous genus term (*regard,* which can mean both 'look' and 'think of') merely compounds the difficulty:

(27)
    a.   CCEDLD If you admire someone or something . . .
                1.   you like, respect, and approve of them. E.g., *I admire
                    cleverness – courage too . . .*
                2.   look with pleasure at them. E.g., *He went back along the
                    lane, admiring the autumn crocuses.*
    b.   CED   1.   to *regard* with esteem, respect, approval, or pleased sur-
                    prise . . .
    c.   LDOCE   (for) to think of or look at with pleasure or respect.
                I admire (her for) the way she handles her staff . . .
                He's always looking in the mirror, admiring himself!

d. OALD 1. –sb/sth (for sth): *regard* sb/sth with respect, pleasure, satisfaction, etc. *They admired our garden. I admire him for his success in business.*

2. communicate admiration of (sb/sth). *Aren't you going to admire my new hat?*

e. WNWD 1. to *regard* with wonder, delight, and pleased approval.

2. to have a high regard for.

All the dictionaries record the 'feel admiration' sense and (giving CED and OALD the benefit of the doubt about the polysemous regard) all of them include +LOOK as well. However, this receives the status of a full sense only in CCEDLD and WNWD, where the second definition forces us to interpret *regard* in the first as 'look at'; LDOCE, although mentioning 'look' specifically, combines it with 'feel' into one sense; and CED and OALD rely on the polysemy of *regard* to cover both senses. The +COMMUNICATE sense is noted by only one of the dictionaries, OALD.

The way the dictionaries analyze the semantics of *admire* may be summarized thus:

(28)

	FEEL	LOOK	FEEL – LOOK	FEEL + LOOK	COMMU- NICATE
CCELD	x	x	–	–	–
WNWD	x	x	–	–	–
CED	–	–	x	–	–
OALD	–	–	x	–	x
LDOCE	–	–	–	x	–

2.7 More fuzzy sense boundaries: the case of *reel*

Lest it be thought that arbitrary or semi-arbitrary sense distinctions are the prerogative of verbs and abstract nouns, it is worth looking briefly at at least one concrete noun. *Reel* is not a lexicographically complex word, although all the dictionaries under consideration here except for CCELD treat the device and the dance in two distinct headword entries.

(29) Entries for *reel:*

a. CCELD reel

1. A reel is

1.1 a cylindrical object which is used to hold long things such as thread or cinema film. The thread or film is wrapped round the reel so that it can be kept neatly together. E.g., *She took up some scissors and a reel of white string . . . Reels of magnetic tape were piled high on his desk.*

1.2   all the scenes and events that you see on cinema screen when the cinema film on one reel is shown. E.g., *Saigon looked like the final reel of 'On the Beach'*.

1.3   a round device with a handle, attached to a fishing rod. One end of the fishing line is wrapped round the reel, and when you catch the fish, you can pull it toward you by turning the handle.

2.   If you reel . . .

3.   If you say your *mind is reeling* . . . etc.

4.   A reel is also a type of fast Scottish dance.

b. CED reel[1] n

1.   any of various cylindrical objects . . . onto which film, magnetic tape, paper tape, wire, thread, etc. may be wound. U.S. equivalent: spool.

2.   (Angling) a device for winding, casting etc., consisting of a revolving spool with a handle, attached to a fishing rod.

3.   a roll of celluloid exhibiting a sequence of photographs to be projected. . . . vb . . . etc.

reel[2] v

reel[3] n   . . .

1.   any of various lively Scottish dances, such as the *eightsome reel* and *foursome reel,* for a fixed number of couples who combine in square and circular formations.

2.   a piece of music having eight quavers to the bar composed for or in the rhythm of this dance.

c. LDCOCE reel[1] n

1.   a round object on which a length of sewing thread, wire, cinema film, fishing line, recording tape, etc. . . . can be wound – compare BOBBIN.

2.   (of) the amount that any of these will hold: *two whole reels of cotton*.

3.   one of several parts of a cinema film contained on a reel: *They get married at the end of the eighth reel*.

reel[2] v   . . . etc.

reel[3] v   . . . etc.

reel[4] n   (the music for) a quick cheerful Scottish or Irish dance.

d. OALD reel[1] n

1.   cylinder, roller, or similarly shaped object on which thread, wire, fishing line, photographic film, magnetic tape, etc. is wound: *a cotton reel, a cable reel*.

2.   quantity of thread, etc. wound on such a cylinder, roller, etc.: *a six-reel film,* a reel v . . . etc.

reel[2] n   (music for) a lively Scottish or Irish dance, usu. for two
or four couples.

e.   WNWD reel[1] n v . . . etc.

reel[2] n

1.   a) a lively Scottish dance.
b) short for *Virginia reel*.
2.   music for either of these.

reel[3] n

1.   a frame or spool, on which thread, wire, tape, film, a
net etc. is wound.
2.   such a frame set on the handle of a fishing rod, to wind
up or let out the line.
3.   the quantity of wire, thread, tape etc. usually wound on
one reel.
4.   in some lawn mowers, a set of spiral steel blades rotating on a horizontal bar set between wheels.

−v . . . etc.

It will be seen from the above that for the compilers of these dictionaries the
options for the 'device' sense of *reel* lay within the following range:

(30)   GENERAL   a device for holding tape etc. (no further specific
indication of types of reels or what they hold)
QUANTITY   measurement of the quantity of tape etc. on a reel
FISHING   device as an attachment on a rod
CINEMA-FILM   the film held on one reel
CINEMA-SHOW   the showing of film on reel.

In recording the choices made by various lexicographers (no two dictionaries
are the same), a combinatory title GEN-FISH-C/DEV is also required, to cover
definitions which, though general in import, also specifically mention fishing
rods and movie films:

(31)

	GEN'L	QUANT	FISH	C/FILM	C/SHOW	GEN-FISH-C/DEV
CCELD	–	–	x	–	x	x
WNWD	x	–	x	x	–	–
CED	–	x	–	x	–	x
OALD	–	x	–	–	–	x
LDOCE	x	x	x	–	–	–

Instead of allowing us to identify which of these is the 'true' description, the
corpus seems to support all these interpretations:

(32)   GENERAL: e.g., A fine wire trails from a reel attached to the missile.
        QUANTITY: e.g., the advantages of putting that much information
                          onto several reels of video tape
        FISHING: e.g., . . . to turn the crank to reel in the fish, but the reel
                          did not respond.
        CINEMA-FILM: e.g., a twelve-reel epic entitled . . .
        CINEMA-SHOW: e.g., His girlfriend, who walked out on him in reel
                          one . . .

Here again, as with *safety, acknowledge,* and *admire,* we have the case of a word
with a fairly general sense used in contexts that allow for a more specific
definition.

2.8   Systematizing approaches to sense differentiation in the MRD

Semanticists[4] (without whose skills lexicographers may never achieve a semantic
description accurate enough to be of any real use in NLP) will undoubtedly
identify many known factors contributing to these fuzzy sense boundaries found
in existing dictionaries. I will confine myself to mentioning one that appears to
be operating in these examples, and that could certainly be handled in a more
systematic way, if lexicographers knew how to do it and had the space to carry
it out.

This phenomenon has been termed *modulation* by Cruse (1986), who describes it in his discussion of "the ways in which the effective semantic contribution of a word may vary under the influence of different contexts"; he makes the
point that "a single sense can be modified in an unlimited number of ways by
different contexts, each context emphasizing certain semantic traits, and obscuring or suppressing others". My own experience and that of many other lexicographers seems to support this contention, which is exemplified by *acknowledge* in 13–16 above, where the +COMMUNICATE component seems to be
switched on or off by specific contexts. In the citations in 13, the 'neutral'
context results in ambiguity regarding this component; 'to itself' in 14 and
'privately' in 15 modulate the sense to show explicitly that in these citations
acknowledge does not include COMMUNICATE; 'publicly' in 16, on the other
hand, modulates the sense of *acknowledge* so as to include +COMMUNICATE
quite specifically.

Another aspect of meaning that certainly contributes to lack of systematicity in

---

[4]Work particularly relevant to practical lexicography includes Apresjan (1973) and Levin (this volume): all equally relevant in the realm of systematicity, though less specific, is the work of George
Lakoff and his colleagues Lakoff & Johnson (1980) and Lakoff (1987); the ideas in these theoretical
works are directly applicable to dictionary-making. On a different level, the focusing of the linguist's
microscope on various types of word meanings and on the behavior of individual lexical items has
much to offer the training of lexicographers for NLP: here the work of Charles Fillmore and Paul Kay
and their colleagues (see references) is highly relevant to these scholars.

dictionary sense differentiation is the operation of *regular polysemy* (of Apres-jan, 1973); the same phenomenon is included in the *lexical rules* described in Leech (1981) and Cruse (1986), among others. It is linked to but distinct from sense modulation by context, and has been more extensively studied. Lex-icographers are of course aware of this phenomenon, but I know of no compre-hensive description that could be systematically applied during dictionary com-pilation.

In the case of *reel*, two instances of regular polysemy operate, both of which instantiate 'semantic transfer rules', to use Leech's term; they could be roughly formulated thus:

(33)

1. A lexical item that means 'a container' can also be used to mean 'the quantity of a certain object that that container holds'
   e.g., "wind the tape on the reel"   (= container)
         "I've used a whole reel of tape"   (= contents)
   cf. *bottle, box, bucket, plate . . .*
2. A lexical item that means 'a dance' can also be used to mean 'a piece of music designed to accompany that dance'
   e.g., "they danced a reel"   (= dance)
         "the band played a reel"   (= music)
   cf. *waltz, tango, can-can . . .*

It is not clear to me whether it would be possible to systematize a description of the lexical items of the language in such a way as to take account of all known instances of regular polysemy, far less of the operation of modulation (or indeed whether Cruse is justified in his use of 'unlimited' here).[5] What is clear is that to attempt such a task on the scale required, even with the most sophisticated of lexical tools, would demand a program of intensive and long-term research, funded at national or international levels and involving representatives from many disciplines – theoretical linguistics, artificial intelligence, and other branches of cognitive science, computer science, and lexicography among them.

In the meantime, the process of lexical acquisition depends very heavily on the quality of the lexical entries in the MRD's – entries compiled for the most part by lexicographers who, faced with a fairly general word sense found in contexts allowing for a more specific definition, handled the 'modulation' dimension of word meaning in varying and idiosyncratic ways. On the basis of their individual analysis of the word's potential, sometimes – but not always – supplemented by examples of usage from a citation file or an electronic corpus, some of them tended to 'lump' the more specific senses into a loose general sense, whereas

[5]If Pustejovsky (of Pustejovsky, 1990) is right about the generative lexicon, then one may expect certain limits to exist; the postulated generative devices, operating in a system that is recursive and large enough, could generate what would appear to be an infinite number of novel senses from a finite number of core devices.

others more often 'split' off each specific meaning into a dictionary sense of its
own. In none of the dictionaries under review at the moment is there any evidence of an attempt to deal with this aspect of word meaning in a principled way.

2.9   The assignment of lexicographical sense in the MRD

When corpus lexicography began, the lexicographer's (admittedly rather naive)
initial reaction was one of relief: at last, certainty was on the horizon. All that had
to be done was to set up a 'starter pack' of possible senses for the word to be
analyzed, using both one's own knowledge of the language and insights from
existing dictionaries, then work through the citations (sometimes thousands)
dealing them out like playing cards into the correct dictionary sense (of Atkins,
1987). At the end of this process they would all be snugly packed away where they
belonged, and the meaning of the word would be definitively analyzed and
recorded. Disillusion followed promptly. In the case of many – if not most –
lexical items, this proved impossible. A first 'deal' might leave a group of citations
stranded with none of the prepared senses able to receive them. This was predictable, of course, and the analysis must then be worked over again, to take care
of the unplaced citations. Thus for example, in the case of *safety,* having started
with the two senses 'condition of not being in danger' and 'quality of not being
dangerous', one might be forced to reduce these to a single sense in order to find a
unique lexicographical home for 'road safety' (see 8 above). This solution, although removing the original set of outstanding problem citations by clustering
them under the umbrella sense of 'state of being safe', produces in its turn a different problem. The usages of *safety* in 'the safety of the children' and 'the safety of
the product' are clearly capable of more specific, and distinct, definitions: this
distinction is irritatingly lost when the broader sense is the only one to be held.

Safety, danger, risk, acknowledge, admit, admire, reel . . . these are not isolated phenomena for lexicographers: Moon (1987, 1988) discusses similar problems in relation to *mouth, keep, light,* and *time:* Stock (1984) records the same
situation with *culture,* and points out that "not all citational evidence can be
clearly disambiguated in terms of lexicographic senses". And therein, I believe,
lies the heart of the matter. The traditional dictionary entry is trying to do what
the languages imply will not allow. Word meaning cannot be sliced up into
distinct bundles, labeled (however carefully) and packaged into a dictionary
entry that will tell the truth, the whole truth, and nothing but the truth about the
word. This of course is not news: but it did not matter so much when the only
user of the dictionary was a human being, with a human being's innate knowledge of the way language works, of its secret passages from one sense to the next
or one word to another, the ebbing and flowing of its word meanings, its flit-
ting associations and known-but-not-known relationships. The advent of the
machine-readable dictionary and the user-computer changes all that.

2.10   Reconciliation of varying lexicographical approaches to word meaning analysis

In the process of building a large-scale lexicon, the MRD is systematically trawled to supply facts needed to fill the lexical database (LDB) or lexical knowledge base (LKB). The parsed dictionary is minutely examined (Boguraev & Briscoe, 1989a; Byrd et al., 1987), clues are identified and followed up, and morphological (Byrd, 1983) and syntactic (Boguraev & Briscoe, 1989b) facts are found in abundance. The useful semantic information that may be extracted at present is more restricted in scope, and virtually limited to the construction of semantic taxonomies (Chodorow et al., 1985; Calzolari, 1983, 1984), the recording of semantic coding on the arguments of verbs (Klavans, 1990) and the recording of real-world knowledge gleaned from the definition structure of related lexical items (Amsler, 1980; Calzolari & Picchi, 1988).

The comparison of entries for the same word in different MRDs has highlighted discrepancies both in content and in defining technique. Some account of the difficulties posed by these discrepancies is given in Atkins and Levin (1991), and illustrated by an attempted manual mapping of the entry for *whistle* (not a lexicographically complex entry) in two comparable dictionaries. We suggested then that, rather than attempt to map one dictionary entry onto another, a more fruitful technique might consist of designing an 'ideal' LDB entry for the type of lexical item in question, and extracting facts to fill this entry from various MRDs. Levin (in press, this volume) discusses this approach to the verbs of sound.

I am not concerned here with the way in which semantic information is eventually structured as part of an LKB, but simply with ways of facilitating its extraction from existing MRDs. The divergences in lexicographical approach noted for *safety, danger, acknowledge*, etc., and the fact that none of these descriptions actually reflects the complexity of the word in use will greatly reduce the value of mapping dictionary entries as a part of a technique of building LDBs. There is perhaps an interim stage in the process: the construction of the ultimate MRD, an extremely detailed dictionary with many different types of 'ideal' entry structure designed to meet the demands of many different types of lexical item. (The identification of these demands and the design of the custom-made entry structures would of course be the responsibility of the theoretical linguist.) Such a database, 'knowing' what it needed to record for each type of lexical entry, would form an integral part of the lexical tools needed to carry out successfully mapping procedures such as those described in Byrd (1989). With the development of more robust and sophisticated parsers to handle raw text, this database would greatly contribute to the development of tools capable of extracting facts not only from existing non-compatible MRDs (where the idiosyncrasies and blind spots of the lexicographer inevitably detract from the quality of the data) but also from raw text corpora, from which a more objective description of language use many eventually be derived.

2.11   Intermediate lexicographical level between commercial MRDs and the LKB

The first stage in preparing the MRD material semi-automatically would seem to be the construction of a very general or 'major' sense (or more commonly a series of 'major' senses) for each headword entry, by comparing treatment of that headword within each of the MRDs being used, and also across all of them. Techniques (of Byrd, 1989) would be devised to identify items to be recorded at this 'major sense' level. An example of such a major sense for the word *reel* (see 29), would be 'device' whereas another would be 'dance'. This is, in fact, reflected in the dictionaries: CCELD holds the 'device' senses together under sense 1 while the 'dance' sense is numbered 4; the other works divide the material into homonymic headwords. Within these major senses, however, none of the dictionaries is able to show a hierarchical difference in status between the 'general' sense (see 30) on the one hand, and that of the more specific extensions of that sense (quantity, fishing, film, and film-show). Similarly, in CED and WNWD, where the dance and the music for that dance are given distinct definitions of equal status, no hierarchy is possible. The two-dimensional flat structure of the traditional dictionary entry will not allow the recording of any more subtle relationships.

It should be noted here in parentheses that the macrostructure of some existing dictionaries does in fact allow for such a hierarchical approach to the description of word meaning (and indeed, of the dictionaries being studied here, CCELD's *reel* entry would do this if it allowed a definition at the '1' level). An example of a general sense with more specific meanings linked hierarchically to it may be found in sense 1 of *Webster's Ninth New Collegiate Dictionary* (1983) (MW9) entry for ¹reel n:

(34)
1. a revolvable device on which something flexible is wound: as
    a. a small windlass at the butt of a fishing rod for the line.
    b. (chiefly Brit.) a spool or bobbin for sewing thread
    c. a flanged spool for photographic film; esp. one for motion pictures.
2. a quantity of something wound on a reel.
3. a frame for drying clothes usu. having radial arms on a vertical pole.

This hierarchical approach is not, however, implemented systematically throughout the wordlist of the book, as may be seen from the following MW9 entry for *rod:*

(35)
1.a. (1) a straight slender stick growing on or cut from a tree or bush
     (2) OSIER
     (3) a stick or bundle of twigs used to punish;
         also: PUNISHMENT

(4)   a shepherd's cudgel

(5)   a pole with a line and usu. a reel attached for fishing

b.   (1)   a slender bar (as of wood or metal)

(2)   a bar or a staff for measuring . . .

If this *rod* entry were to be made structurally consistent with the *reel* entry, the content would have to be presented in a format that moves the 'major' senses (1a and 1b in 35) to a higher level in the description, so that they become 1 and 2 respectively:

(36)

1.   a straight slender stick growing on or cut from a tree or bush: more specifically:

a.   OSIER

b.   a stick or bundles of twigs used to punish:

also: PUNISHMENT

c.   a shepherd's cudgel

d.   a pole with a line and usu. a reel attached for fishing

2.   a slender bar (as of wood or metal); more specifically:

a.   a bar or a staff for measuring . . .

In terms of the actual *rod* entry, shown in 35 above, the amended version in 36 supplies the missing nodes 1a ("a straight slender stick growing . . .") and 1b ("a slender bar (as of wood or metal)"). These correspond to node 1 ("a revolvable device . . .") in the *reel* entry from the same dictionary, shown in 34. These 'major' senses are then subdivided into more specific senses, such as – for the first sense of *rod* – 'OSIER', "a stick or bundle of twigs . . .", "a shepherd's cudgel" and a "pole with a line . . ."

Although I do not believe that any tree structure can ever do justice to lexical meaning, the one described above, if implemented consistently throughout the vocabulary, would certainly make it easier to map dictionary entries onto one another and extract from them the maximum information for an LDB. Without a hierarchical structure that allows the 'general' or 'major' sense to be stated and defined and more specific usages attached to it to be recorded in a subsidiary numbering system, dictionary entries will never be able to handle either the operation of semantic transfer rules or the phenomenon of sense modulation by context.

2.12   'Ideal' MRD entry structure to be filled semi-automatically from MRDs[6]

The following (37) shows part of a possible entry in a detailed MRD for the noun *reel:* the hierarchical structure of attributes relevant to this lexical item would be

---

[6]The foundation of the work described here was laid during discussions with Beth Levin, although she is not responsible for this draft partial entry nor for this commentary on it.

generated by an automatic interpretation of the contents of the various MRDs being processed, and the values supplied as far as possible by the same process, as briefly outlined in 38 below.

This must be a hierarchically structured entry, potentially able to contain many specific 'levels' of description, representing predictable extensions of meaning (defined by lexical rules such as those shown in 33 above) and able to instantiate simultaneously more than one such level. The category numbering system must record relationships between these levels; thus the first level of decimal points (e.g., 1.1, 1.2 . . . and 2.1, 2.2, etc.) might indicate the operation of some specific lexical rule (semantic transfers, say, or transitivity alternations: see Levin [this volume]), while the first level of lower-case letters (e.g., 1.a, 1.b . . . and 2.a, 2.b, etc.) might indicate the modulation of sense by domain-specific vocabulary in the surrounding context, and so on. A category such as d or e in 37 below shows by its number that it instantiates two types of systematic meaning extensions.

(37)   Part of a hierarchically structured MRD entry for noun *reel:*

a. CATEGORY: 1
    GENUS: device / container / object / cylinder / roller
                           / frame / spool
    DIFF-1: STATUS   autonomous
    DIFF-2: USE   contain / hold / wind
    DIFF-3: FORM   cylindrical / round
    DIFF-4: CONTAINED   thread / film / cinema film / string / mag-
                           netic tape / paper tape / wire / sewing thread
                           / fishing line / recording tape / cotton /
                           photographic film / cable / net /

b. CATEGORY: 1.a
    LINK-RULE: modulation | domain
    EXTENSION: domain-specific
    GENUS: device
    DIFF-1: DOMAIN   angling
    DIFF-2: STATUS   part-of
    DIFF-3: PART-OF   fishing rod
    DIFF-4: CONTAINED   fishing line
    DIFF-5: USE   wrap / wind / cast
    DIFF-6: FORM   cylindrical / round

c. CATEGORY: 1.1
    LINK-RULE: container | contents
    EXTENSION: contained-quantity
    GENUS: quantity / amount

d. CATEGORY: 1.1.b
    LINK-RULE-1:   container | contents

	LINK-RULE-2:	modulation | domain
	EXTENSION-1:	contained-content
	EXTENSION-2:	domain-specific
	GENUS:	film / roll of celluloid (etc.)
	DIFF-2: DOMAIN	cinema
e.	CATEGORY:	1.2.b
	LINK-RULE-1:	activity | time-period
	LINK-RULE-2:	modulation | domain
	EXTENSION-1:	time period
	EXTENSION-2:	domain-specific
	GENUS:	period of time
	DIFF-1: DOMAIN	cinema
f.	CATEGORY:	2
	GENUS:	dance
	DIFF-1: TYPE	group
	DIFF-2: NUMBER	2-couple / 4-couple
	DIFF-3: NATIONALITY	Scottish / Irish
	DIFF-4: SPEED	fast
g.	CATEGORY	2.1
	LINK-RULE:	dance | music
	EXTENSION:	music
	GENUS:	piece of music
	DIFF-1: NATIONALITY	Scottish / Irish
	DIFF-2: SPEED	fast

An entry of this nature would be constructed semi-automatically as an inter-
mediary between existing MRDs and the LDB proper, and filled – as far as
possible automatically (of Byrd, 1989) – from the various relevant entries in
these MRDs, given in 29 above. This assumes a theoretical basis that will offer an
appropriate structure for each lexical item; such an entry structure will be generated for each lexical item as part of the process of building the lexical database; it
will be designed to hold the facts relevant to that type of item and be flexible
enough to respond to the contents of the entries of the MRDs. The generation and
'population' (filling) of these entries should as far as possible be accomplished
by semi-automatic methods such as those sketched in the following explanation
of the sample part-entry for *reel:*

(38)   GENUS 37a,b   'Device' is selected automatically as the
genus term on the basis of "object used
for", "object . . . on which . . . is
wound" in the parsed dictionary entries;
similarly 'container' is generated by "used
to hold" in the CCELD entry (a previous
analysis of lexicographical defining conven-

37f
LINK-RULE
37b,c,d,e,g

37c

37b,d

DIFF:STATUS
37a,b

DIFF:PART-OF
37b

tions is assumed). 'Cylinder', 'roller', 'frame', and 'spool' are picked up from the OALD and WNED definitions.

'Dance' is picked up from every dictionary. This refers to various types of relevant semantic transfer lexical rules, activated by the specific type of lexical item to which – on the basis of the genus term – the headword is identified as belonging.

The value 'container | contents' is generated by the value 'container' at GENUS (see immediately above).

The value 'modulation | domain' is trickier to generate automatically. It would have to be done by a clever combination of factors, such as the presence in three of the parsed MRD entries (CCELD 1.3, CED 2 and WNWD 2) of what are clearly domain-specific senses, and the presence in the lexicon of markers for the same domain (Fishing) against lexical items that appear within the first 'object, device' sense of two other MRD entries (LDOCE 1 and OALD 1). See below at DIFF:DOMAIN for the marking of domains against items in the lexicon.[7]

This attribute is generated by the input GENUS value 'device' (see above at GENUS). Is the device freestanding (as in 37a) or does it stand in some metonymous relationship to another term (as in 37b)? The value 'autonomous' in 37a is assigned on the basis of the absence of 'part of' or a similar phrase in the relevant definitions in the MRDs. The value 'part-of' in 37b is assigned on the basis of definition wording such as 'attached to' in CCELD section 1.3 and in CED section 2 (see full entries at 29 above).

This differentia is generated by input STATUS value 'part-of' (see immediately

---

[7] It is not clear where this information is to come from; ideally, of course, it would be computed on the basis of the frequency/distribution ratio of each item in a very large and comprehensive text corpus.

	above); 'fishing rod', the related term, is picked up from parsed CCELD and CED entries (of "attached to a fishing rod").
DIFF:USE 37a,b	This differentia is generated by the input GENUS value 'device' (see above at GENUS). What use is this device intended for? The items, 'hold' and 'wind' (in 37a) and 'wrap', 'wind', and 'cast' (in 37b) are picked up from the parsed CCELD entry ("used to hold") or the others ("on which . . . is wound").
DIFF:FORM 37a,b	This attribute is generated by the input GENUS value 'device' (see above at GENUS); a device is routinely identified as a concrete object.
37a	The value 'cylindrical' is picked up from "cylinder" in OALD, via the morphological component, and from "cylindrical" in the parsed CCELD and CED entries; "round" in LDOCE produces the value 'round'.
DIFF:CONTAINED	This attribute is generated by the input GENUS value 'container' (see above at GENUS).
37a	The lexical items ('thread', 'film', etc.) listed here have been picked up from the various parsed dictionary entries.
EXTENSION 37b,c,d,e,g	This attribute is generated automatically (every LINK-RULE must have its own EXTENSION sense) for any decimal-point category, in order to relate it to the 'major' sense in a structured way. In, for instance, the entry for *safety*, one value might be 'place', which would be in category 1.3, following upon and generated by the 'state or condition' GENUS of category 1, "the state or condition of no danger".
DIFF:DOMAIN 37b,d,e	This is generated by the input EXTENSION item 'domain-specific'. All legitimate domains will be stored in a closed-set list and marked (as far as possible automatically, from the contents of the MRDs) on lexical items in the computer's lexicon.
37d,e	This DOMAIN value ('cinema') is assigned

	on the basis of the presence in the definition of several lexical items marked in the lexicon as 'DOMAIN – cinema'. Other DOMAIN values are assigned in the same way.
DIFF:TYPE 37f	This differentia is generated by the input GENUS value 'dance'; other TYPE values might be 'partner', 'solo', etc.
DIFF:NUMBER DIFF:SPEED 37F	These differentiae are also generated by input GENUS value 'dance'. Options here would include 'slow', 'moderate', 'unspecified', etc.
DIFF:NATIONALITY 37f,g	This is generated by the input GENUS value 'dance' together with input TYPE value 'group'.
37f	The items 'Scottish' and 'Irish' are picked up from definitions in the parsed MRD entries.
37g	Here, 'Scottish' and 'Irish' are automatically inherited from DIFF-NATIONALITY in 37f.

2.13   "I am speaking of that which words are insufficient to explain"

So wrote Samuel Johnson, in 1755, when discussing word meaning and the ordering of senses in the *Preface* to his great Dictionary. None of the problems of today's lexicographers – as far as I can see – was unknown to him. Of course the idea of setting out the meaning of words in numbered sections is as doomed to failure in the twentieth century (computers or no computers) as it was in the eighteenth. It is instructive to consider the difference in attitude to the task of describing word meaning in his *Plan of a Dictionary*, in 1747, at the start of the enterprise, and the painstaking telling-it-like-it-was that is to be found in the 1755 *Preface* to the published work.

When the dictionary was still at the design stage, Johnson wrote: "The great labour is yet to come, the labour of interpreting these words and phrases with brevity, fulness and perspicuity; a task of which the extent and intricacy is sufficiently shewn by the miscarriage of those who have generally attempted it. This difficulty is increased by the necessity of explaining the words in the same language, for there is often only one word for one idea; and though it be easy to translate the words *bright, sweet, salt, bitter,* into another language, it is not easy to explain them". At that point, the wording of definitions was clearly seen as the most difficult aspect of handling word meaning. Johnson appeared to foresee few problems in analyzing the meaning of a word into distinct senses and in ordering these. Indeed, he goes on to write quite confidently: "In explaining the general and popular language, it seems necessary to sort the several senses of each word, and to exhibit first its natural and primitive signification . . . then to give its consequential meaning . . . then its metaphorical sense . . ." and so on.

In 1755, the picture had changed. ("But these were the dreams of a poet, doomed at last to wake a lexicographer.") I leave the last word to Johnson, who spoke for many succeeding generations of lexicographers when he wrote:

> In every word of extensive use, it was requisite to mark the progress of its meaning, and show by what gradations of intermediate sense it has passed from its primitive to its remote and accidental signification; so that every foregoing explanation should tend to that which follows, and the series be regularly concatenated from the first notion to the last.
> This is specious,[8] but not always practicable; kindred senses may be so interwoven, that the perplexity cannot be disentangled, nor any reason be assigned why one should be ranged before the other. When the radical idea branches out into parallel ramifications, how can a consecutive series be formed of sense in their nature collateral? The shades of meaning sometimes pass imperceptibly into each other, so that though on one side they apparently differ, yet it is impossible to mark the point of contact. Ideas of the same race, though not exactly alike, are sometimes so little different, that no words can express the dissimilitude, though the mind easily perceives it, when they are exhibited together; and sometimes there is such a confusion of acceptations, that discernment is wearied, and distinction puzzled, and perseverance herself hurries to an end, by crowding together what she cannot separate.

Appendix

Acknowledge

Collins Cobuild English Language Dictionary (1987)

acknowledge /ə'knolihdʒ/, **acknowledges, acknowledging, acknowledged. 1**
  If you acknowledge a fact or a situation, you accept or admit that it is true or that
  it exists. EG *The state acknowledged the justice of their cause... Most people
  will now acknowledge that there is a crisis.*
  2 If people or their status, qualities, or achievements are **acknowledged** by
  other people, they are widely known about and admired. EG *Edwin Lawrence
  Godkin was acknowledged as America's finest editorial writer... ...a woman of
  acknowledged charm and personality.*
  3 If you **acknowledge** someone, for example, with a nod or a smile, you show
  that you have seen and recognized them. EG *I took care not to acknowledge
  Janet with more than a nod... He never even bothered to acknowledge her
  presence.*
  4 If you **acknowledge** a message, letter, or parcel, you tell the person who sent
  it that you have received it. EG *The Colonel heard his Operations Officer
  acknowledge the message... You have to sign here and acknowledge receipt.*
  5 If you **acknowledge** applause, compliments, or something which is done for
  you, you show your gratitude for it or your appreciation of it. EG *The president
  stood up to acknowledge the cheers of the crowd... I pushed a drink toward
  him; he acknowledged it, but continued talking.*

---

[8]Snowy; pleasing to the view (S. Johnson, *A Dictionary of the English Language*).

Collins English Dictionary (1986)

acknowledge (ək'nolihdʒ) *vb.* (*tr.*) **1.** (*may take a clause as object*) to recognize or admit the existence, truth, or reality of. **2.** to indicate recognition or awareness of, as by a greeting, glance, etc. **3.** to express appreciation or thanks for: *to acknowledge a gift.* **4.** to make the receipt of known to the sender: *to acknowledge a letter.* **5.** to recognize, esp. in legal form, the authority, rights, or claims of. [C]5: probably from earlier knowledge, on the model of Old English *oncnāwan,* Middle English *aknowen* to confess, recognize] —**ac'knowledgeable** *adj.* —**ac'knowledger** *n.*

Longman Dictionary of Contemporary English (1987)

ac·knowl·edge /ək'nolihdʒ‖-'nɑ:-/ *v* [T] **1** [(as)] to accept or admit (as); recognize the fact or existence (of): *When the results of the vote were announced the Prime Minister acknowledged defeat.* | *The terrorists refused to acknowledge the court.* | *She is acknowledged as an expert on the subject.* | *an acknowledged expert* [+ *v-ing/that*] *He grudgingly acknowledged having made a mistake/that he had made a mistake.* [+ *obj* + *to-v*] *He is generally acknowledged to have the finest collection of Dutch paintings in private hands.* [+obj +adj] *She acknowledged herself puzzled.* **2** to show that one is grateful for: *The producer wishes to acknowledge the assistance of the Los Angeles Police Department in the making of this film.* **3** to state that one has received (something): *We must acknowledge his letter/acknowledge receipt of his letter.* **4** to show that one recognizes (someone) by smiling, waving, etc.: *She walked right past me without even acknowledging me.*

Oxford Advanced Learner's Dictionary (1989)

ac·know·ledge /ək'olihdʒ/ *v* **1** [Tn, Tf, Tw, Cn·a, Cn·t] accept the truth of (sth); admit (sth): *acknowledge the need for reform* ○ *a generally acknowledged fact* ○ *He acknowledged it to be true/that it was true.* ○ *They refused to acknowledge defeat/that they were defeated/themselves beaten.* **2** [Tn] report that one has received (sth):

acknowledge (receipt of) a letter. **3** [Tn] express thanks for (sth): *acknowledge help* ○ *His services to the country were never officially acknowledged.* **4** [Tn] show that one has noticed or recognized (sb) by a smile, nod of the head, greeting, etc: *I was standing right next to her, but she didn't even acknowledge me/my presence.* **5** (a) [Cn·n/a, Cn·t] ~ sb (as sth) accept sb (as sth): *Stephen acknowledged Henry as* (ie recognized his claim to be) *his heir.* ○ *He was generally acknowledged to be the finest poet in the land.* (b) [Tn] accept or recognize (sth): *The country acknowledged his claim to the throne.*

Webster's New World Dictionary (1988)

ac·knowl·edge (ak näl'ij, ək-) *vt.* **-edged, -edg·ing** [earlier *aknowledge* < ME *knowlechen* < *knowleche* (see KNOWLEDGE): infl. by ME *aknowen* < OE *oncnawan,* to understand, know, with Latinized prefix] **1** to admit to be true or as stated; confess **2** to recognize the authority or claims of **3** to recognize and answer (a greeting or greeter, an introduction, etc.) **4** to express thanks for **5** to state that one has received (a letter, gift, favor, payment, etc.) **6** *Law* to admit or affirm as genuine; certify in legal form [*to acknowledge* a deed] —**ac·knowl'edge·able** *adj.*

SYN. —**acknowledge** implies the reluctant disclosure of something one might have kept secret [*he acknowledged* the child as his]; **admit** describes assent that has been elicited by persuasion and implies a conceding of a fact, etc. [I'll *admit* you're right]; **own** denotes an informal acknowledgment of something in connection with oneself [to *own* to a liking for turnips]; **avow** implies an open, emphatic declaration, often as an act of affirmation; **confess** is applied to a formal acknowledgment of a sin, crime, etc., but in a weakened sense is used interchangeably with admit in making simple declarations [I'll *confess* I don't like him] —*ANT*. deny

ack·nowl·edged (-ijd) *adj*. commonly recognized or accepted [the *acknowledged* leader of the group]

Admire

Collins Cobuild English Language Dictionary (1987)

admire /ə'dmaɪə/, **admires, admiring, admired.** If you admire someone or something, you **1** like, respect, and approve of them. ○ *I admire cleverness-and courage too... They had been admired for their discipline.* **2** look with pleasure at them. EG *He went back along the lane admiring the autumn crocuses.*

Collins English Dictionary (1986)

admire (əd'maɪə) *vb.* (*tr.*) **1.** to regard with esteem, respect, approval, or pleased surprise. **2.** *Archaic.* to wonder at. [C16: from Latin *admirari* to wonder at, from *ad-* to, al + *mirari* to wonder, from *mirus* wonderful] —**ad'mirer** *n.* —**ad'miring** *adj.* —**ad'miringly** *adv.*

Longman Dictionary of Contemporary English (1987)

ad·mire /əd'maɪə'/ *v* [T (for)] to think of or look at with pleasure and respect: *I admire (her for) the way she handles her staff.* | *You may not like him, but you've got to admire his persistence.* | *He gave her an admiring look.* | *He's always looking in the mirror, admiring himself!* —see WONDER (USAGE)

Oxford Advanced Learner's Dictionary (1989)

ad·mire /əd'maɪə(r)/*v* **1** [Tn, Tn·pr, Tsg] ~ sb/sth (for sth) regard sb/sth with respect, pleasure, satisfaction, etc: *They admired our garden.* ○ *I admire him for his success in business.* **2** [Tn] express admiration of (sb/sth): *Aren't you going to admire my new hat?*
▷ **ad·mirer** *n* (a) person who admires sb/sth: *I am not a great admirer of her work.* (b) man who admires and is attracted to a woman: *She has many admirers.*
ad·mir·ing *adj* showing or feeling admiration: *give/sb/receive admiring glances* ○ *be welcomed by admiring fans.* **ad·mir·ingly** *adv.*

Webster's New World Dictionary (1988)

ad·mire (ad mir', ed-) *vt.* **-mired', -mir'ing** [OFr *admirer* < L *admirari* < *ad-*, at + *mirari*, to wonder: see MIRACLE] **1** to regard with wonder, delight, and pleased approval **2** to have high regard for ★**3** [Dial.] to like or wish (*to* do something) **4** [Archaic] to marvel at —*SYN.* REGARD —**ad·mir'er** *n.* —**ad·mir'ingly** *adv.*

Admit

Collins Cobuild English Language Dictionary (1987)

admit /ə'dmɪt/, **admits, admitting, admitted. 1** If you **admit** something you **1.1** agree, often reluctantly, that it is true. EG *I must admit I had my doubts... It is not, I admit, a good way of selling newspapers... 'I don't know,' he admitted.* **1.2** agree or confess that you have done something that you should not have done. EG *The Vice President admitted taking bribes.*
2 If you **admit** defeat, you accept that you cannot do something which you have started. EG *Her imagination failed her: she had to admit defeat.*
3 To **admit** someone or something to a place means to allow them to enter it. EG *The Sovereign has never been admitted to the House of Commons... This ticket admits two... The door was opened, admitting a shaft of daylight.*
4 If someone is **admitted** to hospital, they are taken there because they are ill and stay there for one or more nights. EG *He was admitted to hospital with an ulcerated leg.*
5 If you **admit** someone to an organization or group, you allow them to join it or become part of it. EG *He was admitted to full membership of the academy... Soon afterwards he was admitted to British citizenship.*
6 If a room or building **admits** a particular number of people, it has room for that number; a formal use. EG *The new theatre will admit 400 people.*
7 If an event or situation **admits** of something, it makes it possible for that thing to happen or be true; a formal use. EG *The relevant statute admitted of one interpretation only.*

Collins English Dictionary (1986)

admit (əd'mɪt) *vb.* **-mits, -mitting, -mitted.** (*mainly tr.*) **1.** (*may take a clause as object*) to confess or acknowledge (a crime, mistake, etc.). **2.** (*may take a clause as object*) to concede (the truth or validity of something). **3.** to allow to enter; let in. **4.** (foll. by *to*) to allow participation (in) or the right to be part (of): *to admit to the profession.* **5.** (when *intr.,* foll. by *of*) to allow (of); leave room (for). **6.** (*intr.*) to give access: *the door admits onto the lawn.* [C14: from Latin *admittere* to let come or go to, from *ad-* to + *mittere* to send]

Longman Dictionary of Contemporary English (1987)

ad·mit /əd'mɪt/ *v* -tt- **1** [I (to), T] to state or agree to the truth of (usu. something bad); CONFESS: *He admitted his guilt/admitted to the murder.* [+ *v-ing*] *She admitted stealing the bicycle/admitted having stolen the bicycle.* [+(*that*)] *She admitted that she had stolen the bicycle.* | *I must admit, it's more difficult than I though it would be.* [+ *obj* + *to-v*] *A fuel leak is now admitted to have been the cause of the trouble.* —compare DENY (1) **2** [T (into, to)] to permit to enter, let in: *he was admitted to hospital suffering from burns.* **3** [I + of: T] *fml* to leave a chance for being possible; allow: *The facts admit (of) no other explanation.*

Oxford Advanced Learner's Dictionary (1989)

ad·mit /əd'mɪt/ *v* (-tt-) **1** [Tn, Tn·pr] ~ sb/sth (into/to sth) (a) allow sb/sth to enter: *That man is not to be admitted.* ○ *Each ticket admits two people to the party.* ○ *The small window admitted very little light.* (b) accept sb into a hospital as a patient, or into a school, etc as a pupil: *The school admits sixty new boys and girls every year.* ○ *He was admitted to hospital with minor burns.* **2** [Tn] (of an enclosed space) have room for (sb/sth): *The theatre admits only 250 people.*

3 [Ipr, Tn, Tf, Tnt, Tg] ~ to sth/doing sth recognize or acknowledge sth as true, often reluctantly; confess sth: *George would never admit to being wrong.* ○ *The prisoner has admitted his guilt.* ○ *I admit my mistake/that I was wrong.* ○ *I admit (that) you have a point.* ○ *He admitted having stolen the car.* ○ *It is now generally admitted to have been* (ie Most people agree and accept that it was) *a mistake.* **4** [Ipr] ~ of sth (*fml*) allow the possibility of sth; leave room for sth: *His conduct admits of no excuse.* ○ *The plan does not admit of improvement,* ie cannot be improved. **5** (idm) be **admitted** to sb's presence (*fml*) be allowed to enter the room, etc where sb (esp sb important) is.

Webster's New World Dictionary (1988)

ad·mit (ad mit', əd'-) *vt.* **-mit'ted, -mit'ting** [ME *admitten* < L *admittere* < *ad-*, to + *mittere,* to send: see MISSION] **1** to permit to enter or use; let in **2** to entitle to enter [this ticket *admits* two] **3** to allow; leave room for **4** to have room for; hold [the hall *admits* 2,500 people] **5** to concede or grant **6** to acknowledge or confess **7** to permit to practice certain functions [he was *admitted* to the bar] —*vi.* **1** to give entrance (*to* a place) **2** to allow or warrant: with *of* **3** to confess or own (*to*) —*SYN.* ACKNOWLEDGE, RECEIVE

Danger

Collins Cobuild English Language Dictionary (1987)

danger money is extra money that is paid to someone for doing dangerous work. EG *He deserves to get danger money for that job.*

danger /ˈdeɪndʒə/, **dangers. 1** Danger is the possibility that someone may be harmed or killed. EG *The child is too young to understand danger... There was widespread danger of disease... My friends were round me. I was in no danger... Danger! Keep away!*

2 A danger is something or someone that can hurt or harm you. EG *Cigarette smoking is a danger to health... They warned us of the dangers of making assumptions.*

3 If someone is on the danger list, they are extremely ill, and may die.

4 If someone is out of danger, they are still ill but are not expected to die.

5 If there is a danger that something unpleasant will happen, it is possible that that thing will happen. EG *There was a danger that she might marry the wrong man... There is a danger of war and holocaust.*

6 If you say 'There's no danger of that', you mean that you do not think that the thing referred to will happen.

Collins English Dictionary (1986)

danger (ˈdeɪndʒə) *n.* **1.** the state of being vulnerable to injury, loss, or evil; risk. **2.** a person or thing that may cause injury, pain, etc. **3.** *Obsolete.* power. **4.** in **danger of.** liable to. **5.** on the **danger** list. critically ill in hospital. [C13 *daunger* power, hence power to inflict injury, from Old French *dongier* (from Latin *dominium* ownership) blended with Old French *dam* injury, from Latin *damnum*] —ˈ**dangerless** *adj.*

danger money *n.* extra money paid to compensate for the risks involved in certain dangerous jobs.

dangerous (ˈdeɪndʒərəs) *adj.* causing danger; perilous —ˈ**dangerously** *adv.* —ˈ**dangerousness** *n.*

Longman Dictionary of Contemporary English (1987)

dan·ger /'deɪndʒə'/ *n* **1** [U (of, to)] the possibility of harm or loss: *The red flag means "Danger!"* | *a danger signal* | *a place where children can play without danger* | *The patient's life is* in danger. | *The operation was a success and she is now* out of danger. | *He is in (great/real) danger of losing his job.* | *Climbing mountains is* fraught with (= full of) danger. **2** [C (of, to)] a case or cause of danger: *the dangers of smoking* | *This narrow bridge is a danger to traffic.* | *Violent criminals like that are a danger to society.*
danger mon·ey /'·· , ··/ *n* [U] additional pay for dangerous work

Oxford Advanced Learner's Dictionary (1989)

dan·ger /'deɪndʒə(r)/ *n* **1** [U] ~ (of sth) chance of suffering damage, loss, injury, etc; risk: *There's a lot of danger in rock climbing.* ○ *Danger—thin ice!* ○ *In war, a soldier's life is full of danger.* ○ *Is there any danger of fire?* ○ *She was very ill, but is now out of danger,* ie not likely to die. ○ *Ships out in this storm are in great danger,* ie very liable to suffer damage, etc. ○ *His life was in danger.* **2** [C] ~ (to sb/sth) person or thing that may cause damage, injury, pain, etc; hazard: *be afraid of hidden dangers* ○ *Smoking is a danger to health* ○ *That woman is a danger to society.* **3** (idm) on the danger list (*infml*) very ill and near to death: *She was on the danger list, but is much better now.*
□ **'danger money** extra pay for dangerous work.
dan·ger·ous /'deɪndʒərəs/ *adj* ~ (for sb/sth) likely to cause danger or be a danger: *a dangerous bridge, journey, illness* ○ *The river is dangerous for swimmers.* ○ *This machine is dangerous: the wiring is faulty.* ▷ **dan·ger·ously** *adv: driving dangerously* ○ *dangerously ill,* ie so ill that one might die.

Webster's New World Dictionary (1988)

dan·ger (dän'jər) *n.* [ME *daunger,* power, domination, arrogance < OFr *danger,* absolute power of an overlord < VL **dominarium* < L *dominium,* lordship < *dominus,* a master: see DOMINATE] **1** liability to injury, damage, loss or pain; peril **2** a thing that may cause injury, pain, etc. **3** [Obs.] power of a lord, esp. to harm
SYN. —**danger** is the general term for liability to injury or evil, of whatever degree or likelihood of occurrence [the *danger* of falling on icy walks]; **peril** suggests great and imminent danger [the burning house put them in *peril* of death]; **jeopardy** emphasizes exposure to extreme danger [liberty is in *jeopardy* under tyrants]; **hazard** implies a foreseeable but uncontrollable possibility of danger, but stresses the element of chance [the *hazards* of hunting big game]; **risk** implies the voluntary taking of a dangerous chance [he jumped at the *risk* of his life] —*ANT.* **safety, security**

Reel

Collins Cobuild English Language Dictionary (1987)

reel /riːl/, **reels, reeling, reeled 1** A reel is **1.1** a cylindrical object which is used to hold long things such as thread or cinema film. The thread or film is wrapped round the reel so that it can be kept neatly together. EG *She took up some scissors and a reel of white string... Reels of magnetic tape were piled high on his desk.* **1.2** all the scenes and events that you see on a cinema screen when the cinema film on one reel is shown. EG *Saigon looked like the final reel of 'On the Beach'.* **1.3** a round device with a handle, attached to a fishing-rod. One end of the fishing line is wrapped round the reel, and when you catch a fish, you can pull it towards you by turning the handle.

2 If you reel **2.1** you move about unsteadily and jerkily as if you are going to fall. EG *I reeled back into the room... She gave him a smack in the face that sent him reeling off the pavement.* **2.2** you are very upset by an unpleasant experience. EG *We reeled from the shock of discovering that our own father was a liar.*

3 If you say that your brain or mind is reeling, you mean that you are feeling very confused because you have too many things which you need to think about. EG *My brain reeled with all my plans for my new house... His mind was dazed and reeling with all that he had seen and heard.*

4 A reel is also a type of fast Scottish dance.

reel in. If you reel in a fish, you pull it towards you by winding the line onto the reel of the your fishing rod. EG *You could throw a bare hook in the water and reel it in, and more often than not you'd catch a fish.*

reel off. If you reel off information, you repeat it from memory quickly and easily. EG *He could reel off the names of all the capitals of Europe.*

Collins English Dictionary (1986)

reel[1] (ri:l, rɪəl) *n.* **1.** any of various cylindrical objects or frames that turn on an axis and onto which film, magnetic tape, paper tape, wire, thread, etc., may be wound. U.S. equivalent: spool. **2.** *Angling.* a device for winding, casting, etc., consisting of a revolving spool with a handle, attached to a fishing rod. **3.** a roll of celluloid exhibiting a sequence of photographs to be projected. ~*vb.* (*tr.*) **4.** to wind (cotton, thread, etc.) onto a reel. **5.** (foll. by *in, out,* etc.) to wind or draw with a reel: *to reel in a fish.* [Old English *hrēol*; related to Old Norse *hrǽll* weaver's rod, Greek *krekein* to weave] —'**reelable** *adj.* —'**reeler** *n.*

reel[2] (ri:l, rɪəl) *vb.* (*mainly intr.*) **1.** to sway, esp. under the shock of a blow or through dizziness or drunkenness. **2.** to whirl about or have the feeling of whirling about: *his brain reeled.* ~*n.* **3.** a staggering or swaying motion or sensation. [C14 *relen*, probably from REEL[1]]

reel[3] (ri:l, rɪəl) *n.* **1.** any of various lively Scottish dances, such as the eightsome reel and foursome reel, for a fixed number of couples who combine in square and circular formations. **2.** a piece of music having eight quavers to the bar composed for or in the rhythm of this dance. [C18: from REEL[2]]

reel-fed *adj. Printing.* involving or printing on a web of paper: a *reel-fed press.* Compare sheet-fed.

reel man *n. Austral. and N.Z.* the member of a beach life-saving team who controls the reel on which the line is wound.

reel off *vb.* (*tr., adv.*) to recite or write fluently and without apparent effort: *to reel off items on a list.*

reel of three *n.* (in Scottish country dancing) a figure-of-eight movement danced by three people.

reel-to-reel *adj.* **1.** (of magnetic tape) wound from one reel to another in use. **2.** (of a tape recorder) using magnetic tape wound from one reel to another, as opposed to cassettes.

Longman Dictionary of Contemporary English (1987)

reel[1] /ri:l/ *n* **1** *BrE* ‖ spool *AmE* – a round object on which a length of sewing thread, wire, cinema film, fishing line, recording TAPE[1] (2a), etc., can be wound –compare BOBBIN **2** [(of)] the amount that any of these will hold: *two whole reels of cotton* **3** one of several parts of a cinema film contained on a reel: *They get married at the end of the eighth reel.*

reel² *v* [T + *obj* + *adv/prep*] to bring, take, etc. by winding: *he reeled in his fishing line.* | *Reel some more thread off the machine.*

reel sthg. ↔ off *phr v* [T] *infml* to repeat (usu. a lot of information) quickly and easily from memory, RATTLE off: *He could reel off the dates of all the kings of England.*

reel³ *v* [I] **1** [+ adv/prep] to walk unsteadily, moving from side to side, as if drunk: *he came reeling up the street.* **2** [(BACK)] to step away suddenly and unsteadily (as if) after being hit or receiving a shock: *When I hit him he reeled (back) and almost fell.* **3** to be in a state of shock, confusion, or uncertainty: *All these statistics make my head reel.* | *The party is still reeling from its recent election defeat.* **4** to seem to go round and round: *The room reeled before my eyes and I became unconscious.*

reel⁴ *n* (the music for) a quick cheerful Scottish or Irish dance

Oxford Advanced Learner's Dictionary (1989)

reel¹ /ri:l/ *n* (*US* **spool**) **1** cylinder, roller or similarly shaped object on which thread, wire, fishing line, photographic film, magnetic tape, etc is wound: *a cotton reel* ○ *a cable reel.* **2** quantity of thread, etc wound on such a cylinder, roller, etc: *a six-reel film.*
▷**reel** *v* **1** [Tn·p] ~ sth in/out wind (sth) on or off a reel; pull (sth) in by using a reel: *reel the line, the hosepipe, etc out* ○ *The angler reeled the trout in slowly.* **2** (phr v) reel sth off say or repeat sth rapidly without pause or apparent effort: *reel off a poem, list of names, set of instructions.*

reel² /ri:l/ *v* **1** [I, Ipr, Ip] move unsteadily or sway; stagger: *reel drunkenly down the road* ○ *She reeled (back) from the force of the blow.* ○ *I reeled round in a daze.* **2** [I, Ipr] (*fig*) (of the mind or head) be or become dizzy or confused; be in a whirl: *The very idea sets my head reeling.* ○ *His mind reeled when he heard the news/at the news.* ○ *be reeling from/with/under the shock* ○ (*fig*) *The street reeled* (ie seemed to go round and round) *before her eyes.*

reel³ /ri:l/ *n* (music for a) lively Scottish or Irish dance, usu for two or four couples.

Webster's New World Dictionary (1988)

reel¹ (rēl) *vl.* [ME *relen* < the *n.*: from the sensation of whirling] **1** to give way or fall back; sway, waver, or stagger as from being struck **2** to lurch or stagger about, as from drunkenness or dizziness **3** to go around and around; whirl **4** to feel dizzy; have a sensation of spinning or whirling —*vt.* to cause to reel —*n.* [ME *rele* < OE *hreol: see* REEL³] a reeling motion; whirl, stagger, etc.

reel² (rēl) *n.* [prob. < prec., *n.*] **1** *a*) a lively Scottish dance *b*) *short for* VIRGINIA REEL **2** music for either of these

reel³ (rēl) *n.* [ME < OE *hreol* < Gmc **hrehulaz* < IE base **krek-*, to strike, make a weaving motion > Gr *krekein,* to weave, Latvian *brekls,* shirt] **1** a frame or spool on which thread, wire, tape, film, a net, etc. is wound **2** such a frame set on the handle of a fishing rod, to wind up or let out the line **3** the quantity of wire, thread, film, tape, etc. usually wound on one reel **4** in some lawn mowers, a set of spiral steel blades rotating on a horizontal bar set between wheels —*vt.* *vi.* to wind on a reel —**reel in 1** to wind on a reel **2** to pull in (a fish) by winding a line on a reel —**reel off** to tell, write, produce, etc. easily and quickly —**reel out** to unwind from a reel —★(right) off the reel without hesitation or pause.

reel-to-reel (-tōō-rēl′) *adj.* designating or of a tape recorder using two separate reels, on which the tape must be threaded.

Webster's Ninth New Collegiate Dictionary (1983)

¹reel \'rē(ə)l *n* [ME, fr. OE *hrēol; akin to ON* hrœll weaver's reed, Gk *krekein* to weave] (bef. 12c) **1:** a revolvable device on which something flexible is wound: as **a :** a small windlass at the butt of a fishing rod for the line **b** *chiefly Brit* : a spool or bobbin for sewing thread **c :** a flanged spool for photographic film; *esp* : one for motion pictures **2 :** a quantity of something wound on a reel **3 :** a frame for drying clothes usu. having radial arms on a vertical pole

²reel *vt* (14c) **1 :** to wind on or as if on a reel **2 :** to draw by reeling a line (~ a fish in) ~ *vi :* to turn a reel —**reel-able** \'rē-lə-bəl\ *adj*

³reel *vb* [ME *relen.* prob. fr. *reel,* n.] *vi* (14c) **1 a :** to turn or move round and round **b :** to be in a whirl **2 :** to behave in a violent dissorderly manner **3 :** to waver or fall back (as from a blow) **4 :** to walk or move unsteadily ~ *vt :* to cause to reel

⁴reel *n* (1572): a reeling motion

⁵reel *n* [prob. fr. *⁴reel*] (1585) **1 :** a lively Scottish-Highland dance; *also* : the music for this dance **2 :** VIRGINIA REEL

reel off *vt* (1952) **1 :** to chalk up usu. as a series **2 :** to tell or recite readily and usu. at length (*reel off* a few jokes to break the ice)

reel-to-reel *adj* (1961) : of, relating to, or utilizing magnetic tape that requires threading on a take-up reel (a ~ tape recorder)

Rod

Webster's Ninth New Collegiate Dictionary (1983)

rod\'räd*n* [ME, fr. OE *rodd;* akin to ON *rudda* club] (bef. 12c) **1 a** (1) : a straight slender stick growing on or cut from a tree or bush (2) : OSIER (3) : a stick or bundle of twigs used to punish; *also* : PUNISHMENT (4) : a shepherd's cudgel (5) : a pole with a line and usu. a reel attached for fishing **b** (1) : a slender bar (as of wood or metal) (2) : a bar or staff for measuring (3) : SCEPTER: *also* : a wand or staff carried as a badge of office (as of marshal) **2 a :** a unit of length – see WEIGHT table **b :** a square rod **3 :** any of the long rod-shaped photosensitive receptors in the retina responsive to faint light **4 :** a rod-shaped bacterium **5** *slang* : PISTOL – **rod-less** \-ləs\ *adj* – **rod-like** \-,lik\ *adj*

Safety

Collins Cobuild English Language Dictionary (1987)

safety/seIfti'/. **1** Safety is **1.1** the state of being safe. EG *He was assured of his daughter's safety.* **1.2** the possibility of your being harmed in a particular situation. EG *Many worried about the safety of their children.* **1.3** a place where you are safe from a particular danger. EG *They were busy helping survivors to safety... They swim to the safety of a small, rock island.*

2 If you are concerned about the safety of a product, course of action, etc, you are concerned that it might be harmful or dangerous. EG *People worry about the safety of nuclear energy.*

3 Safety features, safety measures, etc are intended to make something less dangerous. EG *Every car will come with built-in safety features... Heating was by oil stoves without proper safety measures.*

safety belt, safety belts; also spelled with a hyphen. A safety belt is a belt or strap attached to a seat in a car, aeroplane, etc. You fasten it round your body, and it stops you being thrown forward if there is an accident. EG *He would have been killed if he hadn't been wearing a safety belt.*

safety catch, safety catches; also spelled with a hyphen. **1** The safety catch on a gun stops you firing it accidentally. EG *Charles slipped on the safety catch and pocketed the gun.*
2 The safety catch on a window or door stops it being opened too far, or being opened by a thief.

safety net, safety nets; also spelled with a hyphen. **1** In a circus, a safety net is a large net that performers on trapezes or high wires can fall into if they make a mistake. EG *His most dangerous stunt was walking the tightrope without a safety net.*
2 A safety net is also something that you can rely on to help you if you get into a difficult situation. EG *The Fund is our safety net if anything should go wrong.*

safety pin, safety pins; also spelled with a hyphen. A safety pin is **1** a bent metal pin that is used for fastening two things together. It is designed so that the point of the pin is covered and does not stick into you. EG *My trousers were fastened with a safety-pin... Do it up with a safety pin.* **2** a short piece of metal in a grenade, bomb, etc that has to be removed before the device can explode.

safety-valve, safety-valves; also spelled as two words. **1** A safety-valve allows liquids or gases to escape from a steam engine or other machine when the pressure inside the machine becomes too great.
2 A safety-valve is also anything that allows you to express strong feelings without harming other people. EG *She needed a safety-valve, that was all... ...a safety-valve for the harmless release of rebellious feelings.*

Collins English Dictionary (1986)

safety ('seɪftɪ) *n., pl.* **-ties. 1.** the quality of being safe. **2.** freedom from danger or risk of injury. **3.** a contrivance or device designed to prevent injury. **4.** *American football.* **a.** Also called: 'safety, man. the defensive player furthest back in the field. **b.** a play in which the ball is put down by a player behind his own goal line when the ball is caused to pass the goal line by one of his own team. Compare touchback.

safety belt *n.* **1.** another name for seat belt. **2** a belt or strap worn by a person working at a great height and attached to a fixed object to prevent him from falling.

safety catch *n.* a device to prevent the accidental operation of a mechanism, e.g. in a firearm or lift.

safety chain *n.* a chain on the fastening of a bracelet, watch, etc., to ensure that it cannot open enough to fall off accidentally. Also called: guard.

safety curtain *n.* a curtain made of fireproof material that can be lowered to separate the auditorium and stage in a theatre to prevent the spread of a fire.

safety factor *n.* another name for factor of safety.

safety film *n.* photographic film consisting of a nonflammable cellulose acetate or polyester base.

safety fuse *n.* **1.** a slow-burning fuse for igniting detonators from a distance. **2.** an electrical fuse that protects a circuit from overloading.

safety glass *n.* glass made by sandwiching a layer of plastic or resin between two sheets of glass so that if broken the fragments will not shatter.

Safety Islands *pl. n.* a group of three small French islands in the Atlantic, off the coast of French Guiana. French name: Iles du Salut.

safety lamp n. an oil-burning miner's lamp in which the flame is surrounded by a metal gauze to prevent it from igniting combustible gas. Also called: Davy lamp.

safety match n. a match that will light only when struck against a specially prepared surface.

safety net *n*. **1.** a net used in a circus to catch high-wire and trapeze artists if they fall. **2.** any means of protection from hardship or loss, such as insurance.

safety pin *n*. **1.** a spring wire clasp with a covering catch, made so as to shield the point when closed and to prevent accidental unfastening. **2.** another word for pin (sense 9).

safety razor *n*. a razor with a guard or guards fitted close to the cutting edge or edges so that deep cuts are prevented and the risk of accidental cuts reduced.

safety valve *n*. **1.** a valve in a pressure vessel that allows fluid to escape when a predetermined level of pressure has been reached. **2.** a harmless outlet for emotion, energy, etc.

Longman Dictionary of Contemporary English (1987)

safe-ty /'seɪfti/ *n* [U] the condition of being safe: freedom from danger, harm, or risk: *The safety of the ship is the captain's responsibility.* | *She led the children to a place of safety.* | *There are fears for the safety of the climbers.* (= they might be hurt or dead) | *The management took all reasonable safety precautions.* | *Safety checks are carried out on all industrial machinery.* | *Let's try to stay together as a group: there's safety in numbers.* | *It's very important to teach children about road safety.*

safety belt /'·· ·/ *n* A SEAT BELT

safety catch /'·· ·/ *n* a lock on a gun to prevent it from being fired accidentally

safety cur-tain /'···,··/ is a theatre curtain made of material that will not burn, which may be lowered in front of the stage

safety-de-pos-it box /'·· ·,·· '·/ *n* a SAFE-DEPOSIT BOX

safety-first /,·· '·/ *adj* [A] *sometimes derog* showing a wish to take no risks; CAUTIOUS: *a safety-first attitude*

safety glass /'·· ·/ *n* [U] strong glass that breaks only into small pieces which are not sharp

safety is-land /'···,··/ *n AmE for* ISLAND (2)

safety lamp /'·· ·/ *n* a miner's lamp made so that its flame cannot explode the gases found underground

safety match /'·· ·/ *n* a match which can be lit only by rubbing it along a special surface on its box or packet

safety net /'·· ·/ *n* a large net stretched out below someone performing high above the ground to catch them if they fall: *A safety net was spread below the tightrope walker.* | (fig.) *What happens to the poor people who are not caught by the government's safety net of welfare payments?*

safety pin /'·· ·/ *n* a wire pin that has a cover at one end and is bent round so that its point can be held safely inside the cover —see picture at PIN

safety ra-zor /'·· ,··/ *n* a RAZOR with a cover fitting over the thin blade to protect the skin from being cut —see picture at RAZOR

safety valve /'·· ·/ *n* a part of a machine, esp. of a steam engine, which allows gas, steam, etc., to escape when the pressure becomes too great: (fig.) *Vigorous exercise is a good safety valve if you're under a lot of pressure at work.*

Oxford Advanced Learner's Dictionary (1989)

safety /'seɪftɪ/ *n* [U] **1** being safe; not being dangerous or in danger: *I'm worried about the safety of children,* ie I'm afraid something may happen to them. ○ *I'm worried about the safety of the product,* ie I'm afraid it may be dangerous. ○ *We reached the safety of the river bank,* ie a place where we would be safe. ○ *We're keeping you here for your own safety.* ○ *road safety,* ie stopping accidents on the roads ○ [attrib] *safety precautions* ○ *a safety harness, bolt.* **2** (idm) ‚safety 'first (*saying*) ie safety is the most important thing. there's 'safety in 'numbers (*saying*) being in a group makes one feel more confident: *We decided to go to see the boss together; there's safety in numbers.*

☐'safety-belt *n* **1** = SEAT-BELT (SEAT). **2** strap securing a person, eg sb working on a high building.

'safety-catch *n* device that prevents the dangerous or accidental operation of a machine, etc, esp one that stops a gun being fired accidentally: *Is the safety-catch on?*

'safety curtain fireproof curtain that can be lowered between the stage and the auditorium of a theatre.

'safety glass glass that does not shatter or splinter when broken.

'safety island (also 'safety zone) (*US*) = TRAFFIC ISLAND (TRAFFIC).

'safety lamp miner's lamp in which the flame is protected so that it will not ignite dangerous gases.

'safety match match that will only ignite when rubbed against a special surface, eg on the side of the matchbox.

'safety net **1** net placed to catch an acrobat, etc if he should fall. **2** (*fig*) arrangement that helps to prevent disaster if sth goes wrong: *If I lose my job, I've got no safety net.*

'safety-pin *n* pin like a brooch, with the point bent back towards the head and covered by a guard when closed.

'safety razor razor with a guard to prevent the blade cutting the skin.

'safety-valve *n* **1** valve that releases pressure in a steam boiler, etc when it becomes too great. ◊ illus at PAN. **2** (*fig*) way of releasing feelings of anger, resentment, etc harmlessly: *My hobby is a good safety net.*

Webster's New World Dictionary (1988)

safety (sāf'tē) *n.*, *pl.* -ties [ME *sauvete* < MFr *sauveté* < OFr *salvete* < ML *salvitas*, safety < L *salvus:* see SAFE] **1** the quality or condition of being safe; freedom from danger, injury, or damage; security **2** any of certain devices for preventing an accident or an undesirable effect; specif., *a*) a catch or locking device on a firearm that prevents it from firing (also safety catch or safety lock) *b*) [Slang] a condom ★**3** *Baseball* BASE HIT ★**4** *Football a*) a play in which the ball is grounded by a player behind his own goal line when the ball was caused to pass the goal line by his own team: it scores as two points for the opponents (distinguished from TOUCHBACK) *b*) a player of a defensive backfield whose position is deep, behind the cornerbacks (in full **safety man**) —*adj.* giving safety; reducing danger or harm

safety belt 1 LIFE BELT **2** a belt attaching a telephone lineman, window washer, etc. to a telephone pole, window sill, etc. to prevent falling **3** a restraining belt, as in an airplane or motor vehicle: see SEAT BELT, SHOULDER HARNESS

safety glass glass made to be shatterproof by fastening together two sheets of glass with a transparent, plastic substance between them

★**safety island** SAFETY ZONE

safety lamp a miner's lamp designed to avoid explosion, fire, etc.; specif., DAVY LAMP

safety match a match that will light only when it is struck on a prepared surface

safety net 1 a net suspended as beneath circus aerialists to catch them if they fall **2** any protection against failure or loss, esp. financial loss

safety pin a pin bent back on itself so as to form a spring, and having the point covered and held with a guard

★**safety razor** a razor with a detachable blade fitted into a holder provided with guards and set at an angle which minimizes the danger of cutting the skin

safety valve 1 an automatic valve for a steam boiler, pressure cooker, etc., which opens if the pressure becomes excessive **2** any outlet for the release of strong emotion, energy, etc.

★**safety zone** a platform or marked area in a roadway, from which vehicular traffic is diverted, for protection of pedestrians, as in boarding or leaving buses

References

Amsler, R. A. (1980). *The Structure of the Merriam-Webster Pocket Dictionary*. Doctoral dissertation, University of Texas, Austin, TX.

Apresjan, Ju. D. (1973). "Regular Polysemy." *Linguistics,* 142, Mouton, The Hague.

Atkins, B. T. (1987). "Semantic ID Tags: Corpus Evidence for Dictionary Senses." In *The Uses of Large Text Databases,* Proceedings of the Third Annual Conference of the UW Centre for the New OED, Waterloo, Canada, pp. 45–63.

Atkins, B. T., J. Kegl, & B. Levin. (1986). "Implicit and Explicit Information in Dictionaries." In *Advances in Lexicology,* Proceedings of the Second Annual Conference of the UW Centre for the New OED, Waterloo, Canada.

Atkins, B. T., J. Kegl, & B. Levin. (1988). "Anatomy of a Verb Entry." *International Journal of Lexicography,* Vol. 1, No. 2.

Atkins, B. T. & B. Levin. (1991). "Admitting Impediments." In *Lexical Acquisition: Exploiting On-line Resources to Build a Lexicon,* ed. U. Zernik, Hillsdale, NJ: Lawrence Erlbaum Associates.

Boguraev, B. & T. Briscoe. (1989a). "Introduction." In *Computational Lexicography for Natural Language Processing.* London: Longman.

Boguraev, B. & T. Briscoe. (1989b). "Utilising the LDOCE Grammar Codes." In *Computational Lexicography for Natural Language Processing.* London: Longman.

Byrd, R. J. (1983). "Word Formation in Natural Language Processing Systems." In *Proceedings of the Eighth International Joint Conference on Artificial Intelligence,* Karlsruhe, Germany, pp. 704–706.

Byrd, R. J. (1989). "Discovering Relationships among Word Senses." In *Dictionaries in the Electronic Age,* Proceedings of the Fifth Annual Conference of the UW Centre for the New OED, Waterloo, Canada.

Byrd, R. J. & J. L. Klavans. (1986). "Computer Methods for Morphological Analysis." *Proceedings of the Association for Computational Linguistics,* pp. 120–127.

Byrd, R. J., N. Calzolari, M. Chodorow, J. Klavans, M. Neff, & O. Rizk. (1987). "Tools and Methods for Computational Lexicology." *Computational Linguistics,* 13:219–240.

Calzolari, N. (1983). "Lexical Definitions in a Computerised Dictionary." *Computers and Artificial Intelligence,* 2(3):225–233.

Calzolari, N. (1984). "Detecting Patterns in a Lexical Database." In *Proceedings of the Tenth International Congress on Computational Linguistics,* pp. 170–173, Stanford, CA.

Calzolari, N. & E. Picchi. (1988). "Acquisition of Semantic Information from an On-line Dictionary." In *Proceedings of COLING '88,* Budapest, pp. 87–92.

Chodorow, M. S., R. J. Byrd, & G. E. Heidorn. (1985). "Extracting Semantic Hierarchies from a Large On-line Dictionary." *Computational Linguistics,* 23:299–304.

Cruse, D. A. (1986). *Lexical Semantics.* Cambridge: Cambridge University Press.

Fillmore. C. J. (1975). "An Alternative to Checklist Theories of Meaning." In *Proceedings of the First Annual Meeting of the Berkeley Linguistics Society,* ed. C. Cogen et al., pp. 123–131, Berkeley, CA.

Fillmore, C. J. (1977). "Topics in Lexical Semantics." In *Current Issues in Linguistic Theory*, ed. R. Cole, pp. 76–138, Bloomington: Indiana University Press.

Fillmore, C. J. (1978). "On the Organization of Semantic Information in the Lexicon." In *Parasession on the Lexicon*, Chicago Linguistic Society, University of Chicago.

Fillmore, C. J. & B. T. Atkins (in press: a) "Towards a Frame-based Lexicon: the Semantics of RISK and its Neighbors." In *Frames, Fields and Contrasts*, eds. A. Lehrer and E. Kittay. Hillsdale, NJ: Lawrence Erlbaum Associates.

Fillmore, C. J. & B. T. Atkins. (in press: b). "Starting Where the Dictionaries Stop: The Challenge of Corpus Lexicography." In *Computational Approaches to the Lexicon*, ed. B. T. Atkins & A. Zampolli, Oxford: Oxford University Press.

Fillmore, Charles J., Paul Kay, & Mary Catherine O'Connor. (1988). "Regularity and Idiomaticity in Grammatical Constructions: The Case of Let Alone." *Language*, Vol. 64, No. 4, pp. 501–508.

Kay, Paul. (1984). "The kind of / sort of Construction." In *Proceedings of the Tenth Annual Meeting of the Berkeley Linguistics Society*, eds. C. Brugman, M. Macaulay et al., Berkeley, CA.

Kay, Paul. (1989). "Contextual Operators: Respective, Respectively, and Vice Versa." In *Proceedings of the Fifteenth Annual Meeting of the Berkeley Linguistics Society*, eds. K. Hall, M. Meacham & R. Shapiro, Berkeley, CA.

Kay, Paul. (1990). "Even." *Linguistics and Philosophy*, Vol. 13, pp. 59–111, The Netherlands: Kluwer Academic Publishers.

Kay, Paul. (in press). "At least." In *Frames, Fields and Contrasts*, eds. A. Lehrer & E. Kittay. Hillsdale, NJ: Lawrence Erlbaum Associates.

Klavans, J. L. (1990). "COMPLEX: a Computational Lexicon for Natural Language Systems." In *Proceedings of the 12th International Conference on Computational Linguistics*, 1988, Budapest, Hungary, pp. 815–823.

Lakoff, George. (1987). *Women, Fire and Dangerous Things*, Chicago: University of Chicago Press.

Lakoff, George & Mark Johnson. (1980). *Metaphors We Live By*, Chicago: University of Chicago Press.

Leech, Geoffrey. (1981). *Semantics*. Cambridge: Cambridge University Press.

Levin, B. (in press). *Towards a Lexical Organization of English Verbs*. Chicago: University of Chicago Press.

Lyons, J. (1969). *Introduction to Theoretical Linguistics*. Cambridge: Cambridge University Press.

Moon, R. (1987). "Monosemous Words and the Dictionary." In *The Dictionary and the Language Learner*, ed. A. P. Cowie, Tübingen: Niemeyer.

Moon, R. (1988). " 'Time' and Idioms." In *Zurilex '86 Proceedings*, ed. M. Snell-Hornby, Francke, Tübingen.

Pustejovsky, James. (1990). "The Generative Lexicon." *Computational Linguistics*, Vol. 17.

Stock, P. F. (1984). "Polysemy." In *Lexeter '83 Proceedings*, ed. R. R. K. Hartmann, Tübingen: Niemeyer.

Dictionaries cited

CCELD   *Collins Cobuild English Language Dictionary* (1987), ed. Sinclair, Hanks et al., Collins Ltd., London, UK.

CED   *Collins English Dictionary* (1986), ed. Hanks et al., Collins Ltd., Glasgow, UK.

LDOCE   *Longman Dictionary of Contemporary English* (1987), ed. Summers et al., Longman Group UK Ltd., Harlow, UK.

MW9 *Webster's Ninth New Collegiate Dictionary* (1983), ed. Mish et al., Merriam-Webster Inc., Springfield MA, USA.

OALD *Oxford Advanced Learner's Dictionary* (1989), ed. Cowie et al., Oxford University Press, Oxford, UK.

WNWD *Webster's New World Dictionary* (1988), ed. Neufeldt et al., Simon & Schuster Inc., New York, USA.

3   The contribution of linguistics

BETH LEVIN

3.1   Introduction

The lexicon has come to occupy an increasingly central place in a variety of current linguistic theories, and it is equally important to work in natural language processing. The lexicon – the repository of information about words – has often proved to be a bottleneck in the design of large-scale natural language systems, given the tremendous number of words in the English language, coupled with the constant coinage of new words and shifts in the meanings of existing words. For this reason, there has been growing interest recently in building large-scale lexical knowledge bases automatically, or even semi-automatically, taking various on-line resources such as machine readable dictionaries (MRDs) and text corpora as a starting point, for instance, see the papers in Boguraev and Briscoe (1989) and Zernik (1989a). This chapter looks at the task of creating a lexicon from a different perspective, reviewing some of the advances in the understanding of the organization of the lexicon that have emerged from recent work in linguistics and sketching how the results of this work may be used in the design and creation of large-scale lexical knowledge bases that can serve a variety of needs, including those of natural language front ends, machine translation, speech recognition and synthesis, and lexicographers' and translators' workstations.

Although in principle on-line resources such as MRDs and text corpora would seem to provide a wealth of valuable linguistic information that could serve as a foundation for developing a lexical knowledge base, in practice it is often difficult to take full advantage of the information these existing resources contain. Dictionaries, for example, might seem particularly well-suited as a basis for automatic lexicon construction, since the information they provide is structured within the entry, and it would seem possible to extract certain information, for example, part of speech, fairly trivially. However, this is only a fraction of the information available in a dictionary. Dictionaries are designed for human users by humans. Human users are native speakers of language who know at least

Much of the material on verbs of sound in this chapter grew out of a series of discussions with Sue Atkins that accompanied the writing of Atkins and Levin (1988). I would like to thank Sue Atkins, Chuck Fillmore, Bob Ilson, and Annie Zaenen for their comments on an earlier version of this chapter.

implicitly how the lexicon of their language is structured, and lexicographers exploit the lexical knowledge of potential users in writing dictionary entries. Consequently, dictionary entries only need to say enough about a word to allow native speakers of a language to tap into their general knowledge. Thus entries often leave much implicit or unsaid, something that would be unacceptable in a lexical knowledge base for a natural language system. The missing information must be filled in from somewhere, and linguistic studies into lexical organization can contribute to this task. Even learner's dictionaries, which are intended for learners of a language, take advantage of general properties of language, although typically they do provide fuller information than dictionaries intended for native speakers of that language about syntactic properties, as well as a range of example sentences illustrating word use. For more discussion of this issue see Atkins, Kegl, and Levin (1986, 1988), Boguraev and Briscoe (1989), and McCawley (1986).

These considerations aside, the value of using dictionaries as a starting point for building a lexical knowledge base is diminished by the limitations of dictionary-making itself. Dictionaries are written by lexicographers, who are themselves humans working within rigorous time and space constraints. Consequently, not all words receive the attention they deserve (see Atkins [this volume] for discussion). Even the best dictionaries have flaws; for instance, they are often incomplete and inconsistent (Atkins, Kegl, and Levin, 1988; Boguraev and Briscoe, 1989; Neff and Boguraev, 1989; among others). For instance, words that pattern in the same way are often not given parallel treatment in dictionaries, due either to time and space limitations or to the failure of the lexicographer to recognize the pattern.[1]

The goal of this chapter is to sketch the contribution that linguistics can make to the task of building lexical knowledge bases. Specifically, results of linguistic research into lexical organization have implications for the design of a lexical knowledge base: they both suggest the overall structure of the knowledge base and delineate the type of information that must be available in this knowledge base. This framework in turn should facilitate the extraction of as much information as possible from on-line resources. Specifically, efforts to build lexical knowledge bases automatically or semi-automatically could use template entries for verbs of particular semantic types motivated by linguistic research to guide attempts to extract information about specific verbs from existing on-line resources such as dictionaries and corpora.

Section 3.1 outlines the nature of a native speaker's lexical knowledge from

---

[1]On-line dictionaries are unlikely to serve as a lexical knowledge base, even if, as suggested by some researchers, several dictionaries were merged on the assumption that the result will be more complete than any single dictionary. As pointed out in Atkins and Levin (1988), the process of merging dictionary entries faces many obstacles. Furthermore, there is no guarantee that the result of merging the entries for a given word would be an entry that is substantially better than the entries of individual dictionaries; such an entry is unlikely to approximate a linguistically motivated lexical knowledge base entry for that word.

the perspective of linguistics. Section 3.2 provides a case study of the lexical knowledge of a native speaker of English by focusing on what a native speaker of English knows about verbs of sound. Section 3.3 exemplifies the design of some aspects of linguistically motivated entries for verbs of sound in a lexical knowledge base, drawing to a large extent on earlier work presented by Atkins and Levin (1988). Section 3.4 discusses how the properties of lexical organization can be used to take maximal advantage of the information available in existing lexical resources.

3.2   The nature of lexical knowledge

A prerequisite for the design and creation of lexical knowledge base is an understanding of what constitutes the lexical competence of a speaker of English, since a lexical knowledge base must make this knowledge explicit. Therefore, this section reviews what research in linguistics has uncovered concerning the nature of lexical knowledge, focusing almost exclusively on lexical knowledge associated with verbs, since they are typically the most complex lexical items to deal with. Similar issues arise for lexical items from other parts of speech; for example, Pustejovsky (1990) discusses some of the problems posed by nouns.

First, consider a problem that computational linguists engaged in building natural language systems might face, a problem that arises because of the complex nature of lexical knowledge.[2] The problem involves the two interchanges below.

(1)   Speaker 1: Sally ate a peach.

       Speaker 1: Did Sally eat?

       Speaker 2: Yes.

(2)   Speaker 1: David dressed the baby.

       Speaker 1: Did David dress?

       Speaker 2: I don't know.

If asked *Did Sally eat?* after having been told that Sally ate a peach as in interchange 1, speakers of English would not hesitate to answer *Yes*. But the same speakers would not answer *Yes* if asked *Did David dress?* after being told that David dressed a baby (see interchange 2). Here the appropriate answer would be *I don't know*. Two sequences consisting of a statement followed by a question that appear to be parallel syntactically (transitive use of a verb in the initial statement, intransitive use of the same verb in the question) elicit quite different

---

[2]For more discussion of this problem and related ones, as well as an attempt to design a natural language system that can deal with such problems, see Katz and Levin (1988). The examples in (1) and (2) are taken from this chapter.

responses from speakers of English. The simple syntax of each pair is unlikely to present a challenge to the parsers used in most existing natural language systems. The difficulty is that the intransitive uses of the two verbs receive very different interpretations. The intransitive use of *eat* found in the question *Did Sally eat?* implies the existence of an understood but unexpressed object, some type of food or meal. The question *Did David dress?* on the other hand does not mean 'Did David dress something one typically dresses?'; it means 'Did David dress himself?'. Speakers of English draw on their knowledge of the properties of these verbs to determine the appropriate interpretation of their intransitive use. Similarly, the lexicons of natural language systems must be built to allow these systems to recognize that the relationship between transitive and intransitive *dress* is not the same as that between transitive and intransitive *eat,* so that they can handle interchanges of the type sketched here appropriately.

Although dictionaries are a rich source of information about words, the information needed in dealing with problems of the type described here is often not explicitly signaled, if it is included at all. Most dictionaries indicate whether verbs have a transitive use, an intransitive use, or both, but relationships between transitive and intransitive uses of verbs such as *eat* and *dress* are not as a rule explicitly indicated. However, such relationships are often encoded using a variety of cues in the dictionary entry that involve the grammatical codes, the wording of the definitions, and properties of the example sentences (Atkins, Kegl, and Levin, 1986, 1988). Thus although the relevant information can sometimes be found in a dictionary, it is not trivially accessible, but will require queries formulated in terms of the specific cues in dictionary entries, a problem complicated by the fact that the same cues are not used consistently across the entries of verbs that pattern in the same way.

As the *eat/dress* example illustrates, some verbs may express their arguments in more than one way, sometimes with slightly different semantic interpretations. Any natural language system that aims at substantial coverage of English must be able to handle correctly not only these but the entire range of possible relationships between alternate expressions of the arguments of verbs. The understanding of the lexical organization of English verbs of the type that emerges from linguistic investigations can contribute to the realization of this goal.

Although the lexicon has been considered the domain of the idiosyncratic, there is much evidence that the relationship between the meaning of verbs and their syntactic behavior is governed by quite general principles, with evidence coming from studies in both lexical semantics and syntax (Bresnan and Kanerva, 1989; Carter, 1976, 1988; Fillmore, 1968; Foley and Van Valin, 1984; Gruber, 1976; Hale and Keyser, 1986, 1987; Jackendoff, 1983, 1990; Levin, 1985; Marantz, 1984; Pustejovsky, 1990; Rappaport, Levin, and Laughren, 1988; Talmy, 1985; and many other works in various theoretical frameworks). The *eat/dress* example shows that certain verbs have both transitive and intransitive uses, and that the relationship between the uses is not uniform across all verbs.

However, such a relationship is not merely an idiosyncratic property of a verb; rather it is to a large extent predictable from the verb's meaning. Interchanges parallel to the one described for *eat* are possible with a wide range of verbs, including *type, sew, sweep,* and *read.* These verbs are all activity verbs; most of them describe typical occupations. Another set of verbs including *bathe, change, shave, shower,* and *wash* – all verbs of grooming or bodily care – behave like *dress.*

Linguists have extensively studied a wide range of linguistic phenomena involving the expression of the arguments of verbs, such as the alternations in transitivity exhibited by the verbs *eat* and *dress.* These studies reveal that English verbs are organized into classes on the basis of shared components of meaning. The members of these classes have in common a range of properties, specifically properties concerning the possible expression and interpretation of their arguments, as well as the extended meanings that they can manifest (Levin, 1985).

The long-term goal of much current linguistic research is explaining what a native speaker of a language knows about the lexical properties of verbs, focusing on those aspects of lexical knowledge related to argument structures, the semantic and syntactic properties of verbs tied to their status as argument-taking lexical items. A central concern of linguistic research on the lexicon is the study of the meanings of verbs and the elaboration of a theory of the representation of lexical entries in which the meaning of a verb is properly associated with the syntactic expressions of its arguments. Ideal lexical entries of verbs should embody the full range of linguistic knowledge possessed by an English speaker in relation to those verbs. At the same time, however, any given entry should supply the minimum amount of information necessary to account for the native speaker's linguistic knowledge of it. This dual requirement naturally leads to the investigation of those aspects of the linguistic behavior of lexical items that are determined by general principles of grammar.

Currently, an important part of this research is the rigorous study of diathesis alternations, alternations in the expression of the arguments of verbs. As the discussion of the verbs *eat* and *dress* illustrates, since diathesis alternations reflect the interaction between a representation of the meaning of a verb and the principles that determine the syntactic realization of its arguments, they can be used to probe into both the lexical representation of meaning and the relationship between syntax and semantics. As the distinctive behavior of verbs with respect to diathesis alternations arises from their lexical properties, specifically their meaning, the exploration of the ways in which diathesis alternations distinguish among verbs should reveal semantically coherent verb classes. Once identified, these classes can be examined to isolate the components of meaning common to verbs participating in particular alternations. These components of meaning would be expected to figure prominently in the lexical representation of the meaning of these verbs. Attempts to formulate the principles according to which these elements of meaning determine the syntactic behavior of verbs then become possible. For some work along these lines, see Hale and Keyser (1986, 1987), Laughren (1988), Levin and Rappaport (1988).

For these reasons, the study of diathesis alternations can make a significant contribution to the elucidation of the lexical representation of meaning. These studies have established a range of diathesis alternations relevant to the lexical organization of English and have identified a number of essential semantically coherent classes of verbs, as well as the central properties characterizing verbs of each type. (See Levin [1989] for a description of the lexical properties of English verbs taking noun phrase and prepositional phrase complements.) Nevertheless, much basic research remains to be done in this area.

3.3 A case study of lexical knowledge: verbs of sound

Linguistic investigations into lexical organization of the type described here can be used to form the basis for the systematic treatment of lexical items, which in turn will ensure the completeness and consistency of verb entries in a lexical knowledge base. As an example of what such a treatment entails, this section will provide a case study of the lexical knowledge that a native speaker of English possesses with respect to a certain class of verbs, the verbs of sound. The focus will be on the syntactic and semantic properties of the verb *whistle* and related verbs; morphological and phonological properties, which are also part of a native speaker's lexical knowledge, will be ignored. This section will not attempt to provide an exhaustive analysis of these facets of these verbs, even in the senses considered here. Rather the aim is to provide a picture of the form that the lexical knowledge associated with the members of a given verb class takes. Section 3.4 will begin to explore how this knowledge translates into a lexical knowledge base entry. The discussion of verbs of sound in this and subsequent sections draws and elaborates on the discussion of these verbs in Atkins and Levin (1988).

As discussed in the previous section, current linguistic research on the lexical knowledge of native speakers of a language shows that the human lexicon is highly structured. Verbs fall into classes on the basis of shared meaning components, and the members of these classes have in common a range of properties concerning the expression and interpretation of their arguments. Verbs of sound are no exception. In this section, the structure of the verb lexicon will be explored by focusing primarily on the verb *whistle,* chosen as a representative member of the class of verbs of sound. English possesses a large class of verbs that denote in their basic (simplest) sense the emission or production of a sound in some way. This class includes the verbs *whistle, whine, groan, grunt, snort, hum, hoot, howl, moan.* In their basic sense, the members of this class share the meaning 'emit a sound'; however, the meanings of the members of this class differ from each other in several well-defined ways. The most obvious differences involve the physical properties of the sound produced ('shrill' for *whistle,* 'low' for *grunt,* and 'high' for *bleep*) and the means of producing this sound ('electronically' for *bleep,* 'blowing' for *whistle,* 'vibrating the vocal cords' for *grunt*).

The nature of the differences in meaning among the verbs of sound is not unusual, but reflects one facet of English lexical organization. There are a variety of classes of verbs in English whose members share a basic sense but differ from each other in terms of a means or manner component (Carter, 1976; Fellbaum, 1990). For instance, English has a large class of verbs of manner of motion, which includes *jump, hop, run, skip, walk, waddle,* and a class of verbs of means of removal, which includes *erase, mop, shovel, sweep, vacuum, wipe.* Furthermore, some of the classes of means or manner verbs are opposed to a class of verbs that share the same basic meaning, but combine it with what might be called a 'result' component. For example, English verbs of removal fall into two classes, the class of means of removal verbs just mentioned, and a smaller class of verbs denoting only the result (and not the means) of removal, which includes *clear, clean, empty;* the two subclasses of verbs of removal behave very differently. In fact, the presence or absence of a means or manner component often plays a part in determining the properties of a word.[3] The importance of the notions of means and manner in the organization of the English verb lexicon is also reflected in the verb component of WordNet (Miller et al., 1988, 1990; Miller and Fellbaum, in press), which as described by Fellbaum (1990) is to a large extent structured around means or manner relations between verbs.

An important part of an English speaker's knowledge of the verbs of sound is knowledge of their argument-taking properties. In their basic sense – as verbs denoting the emission or production of a particular sound – these verbs denote events with a single participant, the emitter of the sound. This participant is expressed as the subject of these verbs, so that in this sense these verbs are intransitive. (Some of these verbs can take objects, as in *"he honked the horn"*, but such uses represent different senses of the verbs; see below.)[4]

(3) a. *"I hissed and snarled and ground my teeth at them."*
  b. *"the line of wart-hogs moved snuffling and grunting across the trail"*
  c. *"the wet candles hissed and went out one by one"*
  d. *"cars honked and hummed in the road"*

Most of the verbs of sound impose very tight restrictions on the choice of possible subjects, since the subject must be something that is capable of inherently producing a sound with the appropriate characteristics. An examination of verbs of sound reveals that these verbs may denote the production of that sound

[3]For further discussion with respect to verbs of motion see Levin and Rappaport Hovav (in press a); for discussion with respect to verbs of removal see Levin and Rappaport Hovav (in press b).
[4]The italicized citations in double quotes are taken from the Cobuild Corpus, which is part of the Birmingham Collection of English Text, held at the University of Birmingham, England, and jointly owned by the University of Birmingham and by Collins Publishers Ltd.

by a human ("*I put back my head and howled*"), another animate entity ("*I could hear a wolf howl*"), or an inanimate entity ("*the wind howled in the trees*"). However, no verb of sound can have an abstract noun as a subject (**the despair growled, *the clarity cooed*). Furthermore, verbs of sound differ in the selectional restrictions on their subjects. That is, it appears to be a property of a particular verb of sound which of the possible subjects it allows, with members of this class differing from each other in this respect. The verb *whistle* permits all three types of subject, *bleep* is rarely if ever found with animate subjects, and *grunt* is rarely if ever found without them.[5] As we shall see, the choice of subject plays a part in determining whether the verb shows certain extended senses.

Verbs of sound in their basic sense do not show a variety of ways of expressing their arguments, probably because they take a single argument. However, they manifest a range of extended senses – additional senses that are systematically related to the basic sound emission sense. As discussed further below, individual verbs vary as to which of the possible extended senses they manifest, so that not all possible senses are shown by every verb in the class. Taking the verb *whistle* as an example where possible, we see the following possibilities:

(4) a. 'emit a sound in a particular way'
   e.g., *the girl whistled / grunted / hissed*
   b. 'emit the sound as a reaction'
   e.g., *the boy whistled / grunted / shrieked at the dog*
   c. 'utter by emitting the sound'
   e.g., *he whistled / hummed / yodelled a tune*
   d. 'signal by emitting the sound'
   e.g., *they whistled / grunted / hissed a warning*
   e. 'express (an emotion) by emitting the sound'
   e.g., *she whistled / grunted her disgust*
   f. 'communicate verbally by emitting the sound'
   e.g., *he grunted / hissed that the meeting was over*
   g. 'move while causing the sound to be emitted'
   e.g., *the rope whistled / hissed through the air*
   h. 'cause to emit the sound'
   e.g., *the postman rang / buzzed the doorbell*
   i. '(of a place) be full of the sound'
   e.g., *the air whistled / hummed with bullets*

---

[5]Selectional restrictions are sometimes violated under particular conditions. For instance, in the context of a science fiction movie it might be possible to say *The man bleeped*. In general, acceptable violations of selectional restrictions arise (i) in contexts where certain beliefs about the word are suspended or modified or (ii) through the operation of specific lexical processes such as metonymy or coercion, whose operation crucially takes advantage of the underlying selectional constraints (Pustejovsky, 1990). Therefore, violations of selectional restrictions should not be taken as evidence for the point of view that stating the restrictions in the first place is futile.

This set of senses was identified because of properties that differentiate them from other senses (selectional restrictions on arguments, expression of arguments, other syntactic properties). Some of these properties will be discussed further in the remainder of this section. Except that the basic sense of a verb of sound is listed first, no particular importance should be attached to the order of presentation of these senses.

What is important for this chapter is that there is a set of senses that can be manifested by verbs belonging to a particular semantic class, since their existence can be exploited in the design of a lexical knowledge base as discussed in Section 3.5. It is likely that further study will show that some of the senses distinguished here might prove to overlap with or be subsumed under others, but as a first approximation it seems preferable to distinguish too many senses than too few. Senses (4b)–(4f), in particular, could use further refinement, possibly using corpus-based lexicography techniques of the type described by Atkins (this volume) and Fillmore and Atkins (in press).

A full account of the extended senses of a verb should identify the factors that allow that verb to show a specific extended sense, whether or not it is actually attested. Some of the senses identified here may be interdependent; that is, their existence may depend on the existence of other senses. Although some factors that determine the availability of particular extended senses are identified here, a full study of this issue is outside the scope of this chapter.

Several of the extended senses of verbs of sound are available only to verbs denoting sounds that can be made by animates, as in (4b)–(4f). However, even when the sound is emitted by an inanimate entity, verbs of sound in their basic sense, as well as in some of their extended senses, are not necessarily verbs of communication. That is, in some senses they simply describe the emission of a sound by some entity without any intent to communicate something through the emission of this sound. Those verbs that may take animate subjects may denote the intentional emission of a sound, and the sound may be emitted with communicative intent. Sometimes, as in extended sense (4b) above, the sound is simply intended as a reaction directed at a certain target. The target may be expressed in an *at* phrase, as in "*A marmot whistled at us and withdrew*" or "*they didn't whistle at her*". Although the target is the intended recipient of the sound, there is no indication that the actual emitter of the sound succeeds in conveying anything to the target; it is in this respect that verbs of sound are not necessarily verbs of communication in all their senses.

However, among the extended senses of verbs of sound that allow human subjects, there is often a sense that might be characterized as in (4f): 'communicate verbally by emitting a sound'. On this sense, which is not typically observed with the verb *whistle* since physically a whistle precludes speech, the verbs denote what Zwicky (1971: 223) calls "intended acts of communication by speech'. When used as verbs of manner of speaking, these verbs take a variety of sentential complements.

(5) a. Susan bellowed that the party would be tonight.
    b. Susan bellowed how to avoid the crowd.
    c. Susan bellowed for me to come.
    d. Susan bellowed to Rachel to come.
    e. Susan bellowed to come.
    f. Susan bellowed, 'Come'.
    g. 'Come', bellowed Susan.

As (5d) illustrates, verbs of sound may also take a *to* phrase indicating the recipient of the communication on this sense. The use of a *to* phrase with this sense contrasts with the use of the *at* phrase found in sense (4b), where there is no necessary implication that the target is a cooperating participant in the event. See Zwicky (1971) and Mufwene (1978) for a detailed exposition of the properties of verbs of sound when used as verbs of manner of speaking.[6]

Many verbs of sound have extended senses as verbs of motion, as in "*A rocket whistled by, missing the hill . . .*", where *whistle* means 'move while causing a whistling sound to be emitted'. This type of meaning extension is relatively productive across verbs of sound, although it is restricted to sounds that are made when a physical entity − whether it be human, animate, or inanimate − moves (and is not manifested with sounds such as *grunt*, which can only be made by the vocal tract). The verbs showing this extended sense are those verbs that can take inanimate subjects (although animate subjects are possible in this extended sense precisely when they make these sounds by moving rather than through their mouth or nose).

Some of those verbs of sound that denote sounds that can be emitted by inanimate objects, including those in (6), manifest a causative meaning, 'cause to emit a particular sound'. This possibility is open to those sounds that can be brought about by an outside cause and are not only emitted due to the inherent properties of the entity producing them.

(6)   bang, beat, beep, buzz, clatter, crack, crunch, jangle, jingle, knock, rattle, ring, roar, rustle, toll, toot, twang, . . .

Many of the extended senses manifested by verbs of sound are not limited to the members of this class. Certain sounds are associated with particular emotions and are emitted to express the associated emotion. For instance, a whistle can indicate surprise or admiration, whereas a hiss might indicate anger. These associations give rise to extended sense (4e), characterized as 'express (an emotion) by emitting the sound'. This extended sense is really an instantiation of the more general meaning 'express (an emotion) in some way'; one way of expressing an emotion is through the emission of a sound that expresses that emotion.

---

[6]Although the complement-taking properties of verbs of sound used as verbs of manner of speaking parallel those of simple verbs of speaking such as *say*, there are some differences between the two in syntactic behavior. Specifically, verbs of manner of speaking, unlike the verb *say*, are what are known as 'non-bridge' verbs (Erteschik, 1973; Stowell, 1981, among others).

This extended sense is found not only with verbs of sound but also with verbs of gestures and signs such as *nod* (*nod one's approval*) or *frown* (*frown one's dismay*), as the examples below illustrate. Gestures and signs, like certain sounds, can also be used to convey certain emotions.

(7) a. *"the men in the audience whistled their appreciation of her figure"*
   b. Marlowe roared approval in his characteristic way, . . .
      (D. Sayers, *The Documents in the Case,* Perennial, 1987, p. 94)
(8) a. She sniffed her disapprobation of the police in general . . .
      (M. Grimes, *The Man with a Load of Mischief,* 1981, p. 132)
   b. Instead, he snorted derision.
      (L. Grant-Adamson, *The Face of Death,* Scribner's, 1986, p. 108)

The process that is involved in creating many of these extended senses is also responsible for creating extended senses of English verbs associated with other semantic classes. This process, called 'lexical subordination' by Levin and Rapoport (1988), involves 'subordinating' the meaning of the verb associated with the basic sense under an additional component of meaning to give the extended sense; typically the meaning associated with the basic sense is a means of bringing the additional meaning about (Jackendoff, 1990; Levin and Rapoport, 1988; as well as Talmy, 1985). For instance, in the extended sense described as 'express (an emotion) by emitting the sound', the basic sense 'emit a sound' is subordinated under the meaning 'express'. The process of lexical subordination is also manifested outside of the verb of sound class. For example, the cooking verb *bake,* which is basically a change of state verb, has an extended sense as a creation verb, with the meaning 'create by means of change of state *bake*' (Atkins, Kegl, and Levin, 1988; Ilson and Mel'čuk, 1989).

Another sense of *whistle,* '(of a place) be full of the sound', is exemplified in *The air whistled with bullets,* which appears to be a near paraphrase of the basic sense of the verb *whistle* found in *The bullets whistled in/through the air.* In this extended sense, the sound is attributed to the location in which it is emitted, with the actual entities emitting the sound expressed in a *with* phrase. Such pairs of sentences are instances of the intransitive variant of the locative alternation characteristic of such verbs as *swarm* (*The garden is swarming with bees/Bees are swarming in the garden*).[7] This sense of *whistle* represents an extended sense of a verb of sound that is manifested very productively across the whole class.

[7]Not every use of a verb of sound in its basic sense can be paraphrased using this extended sense; a variety of factors determine when such pairs are possible. For an extensive discussion of the properties associated with this sense see Salkoff (1983). This sense is not present in any of the dictionaries I have examined, nor are there citations for it among the uses of *whistle* in the Cobuild Corpus. The alternative expressions of the arguments of *swarm* manifested in *The garden is swarming with bees/Bees are swarming in the garden* are the intransitive version of the locative alternation found with verbs like *spray* or *load* (*spray the wall with paint/spray paint on the wall*). This alternation is discussed by Jeffries and Willis (1984), Rappaport and Levin (1988), Schwartz-Norman (1976), among many others.

In their basic sense, the verbs of sound are part of a larger class of verbs of stimulus emission. This larger class includes three additional major subclasses, which can be distinguished by the nature of the stimulus: smell, light, or substance. Representative verbs from these subclasses are listed below:

(9) LIGHT: flicker, gleam, glitter, glow, shimmer, shine, sparkle, twinkle
(10) SMELL: reek, smell, stink
(11) SUBSTANCE: bubble, gush, ooze, puff, spew, spout, squirt

Many of the properties of verbs of sound are shared with the members of the larger class of verbs of stimulus emission. For instance, all are single argument verbs, taking only a subject in their basic sense. Members of all the subclasses are open to the causative extended sense described above (e.g., *The driver flashed the headlights*), although because of the constraints on this meaning only a limited number of verbs in any subclass exhibit this sense. A more general form of the extended sense '(of a place) be full of the sound' – '(of a place) to be full of the stimulus' – is also manifested by verbs from other subclasses of verbs of stimulus emission (e.g., *The sky twinkled with stars*). However, the verbs of sound have a wider range of extended senses than other verbs of stimulus emission: since only sounds can be used for communication, only the verbs of sound have the extended senses associated with communication.

This section has exemplified the close correlation between the basic semantic class of a verb and the way it behaves in the language (expression of arguments, selectional restrictions, extended senses, etc.). As the next section demonstrates, again with verbs of sound, research into lexical organization clarifies not only the basic properties of the verbs, as described in this section, but also the necessary organization and components of lexical entries for verbs of particular types.

3.4 The design of a lexical knowledge base entry for verbs of sound

A lexical knowledge base should make explicit what a native speaker knows about a word. To ensure that a full and systematic presentation of relevant facts is provided, this presentation must be informed by an understanding of lexical organization. Leaving aside phonological and morphological information, a verb entry must give information about each of its sense categories. For each of these, it must give information and examples, when appropriate, about:[8]

(12) a. Semantic class, aktionsart, and arguments
     b. Selectional restrictions on the arguments
     c. Syntactic properties and expression of arguments
     d. Related extended senses

---

[8]Many people have discussed the issue of what types of information should be included in an ideal dictionary entry. For another recent list of such information, which overlaps substantially with the list provided here, see Hudson (1988).

e. Morphologically related nouns, adjectives, and verbs
f. Related idiomatic uses
g. Collocates
h. Pragmatic force

It is worth noting that only some of these facts about a verb can be learned from its dictionary entry. Existing dictionaries might provide a starting point for the construction of a lexical knowledge base entry for a verb, but they do not provide all the information that such a knowledge base should ideally make available.

This section describes lexical knowledge base entries that handle the first four types of facts. The entries developed in this section and the next section again draw on the study of verbs of sound described in Atkins and Levin (1988), which tries, by studying certain aspects of this class, to take the first steps toward defining some of the structure of a template for a lexical knowledge base entry for such verbs.

An essential part of the lexical knowledge base entry for any lexical item is a description of its meaning. Prototypical dictionary definitions consist of two parts, a genus word and differentiae; the genus word is that part of its meaning that a word shares with other hyponyms of the particular genus term selected, and the differentiae are properties that distinguish that word from these co-hyponyms, and this particular sense of the word from other senses of the same word. The discussion of the meaning of verbs of sound in their basic sound emission sense shows that definitions of their meaning conform to this scheme. With verbs of sound, the genus is 'emit a sound' and the differentiae describe the type of sound produced (low, high, loud, soft, shrill, etc.), the means of producing the sound (by blowing, vibration, impact, etc.), what produces the sound (a person, animal, device), and, if a person produces the sound, whether or not an instrument is used to produce it. The first two of these, sound-type and means, were discussed in the previous section. They could be indicated in a lexical knowledge base entry as follows:[9]

	WHISTLE	GRUNT	BLEEP
genus	emit sound	emit sound	emit sound
diff-1: sound-type	shrill	low	high
diff-2: means	by blowing	by vibration	electronically

[9]The lexical knowledge base entries given here are intended only to be suggestive, and actual entries might look rather different. The use of items such as 'shrill' or 'by blowing' as fillers of the differentiae slots may seem a cause for concern to some readers, since they are not themselves 'primitive' notions. However, the concern in this chapter is with the representation of linguistically relevant information, and, from this point of view, it is the existence of specific components of meanings (the nature of the differentiae slots in an entry), rather than the specific instantiation of the components (the fillers of the slots), that is important. For instance, as mentioned, earlier, a verb whose meaning involves a notion of means or manner demonstrates certain linguistic properties independent of the specific means or manner associated with that verb.

As discussed in the previous section, the verbs of sound differ in the types of subjects they allow; therefore, the knowledge base will need to identify the potential subjects of these verbs. For simplicity, the possibilities are indicated using features to encode the possibilities.

	WHISTLE	GRUNT	BLEEP
genus	emit sound	emit sound	emit sound
diff-1: sound-type	shrill	low	high
diff-2: means	by blowing	by vibration	electronically
select-restrns subj	+concrete	+animate	+concrete
	(+/−animate)	(+/−human)	−animate
	(+/−human)		

There is one additional differentia that was not discussed in the previous section. When a person produces a sound, an instrument may or may not be involved. A person can whistle either by blowing air through the lips or by forcing the air through a device (*a whistle*), but a person does not use a device to grunt. Electronic devices bleep, but people typically do not, so the use of an instrument is not relevant to the verb *bleep*. However, because the use of an instrument is pertinent to many verbs of sound, this possibility, which is really a refinement of the means differentia, must be incorporated into a lexical knowledge base entry.

	WHISTLE	GRUNT	BLEEP
genus	emit sound	emit sound	emit sound
diff-1: sound-type	shrill	low	high
diff-2: means	by blowing	by vibration	electronically
diff-3: instrument	+/−device	—	—
select-restrns subj	+concrete	+animate	+concrete
	(+/−animate)	(+/−human)	−animate
	(+/−human)		

Finally, it is important for a verb's entry to contain information regarding its argument-taking properties, and the syntactic expression of these arguments. As discussed in the previous section, in their basic sense, verbs of sound are intransitive. There are a variety of ways in which the syntactic argument-taking properties can be expressed. The entries below represent these properties via a subcategorization frame (Chomsky, 1965).

	WHISTLE	GRUNT	BLEEP
genus	emit sound	emit sound	emit sound
diff-1: sound-type	shrill	low	high
diff-2: means	by blowing	by vibration	electronically
diff-3: instrument	+/−device	—	—

	WHISTLE	GRUNT	BLEEP
select-restrns subj	+concrete (+/−animate) (+/−human)	+animate (+/−human)	+concrete −animate
subcategorization	+[—]	+[—]	+[—]

Alternatively, the argument-taking properties could be represented in terms of the various argument structure representations that have replaced subcategorization frames in recent work in syntax. One possibility is to use the notions of external, internal, direct, and indirect arguments (Williams, 1981; Rappaport, Levin, and Laughren, 1988, among others); on this approach, verbs of sound in the sound emission sense would be characterized as taking only an external argument (the analogue of a subject). Alternatively, the notion of argument classification recently introduced into Lexical Functional Grammar (LFG) could be used (Bresnan and Kanerva, 1989).

In order to introduce the structure of the lexical knowledge base, the focus has been on a single major sense of the verb *whistle,* setting out similarities and differences between this verb and other verbs of sound. Since the goal of this chapter is not to present an exhaustive analysis of these verbs, many additional facts that an ideal lexical knowledge base entry must include for such verbs, even in the sense represented in the template, have been omitted.

3.5   The contribution of on-line resources to a lexical knowledge base

Although the design of an effective and successful lexical knowledge base should be informed by work in linguistics, the knowledge base itself does not need to be completely built up from scratch. The construction of such a knowledge base should take advantage of existing on-line resources, both MRDs and text corpora, extracting whatever information possible from them. Having outlined the contribution that linguistics can make to the design of lexical knowledge base entries of verbs of a particular type, this section will consider how linguistics can also enhance the contribution that on-line resources can make to the creation of lexical knowledge base entries. Specifically, a comprehensive model of the lexicon will enable the designers of a knowledge base to predict the type of facts about a verb that might be expected to be found in dictionaries and corpora once a verb's class has been established. Using such a model, the knowledge base designers can define accurately the type of information that might be expected to be retrieved.

As Section 3.3 makes clear, knowing a verb's semantic class membership is crucial to understanding the properties of a given word and to determining its relation to other words. To state this differently, certain aspects of a verb's meaning serve as a pointer to its place in the organizational scheme of English verbs. Once this place is identified, various properties of the verb can be determined. For example, turning again to verbs of sound, it is clear that there are certain properties that would be expected to be recorded in the lexical knowledge base entry of any verb of this type. These properties can be used to construct a template lexical knowledge base entry for all verbs of sound. An instance of this template entry can then be instantiated for each verb using on-line lexical resources as a source of information, with the template entry-serving in some sense as a guide to the required information.

The partial lexical knowledge base entry for the verb *whistle* presented in the previous section identified certain properties that this verb shares with other verbs of sound and that, therefore, must be taken into account in the design of a knowledge base entry for such verbs. For example, all verbs of sound have a basic sense that can be characterized as emitting or producing a particular sound, and many of them will also have some or all of the extended senses listed in Section 3.3. Information about each of these senses must be included in the knowledge base.

The properties common to all verbs of sound can be incorporated directly into a template lexical entry generated for such verbs. The entry for the basic sense ('emit a sound') must indicate that the genus is of a particular nature ('emit sound') and that the possible differentiae are of predictable types (sound-type, means, instrument), their exact nature depending on the properties of each individual verb. The template entry must also specify that such verbs require a non-abstract subject (with individual verbs imposing additional restrictions). The following is a possible template for the basic sound emission sense of verbs of sound:

genus	emit sound
diff-1: sound-type	
diff-2: means	
diff-3: instrument	
select-restrns subj	−abstract
subcategorization	+[—]

The lexical knowledge base entry for a specific verb of sound in this basic sense can be completed by the addition to this template entry of the differentiae and, if required, further selectional restrictions on the subject. On-line resources would be used to furnish this data in order to complete the description, as well as to provide corroboration for the existence of specific options for specific words.

Similar template entries will have to be constructed for the extended senses of the verbs of sound. The existence of these senses depends in part on certain properties of the basic sense. To the extent that the factors determining the availability of each extended sense are known, the extended senses can be linked to the template entry of the basic sense in such a way that if information obtained about the basic sense precludes a certain extended sense, there would be no need to look for evidence that it exists. For example, a verb of sound can only show an extended sense as a verb of verbal communication if it can denote a sound made by a human; therefore, if the verb under consideration does not take a human subject, the potential existence of this extended sense does not need to be posited for that verb.

The use of a template entry makes it possible to define the type of information being sought from on-line resources, whether MRDs or text corpora, before an attempt is made to extract data. The template defines the specific queries that are being made for any particular word. Given the structured basis of dictionary entries, this type of semi-automatic lexical knowledge base construction is more likely to be successful than attempts to create lexical knowledge bases in some other ways.

3.5.1   The contribution of dictionaries

A model of lexical organization can suggest the properties that a given verb might be expected to show, and hence it can give rise to expectations about what properties might be illustrated in the dictionary entry of that verb. These expectations will help make sense of the information in dictionary entries, allowing information in entries to be exploited beyond what might have been possible in the absence of such a model. Such a model can help overcome certain shortcomings that arise because words in existing dictionaries are treated in isolation. Existing dictionary entries do not fit words into the larger organizational scheme of the English lexicon, nor do they impose any internal structure on the sense categories given in their entries. Learners' dictionaries often present properties that reflect a verb's semantic class through the use of a combination of grammar codes, stylized definitions, and example sentences, but information about the class itself is implicit in an entry (Atkins, Kegl, and Levin, 1986). A model of lexical organization can contribute such information, which is a central component of what a native speaker knows about words.

There are various types of dictionaries, and every dictionary has its own contribution to make to the construction of a lexical knowledge base due to its individual nature and design. Among other things, a dictionary entry includes some or all of the following elements, depending on its individual nature and design: a definition, prototypically structured into genus and differentiae sections; examples of usage, with or without glosses or translations; and metalinguistic information relating to subcategorization and selectional restrictions. Differences among dictionaries should be exploited to obtain as much information as possible from them.

Monolingual collegiate-sized dictionaries of a language can contribute information about a word's possible senses, and, for each sense, the relevant semantic class and the genus and differentiae that constitute its definition. Entries in the dictionaries designed for the foreign learner of English typically contain very specific grammar information, usually in the form of codes, as well as many examples of use of the headword, carefully constructed in order to enrich the information provided by the entry. Some MRDs also contain explicit indicators of semantic domains and of selectional restrictions.

Certain information required for filling in the template entry for a verb of sound is available in existing dictionaries, where, although this information is not overtly identified, it is often presented in a reasonably structured way, a prerequisite for automatic extraction and transfer into the lexical knowledge base entry. Dictionary definitions frequently use formulaic expressions that allow information of certain types to be identified relatively easily (Fox et al., 1986; Markowitz et al., 1986, among others). For instance, various researchers have shown that genus terms can be identified relatively successfully (Amsler, 1980; Byrd et al., 1987; Chodorow et al., 1985; Klavans, 1988; Markowitz et al., 1986, among others), allowing the initial identification of a verb's semantic type. Once a verb of sound has been identified in this way, it should then be possible to use automatic methods to pinpoint within a parsed MRD entry the means differentia, since it is usually expressed in a *by* phrase, as in sense 1 of the *Collins English Dictionary* (CED) (Hanks, 1986) entry for the verb *whistle,* which includes the phrase 'by passing breath through a narrow constriction'. Similarly, the contents of examples (e.g. in CED *whistle* 1 *"he whistled a melody")* or the metalanguage (e.g. in CED *whistle* 3 'of a kettle, train etc.' or CED *whistle* 5 'of animals, esp. birds') provide more detailed information about the selectional restrictions associated with the various senses of the word.

Certain extended senses can also be identified and extracted fairly easily. For instance, the sense of *whistle,* characterized as 'express (an emotion) by emitting the sound', can be found by searching for definitions including the string 'express'. In fact, a search of *The Longman Dictionary of Contemporary English* (Procter et al., 1978) for verbs having both transitive and intransitive uses whose definition includes the word 'express' yields a number of verbs of sound, including *babble, cluck, giggle, growl, howl, moan, purr, roar, scream, snort.* The extended sense of a verb of sound as a verb of motion ('move while causing the sound to be emitted') can also be identified, as it is occasionally signaled in the dictionary entries of such verbs. However, an examination of entries for verbs of sound reveals that this sense has posed a problem for lexicographers, who are not always sure whether to define this sense as a sound or a movement, leading to inconsistencies in and across dictionaries in the treatment of this sense (sense 1c of the *Webster's Ninth* [Mish, 1986] entry for the verb *whistle* is 'to make a shrill clear sound, esp. by rapid movement ⟨the wind whistled⟩'; sense 4 in CED is 'to move with a whistling sound caused by rapid passage through the air'). Although these inconsistencies might complicate the process of identifying this sense, once the source of the inconsistency is understood, they need not prevent its automatic identification in a MRD, assuming that the appropriate clues are searched for.

Bilingual dictionaries are also a rich source of material for monolingual lexical knowledge base entries. A monolingual dictionary intended for native speakers, such as the CED or *Webster's Ninth,* is obliged to contain real definitions; therefore, it provides explicit information regarding genus terms and differentiae. The parallel part of a bilingual dictionary entry contains target language equivalents of the headword. Thus a bilingual dictionary, although it does not provide genus terms or differentiae, does distinguish between two non-identical target language equivalents. This differentiation is often achieved by indicating selectional restrictions on the subject and/or object of verbs, and these indications in turn provide systematic information for the knowledge base. As an example consider section 3 of the *Collins-Robert English–French Dictionary* (Atkins et al., 1987) entry for *whistle:*

(13)   3 *vi* [*person*] siffler, (*tunefully, light-heartedly*) siffloter; (*blow a–*) donner un coup de sifflet; [*bird, bullet, wind, kettle, train*] siffler . . .

In this part of the entry, the material in square brackets sets out typical subjects of the verbs that follow, showing that all are possible subjects of the English headword *whistle*. This information may also be found in monolingual dictionaries but is often implicitly held in the form of examples. The explicit treatment that it often receives in dictionaries for the foreign learner renders such works a valuable source of material for the semi-automatic acquisition of information for a lexical knowledge base.

Bilingual dictionaries can also be used to provide information about whether certain verbs of sound have extended senses as verbs of motion. French differs from English in not allowing verbs of sound, and, in fact, verbs from a variety of other classes, to become verbs of motion (Carter, 1988; Talmy, 1985; Levin and Rapoport, 1988). For example, in French, *to roar down the driveway* would be expressed as 'to go down the driveway roaring'. Consequently, an English–French dictionary is likely to provide information about this sense. As discussed by Boguraev et al. (1989), this information does, in fact, tend to be provided in a fairly structured way, allowing the verbs that show this sense to be readily identified.

3.5.2   *The contribution of text corpora*

Text corpora of both written and spoken language also provide a rich resource that has much to offer to the construction of a lexical knowledge base. Tools for taking advantage of these resources are only now beginning to be developed (Church and Hanks, 1989; Hindle, 1989; Zernik, 1989b,c, among others), but it is clear that corpora will eventually offer much more detail about the properties of words than can be found in their dictionary entries, although dictionaries will still be essential to any attempt to construct a lexical knowledge base automatically.

Text corpora are an excellent source of information about the selectional restrictions on the arguments of verbs. The information provided by corpora would be enhanced if the corpus citations were tagged with a sense from the lexical knowledge base, but it is possible that the selectional information derived from the corpus might itself provide a basis for the identification of the senses of the occurrences of a given word in a corpus. Also interesting are the examples of the possible uses of a word that a corpus can provide, since these might exemplify some of the syntactic properties of that word that are necessary to pigeonhole it appropriately. Even if a word's semantic type has already been identified, these facts could be used at least to confirm a classification previously reached on the basis of the genus term in a dictionary definition, and possibly also to fill in additional properties that were not noted in the dictionary. For instance, the citations in the Cobuild Corpus show that the verb *whistle* is found with both *at* and *to* phrases.

(14)   *"A man whistled AT her"*
         "we hate being whistled AT in the street"
(15)   *"He whistled TO his partner"*
         "I whistled TO her"

The presence of *to* phrase complements to the verb, for example, could be used either to confirm or to determine that *whistle* does indeed have an extended sense as a verb of verbal communication, whereas the presence of *at* phrase complements signals the 'emit a sound as a reaction' sense. Similarly, a corpus could be used to determine whether a verb of sound has an extended sense as a verb of motion by searching for instances of intransitive uses of the verb followed by directional phrases, such as the following.

(16)   *"A shot whistled past Bond's head."*
         "A rocket whistled by, missing the hill . . ."

3.6   Conclusion

This chapter explores the use of results of linguistic research into the lexicon in the construction of a lexical knowledge base by showing how the information regarding a word is structured. The chapter proposes that a linguistically-motivated template entry should be designed for each type of word, and that these entries might then be instantiated for individual words. The use of such template entries does not preclude the use of on-line dictionaries or text corpora to aid the process of lexical acquisition. Rather the information available in such on-line resources is essential for building lexical knowledge base entries for specific verbs from the appropriate template. However, the template entries will guide the search for information within these resources, allowing them to be exploited as fully as possible.

References

Amsler, R. A. (1980). *The Structure of the Merriam-Webster Pocket Dictionary*, Ph.D. thesis, University of Texas, Austin, TX.

Atkins, B. T., Duval, A., Milne, R. M., et al. (1987). *Collins-Robert English-French Dictionary*. London and Glasgow: Collins Publishers. Second edition.

Atkins, B. T., Kegl, J., and Levin, B. (1986). 'Implicit and Explicit Information in Dictionaries', *Advances in Lexicology,* Proceedings of the Second Conference of the Centre for the New OED, University of Waterloo, 45–63.

Atkins, B. T., Kegl, J., and Levin, B. (1988). 'Anatomy of a Verb Entry: from Linguistic Theory to Lexicographic Practice', *International Journal of Lexicography* 1: 84–126.

Atkins, B. T. and Levin, B. (1988). 'Admitting Impediments', *Information in Text*, Fourth Annual Conference of the Centre for the New OED, University of Waterloo, 97–113. Also to appear in Zernik, U. (ed.). *Using On-line Resources to Build a Lexicon.* Hillsdale, NJ: Lawrence Erlbaum Associates.

Boguraev, B. and Briscoe, T. (eds.). (1989). *Computational Lexicography for Natural Language Processing*. Harlow: Longman.

Boguraev, B., Byrd, R. J., Klavans, J. L., and Neff, M. (1989). 'From Structural Analysis of Lexical Resources to Semantics in a Lexical Knowledge Base', position paper prepared for the Workshop on Lexicon Acquisition, IJCAI, Detroit.

Bresnan, J. and Kanerva, J. (1989). 'Locative Inversion in Chichewa: A Case Study of Factorization in Grammar', *Linguistic Inquiry* 20: 1–50.

Byrd, R. et al. (1987). 'Tools and Methods for Computational Lexicology', *Computational Linguistics* 13: 219–240.

Carter, R. J. (1976). 'Some Constraints on Possible Words', *Semantikos* 1: 27–66.

Carter, R. (1988). *On Linking: Papers by Richard Carter* (edited by Levin, B. and Tenny, C.), Lexicon Project Working Papers 25, Center for Cognitive Science, MIT, Cambridge, MA.

Chodorow, M. S., Byrd, R. J., and Heidorn, G. E. (1985). 'Extracting Semantic Hierarchies from a Large On-line Dictionary', *Proceedings of the 23rd Annual Meeting of the Association for Computational Linguistics:* 299–304.

Chomsky, N. (1965). *Aspects of the Theory of Syntax*. Cambridge, MA: MIT Press.

Church, K. C. and Hanks, P. (1989). 'Word Association Norms, Mutual Information and Lexicography', *Proceedings of the 27th Annual Meeting of the Association for Computational Linguistics:* 76–83.

Erteschik, N. (1973). *On the Nature of Island Constraints*, Ph.D. thesis, MIT, Cambridge, MA.

Fellbaum, C. (1990). 'English Verbs as a Semantic Net', *International Journal of Lexicography* 3.

Fillmore, C. J. (1968). 'The Case for Case'. In Bach, E. and Harms, R. T. (eds.). *Universals in Linguistic Theory*. New York: Holt, Rinehart and Winston, 1–88.

Fillmore, C. J. and Atkins, B. T. (in press). 'RISK: The Challenge of Corpus Lexicography'. In Atkins, B. T. and Zampolli, A. (eds.). *Computational Approaches to the Lexicon: Automating the Lexicon II*. Oxford: Oxford University Press.

Foley, W. A. and Van Valin, R. D., Jr. (1984). *Functional Syntax and Universal Grammar*. Cambridge: Cambridge University Press.

Fox, E. A. et al. (1986). 'Building the CODER Lexicon: *The Collins English Dictionary* and its Adverb Definitions', Technical Report 86–23, Department of Computer Science, Virginia Tech, Blacksburg, VA.

Gruber, J. S. (1976). *Lexical Structures in Syntax and Semantics*. Amsterdam: North-Holland.

Hale, K. L. and Keyser, S. J. (1986). 'Some Transitivity Alternations in English', Lexicon Project Working Papers 7, Center for Cognitive Science, MIT, Cambridge, MA.

Hale, K. L. and Keyser, S. J. (1987). 'A View from the Middle', Lexicon Project Working Papers 10, Center for Cognitive Science, MIT, Cambridge MA.

Hanks, P. (ed.). (1986). *Collins English Dictionary*. London and Glasgow: Collins Publishers. (CED)

Hindle, D. (1989). 'Acquiring Disambiguation Rules from Text', *Proceedings of the 27th Annual Meeting of the Association for Computational Linguistics:* 118–125.

Hudson, R. (1988). 'The Linguistic Foundations for Lexical Research and Dictionary Design', *International Journal of Lexicography* 1: 287–312.

Ilson, R. and Mel'čuk, I. (1989). 'English *Bake* Revisited', *International Journal of Lexicography* 2: 325–346.

Jackendoff, R. S. (1983). *Semantics and Cognition*. Cambridge, MA: MIT Press.

Jackendoff, R. S. (1990). *Semantic Structures*. Cambridge, MA: MIT Press.

Jeffries, L. and Willis, P. (1984). 'A Return to the Spray Paint Issue', *Journal of Pragmatics* 8: 715–729.

Katz, B. and Levin, B. (1988). 'Exploiting Lexical Regularities in Designing Natural Language Systems', *Proceedings of the 12th International Conference on Computational Linguistics:* 316–323.

Klavans, J. (1988). 'Building a Computational Lexicon Using Machine-Readable Dictionaries', paper presented at the EURALEX Third International Congress, Budapest, Hungary.

Laughren, M. (1988). 'Towards a Lexical Representation of Warlpiri Verbs'. In Wilkins, W. (ed.). (1988), *Thematic Relations*. New York: Academic Press 215–242.

Levin, B. (1985). 'Introduction'. In Levin, B. (ed.). *Lexical Semantics in Review*, Lexicon Project Working Papers 1, Center for Cognitive Science, MIT.

Levin, B. (1989). 'Verbal Diathesis', Lexicon Project Working Papers 32, Center for Cognitive Science, MIT, Cambridge, MA.

Levin, B. (in press) 'Approaches to Lexical Semantic Representation'. In Walker, D., Zampolli, A., and Calzolari, N. (eds.). *Automating the Lexicon*. Oxford: Oxford University Press.

Levin, B. (unpublished ms.) *Towards a Lexical Organization of English Verbs*, Northwestern University, Evanston, IL.

Levin, B. and Rapoport, T. (1988). 'Lexical Subordination', *Proceedings of the 24th Annual Meeting of the Chicago Linguistic Society*, 275–289.

Levin, B. and Rappaport, M. (1989). 'Approaches to Unaccusative Mismatches', *Proceedings of the 19th Annual Meeting of the North-Eastern Linguistics Society:* 314–328.

Levin, B. and Rappaport Hovav, M. (in press: a). 'The Lexical Semantics of Verbs of Motion: The Perspective from Unaccusativity'. In Roca, I. (ed.). *Thematic Structure: Its Role in Grammar*. Dordrecht: Foris.

Levin, B. and Rappaport Hovav, M. (in press: b). 'Wiping the Slate Clean: A Lexical Semantic Exploration', *Cognition*.

Marantz, A. P. (1984). *On the Nature of Grammatical Relations*. Cambridge, MA: MIT Press.

Markowitz, J., Ahlswede, T., and Evens, M. (1986). 'Semantically Significant Patterns in Dictionary Definitions', *Proceedings of the 24th Annual Meeting of the Association for Computational Linguistics:* 112–119.

McCawley, J. (1986). 'What Linguists Might Contribute to Dictionary-making if They Could Get Their Act Together'. In Bjorkman, P. C., and Raskin, V. (eds.). *The Real-World Linguist*. Norwood, NJ: Ablex, 1–18.

Miller, G. A., Beckwith, R., Fellbaum, C., Gross, D., and Miller, K. (1990). 'Introduction to WordNet: An On-Line Lexical Database', *International Journal of Lexicography* 3.

Miller, G. A., Fellbaum, C., Kegl, J., and Miller, K. (1988). 'WORDNET: An Electronic Lexical Reference System Based on Theories of Lexical Memory', *Revue Quebecoise de Linguistique* 17: 181–211.

Miller, G. A. and Fellbaum, C. (in press). 'Semantic Networks of English', *Cognition*.

Mish, F. C. (ed.). (1986). *Webster's Ninth New Collegiate Dictionary*. Springfield, MA: Merriam-Webster.

Mufwene, S. (1978). 'English Manner-of-speaking Verbs Revisited'. *Papers from the Parasession on the Lexicon*. Chicago: Chicago Linguistic Society, 278–289.

Neff, M. and Boguraev, B. (1989). 'Dictionaries, Dictionary Grammars and Dictionary Entry Parsing', *Proceedings of the 27th Annual Meeting of the Association for Computational Linguistics*.

Procter, P., et al. (eds.). (1978). *Longman Dictionary of Contemporary English*. London: Longman Group. First edition. (LDOCE)

Pustejovsky, J. (1990). 'Towards a Generative Lexicon', *Computational Linguistics* 17.

Rappaport, M. and Levin, B. (1988). 'What to Do with Theta-Roles'. In Wilkins, W. (ed.). (1988), *Thematic Relations*. New York: Academic Press 7–36.

Rappaport, M., Levin, B., and Laughren, M. (1988). 'Niveaux de representation lexical', *Lexique* 7: 13–32. To appear in English as 'Levels of Lexical Representation'. In Pustejovsky, J. (ed.). *Semantics and the Lexicon*. Dordrecht: Kluwer.

Salkoff, M. (1983). 'Bees Are Swarming in the Garden', *Language* 59: 288–346.

Schwartz-Norman, L. (1976). 'The Grammar of "Content" and "Container"', *Journal of Linguistics* 12: 279–287.

Stowell, T. (1981). *Origins of Phrase Structure*, Ph.D. thesis, MIT, Cambridge, MA.

Talmy, L. (1985). 'Lexicalization Patterns: Semantic Structure in Lexical Forms'. In Shopen, T. (ed.). *Language Typology and Syntactic Description 3*, Grammatical Categories and the Lexicon. Cambridge: Cambridge University Press, 57–149.

Wilkins, W. (ed.). (1988). *Thematic Relations*. New York: Academic Press.

Williams, E. (1981). 'Augment Structure and Morphology', *The Linguistic Review* 1: 81–114.

Zernik, U. (ed.). (1989a). *Proceedings of the First International Lexical Acquisition Workshop*, Detroit, Michigan.

Zernik, U. (1989b). 'Paradigms in Lexical Acquisition'. In Zernik, U. (ed.). *Proceedings of the First International Lexical Acquisition Workshop*, Detroit, Michigan.

Zernik, U. (1989c). 'Lexical Acquisition: Learning from Corpus by Capitalizing on Lexical Categories', *Proceedings of the Eleventh International Joint Conference on Artificial Intelligence*, Detroit, Michigan.

Zwicky, A. M. (1971). 'In a Manner of Speaking', *Linguistic Inquiry* 2: 223–232.

4   The contribution of computational lexicography

BRANIMIR K. BOGURAEV

4.1   Introduction

This chapter presents an operational definition of *computational lexicography*, which is emerging as a discipline in its own right. In the context of one of its primary goals – facilitation of (semi-)automatic construction of lexical knowledge bases (aka computational lexicons) by extracting lexical data from on-line dictionaries – the concerns of dictionary analysis are related to those of lexical semantics. The chapter argues for a particular paradigm of lexicon construction, which relies crucially on having flexible access to fine-grained structural analyses of multiple dictionary sources. To this end, several related issues in computational lexicography are discussed in some detail.

In particular, the notion of structured dictionary representation is exemplified by looking at the wide range of functions encoded, both explicitly and implicitly, in the notations for dictionary entries. This allows the formulation of a framework for exploiting the lexical content of dictionary structure, in part encoded configurationally, for the purpose of streamlining the process of lexical acquisition.

A methodology for populating a lexical knowledge base with knowledge derived from existing lexical resources should not be in isolation from a theory of lexical semantics. Rather than promote any particular theory, however, we argue that without a theoretical framework the traditional methods of computational lexicography can hardly go further than highlighting the inadequacies of current dictionaries. We further argue that by reference to a theory that assumes a formal and rich model of the lexicon, dictionaries can be made to reveal – through guided analysis of highly structured isomorphs – a number of lexical semantic relations of relevance to natural language processing, which are only encoded implicitly and are distributed across the entire source.

This paper was originally presented at a *Symposium on Natural Language – Language and Action in the World,* held in December 1989 at Bolt, Beranek and Neumann Laboratories, Cambridge, Mass. Some preliminary results were reported at the First International Workshop on Lexical Acquisition, held during the 11th International Conference on Artificial Intelligence in Detroit. I have benefited greatly from discussions with Sue Atkins, Ted Briscoe, Beth Levin, and James Pustejovsky. Most of the results in this chapter were obtained from the machine-readable versions of the *Longman Dictionary of Contemporary English* and the *Collins Thesaurus:* thanks are due to the publishers for granting access to the sources for research purposes.

One approach to scaling up the lexical components of natural language systems prototypes to enable them to handle realistic texts has been to turn to existing machine-readable forms of published dictionaries. On the assumption that they not only represent (trivially) a convenient source of words, but also contain (in a less obvious, and more interesting way) a significant amount of lexical data, recent research efforts have shown that automated procedures can be developed for extracting and formalizing explicitly available, as well as implicitly encoded, information – phonological, syntactic, and semantic – from machine-readable dictionaries (MRDs).

The appeal of using on-line dictionaries in the construction of formal computational lexicons is intuitively obvious: dictionaries contain information about words, and lexicons need such information. If automated procedures could be developed for extracting and formalizing lexical data, on a large scale, from existing on-line resources, natural language processing (NLP) systems would have ways of capitalizing on much of the lexicographic effort embodied in the production of reference materials for human consumption. On the other hand, there are at least two classes of disadvantages to the use of MRDs in natural language processing. First, because these are produced with the human user in mind, there is a strong assumption about the nature of understanding and interpretation required to make use of a dictionary entry; second, due to the very nature of the process of (human) lexicography, present-day dictionaries are far from complete, consistent, and coherent, certainly with respect to virtually any of the numerous kinds of lexical data they choose to represent and encode. An important question then becomes: where is the line between useful and relevant data to be extracted from existing machine-readable sources, on the one hand, and the level of 'noise' (inconsistencies, mis-representations, omissions) inherent in such sources and detrimental to the enterprise of deriving computational lexicons by (semi-)automatic means, on the other?

A number of arguments have been put forward in support of a claim that, in effect, a dictionary is only as good as its worst (or least experienced) lexicographer – and by that token, it is not much good for developing systematic procedures for extraction of lexical data. For instance, in the process of giving a descriptive introduction to the discipline of *computational lexicography*,[1] Atkins (1990) not only summarizes the process of building a large-scale lexicon[2] as

---

[1]There is still no widely accepted term covering the kinds of activities discussed here. A common practice is to use *computational lexicology*. In recognition of the fact that the ultimate goal of this, and related, research is to produce dictionaries – albeit by means different from the traditional ones (computer-based semi-automatic analysis of existing human dictionaries) and intended for a different kind of 'user' (natural language processing programs) – we prefer *computational lexicography*.

[2]In the rest of this paper, *dictionary* is going to be systematically used to refer to a (published) dictionary, or its machine-readable equivalent, compiled by humans for human use. In contrast, in order to emphasize the (semi-)automatic nature of compiling a formal repository of lexical data for use by a computer program for any natural language processing task, we call such a structure a *lexicon* (or *computational lexicon*).

"trawling" a machine-readable dictionary in search for lexical facts, but points out an imbalance between the kinds of syntactic and semantic information that can be identified by "minutely examining" existing dictionaries: "the useful semantic information which may be extracted at present is more restricted in scope, and virtually limited to the construction of semantic taxonomies".

Although we agree with Atkins' assessment of the state of the field, we ascribe this to the predominant paradigm of computational lexicography. More specifically, several factors are instrumental to the relative inadequacy of the semantic information derived from dictionaries.

First, from the perspective of building formal systems capable of processing natural language texts, there is (currently) a much better understanding of the nature of the syntactic information required for implementing such systems than of its semantic counterpart. In other words, the state of the art of (applied) computational linguistics is such that syntactic analyzers are much better understood than semantic interpreters; consequently, there is a fairly concrete notion of what would constitute necessary, useful, and formalizable syntactic information of general linguistic nature. Consequently, given the well-defined lexical requirements at syntactic level, there is that much more leverage in searching for (and finding) specific data to populate a lexicon at the syntactic level (see, for instance, Boguraev and Briscoe, 1989, for an elaboration of this point).

Second, most of the investigations aimed at recovery of lexical data from dictionaries fall in the category of 'localist' approaches. The notion is that if our goal is to construct an entry for a given word, then all (and the only) relevant information as far as the lexical properties of this word are concerned is to be found, locally, in the source dictionary entry for that word. This observation explains why constructing taxonomic networks on the basis of the general genus-differentiae model of dictionary definitions (as exemplified by the work of e.g., Amsler, 1981; Calzolari, 1984; and Alshawi, 1989) is essentially the extent to which identification of semantic information has been developed. It also underlies the pessimism (expressed by, e.g., Atkins, 1990) concerning the useful semantic information extractable from a dictionary. Most dictionary entries are, indeed, impoverished when viewed in isolation; therefore, the lexical structures derived from them would be similarly under-representative.

Third, it is important to take into account the relationship between the expressive power of on-line dictionary models and the scope of lexical information available via the access methods such models support. In particular, mounting a dictionary on-line only partially (as when leaving out certain fields and segments of entries) and/or ignoring components of an entry whose function is apparently only of typographical or aesthetic nature (such as typesetter control codes) tends to impose certain limitations on the kinds of lexical relationships that can be observed and recovered from a dictionary. Although, in principle, computational lexicography is concerned not only with developing techniques and methods for extraction of lexical data but also with building tools for making lexical resources available to such techniques and methods, in reality often the on-line dictionary model is not an adequate representation of lexical information on a large scale. (Boguraev et al., 1990a, discuss this issue at some length.)

Finally, there is an alternative view emerging concerning a more 'realistic' definition of computational lexicography. Hoping to derive, by fully automatic means, a computational lexicon – from one, or several, dictionary sources – is overly optimistic, and provably unrealistic. On the other hand, discarding the potential utility of such sources on the grounds that they have not yielded enough consistent and comprehensive information is unduly pessimistic. Between these two extremes there is an opinion that the potential of on-line dictionaries is in using them to facilitate and assist in the construction of large-scale lexicons (see, for instance, Levin, this volume). The image is not that of 'cranking the handle' and getting a lexicon overnight, but that of carefully designing a lexicon and then, for each aspect of lexical data deemed to be relevant for (semantic) processing of language, using the dictionary sources – *in their entirety* – to find instances of, and evidence for, such data. This paradigm relies on directed search for a number of specific lexical properties, and requires a much stronger notion of a theory of lexical semantics than assumed by computational lexicography to date.

The remainder of this chapter addresses these issues in some detail. Section 4.2 presents the highlights of a particular model for an on-line dictionary, which promotes fine-grained analysis as an important prerequisite for fully exploiting the semantic content of dictionaries. Section 4.3 introduces the concept of distributed lexical knowledge and demonstrates the relationship between configurational patterns occurring regularly across the entire dictionary source, and lexical semantic relations that underlie – and hence can be recovered by exploiting – these patterns. Section 4.4 discusses the importance of lexical semantic theories. The emphasis, however, is not on promoting a particular theory; rather, we show how the model of lexical data extraction developed in the preceding sections can be put to use to populate the semantic component of lexical entries as stipulated by the theory.

Overall, the chapter argues that just as in the case of building a syntactic lexicon from a machine-readable source, there is far more in a dictionary than meets the eye; however, this wealth of information typically cannot be observed, nor extracted, without reference to a formal linguistic theory with very precise lexical requirements, and without a set of tools capable of making very explicit the highly compacted and codified information at source.

4.2   Structure and analysis of machine-readable dictionaries

Prior to seeking interesting and meaningful generalizations concerning lexical information, repositories of such information – and more specifically, machine-readable dictionaries – should be suitably analyzed and converted to lexical

databases (LDBs). We use the term "lexical database" to refer to a highly structured isomorph of a published dictionary, which, by virtue of having both its *data*
and *structure* made fully explicit, lends itself to flexible querying. One of the
arguments in this chapter is that only such a general scheme for dictionary
utilization would make it possible to make maximal use of the information
contained in an MRD.

4.2.1 Machine-readable dictionaries and lexical databases

Dictionary sources are typically made available in the form of publishers' typesetting tapes. A tape carries a flat character stream where lexical data proper is
heavily interspersed with special (control) characters. The particular denotation
of typesetter control characters as font changes and other notational conventions
used in the printed form of the dictionary is typically highly idiosyncratic and
usually regarded as 'noise' when it comes to mounting a typesetting tape on-line
for the purposes of computational lexicography.

None of the lexical database creation efforts to date addresses, explicitly, the
question of fully utilizing the structural information in a dictionary, encoded in
the control characters at source. Consequently, little attention has been paid to
developing a general framework for processing the wide range of dictionary
resources available in machine-readable form.

In situations where the conversion of an MRD into an LDB is carried out by a
'one-off' program (such as, for instance, described by Alshawi et al., 1989 and
Vossen et al., 1989 in Boguraev and Briscoe, 1989), typesetter information is
treated mostly as 'noise' and consequently discarded. More modular (and, by
design, customizable) MRD-to-LDB conversion schemes consisting of a parser
and a grammar – best exemplified by Kazman's (1986) analysis of the *Oxford
English Dictionary* (OED) – appear to retain this information; however, they
assign only minimal interpretation to the 'semantics' of control codes. As a
result, such efforts so far have not delivered the structurally rich and explicit LDB
ideally required for easy and unconstrained access to the source data, as they
have been driven by processing demands of a different nature from ours.[3]

The majority of computational lexicography projects to date fall in the first of
the above categories, in that they typically concentrate on the conversion of a
single dictionary into an LDB. Even work based on more than one dictionary
(e.g., in bilingual context: see Calzolari and Picchi, 1986) tends to use spe-

---

[3]The computerization of the OED had, as its primary goal, setting up a dictionary database to be used
by lexicographers in the process of (re)compiling a dictionary for human, and human only, use. As a
particular consequence, mapping from database representation to visual form of dictionary entries
was a central concern of the design; so was efficiency in access. Another consequence of the same
design was a highly idiosyncratic query language, making the kind of structure analysis discussed
below difficult and unintuitive (see Neff and Boguraev, 1989, 1990; and Boguraev et al., 1989, for
more details).

cialized programs for each dictionary source. In addition, not an uncommon property of existing LDBs is their completeness with respect to the original source: there is a tendency to extract, in a pre-processing phase, only some fragments (e.g., part of speech information or definition fields) while ignoring others (e.g., etymology, pronunciation, or usage notes).

This reflects a particular paradigm for deriving computational lexicons from MRDs: on the assumption that only a limited number of fields in a dictionary entry are relevant to the contents of the target lexicon, these fields are extracted by arbitrary means; the original source is then discarded, and with it the lexical relationships implicit in the overall structure of an entry are lost. Such a strategy may be justified in some cases; in particular, it saves time and effort when a very precise notion exists of what information is sought from a dictionary *and* from where and how this is to be identified and extracted. In the general case, however, when a dictionary is to be regarded as a representative 'snapshot' of a language, containing a substantial amount of explicit and implicit information about words, selective analysis and partial load inevitably loses information. Although this process of 'pre-locating' lexical data in the complete raw source is occasionally referred to as "parsing" a typesetting tape, it is substantially different from the use of the same term below, where a parser is essentially a convertor of the flat character stream into an arbitrarily complex structured representation, and parsing is both constrained never to discard any of the source content, and augmented with interpretations of the typesetter control codes in context.

Partial LDBs may be justified by the narrower, short-term requirements of specific projects; however, they are ultimately incapable of offering insights into the complex nature of lexical relations. The same is true of computerized dictionaries, which are available on-line, but only via a very limited, narrow bandwidth interface (typically allowing access exclusively by orthography). Even a functionally complete system for accessing an analyzed dictionary rapidly becomes unintuitive and cumbersome, if it is not based on fine-grained structural analysis of the source. For instance, the query processor designed to interact with the fully parsed version of the OED (Gonnet, 1987; Raymond and Blake, 1987) and capable of supporting a fairly comprehensive set of lexical queries, still faces problems of formulation and expressive power when it comes to asking questions concerning complex structural relationships between fields and components of dictionary entries. We argue this point in some detail in the next section.

4.2.2   *Parsing dictionaries into LDBs*

An example of the functionality require for converting to a common LDB format a range of MRDs exhibiting a range of phenomena, is provided by the general mechanism embodied in the design of a Dictionary Entry Parser (DEP). A specific implementation, described in detail by Neff and Boguraev (1989, 1990) has been applied to the analysis of several different dictionaries.

DEP functions as a stand-alone parsing engine, capable of interpreting a dictionary tape character stream with respect to a grammar of that particular dictionary, and building an explicit parse tree of the entries in the MRD. In particular, rather than just tagging the data in the dictionary to indicate its structural characteristics, the grammar explicitly controls the construction of rather elaborate tree representations denoting deeper configurational relationships between individual records and fields within an entry. Two processes are crucial for 'unfolding', or making explicit, the structure of an MRD: identification of the structural markers, and their interpretation in context resulting in detailed parse trees for entries.

Neff and Boguraev (1989, 1990) present at some length a detailed motivation for the overall system architecture, give considerations leading to the design of a dictionary grammar formalism, and discuss analyses of typical dictionary configurations across a range of different MRD sources within the DEP framework. Here we only illustrate the kind of structure assignment carried out by one of our grammars to a (fragment) of a sample dictionary entry (this, and the majority of the examples in the rest of the paper, are taken from the *Longman Dictionary of Contemporary English* – see Procter, 1978).

> **book**[1] / . . . / *n* **1** a collection of sheets of paper fastened together as a thing to be read, or to be written in . . . **3** the words of a light musical play: *Oscar Hammerstein II wrote the book of "Oklahoma", and Richard Rodgers wrote the music* – compare LIBRETTO . . .

```
entry
+ − hdw: book
|
+ − homograph
    + − print_form: book
    + − hom_number: 1
    + − syncat: n
    |
    + − pronunciation
    |   + − primary
    |       + − pron_string: bUk
    |
    + − sense_def
    |   + − sense_no: 1
    |   + − defn
    |       + − def_string: a collection of sheets of paper
    |                       fastened together as a thing to
    |                       be read, or to be written in
    + −  . . . . . . . .
    |
    + − sense_def
    |   + − sense_no: 3
```

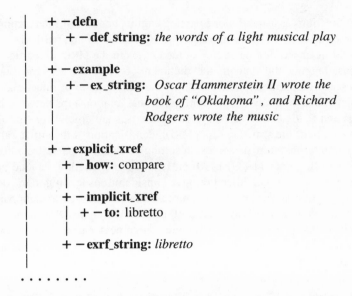

```
|    + − defn
|    |   + − def_string: the words of a light musical play
|    |
|    + − example
|    |   + − ex_string:  Oscar Hammerstein II wrote the
|    |                   book of "Oklahoma", and Richard
|    |                   Rodgers wrote the music
|    |
|    + − explicit_xref
|    |   + − how: compare
|    |   |
|    |   + − implicit_xref
|    |   |   + − to: libretto
|    |   |
|    |   + − exrf_string: libretto
|
```
· · · · · · · ·

In this representation, lexical data are encoded as a set of values associated with terminal nodes in the entry parse tree. In addition to the usual observations relating to structured representations of this kind, there are two important points to be made for dictionary entry parsing in particular.

First, it is not *only* the set of terminal values that fully represents the complete lexical content of the original entry, even though by a process conceptually equivalent to 'tree walking' we would be able to recover virtually everything that is presented visually at source. On the contrary: the global picture of the structure of a dictionary entry, only intuitively inducible from the typographic properties of a dictionary, now becomes visibly marked by the system of embedded labels.

Furthermore, this embedding of labels is systematic (it is ultimately defined by the particular grammar used by DEP to assign structure to the dictionary) and maps to the notion of a *path* – namely, a step-wise refinement of the function performed by a particular terminal value.

Take, for instance, the string "LIBRETTO" in the entry for "book" above. On the face of it, the change of typeface to small capitals indicates the use of a word outside of the controlled core vocabulary employed by the lexicographers during dictionary compilation. This is the minimal analysis that might be assigned to the particular font-controlled character, and carried over to the dictionary representation. At a deeper level of interpretation, however, is the realization that the typographical convention here is used to signal an (implicit) cross-reference to another entry. In terms of representation, we are faced with several possibilities. Discarding the 'noisy' typesetter control might result in a data structure that represents the fact that "libretto" is an (explicit) cross-reference of the straightforward *see* category (as opposed to, for instance, *compare*, *opposite*, or *see picture at*). Alternatively, we might follow the minimal analysis and retain a trace of the font change:

> . . . **[begin[small_caps]]libretto[end[small_caps]]** . . .

Both of these representations are clearly impoverished; of special interest here, however, is the fact that an alternative

> . . . **implicit_xref = "libretto"**

is equally lacking: it fails to capture the fact that the string in question is an implicit cross-reference within an explicit cross-reference applying to the third sense definition of the first homograph for "book". This knowledge is encoded in the path from the root of the entry tree to this particular terminal node:

> **LDOCE:**
>   **entry**
>   **.homograph**
>   **.sense_def**
>   **.explicit_xref**
>   **.implicit_xref**
>   **.to: "libretto"** ;

It is this notion of context-driven decoding of a simple font change code, such as small_caps, that assigns non-atomic 'labels' (i.e., composite paths) to pieces of text within an entry. Having functional properties of entry components defined decompositionally is important, because now fragments of dictionary entries can contribute to the lexical content of our target computational lexicon (or lexical knowledge base) not only by an interpretation of the immediate tag (terminal label) they carry, but by considering a complete or partial path, which indicates their overall participation in the lexical make-up of a language. We come back to this point in the next section, when we discuss in some detail the interpretation of the 'semantics' of path specifications, crucial to our notion of distributed lexical knowledge.

An immediate application of the path concept is its use in the design of an access mechanism for browsing through, and extracting data from, lexical databases. More specifically, if we assume a database model that holds instances of the structured representations produced by a mechanism similar to DEP, it is possible to specify, to arbitrary depth of detail, entries to be retrieved from the database by composing any number of paths into a declarative specification of a set of properties required of the entries sought. Paths can be fully instantiated, by 'quoting' literal strings to be found at terminal positions; alternatively, partially instantiated paths can be defined by assigning variables to terminal nodes or by leaving certain intermediate nodes in the path unspecified. A mechanism essentially equivalent to string calculus allows the specification of restrictions on, and constraints among, variables. Paths can be viewed as projections onto sets of entries that fulfill such constraints; composing more than one path to a query and suitably interpreting the constraints associated with them makes it possible to combine statements concerning both content and structure of entries into arbitrarily complex search expressions. The process of search, or interpretation of the declarative specification of target entries, can be viewed as driven by unification. Neff et al. (1988) and Byrd (1989a) discuss a particular implementation of a query processor in some detail.

As an example, consider the following simple query designed to extract all (and only) nouns from a database constructed from a dictionary source.

> **LDOCE:**
> **entry**
>   (.hdw: _word ;
>   .homograph
>   .syncat: "n" ;)

Without going into a detailed description of its syntax, this expression effectively specifies that all entries in the database (uniquely identified by the specified "**LDOCE**"), which contain an **entry . homograph . syncat** path with a terminal value of noun ("**n**") are valid search targets. Using a variable (_pos), the same effect – namely, extracting all noun entries – can be achieved by the following query.

> **LDOCE:**
> **entry**
>   (.hdw: _word ;
>   .homograph
>   .syncta: _pos ;)
> **CONDITION** (_pos = "n")

As an example of a more complicated query, designed to find all noun entries whose explicit cross-reference fields themselves include a non-empty implicit cross-reference (such as the "book" entry exemplified earlier), the query specification below merges the two paths leading to, respectively, **syncat** and to **implicit_xref . to**.

> **LDOCE:**
> **entry**
>   (.hdw: _word ;
>   .homograph
>   (.syncat: "n" ;
>   .sense_def
>   .explicit_xref
>   .implicit_xref
>   .to: _ixref ;))
> **CONDITION** (_ixref \= "")
> **FORMAT**   (_word)

4.2.3 Structural properties of on-line MRD representations

The kind of structural analysis of dictionaries argued for here seeks to unfold *all* the functional implications of the font codes and other special characters controlling the layout of an entry on the printed page. As data is typically compacted to save space in print, and as it is common for different fields within an entry to employ radically different compaction schemes and abbreviatory devices, dictionary analysis faces non-trivial decompaction tasks. Furthermore, it is not uncommon for text fragments in a dictionary entry to serve more than one function; in such cases the analysis process should both identify the nature of the function and assign it proper structural representation. Neff and Boguraev (1989, 1990) present a detailed account of a comprehensive set of lexicographic conventions implemented via topography and carrying largely a semantic load; for illustrative purposes, as well as for reference in the next section, below are some examples of particular phenomena, together with the kind of fine-grained structural presentations assigned to them.

A particularly pervasive space-saving device in dictionary entries is the factoring out of common substrings in data fields. A definition-initial common fragment can be routinely shared by more than one sub-definition, as in "**incubator** . . . a machine for **a** keeping eggs warm until they HATCH **b** keeping alive babies that are too small to live and breathe in ordinary air". Similarly, a translation final fragment is not uncommon in bilingual dictionaries: "**Bankrott** . . . ~ **machen** to become *or* go bankrupt". A dictionary database should reflect this by duplicating the shared segments and migrating the copies as appropriate.

A more complex example of structure duplication is illustrated by a possible treatment of implicit cross-references, discussed earlier and exemplified here by a fragment of the entry for "nuisance".

> **nui.sance** /'nju:səns ‖ 'nu:-/ *n* **1** a person or animal that annoys or causes trouble, PEST: *Don't make a nuisance of yourself: sit down and be quiet!* **2** an action or state of affairs which causes trouble, offence, or unpleasantness: *What a nuisance! I've forgotten my ticket* **3 Commit no nuisance** (as a notice in a public place) Do not use this place as **a** a lavatory **b** a TIP[4]

The dual purpose served by e.g., "TIP" requires its appearance on at least two different nodes in the structured representation of the entry, **def_string** and **implicit_xfr . to,** as shown in the figure below.

```
entry
+ − hdw: nuisance
+ − homograph
    + − print_form: nuisance
    + − pronunc    . . . . . . .
    + − syncat: n
    + − sense_def
    |    + − sense_no: 1
```

```
|   + − defn
|   |   + − implicit_xrf
|   |   |   + − to: pest
|   |   + − def_string: a person or animal that annoys
|   |                       or causes trouble: pest
|   + − example
|   + − example
|       + − ex_string: Don't make a nuisance of your-
|                          self sit down and be quiet!
. . . . . . . .
+ − sense_def
    + − sense_no: 3
    + − defn
        + − hdw_phrase:  Commit no nuisance
        + − qualifier:    as a notice in a public
                            place
    + − sub_defn
    |   + − seq_no:     a
    |   + − defn
    |       + − def_string: Do not use this place as a
    |                          lavatory
    + − sub_defn
        + − seq_no:    b
        + − defn
            + − implicit_xrf
            |   + − to: tip
            |   + − hom_no: 4
            + − def_string: Do not use this place as
                               a tip
```

The sub-tree associated with the third sense definition of "nuisance" illustrates certain aspects of our analysis.

For instance, common substrings get replicated as many times as necessary and propagated back to their conceptually original places, as with *"Do not use this place as"*. Multi-function entry components, such as implicit cross-reference kernels, now participate in more than one structure representation: the definition string itself, as well as the **implicit_xref cluster.** Note that an implicit cross-reference may itself be a structurally complex unit: in the example above, it consists of a kernel, *"tip"*, and an annotation for the homograph number, *"4"*, under which the relevant definition for the reference lexical item is to be found; in general, cross-references may also be annotated by sense number and additional morphological information.

Parenthetical strings are assigned functional labels: thus the string that appears in italics at source, "**as a notice in a public place**", is tagged as a **qualifier**. In general, parentheticals are commonly used by lexicographers to specify domains of use, selectional restrictions, typical collocations, and so forth; they also help in conflating more than one (related) definition under a single sense number (see Hanks, 1987, for an account of the use of parentheses in dictionary definitions). Additionally, or alternatively, a parenthesized fragment of a definition field can also be genuinely part of the definition string (for instance, "**clamour** . . . to express (a demand) continually, loudly and strongly"), in which case our grammar performs similar analysis to the one for implicit cross-references: the fragment is retained as part of the definition, as well as assigned a separate structural slot. The analysis of the entry for "accordion" illustrates this (note the replication of the string **key** as an implicit cross-reference and a parenthetical expression, in addition to its being part of the definition proper).

> **ac.cor.di.on** / . . . / *n* a musical instrument that may be carried and whose music is made by pressing the middle part together and so causing air to pass through holes opened and closed by instruments (KEYs[1] (2)) worked by the fingers – compare CONCERTINA[1] – see picture at KEYBOARD[1]

```
entry
+ − hdw: accordion
|
+ − homograph
    + − print_form: ac.cor.di.on
    + − pronunciation . . . . . . . .
    + − syncat: n
    |
    + − sense_def
        + − sense_no: 1
        |
        + − defn
        |   |
        |   + − implicit_xref
        |   |   + − to:          key
        |   |   + − x_morph:  s
        |   |   + − how_no:    1
        |   |   + − s_no:        2
        |   |
        |   + − par_string:  keys
        |   + − def_string:  a musical instrument that may be carried and
        |                     whose music is made by pressing the middle
        |                     part together and so causing air to pass through
        |                     holes opened and closed by instruments (keys)
        |                     worked by the fingers
        + − explicit_xref
        |   + − how: compare
        |   |
        |   + − implicit_xref
        |   |   + − to: concertina
        |   |   + − hom_no: 1
        |   |
```

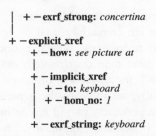

```
        |   + − exrf_strong: concertina
        |
        + − explicit_xref
             + − how: see picture at
             |
             + − implicit_xref
             |   + − to: keyboard
             |   + − hom_no: 1
             |
             + − exrf_string: keyboard
```

To summarize, the approach to dictionary analysis illustrated above expresses the crucial difference between our definition of *parsing,* and that of *tagging:* the latter involves, in principle, no more than identification of entry-internal field delimiters, their interpretation in context and markup of individual components by 'begin-end' brackets. It does not, however, extend to recovery of elided information; nor does it imply explicit structure manipulation (Boguraev et al., 1990, discuss the relationship between decompaction processes in dictionary analysis and the representational frameworks encoding the results of these processes).

The next section looks at the kind of generalizations of a semantic nature that can be made precisely because of the insights offered by an analysis of structural (and specifically, configurational) regularities of entries across the entire LDB representation of a dictionary.

4.3   Lexical knowledge in MRDs

Most of the work on deriving computational lexicons from machine-readable sources to date focuses on the individual lexical item. This particular perspective is especially visible in the context of providing phonological or syntactic information on a word-by-word basis. For instance, techniques have been developed for extracting from the pronunciation fields in a dictionary annotations suitable for driving speech recognition and synthesis systems; for mapping part of speech information to feature lists used for syntactic analysis; and even for constructing fully instantiated feature clusters, of the type posited by contemporary formal theories of grammar, from certain kinds of encodings of syntactic idiosyncrasies of words. Using such techniques, lexicons of non-trivial size have been constructed, thus providing 'proof of concept': fragments of dictionary entries can be formalized for the purposes of automated natural language processing.

4.3.1   Structure and organization of the lexicon

Most of the current work on fleshing out the semantic component of computational lexicons mimics the localist approach outlined above, by seeking to extract and formalize the information in certain fragments of dictionary definitions.

Typically, the target lexical entries encode, in a variety of ways, notions like category (type) information, selectional restrictions, polyadicity, case roles of arguments, and so forth. Although the utility of this kind of information for natural language processing is beyond doubt, the emphasis on the individual entry in separation misses out on the issue of global lexicon organization.

This is not to dismiss ongoing work that does focus precisely on this issue, for instance the attempts to relate grammatical nature with diathesis (e.g., Levin, 1985, 1990a, 1990b). Whether aspects of a verb's subcategorization, and specifically the range of alternative complement structures it can take, can be predicted from the semantic class of the verb and its predicate argument structure is not at issue here; rather, this is the kind of a question that can only be answered on the basis of applying strong methods of computational lexicography for analyzing data *across* entire dictionary sources.

Questions concerning the structure and organization of the lexicon are not uncommonly brought up in the context of studying linguistic and/or cognitive phenomena. Much of contemporary psycholinguistic research, in fact, exploits the assumption that the lexical component of language strongly interacts with the machinery (strategies and processes) underlying both language comprehension and generation. By that token, machine-readable dictionaries should, and have, become part of the methodology for studying the interactions between the (human) lexicon and the other language components. This is, however, outside of the scope of this chapter.

Of more immediate relevance are two related facts. First, studies in lexical semantics, even at a level where no richer representation is offered than named roles (Levin and Rappaport, 1986), have been shown to have immediate applications for improving the robustness of NLP systems (see, for instance, Katz and Levin, 1988). Second, an orthogonal view of MRDs, namely, regarding them as repositories of lexical knowledge and seeking to map their content onto a lexical knowledge base (Boguraev et al., 1989), inevitably commits to blurring the boundaries of individual lexical entries. A lexical knowledge base, in the sense of 'knowledge base' as used by the Artificial Intelligence community and employing representation techniques developed for the purpose, is likely to evolve as a highly interconnected tangled network. Hence it needs a richer notion of lexical relation than the conventional dictionary categories (of e.g., antonymy, synonymy, taxonomy, and so forth) provide.

The two issues above link work of a more theoretical flavor in the area of lexical semantics with the applied question of representation. It is not only the case that both of them require a better understanding of the global organization of the lexicon; it is also true that until it is well known what facts about the lexicon need to be represented formally, there is very little to be said (in specific terms) of the descriptive adequacy of existing representations.

Thus we arrive at the question of distributed lexical knowledge, because this is where we are most likely to find clues for imposing structure on the lexicon. Examples here would be, for instance, facts like

1. the choice of a word usually carries with it a set of implications of semantic nature (Gruber, 1976);
2. partitioning verbs into classes on the basis of common semantic properties seems to have implications for the types of syntactic constructions that each class admits (Levin, 1990a, 1990b);
3. the notion of subtle shifts of meaning, such as lexical coercion, depends on the particular lexical decomposition assigned to a word (Pustejovsky, 1989; 1990).

In the remainder of this section we look at some examples illustrating ways in which such clues can be derived simply as configurational patterns over entry tree representations, described in terms provided by our detailed analyses of machine-readable dictionaries, and learned by studying the spread of different tree shapes across entire dictionary sources.

4.3.2 *Paths in lexical databases and semantic fields*

The discussion of global organization of the lexicon above and our search for a richer notion of lexical relation suggests that, informally, we assume a field structure for the lexicon. It turns out that this allows a particular interpretation of the 'path' concept, introduced in Section 4.2.2 above.

Consider the use of the implicit cross-reference notation, as exemplified in the entry for "book" (Section 4.2.2). As the guide for the dictionary states, implicit cross-references are used to draw the reader's attention to "related words in other parts of the dictionary". However, the convention is one of the most pervasive in the dictionary; consequently, implicit cross-references can be found in examples (as in the use of "SEAL" in the entry for "hermetic"), as part of definition strings (e.g. "ALCHEMY" in the entry for "hermetic"), as components of parenthetical expressions (e.g., "HYMN" in the definition of "chorale[1]", or "CAPITAL" in "stock[10]"), as auxiliary definitions (e.g., "CHORUS in "chorale[2]" or "LIVE-STOCK" in "stock[7]" and so forth:

> **cho.rale** / . . . / *n* **1** (a tune for) a song of praise (HYMN) sung in a church: *a Bach chorale* **2** CHOIR(1); CHORUS[1](1)

> **her.metic** . . . *adj* **1** concerning magic or ALCHEMY **2** very tightly closed; AIR-TIGHT: *a hermetic SEAL[2](4) is used at the top of this glass bottle*

> **stock** . . . **7** farm animals, usu. cattle; LIVESTOCK . . . **10** the money (CAPITAL) owned by a company, divided into SHAREs

A superficial analysis of a dictionary, simply assigning **implicit_xref** labels to all instances above, would miss the different functions these serve in their respective definitions. Alternatively, an analysis that not only decomposes explicit cross-references, but also factors out implicit cross-references (as described in

Section 4.2.3), as well as parenthetical expressions and embedded (auxiliary) definitions (as introduced by ";" in "chorale[2]", "hermetic[2]", "stock[7]" above), naturally associates different semantics to the **implicit_xref** pre-terminal nodes. These interpretations can be read off directly from the path specifications, and the constraints associated with them: thus the case already discussed in Section 4.2 above ("LIBRETTO" in the definition of "book") is represented by the following path.

> **LDOCE:**
> **entry**
> **.homograph**
> **.sense_def**
> **.explicit_xref**
> **.implicit_xref**
> **.to: _ixref ;**

The use of an implicit cross-reference as an auxiliary definition, as in "chorale[2]" ("CHORUS") and "hermetic[2]" ("AIRTIGHT") gives rise to

> **LDOCE:**
> **entry**
> **.homograph**
> **.sense_def**
> **.aux_def**
> **.implicit_xref**
> **.to: _ixref ;**

Finally, for the cross-reference functioning as a parenthetical remark as well, as in "chorale[1]" ("HYMN") and "stock[10]" ("CAPITAL") have

> **LDOCE:**
> **entry**
> **.homograph**
> **.sense_def**
> **(.par_string: _par ;**
> **.implicit_xref**
> **.to: _ixrf ;)**
> **CONDITION (_par = _ixrf)**

These different structural analyses correspond to the different functions associated with the uses of the 'small caps' notation. In the first case above, the lexical item 'pointed to' as a cross-reference introduces a related word within a larger notion of domain: consider the lexical relationship between "book" and "libretto". In the second case, the relationship is that of an apposite synonym: "chorale" and "chorus", "hermetic" and "airtight", "stock" and "livestock". In the third case, an embedded defining pointer (denoted by its inclusion in parenthesis without any auxiliary text) punctuates a concept used in the definition string proper: "stock" in its finance-related sense is defined not only as "money" (via the genus relation), but also as "capital" – the latter concept being a specialization of the former.

Such analyses help to explain our intuitive understanding of the different nature of the semantic classes of items that might occur in the respective fields of the dictionary. For instance, given the cluster of words (concepts) related to "libretto" (e.g., "PLAY", "SCORE", and so forth), it would not be surprising to find any of them in the same field, or textually in an adjacent position, in the entry for "book". Similarly, "BEGINNER" and "NOVICE" (in the entry for "neophyte" below) are fairly interchangeable with e.g., "APPRENTICE", "PUPIL", "LEARNER", precisely because the part of an entry they are to be found in is that denoting a synonymy relationship. On the other hand, because words like "MANUAL," "PUBLICATION", "ALBUM", or "DIARY" are not semantically related to "book³", they are unlikely to be found in the same position as "LIBRETTO".

> **ne.o.phyte . . .** a student of an art, skill, trade, etc., with no experience; BEGINNER; NOVICE

Viewed from an alternative perspective, the path specifications above, when suitably constrained and applied to appropriate dictionary entry contexts, can be embedded in queries to the database that would retrieve sets of words closely related along a particular semantic dimension – achieving in this way a mapping from a structural configuration (i.e., an LDB path) to a semantic field. A very simple example would be to use the second path above for extracting a fairly precise list of synonyms: a small sample of this list looks as follows:

hermetic	AIRTIGHT
hyperbole	EXAGGERATION
keep back	WITHHOLD
lead	CLUE
impoverish	DEPLETE
meddle	INTERFERE
metempsychosis	TRANSMIGRATION
shrink	PSYCHIATRIST
skin	PEEL
skin	FLEECE
percentage	PROPORTION
apparition	GHOST
coterie	CLIQUE

A different example would use the third path configuration above to refine a perhaps already existing taxonomic structure. Although methods have been developed for extracting such structures from dictionary sources (most notably by

Amsler, 1981, and Chodorow et al., 1985), the resulting taxonomies are typically broad and shallow, lacking in detail along the specialization dimension. However, extra depth in such structures can be introduced by observing that the configurational pattern exemplified in the definition of "stock[10]" (and "chorale[1]") above is quite common in the dictionary:

> **dandelion** . . . sometimes eaten but often considered a useless plant (WEED)
>
> **claymore** . . . a type of explosive weapon (MINE) for setting into the ground, . . .

These entries support the following semantic relationships, which introduce an additional level of specialization into a taxonomic structure (the symbol = > denotes an **is_a** link):

dandelion	= >	weed	= >	plant
claymore	= >	mine	= >	weapon
chorale	= >	hymn	= >	song (of praise)
stock	= >	capital	= >	money

In these examples, semantic fields are defined by sets of words collected, on the basis of a structurally defined common semantic function, from across the entire dictionary source. This is precisely the sense in which we define the notion of distributed lexical/semantic knowledge. Even though distributed semantic knowledge ultimately is compiled on an entry-by-entry basis, by collecting together suitable fragments of certain entries, the insights of what constitutes a 'suitable fragment', as well as the nature of the semantic relationship between such fragment(s) and/or headwords, can only come from fully exploiting the ability to cast very specific projections (or, equivalently, to look from very different perspectives) at a multi-dimensionally structured dictionary source.

4.3.3   *Entry configurations and semantic regularities*

With a structured dictionary representation available on-line, queries can be constructed to exploit the fact that configurational features of dictionary definitions have a mapping onto a unifying semantic property. In the following example, the internal structure of subdefinitions reflects a linguistic generalization that holds for a class of English verbs.

Case study – transitivity alternations

Katz and Levin (1988) make a strong case for the need to exploit lexical regularities in the design of natural language processing systems. The emphasis of their analysis rests with a class of verbs that undergo a number of transitivity alternations (Levin, 1985, 1990a). Levin further argues not only that machine-readable dictionaries *could* be used to evaluate hypotheses concerning the global organization of the lexicon, but also that they *should* be used as major resources in the construction of (computational) lexicons (Levin, 1990b).

On the assumption that one aspect of lexical knowledge required for full-scale language processing would involve information concerning ergativity, it is not surprising that various attempts have been made to extract lists of verbs participating in a transitivity alternation from dictionary sources (e.g., by Levin, and by Klavans, personal communication). Such attempts have hitherto looked at flat (unanalyzed) dictionary sources and exploited various 'transparent' notational devices in the verb entries: for instance, grammar code collocations denoting both transitive and intransitive use of a verb in the same sense and/or the inclusion of a parenthetical "cause to" phrase in the verb definition. Strategies like this one have been designed to be triggered by the causative construction which, intuitively, might have been employed by lexicographers to express the alternation property. The resulting lists, however, turned out to be of a heterogeneous nature, including a large number of verbs that do not participate in a transitivity alternation, e.g.:

> **foul**[1] / . . . / *v* [T1;I0] **1** to (cause to) become dirty, impure, or blocked with waste matter: *The dog's fouled the path. One pipe has fouled, and the water won't go down.*

Even careful analysis of the range of defining patterns underlying the 'deep' semantics of transitivity alternations (such as carried out by Fontenelle and Vanandroye, 1989) fails to capture a particular structural regularity employed by the lexicographers to represent precisely the nature of a transitivity alternation. Yet we would expect that since regular linguistic properties of language (of which transitivity alternations are one example) tend to get reflected in the structure of dictionary definitions, an analysis like the one cited above would be enhanced by exploiting the structured representation of (verb) entries.

The query below, run against the *Longman Dictionary of Contemporary English* (LDOCE), is designed to extract those verbs marked both transitive (T1) and intransitive (I0) in the same sense, which also have two sub-senses (sub_defn).

```
LDOCE:
  entry
    .homograph
      (.word: _hw;
       .syncat: _pos;
       sense_def
         (.sense_no: _sno;
          .sub_defn
          (.seq_no: _sa;
           .defn.def_string: _defa;)
          .sub_defn
          (.seq_no: _sb;
```

.defn.def_string; _defb;)
.g_code_field: _gc;))
CONDITION (_pos('v',_pos) = 1 &
_sa = 'a' &
_sb = 'b' &
pos('I0',_gc)>0 &
pos('T1',_gc)>0)

The results, a sample of which is given below, show a pervasive pattern: most of the subdefinitions contain a parenthetical expression, denoting the same object as the (syntactic) object and subject appropriate to the transitive and intransitive sub-senses of the verb. This pattern maps precisely onto the linguistic definition of a 'transitivity alternation' – the typical object in transitive use of the verb, e.g. "to cause (a horse) to go at the fastest speed", "to confuse (someone or someone's brain)" is the same as the typical subject in the intransitive form: "(of someone's brain) to become confused", "(of a horse) to go at the fastest speed" – but can only be expressed in structural terms. In addition, the sample definitions below demonstrate why the simpler queries of the earlier strategies failt to be triggered by a number of suitable verb candidates. In the case of searching for a "cause to" phrase in the definition, semantically related "to allow" or "to become" would miss out the entries for "float" and "addle(2)". Even enhancing a query to reflect such a relatedness (as, for instance, embodied in the search patterns of Fontenelle and Vanandroye who cast a wider net by positing lexicalizations of causativity to be denoted by phrases like "to become", "to allow", "to help", "to make", "to bring", and so forth) still would miss (the more naturally sounding) "loosen" and "separate" in the definition of "disengaged".

addle(1)	**a:** to cause (an egg) to go bad
	b: (of an egg) to go bad
addle(2)	**a:** to confuse (someone or someone's brain)
	b: (of someone's brain) to become confused
adjourn(1)	**a:** to bring (a meeting, trial, etc.) to a stop, esp. for a particular period or until a later time
	b: (of people at a meeting, court of law, etc.) to come to such a stop
careen(1)	**a:** (of a ship) to lean to one side
	b: to cause (a ship) to lean to one side
carry(18)	**a:** (esp. of a law or plan) to be approved; PASS
	b: to cause (esp. a law or plan) to be approved; (cause to) PASS
curl(1)	**a:** (of hair) to twist into or form a curl or curls
	b: to cause (hair) to twist into or form a curl or curls
disengage(1)	**a:** (esp. of parts of a machine) to come loose and separate

	b: to loosen and separate (esp. parts of a machine)
float(7)	**a:** to allow the exchange value of (a country's money) to vary freely from day to day
	b: (of a country's money) to vary freely in exchange value from day to day
flutter(4)	**a:** (of a thin light object) to wave quickly up and down or backwards and forwards
	b: to cause (a thin light object) to do this
gallop(1)	**a:** (of a horse) to go at the fastest speed
	b: to cause (a horse) to go at the fastest speed

4.4   Computational lexicography and lexical semantics

Structural analysis of on-line dictionary sources is only a necessary condition for setting up a framework for extracting lexical data and populating a lexical knowledge base. Just as no effective lexicon can be constructed from an MRD without reference to a formal theory of grammar (Boguraev and Briscoe, 1989), a semantic component of lexical knowledge cannot be derived outside a theory of lexical semantics. Without such a theory, any collection of dictionary LDBs is no more than a heterogenous body of seemingly *ad hoc,* and apparently incomplete and inconsistent, lexical annotations of words (see e.g., Atkins, 1990, for an analysis of the impoverished nature of individual dictionary definitions).

Furthermore, lexical databases, even though better suited for locating arbitrary fragments of lexical data, ultimately mimic the overall organization of dictionaries for humans – namely, that of individual entries, in alphabetical order, and with very little indication of interrelations between different words, as well as between word senses within an entry. Still, there is no reason to attempt to mimic this organization for the purposes of computational lexicons. Not only the nature of lexical access and language analysis is different from that of essentially consulting a reference book, but the technology of, e.g., knowledge representation (KR) makes it possible to consider novel ways of structuring lexical knowledge on a large scale. To quote Randolph Quirk: "we should re-evaluate lexicographic practice not to suit the computer, but because of it".[4] Indeed, a number of proposals already exist for importing tools and methodologies of KR into the design of computational lexicons (see e.g., Evans and Gazdar, 1989; Boguraev and Pustejovsky, 1990); as a parallel development lexicographers are also becoming increasingly dissatisfied with the limitations of the conventional form and media of dictionaries: "the traditional dictionary entry is trying to do what the language simply will not allow to be done" (cf. Atkins, 1990, on the inadequacy of the linear sense definition, subordinated by hierarchically organized

---

[4]From an invited speech at the Fifth Annual Conference of the University of Waterloo Center for the *New Oxford English Dictionary*, September 1989, Oxford.

sense distinctions, to convey the rich interdependencies between words and word senses).

4.4.1 From lexical description to language processing

From the perspective of natural language processing, the value of any lexical knowledge base is ultimately to be judged by the degree of support it offers for tasks like syntactic analysis and semantic interpretation. For the purposes of effective integration of the representation of lexical semantic information with its use in a compositional semantics model of interpretation, it is necessary to adopt a theory of lexical semantics that satisfies at least two criteria. It should be amenable to strict formalization; i.e., it should go beyond just descriptive adequacy. At the same time, it should fit naturally into a general framework of linguistic description and processing.

This is, arguably, the only way in which the distributed lexical information available in machine-readable dictionaries can be made directly usable for natural language processing. It follows that any questions concerning the contribution of computational lexicography to the enterprise of building a (computational) lexicon can be answered in a positive way only by incorporating into its framework a particular view on the issue of lexical decomposition. Some remarks concerning the view taken in this research were already made in the previous section.

To summarize here, the approach underlying this particular exercise in computational lexicography takes as starting points current research in lexical semantics. Of specific relevance are two lines of work. Pustejovsky's notion of generative lexicon, designed to cope naturally with phenomena underlying the creative use of language – such as ambiguity and lexical coercion – provides a framework for his proposal for different levels of lexical representation, and an especially rich lexical semantics for nominals, based on qualia theory (Pustejovsky, 1989, 1990). Levin's study of verbal diathesis (Levin, 1985, 1990a) looks at the global organization of the lexicon; more specifically, one question concerns the ways in which the relationship between semantic categorization and syntactic behavior reveals semantically interesting classes of verbs.

There is a particular justification for attempting to develop a model of the lexicon that encodes the kinds of lexical properties and generalizations posited by these theories. If such a lexicon can be made to support a processing model of language within the current (unification-based) accounts, and if its structure naturally fits the kind of a (lexical) semantic taxonomy underlying the incorporation of global semantic constraints into such accounts (as proposed by e.g., Moens et al., 1989), then at least two propositions hold.

First, the kinds of lexical distinctions highlighted as relevant from a theoretical standpoint (and required by the processing framework) offer substantial direction to the efforts of extracting lexical data from MRDs, by means of the tools and methodologies developed by computational lexicography. Second, since these theories embody to a certain extent the notion of distributed lexical knowledge, they provide, by the same token, a hitherto uncharted route for exploring the lexical data in MRDs, itself distributed across entire dictionary sources.

Briscoe et al. (1990) present a proposal for integrating current research on lexical semantics with a unification-based account of language processing along the lines sketched above. More specifically, the approach is to develop "a model of lexical semantic representation which supports a (somewhat enriched) compositional account of (sentence) meaning by enriching lexical representations of nouns and collapsing those for verbs with alternate grammatical realisations". Starting from a position like this, the task of computational lexicography shifts in emphasis: now we are concerned not so much with local questions like what might constitute an acceptable (semantic) definition of a given word, but with more global ones like what words might be grouped together under a particular projection of lexical meaning.

For more details on the processing framework itself, and the support it offers for the treatment of e.g. lexical coercion, logical metonymy and so forth, the reader is referred to Briscoe et al. (1990). Below we illustrate specifically how the tools of computational lexicography facilitate the location and extraction, from structured dictionary representations, of lexical data required by such a framework. We sketch two possible applications of these tools: fleshing out qualia structures and seeking verbs which induce type coercion.

What can be done to a book?

Central to the issues brought above is the notion of 'spreading the semantic load' equally among the different category types. In such a framework nouns and adjectives, for instance, have a better founded notion of the kinds of semantic contexts in which they can function. As a result, problems of, e.g., lexical ambiguity and underspecification can be tackled on the basis of a richer characterization of an entry in terms of a set of distinctions that generalize on established notions like predicate-argument structure, primitive decomposition, conceptual organization and selectional constraints. In essence, the answer to the question "what can be done to a book?" – namely, in the absence of other overriding information, books can be read, written, reviewed, criticized, and so forth – can be used to guide an analysis and interpretation procedure in the derivation of a semantic structure for inputs like "a long book" and "he enjoyed the book". Such functional specifications of nominals – together with other aspects of their lexical semantics, such as physical attributes, distinguishing characteristics, and so forth – constitute a system of relations (Pustejovsky calls these "qualia structures") that characterize the meaning of a noun, much in the same way as a system of arguments characterizes the meaning of a verb. (For a more detailed account of a theory of lexical semantics instrumental in derivations equivalent to "a long book to read" and "he enjoyed reading the book", see Pustejovsky, 1989, 1990.)

Our approach to dictionary analysis, as discussed in Section 4.2, takes the view that entry fragments performing more than one function are replicated as many times as necessary in the LDB representation; furthermore, the functions of a fragment are made explicit through the appropriate path specifications. In particular, since phrases in parentheses serve, among other things, to denote typical arguments of verbs, parenthetical expressions in dictionary definitions are factored out as separate terminal nodes in the LDB representations. Consider, for example, the (fragment of) the entry for "censor" below, together with its structured analysis that assigns a separate path to the parenthetical expression "books, films, letters, etc." denoting a range of typical objects.

> **censor** . . . to examine (books, films, letters, etc.) with the intention of removing anything offensive

entry
|
+ − **homograph**
  + − **word:** *censor*
  |
  . . . .
  |
  + − **sense_def**
   |
   + − **defn**
    + − **par_string:** *books, films, letters, etc.*
    + − **def_string:** *to examine (books, films, letters, etc.) with the*
                intention of removing anything offensive

On the basis of this analysis, and following an observation that a fairly precise distinction between a parenthetical denoting typical subject(s) and one denoting typical object(s) can be drawn both on the basis of its position in the definition string, and on its internal structure (consider the entry for "sag" below), it is possible to construct a query against the dictionary database that effectively lists a number of verbs (actions) typically applied to books.

> **sag** . . . (of a book, performance, etc.) to become uninteresting during part of the length

The query extracts from the database those verbs that have a non-empty, not definition-initial, parenthetical expression containing the string "book".

> **LDOCE:**
>   **entry:**
>   **(hdw: _hw ;**
>   **homograph:**
>   **(syncat: 'v' ;**
>   **sense_def:**
>   **(defn:**

```
            (par_string: _par;
             def_string: _def ))));
CONDITION (_def \= '''' &
          _par \= '''' &
          pos (_par,  _def) > 1
          pos ("book", _par) > 0 );
```

The resulting list, a sample of which is given below, is a (not necessarily complete) answer to the question of the title.

annotate, censor, consult, excoriate, autograph, classify, cross-index, expurgate, bowdlerize, collate, dramatize, footnote, catalogue, compile, entitle, page, pirate.

It is worth emphasizing the similarity between the nature of the query and the type of data retrieved from the dictionary, in this case and in the earlier search for ergative verbs (Section 4.3.3). Due to the fine-grained analysis of a dictionary, carried out in the process of converting it into a lexical database, we are able to express a semantically interesting query in purely structural terms.

A sample from a similar query, tailored to the specific structural properties of the *Collins English-French Dictionary,* is illustrated below.

abridge, ban, bring out, castrate, abstract, bang about, burlesque, chuck away, appreciate, borrow, call in, churn out, autograph, bowdlerize, castigate, commission.

A very similar query from the *Collins English-German Dictionary* results in even more verbs.

Although techniques like this seem to yield significant data, it is clear that they could, and should, be improved. Further level of detail in the queries, yielding richer results, can be achieved in at least two ways. An obvious improvement is to refine the ways in which typical objects are introduced in dictionary definitions, as had to be done in the case of the *Collins* bilinguals. Even more coherent data is obtained by 'spreading the net wider', which overcomes two inherent problems of dictionary sources: their inconsistency and economy of representation. Since it is unrealistic to expect an entirely uniform pattern of dictionary definitions across the entire dictionary, the original question is generalized by expanding the set of preferred (typical) objects from a single "book" to include suitably semantically related concepts: "literature", "something written", "something printed", and so forth. Such sprouting techniques have been proposed earlier in different contexts (e.g., by Byrd et al., 1987), and they are particularly well-suited to our concerns here. The parameters of the sprouting – namely, the set of semantically close terms and phrases – can be identified on the basis of an analysis of the defining vocabulary and the related conceptual structure underlying the dictionary definitions.

Why is regretting similar to enjoying?

In the processing framework assumed here, the interpretation of a phrase like "enjoy the book" is not triggered only by the specific knowledge of what can be done to books; that is, the qualia structure alone is insufficient to activate the process of type-raising an object (e.g., as that denoted by "book") to an event (such as "reading the book"). Rather, it is the composition of a particular category of verb with the lexical semantics of its object that triggers this process. It follows that "enjoy", and a number of verbs similar to it in that they denote type-coercing predicates, have to be suitably marked. We are then faced with the question of how well the methods of computational lexicography might find such verbs in our dictionary sources.

We approach the problem from two angles. On the one hand, we start with a lexical 'seed' – that is, a set of verbs representative of the phenomenon we seek – and apply suitably constrained sprouting techniques to grow the sample. On the other hand, we design a query against a structured lexical database, incorporating salient properties of the lexical class in question. The query is then incrementally refined, as we intersect the two search/retrieval strategies.

In this particular case, one way of deriving an initial lexical seed is to consult Levin's verb classification system. One of the fundamental assumptions behind that work is that the organization of lexical items (verbs) into classes reflects shared components of meaning. More specifically, commonalities within a class cover, among other things, possible expressions of arguments and possible extended meanings. Even allowing for multiple class membership, it is likely that a set of verbs 'similar' to "enjoy" (where similarity is along some unspecified dimension) will contain more than one entry representative of a type-coercing predicate. Levin (1990a) categorizes, under the exemplary member "admire", a set of psychological verbs (the class is subdivided into two groups, representative of positive and negative emotions):

admire, adore, appreciate, cherish, enjoy, esteem, exalt, fancy, idolise, like, love, miss, respect, revere, stand, support, tolerate, value, worship, . . .

abhor, deplore, despise, detest, disdain, dislike, distrust, dread, envy, fear, hate, lament, loathe, mourn, pity, resent, scorn, . . .

Although not all members of this class resemble "enjoy" fully, items like "appreciate", "fancy", "hate", "lament", "like", "loathe", "love", "miss", "tolerate" are capable, in some of their senses, of demanding type-raising of their arguments in object position for full interpretation of verb phrases. Consider, for instance,

> *Do you fancy a cup of tea?*
> *I find I miss the telephone, since we've moved,*
> *I particularly loathed team games at school,* and
> *It is not unheard of to tolerate opinions other than your own.*

There are a number of ways in which a lexical seed can be grown; we follow the general method of Byrd et al. (1987), which involves traversing, perhaps bidirectionally, a lexical network along hypernym, synonym, and antonym links. Thus the initial set can be expanded[5] to include, for instance,

1. "imagine" and "desire" (as "fancy" is defined in LDOCE to be "to form a picture of; imagine", while COBUILD (Sinclair, 1987) gives "desire" as its superordinate),
2. "relish", "permit", and "allow" (as "to relish" is "to enjoy; be pleased with", and "to tolerate" is "to allow (something that one does not agree with) to be done freely and without opposition; permit"),
3. "prefer", "be partial to", "wish", "incline towards" (as these, together with "fancy" and "desire", are synonyms in the *Collins Thesaurus;* see McLeod, 1984).

One problematic issue in traversing networks derived from MRD sources is that of ambiguity: since the relationships embodied in a lexical relation structure (e.g., one representing taxonomy or synonymy) are between words, we still have to determine the exact word senses (with respect to a dictionary) for which the relationship holds. Although in principle this may turn out to be an arbitrarily complex problem to solve, in this particular case we can use additional information to constrain our search.

Starting from the position that there is some correlation between semantic properties of verbs and their syntactic behavior, we only consider those senses of the words derived by sprouting that are marked in the dictionary to take NP objects and/or progressive or infinitive verb phrase complements.[6] This considerably narrows down the search space. In fact, looking for verbs with particular predicate-taking properties is the basis of the second strategy for extracting type-coercing verbs similar to "enjoy".

In essence, we construct a query against a lexical database that encapsulates salient syntactic and semantic properties of such verbs. In addition to specifying subcategorization frames, the query embodies properties of dictionary definitions that reflect the common, representative semantics of this verb class. Thus we look for words like "experience", "action", "event" used to denote the object of a verb in its definition. This finds entries like

[5]Even though the data structures used in such traversal are, logically, equivalent to networks, they are represented using the LDB format described earlier; consequently, suitably constrained and chained queries against lexical databases can be used to emulate chain traversal.

[6]A number of English monolingual dictionaries utilize some system of encoding the complement-taking properties of verb entries. Examples here are the grammar coding systems of the *Longman Dictionary of Contemporary English* and the *Oxford Advanced Learner's Dictionary of Current English* (Hornby, 1974), as well as the more mnemonic notation used by the Collins COBUILD dictionary: consider for instance, the entry for "enjoy" in COBUILD, which is annotated V+O or V+-ING.

enjoy . . . **1** [T1,4] to get happiness from (things and experiences)

finish . . . **1** [I0; T1,4] to reach or bring to an end; reach an end of (an activity)

prefer . . . **1** [T1(*to*),3,4(*to*) . . .] to choose (one thing or action) rather than another; like better

regret . . . **1** [T1,4,5a] be sorry about (a sad thing or event)

The above definitions are similar in many respects: they share common grammar code descriptions ("T1" and "T4" are the Longman equivalent of the COBUILD "V+O" and "V+-ING" annotations) and parenthetical expressions impose type restrictions of the kind we seek on their objects. Furthermore, we observe from the initial response to the query another configurational regularity: there is a trailing preposition at the end of the definition proper (occasionally followed by the object denoting parenthetical expression). This suggests a further refinement to the query; in effect, we are again 'spreading the net', but rather than using sprouting techniques over lexical networks, we are elaborating a set of queries that return different, and partly overlapping, projections of a lexical database. For instance, one way of 'relaxing' the query would be to allow for an underspecified object: this technique yields entries like

allow . . . **1** [T1,4;V3] to let (somebody) do something; let (something) be done;
permit . . . **2** [T1;V3] to make possible (for); provide (for): *This plan allows 20 minutes for dinner* . . .

After incorporating the specification for a trailing preposition in the definition string, we obtain a new set of candidate type-coercing verbs including

hate . . . **1** [T1,3,4;V3,4] to have a great dislike of . . . **2** [T1,3,4;V3,4] (*infml*) dislike: *She hates fish* . . .

fancy . . . **1** [T1;V4;X(*to be*)1] to form a picture of; imagine 3[T1;X(*to be*)1] to have a liking for; wish for: *I fancy a swim*

loathe . . . [T1,4] to feel hatred or great dislike for

relish . . . [T1,4] enjoy; be pleased with: *to relish a funny story*

Even with this small sample of the results, we can observe that the two strategies outlined above begin to converge. Thus, there are direct overlaps between the lists produced by sprouting and query refinement: for instance, both "fancy" and "allow" are found by either method. In addition, indirect, but strong, evidence in support of entries on the lists is furnished by the lexical overlaps underlying the network traversal: all of "visualise", "envisage" and "imagine", which have been identified as candidates by the criteria encoded in the lexical query, are listed as synonyms in the *Collins Thesaurus*. Note that this is in addition to yet more links being provided by the dictionary itself, via the mechanism of indirect synonym introduction within dictionary definitions discussed in 4.3.2 above.

A more representative (but still incomplete) list of type-coercing verbs similar to "enjoy" extracted by the methods described here is illustrated below:

acknowledge, advise, advocate, avoid, be partial to, begin, deny, desire, discourage, endure, enjoy, envisage, fancy, finish, forbid, hate, imagine, incline towards, justify, lament, like, loathe, love, necessitate, prefer, propose, regret, relish, resume, suggest, tolerate, warrant, wish.

From a dictionary to a lexicon

One final point needs to be made here. Dictionaries are incomplete and unreliable, as well as not fully consistent in form and content of definitions. This is an uncontroversial statement, and has been argued for (and against) quite extensively. Thus it is hardly surprising to find the lists derived in the two earlier sections missing certain (more or less obvious) necessary elements. For instance, in the case of looking for the default predicates naturally composable with "book", the most common – and by that token the most relevant – ones, namely, "read" and "write", are not part of any of the answers.

One of the concerns of computational lexicography is to remain aware of this fact, and consequently to develop techniques and methods for ensuring that the computational lexicons derived from machine-readable sources are more consistent, as well as fully representative with respect to the various lexical phenomena encoded in them.

In the general case, the real issue here is not about any particular verbs; in fact, enhancing the techniques for elaborating the lexical semantics of nominals (as in the case of "book" above) along the lines presented earlier does give reading and writing as actions suitable for composition with books. Rather, the question is: how can we make absolutely certain that complete lists of collocationally appropriate forms, ranked by relevance, can be derived systematically for any kind of input? The answer to this question comes from a separate line of research, becoming integral to the study of word meaning and already beginning to extend the definition of "computational lexicography" given in the beginning of this chapter. Machine-readable dictionaries are not the only type of large-scale lexical resource available; equally important, and arguably richer and more representative of real language use, are the text corpora. Traditionally the basis for inducing stochastic models of language (see e.g., Garside et al., 1987), text corpora more recently have been used for extraction of a variety of lexical data (e.g., by Atkins, 1987; Wilks et al., 1989; Church and Hanks, 1990; and Hindle, 1990).

This chapter has looked specifically into a particular framework for populating a lexical knowledge base with data extracted from MRD sources. The complementary aspect of this same question, namely the use of corpora for enhancing dictionary data, is the subject of separate studies. The reader is referred to Boguraev et al. (1990a,b) for more specific remarks on applying methodologies similar to the ones discussed here, in the context of deriving semantics of nominals, to large-scale machine-readable corpora; similarly, Briscoe et al. (1990) discuss the role of corpora in evaluating the results of type-coercing predicate extraction procedures.

4.5 Conclusion: what computational lexicography is and isn't

In this chapter we have attempted to place computational lexicography in the larger context of related studies of lexical semantics and, to a lesser extent, knowledge representation. From the perspective of one particular goal in applied computational linguistics – namely, that of building large-scale, comprehensive lexicons for natural language processing – we propose a framework for locating and extracting a range of lexical semantic relations, ultimately of use to practical implementations of formal accounts of language.

This framework substantively relies on detailed analysis of existing machine-readable sources, followed by theory-driven search for lexical properties across the entirety of these sources. In particular, strong connections are sought between a lexical characteristic and ways(s) in which it might be encoded configurationally, i.e., as a structural pattern common to a set of dictionary entries. Such connections, once established, are then used to 'carve out' projections from the dictionary, by suitably composing arbitrarily complex queries against structured dictionary database(s).

We put forward a view that the tools and methods of computational lexicography are best put to use in such a goal-driven context: rather than attempting to develop a procedure (or a set of procedures) for automatically constructing a lexicon on the basis of the information available in published dictionaries, the emphasis should be on striving for better understanding of the mapping between language description and dictionary design, and exploiting this for fleshing out components of the lexicon as required by any particular theory of (formal) lexical semantics.

The methods and techniques outlined in this chapter fall in the category of 'weak strategies', insofar as they can never be trusted to deliver complete and coherent results. Ultimately, two independent lines of work are needed to expand the scope of what has been traditionally considered the subject area of computational lexicography.

There is a natural extension of the notion of distributed lexical knowledge, in that any large text sample contains such knowledge – albeit in even less structured form than a dictionary. Given that one of the characteristics of lexical information extracted from dictionary sources is its incompleteness, it is clear that more raw data is required. Text corpora provide such data, and techniques for large corpus studies (many of them, in fact, parallel to the structured analysis paradigm proposed here) should rightly belong to the arsenal of computational lexicography. A different kind of concern is that, given the inherently noisy nature of any data derived (whether from a dictionary or from a corpus), it is imperative to develop methodologies for its evaluation and validation.

Unlike developments in corpus analysis, this latter line of work is still in very early stages. However, there is a growing realization that before a (practical) computational lexicon is instantiated with semantic information on a large scale, it is necessary to go through an intermediate stage of a lexical knowledge base: a holding store for information concerning words and their use of language (see, for instance, Boguraev and Levin, 1990). The enterprise of constructing such a knowledge base should exploit recent developments in the area of knowledge representation; one side effect of this strategy would be the ability to exploit, and build on, an inventory of general purpose data validation techniques.

In this chapter, then, we take the position that computational lexicography is not all there is to constructing a large-scale lexicon for natural language processing; however, it is an essential part of the enterprise.

References

Alshawi, H. (1989). "Analyzing the Dictionary Definitions", in B. Boguraev and E. Briscoe (Eds.), *Computational Lexicography for Natural Language Processing*, Longman, London, 153–170.

Alshawi, H., Boguraev, B., and Carter, D. (1989). "Placing LDOCE On-line", in B. Boguraev and E. Briscoe (Eds.), *Computational Lexicography for Natural Language Processing*, Longman, London, 41–64.

Amsler, R. A. (1981). "A Taxonomy for English Nouns and Verbs", *Proceedings of the 19th Annual Meeting of the Association for Computational Linguistics*, Stanford, California, 133–138.

Atkins, B. T. (1987). "Semantic ID Tags: Corpus Evidence for Dictionary Senses", *The Uses of Large Text Databases*, Third Annual Conference of the University of Waterloo Centre for the New Oxford English Dictionary: Waterloo, Canada, 17–36.

Atkins, B. T. (1990). "Building a Lexicon: Beware of the Dictionary", MS, Oxford University Press (paper presented at a BNN Symposium on Natural Language Processing, Cambridge, MA) (this volume).

Boguraev, B. and Briscoe, E. J. (Eds.). (1989). *Computational Lexicography for Natural Language Processing*, Longman, London.

Boguraev, B. et al. (1989). "Acquisition of Lexical Knowledge for Natural Language Processing Systems", Technical Annexe, ESPRIT Basic Research Action No. 3030, Brussels.

Boguraev, B., Briscoe, T., Carroll, J., and Copestake, A. (1990a). "Database Models for Computational Lexicography", *Proceedings of Euralex-VOX – Fourth International Congress on Lexicography*, Malaga, Spain.

Boguraev, B., Byrd, R., Klavans, J., and Neff, M. (1990b). "From Structural Analysis of Lexical Resources to Semantics in a Lexical Knowledge Base", RC #15427, IBM T. J. Watson Research Center, Yorktown Heights, New York.

Boguraev, B. and Pustejovsky, J. (1990). "Lexical Ambiguity and the Role of Knowledge Representation in Lexicon Design", *Proceedings of the 13th International Conference on Computational Linguistics*, Helsinki, Finland.

Boguraev, B. and Levin, B. (1990). "Models for Lexical Knowledge Bases", *Proceedings of the 6th Annual Conference of the UW Centre for the New OED*, Waterloo, Ontario.

Briscoe, T., Copestake, A., and Boguraev, B. (1990). "Enjoy the Paper: Lexical Semantics via Lexicology", *Proceedings of the 13th International Conference on Computational Linguistics*, Helsinki, Finland.

Byrd, R. J. (1989a). "LQL User Notes: An Informal Guide to the Lexical Query Language", Research Report RC 14853, IBM Research Center, Yorktown Heights, New York.

Byrd, R. J., Calzolari, N., Chodorow, M., Klavans, J., Neff, M., and Rizk, O. (1987). "Tools and Methods for Computational Lexicology", *Computational Linguistics*, vol. 13(3–4), 219–240.

Calzolari, N. (1984). "Detecting Patterns in a Lexical Database", *Proceedings of the 10th International Conference on Computational Linguistics*, Stanford, California, 170–173.

Calzolari, N. (1988). "The Dictionary and the Thesaurus Can Be Combined", in M. Evens (Ed.), *Relational Models of the Lexicon*, Cambridge University Press, Cambridge,UK, 75–96.

Calzolari, N.and Picchi, N. (1986). "A Project for a Bilingual Lexical Database System", *Advances in Lexicology*, Second Annual Conference of the UW Centre for the New Oxford English Dictionary, Waterloo, Ontario, 79–92.

Calzolari, N. and Picchi, N. (1988). "Acquisition of Semantic Information from an On-Line Dictionary", *Proceedings of the 12th International Conference on Computational Linguistics*, Budapest, Hungary, 87–92.

Chodorow, M. S., Byrd, R. J., and Heidorn, G. E. (1985). "Extracting Semantic Hierarchies from a Large On-line Dictionary", *Proceedings of the Association for Computational Linguistics*, Chicago, Illinois, 299–304.

Church, K. and Hanks, P. (1990). "Word Association Norms, Mutual Information and Lexicography", *Proceedings of the 27th Annual Meeting of the Association for Computational Linguistics*, Vancouver, British Columbia, 76–83. (Full version in *Computational Linguistics*, 16[1].)

Evans, R. and Gazdar, G. (1989). "Inference in DATR", *Proceedings of the Fourth Conference of the European Chapter of the ACL*, Manchester, 66–71.

Fontenelle, T. and Vanandroye, J. (1989). "Retrieving Ergative Verbs from a Lexical Data Base", MS, English Department, University of Liege.

Garside, R., Leech, G., and Sampson, G. (1987). *The Computational Analysis of English: A Corpus-Based Approach*, Longman, London and New York.

Gonnet, G. (1987). "Examples of PAT", Technical Report OED-87-02, University of Waterloo Center for the New Oxford English Dictionary, Waterloo, Ontario.

Gruber, J. (1976). *Lexical Structures in Syntax and Semantics*, North-Holland, Amsterdam.

Hanks, P. (1987). "Definitions and Explanations", in J. M. Sinclair (Ed.), *Looking Up: An Account of the COBUILD Project in Lexical Computing*, Collins ELT, London and Glasgow, 116–136.

Hindle, D. (1990). "Noun Classification from Predicate-Argument Structures", *Proceedings of the 28th Annual Meeting of the Association for Computational Linguistics*, Pittsburgh, PA, 268–275.

Hornby, A. S. (1974). *Oxford Advanced Learner's Dictionary of Current English* (Third Edition), Oxford University Press, Oxford, UK.

Katz, B. and Levin, B. (1988). "Exploiting Lexical Regularities in Designing Natural Language Systems", *Proceedings of the 12th International Conference on Computational Linguistics*, Budapest, Hungary, 316–323.

Kazman, R. (1986). "Structuring the Text of the Oxford English Dictionary through Finite State Transduction", University of Waterloo Technical Report No. TR-86-20.

Levin, B. (1985). "Lexical Semantics in Review: An Introduction", in B. Levin (Ed.), *Lexical Semantics in Review*, Lexicon Working Papers 1, Massachusetts Institute of Technology, 1–62.

Levin, B. (1990a). *The Lexical Organization of English Verbs,* Department of Linguistics, Northwestern University, Evanston, Illinois.

Levin, B. (1990b). "Building a Lexicon: the Contribution of Linguistic Theory", MS, Oxford University Press (paper presented at a BBN Symposium on Natural Language Processing, Cambridge, MA) (this volume).

Levin, B. and Rappaport, M. (1986). "The Formation of Adjectival Passives", *Linguistic Inquiry,* 17(4), 623–661.

McLeod, W. T. (1984). *The Collins New Thesaurus,* Collins, London and Glasgow.

Moens, M., Calder, J., Klein, E., Reape, M., and Zeevat, H. (1989). "Expressing Generalisations in Unification-Based Grammar Formalisms", *Proceedings of the Fourth Conference of the European Chapter of the ACL,* Manchester, 174–181.

Neff, M. and Boguraev, B. (1989). "Dictionaries, Dictionary Grammars and Dictionary Entry Parsing", *Proceedings of the 27th Annual Meeting of the Association for Computational Linguistics,* Vancouver, British Columbia, 91–101.

Neff, M. and Boguraev, B. (1990). "From Machine-Readable Dictionaries to Lexical Databases", *International Journal of Lexicography.*

Neff, M., Byrd, R., and Rizk, O. (1988). "Creating and Querying Hierarchical Lexical Data Bases", *Proceedings of the Second Conference on Applied Natural Language Processing,* Austin, Texas, 84–93.

Procter, P. (1978). *Longman Dictionary of Contemporary English,* Longman, Harlow, UK.

Pustejovsky, J. (1989). "Current Issues in Computational Lexical Semantics", Invited Lecture, *Proceedings of the Fourth Conference of the European Chapter of the ACL,* Manchester, England, xvii–xxv.

Pustejovsky, J. (1990). "The Generative Lexicon", *Computational Linguistics,* vol. 17.

Raymond, D. and Blake, E. G. (1987). "Solving Queries in a Grammar-Defined OED", Unpublished Technical Report, University of Waterloo Centre for the New Oxford English Dictionary, Waterloo, Ontario.

Sinclair, J. (Ed.). (1987). *Collins COBUILD English Language Dictionary,* Collins, London and Glasgow, UK.

Vossen, P., Meijs, W. and den Broeder, M. (1989). "Meaning and Structure in Dictionary Definitions", in B. Boguraev and E. Briscoe (Eds.), *Computational Lexicography for Natural Language Processing,* Longman, London, 171–192.

Wilks, Y., Fass, D., Guo, C.-M., McDonald, J., Plate, T., and Slator, B. (1989). "A Tractable Machine Dictionary as a Resource for Computational Semantics", in B. Boguraev and E. Briscoe (Eds.), *Computational Lexicography for Natural Language Processing,* Longman, London, 193–228.

PART III

Semantics and knowledge representation

5   Events, situations, and adverbs

ROBERT C. MOORE

5.1   Introduction

This chapter concerns a dispute about the relationship of sentences to the events they describe, and how that relationship is manifested in sentences with adverbial modifiers. The two sides to the argument might be called the "Davidsonian position" and the "situation semantics position"; the former being chiefly represented by Donald Davidson's well-known paper "The Logical Form of Action Sentences" (Davidson, 1980) and the latter by John Perry's critique of Davidson's view, "Situations in Action" (Perry, unpublished manuscript).[1]

The issue turns on Davidson's analysis of how a sentence such as (1) is related to a similar sentence with an adverbial modifier, such as (2).

(1)   Jones buttered the toast.
(2)   Jones buttered the toast in the bathroom.

Stated very informally, Davidson's position is this: (1) claims that an event of a certain type took place, to wit, a buttering of toast by Jones, and that (2) makes a similar claim but adds that the event took place in the bathroom. Put this way, an advocate of situation semantics could find little to complain about. Perry and Barwise themselves say rather similar things. The dispute is over the way that (1) and (2) claim that certain events took place. Davidson suggests that the event in question is, in effect, a hidden argument to the verb "butter". As he would put it, the logical form of (1) (not analyzing the tense of the verb or the structure of the noun phrase) is not

(3)   Buttered (Jones, the toast)

but rather

(4)   ∃x(Buttered(Jones, the toast, x)),

where the variable x in (4) ranges over events. Adding the adverbial modifier is then quite straightforward; it is simply an additional predication of the event:

This research was supported in part by the Air Force Office of Scientific Research under Contract No. F49620-85-K-0012 and in part by a gift from the System Development Foundation.

[1]This dispute is a special case of a much deeper disagreement about semantics that is treated in depth by Barwise and Perry in *Situations and Attitudes* (1983).

(5)   ∃x(Buttered(Jones, the toast, x) ∧ In(the bathroom, x))

Perry objects strenuously to making the event described by the sentence an explicit argument to the relation expressed by the verb. He says:

> If we ask what about the statement tells us that there was an event of that type, the only reasonable answer is that the whole statement does. It is not that part of the statement refers to an event, and the other part tells us what it was like. Part of the statement refers to Jones and the other part tells us what he did. Both parts working together tell us that an event of a certain sort occurred. The simple parts of the sentence refer to basic uniformities across events: Jones, buttering, and the toast. The way the simple parts are put together in the sentence describes the event. (Perry, 1983, p. 2)

Now it happens that Davidson considers but rejects an analysis derived from Reichenbach (1947, pp. 266–274) that is in the spirit of Perry's objection. On this analysis, (1) and (2) would be rendered by (6) and (7), respectively:

(6)   ∃x(x consists in the fact that Jones buttered the toast)
(7)   ∃x(x consists in the fact that Jones buttered the toast and x took place in the bathroom)

This seems to meet Perry's objection in that it is the whole statement "Jones buttered the toast" that gives rise to the reference to the event, rather than a hidden argument to the verb. Davidson rejects the analysis, however, on the grounds that its logical properties are problematical. Davidson notes that, from the identity of the Morning Star and Evening Star, we would want to be able to infer that, if I flew my spaceship to the Morning Star, I flew my spaceship to the Evening Star. On the analysis under consideration, this requires being able to infer (9) from (8).

(8)   ∃x(x consists in the fact that I flew my spaceship to the Morning Star)
(9)   ∃x(x consists in the fact that I flew my spaceship to the Evening Star)

Davidson argues that the only reasonable logical principles that would permit this inference would entail the identity of all actually occurring events, which would be absurd. Barwise and Perry's (1983, pp. 24–26) rejoinder to this is that Davidson makes the unwarranted assumption that logically equivalent sentences would have to be taken to describe the same event, an idea they reject. Perry (1983) goes on to develop, within the framework of situation semantics, an analysis of event sentences and adverbial modification that is faithful to the idea that, in general, it is an entire sentence that describes an event.[2]

To summarize the state of the argument: Davidson and Perry agree that sentences describe events, but Davidson thinks that it is virtually incoherent to view

---

[2]We omit the details of Perry's own analysis of adverbial modification, as it is not really needed for the points we wish to make.

the event as being described, as it were, "holistically" by the entire sentence, whereas Perry views it as "the only reasonable answer." Barwise and Perry pinpoint where they think Davidson's argument goes wrong, and Perry provides an analysis of adverbial modification consistent with the holistic view.

5.2   Some facts about adverbs and event sentences

One of the things that Perry's and Davidson's analyses have in common is that neither is based on a very extensive survey of the linguistic data to be explained by a theory of adverbial modification; their arguments are based more on general logical and metaphysical concerns. A close examination of the relevant linguistic phenomena, however, shows that neither Davidson nor Perry have the story quite right, and that a more complete account of adverbial modification has to include at least two possible relations between sentences and events, one close to Davidson's account and the other close to Perry's.

The key set of data we will try to explain is that there exists a significant class of adverbs that can be used to modify event sentences in two quite distinct ways:

(10)   (a)   John spoke to Bill rudely.
      (b)   Rudely, John spoke to Bill.
(11)   (a)   John stood on his head foolishly.
      (b)   Foolishly, John stood on his head.
(12)   (a)   John sang strangely.
      (b)   Strangely, John sang.

The difference between the first and second member of each pair should be clear. For instance, (10a) suggests that it was the way that John spoke to Bill that was rude, whereas (10b) says that the very fact that John spoke to Bill was rude. Thus (10a) leaves open the possibility that John could have spoken to Bill without being rude, but (10b) does not. Similar remarks apply to the other pairs. With this class of adverbs, in general, "X did Y Adj-ly" means that the way X did Y was Adj, and "Adj-ly, X did Y" means that the fact that X did Y was Adj. We will therefore say that the (a) sentences involve a "manner" use of adverb and that the (b) sentences involve a "fact" use.

One notable observation about the fact use of these adverbs is that they are indeed "factive" in the sense that the truth of the sentence with the adverb entails the truth of the sentence without the adverb. This is in contrast to other "sentential" adverbs like "allegedly" or "probably":

(13)   Probably John likes Mary.
(14)   John likes Mary.

The truth of (13) would not necessarily imply the truth of (14). This factivity extends to the adjective forms from which the adverbs derive:

(15)   It was rude for John to speak to Bill.

(16)   It was foolish for John to stand on his head.
(17)   It was strange for John to sing a song.

Another significant fact is that with copular constructions, only the fact use is possible; the manner use doesn't exist:

(18)   Strangely, John is tall.
(19)   *John is tall strangely.

Copular constructions accept the fact use of adverbs, as is shown by (18). If we move the adverb to the end of the sentence to try to obtain a manner interpretation as in (19), the sentence is unacceptable.

Finally, perhaps the most important logical difference between the fact and manner uses of these adverbs is that the manner sentences are extensional with respect to the noun phrases in the sentence, whereas the fact sentences are not. That is, we may freely substitute coreferential singular terms in the manner sentences, but not in the fact sentences. Suppose it is considered rude to speak to the Queen (unless, say, she speaks to you first), and suppose John is seated next to the Queen. Then it could well be that (20) is true, whereas (21) is false, although they differ only in substituting one singular term for a coreferring one.

(20)   Rudely, John spoke to the Queen.
(21)   Rudely, John spoke to the woman next to him.

Thus (21) can differ in truth-value from (20) because, on at least one interpretation, it seems to entail that it was rude for John to speak to the woman next to him, whoever she was, i.e., even if she were not the Queen. The issue is somewhat complicated by the fact that these sentences also exhibit the sort of *de dicto/de re* ambiguity common to most nonextensional constructs. That is, (20) and (21) seem to be open to an additional interpretation that there is a certain woman, whom we may identify either as the Queen or the woman next to John, and that it was rude for John to speak to that particular woman.

On the other hand, it seems that (22) and (23) must have the same truth-value on any interpretation, so long as the Queen and the woman next to John are the same person. Moreover, no *de dicto/de re* distinction seems to obtain.

(22)   John spoke to the Queen rudely.
(23)   John spoke to the woman next to him rudely.

Note, however, that (22) and (23) are not completely extensional in the sense that first-order logic is extensional. That notion of extensionality requires, not only intersubstitutivity of coreferring singular terms, but also intersubstitutivity of sentences with the same truth-value. But even if (24) and (25) have the same truth-value, it does not follow that (26) and (27) do.

(24)   John spoke to the Queen.
(25)   John spoke to the Prince.

(26)   John spoke to the Queen rudely.
(27)   John spoke to the Prince rudely.

This sort of behavior is quite general with these adverbs. Examples similar to (20) through (27) can be constructed for "foolishly", "strangely", and all the other adverbs in this class.

5.3   Situations and events

Before we can give a semantic analysis of event sentences that accounts for these observations, we must develop the framework within which the analysis will be couched. As this will require technical notions of situation and event, this section is devoted to explaining those concepts.

A word of caution is in order before proceeding further. The goal of this exercise is semantic analysis of natural language, not the discovery of Deep Metaphysical Truths. If we postulate situations or events as entities in the world, it is not necessarily because we believe they objectively exist, but because postulating them gives the most natural analysis of the meanings of the class of sentences we are trying to analyze. Our real concern is to identify the metaphysics embedded in the language, not to decide whether that metaphysics is true.

A second word of warning concerns our use of the term "situation". This term is so closely identified with the work of Barwise and Perry that one might be misled into assuming that the theory of situations assumed here is simply Barwise and Perry's theory. That is emphatically not the case. Yet it seems so clear that both Barwise and Perry's theory and the theory presented here are attempts to formalize a single intuitive notion, that in the end it would probably be even more misleading to employ a different term.

5.3.1   *Situations and propositions*

Relatively little in the way of a theory of situations is actually needed to construct an analysis of the linguistic data that we have presented. We really need to say little more than (1) that situations are part of the causal order of the world rather than an abstraction of it, and (2) that situations are in one-to-one correspondence with true propositions. To leave the theory of situations at this, however, would leave open so many questions about what sort of objects situations and propositions were that it might cast serious doubt over the application of the theory to the analysis of event sentences.

In our theory, situations are simpler entities than in Barwise and Perry's theory. For us, a situation is a piece of reality that consists of an *n*-tuple of entities having an *n*-ary property or relation.[3] Like Barwise and Perry, then, we take properties

---

[3]We might want to add "at a spatio-temporal location", but we will ignore this aspect of the problem, as the issue seems independent of the others considered here.

to be first-class entities. A proposition is simply an abstraction of a situation: a way that a situation could be. We will assume that for every *n*-ary property and every *n*-tuple of entities, there exists the proposition that those entities satisfy that property. That is, suppose we have an individual John and the property of being tall. If John is tall, then there is an actual situation of John being tall. Even if John is not tall, however, there is the abstract possibility of John being tall: i.e., there might have been a John-being-tall situation, but as things turn out, there was not. This abstract possibility is what we take a proposition to be. A true proposition is one that is the abstraction of an actual situation. We can ask what would be the individuation criteria for situations and for propositions in this theory, and although various answers are possible, the most natural one would be that the identity of the properties and each pair of corresponding arguments are required for the identity of two situations or propositions.

The theory so far satisfies both of the requirements that we previously placed on situations. They are part of the causal order of the world, because they are taken to be pieces of reality, just as Barwise and Perry take real situations to be. They are in one-to-one correspondence with the true propositions, because they have been individuated in such a way that there is exactly one situation for every proposition that accords with reality. What may be in doubt, however, is that there will be enough propositions to do the work that notion normally does in semantics. Elsewhere (Moore, 1989), we show how the theory can be extended to handle first-order quantification, propositional connectives, and propositional attitude attributions, by admitting propositions and propositional functions among the entities to which properties and relations can be applied.

To summarize the extensions briefly: Propositional connectives become properties of propositions. Negation, for example, would be a unary property of propositions. A proposition has the negation property just in case it is false. For every false proposition, there is an actual situation of it being false, and for every proposition there is the additional proposition that it is false. Conjunction, disjunction, etc., become binary relations between propositions. First-order quantifiers become properties of functions from individuals to propositions.[4] For example, in standard logic "All men are mortal" is rendered as "Everything is such that, if it is a man, then it is mortal". In our framework this would be analyzed as the proposition: every individual is mapped into a true proposition by the function that maps an entity into the proposition that, if the entity is a man, then it is mortal.

Within this theory there is a natural semantics for first-order logic with formulas taken to denote propositions, with distinct formulas denoting distinct propositions unless they can be made identical by renaming of variables. We will

[4]A generalized quantifier treatment where quantifiers are considered to be binary relations on pairs of properties is probably preferable, but we present the simpler treatment in this chapter to be consistent with standard logic and with Davidson.

therefore use the notation of standard logic freely in the rest of this chapter, but with the semantics sketched here rather than the normal Tarskian semantics.

5.3.2   Situations and events

The preceding discussion makes an attempt to clarify the relation between situations and propositions, but what of events? Although we have claimed that situations are parts of the real world, they may seem rather abstract. Events, on the other hand, may seem much more real and familiar. For instance, if a bomb goes off, there seems little doubt that there really is such a thing as the explosion. We can see it and feel it, and it has undoubted causal effects. We will maintain, however, that situations and events are intimately related; that, in fact, robust large-scale events such as explosions consist of nothing more than the sum of (literally) uncountably many simple situations.

Suppose an object moves from point P1 to point P2 between T1 and T2. Consider the situation of the object being at P1 at T1, the situation of it being at P2 at T2, and all of the situations of it being at some intermediate point at the corresponding intermediate time. We claim that the event of the object moving from P1 to P2 between T1 and T2 consists of nothing more than the sum of all these situations. The argument is really quite simple: if all these situations exist – that is, if the object is at P1 at T1 and at P2 at T2 and at all the intermediate points at the corresponding intermediate times – then the movement in question exists. Nothing more needs to be added to these states of affairs for the moving event to exist; therefore it is gratuitous to assert that the moving event consists of anything beyond these situations.

The only qualification that needs to be mentioned is that the verb "consist" is used quite deliberately here, instead of the "be" of identity. That is because, according to common sense, one and the same event could have consisted of slightly different smaller events, and hence of a slightly different set of situations. World War II would not have been a different war merely if one fewer soldier had been killed. But this is no different than the observation that changing one screw on a complex machine does not make it a different machine. Therefore we will say that situations are the stuff out of which events are made, just as material substances are the stuff out of which objects are made. The exact identity criteria for events in terms of situations are likely to be just as hard to define as for objects in terms of their material. But by the same token, there is no reason to conclude that there is something to an event over and above the situations it includes, any more than there is to conclude that there is something to an object over and above the material of which it is made.

5.4   The analysis

With this framework behind us, let us look again at "Jones buttered the toast". Perry begins his analysis by saying

"Jones" refers to Jones, "the toast" refers to some piece of toast, and "buttered" refers to a relational activity, with the tense constraining the location. (Perry, 1983, p. 2)

This certainly seems unobjectionable. We have two objects and a binary relation, ignoring tense, as we do throughout this chapter. If the objects in question actually satisfy the relation, then there is a corresponding situation. But how is this situation related to the commonsense event of Jones buttering the toast? The buttering event is surely a complex motion, so by the argument of the last section it must consist of countless situations of the butter, the toast, the knife, Jones's arm, etc. being in certain positions at certain times. According to the identity criterion we have given for situations, those situations and the event that is constituted by their sum are distinct from the single situation of the buttering relation holding between Jones and the toast.

Clearly the buttering situation and the buttering event are closely related, but according to the principles we have adopted, they cannot be one and the same. Davidson's analysis of event sentences turns out to provide a very attractive way of expressing the relation between them. If we analyze an event sentence as asserting the existence of an event, as he suggests, then according to our semantic framework, the sentence asserts that a certain property of events is instantiated.[5] In the buttering toast example, the sentence says that the property of being a buttering of the toast by Jones is instantiated. The situation that the whole sentence describes then, is the situation of the property of being a buttering of the toast by Jones being instantiated. Thus, on the one hand, we have a situation of a certain property of events being instantiated, and on the other hand we have the event that actually instantiates the property.

On first exposure, this may seem like an artificial distinction imposed to solve an artificial problem. In point of fact, however, this distinction is exactly what is needed to explain the two types of adverbial modification discussed in Section 5.2. Moreover, all the data presented there can then be quite straightforwardly accounted for within the framework we have developed.

Let us look again at perhaps the simplest pair of sentences illustrating these two types of modification:

(12) (a) John sang strangely.
      (b) Strangely, John sang

The manner use of the adverb in (12a) seems to fit quite comfortably within the Davidsonian pattern of treating adverbs as making additional predications of the event whose existence is asserted by the basic sentence. If John sang strangely, it seems most definitely to be the singing event itself that is strange. With (12b), though, the singing event itself may be quite ordinary as singing events go. It

---

[5]Strictly speaking, the theory says the sentence asserts there is an event mapped into a true proposition by certain propositional functions, but for simplicity we will paraphrase this in terms of the corresponding property of events.

seems to be the fact that there is any singing by John at all that is strange. But this is precisely what we are saying if we analyze (12b) as predicting strangeness of the situation of the property of being-a-singing-by-John being instantiated.

We can represent this symbolically by making a minor extension to ordinary logic; (12a) can be represented in the way Davidson has already suggested.

(28) $\exists x(\text{Sang}(\text{John}, x) \wedge \text{Strange}(x))$

The extension is required to represent the fact use of the adverb in (12b). That sentence attributes strangeness to a situation, and because we have decided to let formulas denote propositions, we do not yet have any notation for situations. One remedy for this is to let situations be in the domain of individuals, as Davidson already assumes events to be, and to introduce a relation "Fact" that holds between a situation and the corresponding true proposition. The name "Fact" is chosen because this relation quite plausibly provides the semantics of the locution "the fact that P." Note that although "Fact" denotes a relation between a situation and a proposition in our semantics, it will be an operator whose first argument is a singular term and whose second argument is a formula, rather than an ordinary relation symbol. (12b) would then be represented by

(29) $\exists y(\text{Fact}(y, \exists x(\text{Sang}(\text{John}, x))) \wedge \text{Strange}(y))$

This says literally that there exists a fact (or situation) of there being a singing-by-John event and that fact is strange, or more informally, the fact that John sang is strange.

If there is a distinct situation corresponding to every true proposition, it may be worrying to allow situations into the domain of individuals. There are various foundational approaches that could be used to justify this, but we will merely note that the logical principles needed for our use of situations are so weak that no inconsistency seems threatened. The only general principle that seems appropriate is the schema

(30) $\exists y(\text{Fact}(y, P)) \equiv P$

This schema can easily be shown to be consistent by giving "Fact" a simple syntactic interpretation that makes the schema true.

Under this analysis of event sentences and adverbial modification, all the other data are easily explained. The factivity of the fact use of adverbs and their related adjectives arises because the adverbs and adjectives express properties of situations, which are real pieces of the world that do not exist unless the corresponding propositions are true.

Copular sentences do not exhibit the fact/manner distinction in their adverbial modifiers, because they do not involve event variables; only the overall situation is available for the adverb to be predicated of. This provides one answer to Perry's objection to the Davidsonian treatment of event sentences: "The idea that 'Sarah was walking' gets a cosmically different treatment than 'Sarah was agile' strikes me as not very plausible" (Perry, 1983, p. 3). The first of these can take manner adverbials, and the second cannot, a fact that seems to require *some* difference in analysis to explain.

The extensionality with respect to noun phrases of sentences with manner adverbials follows directly from Davidson's original proposal. The noun phrases do not occur within the adverbial's ultimate scope, which is only the event variable. Changing the entire sentence, as in (24) through (27), changes the event, though, so we do not get that sort of extensionality.

The nonextensionality of sentences with fact adverbials follows from the fact that changing a description of a participant in an event changes the particular property of the event that goes into determining what situation is being discussed, even though the event itself does not change. If we compare (20) and (21),

(20)   Rudely, John spoke to the Queen.
(21)   Rudely, John spoke to the woman next to him.

we see that the two sentences describe a single event, John's speaking to the Queen, who is also the woman next to him. The sentences describe the event in two different ways, though, so they ascribe two different properties to it.[6] If we leave out the adverb, the unmodified sentences assert that these two properties of events are instantiated. Since these properties are different, the situation of one of them being instantiated is a different situation from that of the other one being instantiated. Hence one of those situations might be rude (of John) without the other one being so.

5.5   Conclusions

Let us return to Davidson's and Perry's analyses of event sentences, to see how they fare in the light of the data and theory presented here. We have adopted Davidson's analysis of manner adverbials wholesale, so we are in complete agreement with him on that point. We sharply disagree with him, however, on the possibility of associating event-like entities, i.e., situations, with whole sentences, and we find them absolutely necessary to account for the fact use of adverbs, a case Davidson fails to consider. Perry, on the other hand, rightly takes Davidson to task for his faulty argument against associating situations with whole sentences, but then fails to look closely enough at the data to see that something like Davidson's analysis is still needed to account for the detailed facts about manner adverbials.

---

[6]To make sure these two properties do come out nonidentical in our semantics, we need to treat "the" as a quantifier. There are many independent reasons for doing this, however.

References

Barwise, J., and Perry, J. (1983). *Situations and Attitudes* (The MIT Press, Cambridge, Massachusetts).

Davidson, D. (1980). *Essays on Actions and Events, Essay 6,* pp. 105–148 (Clarendon Press, Oxford, England).

Moore, R. C. (1989). "Propositional Attitudes and Russellian Propositions," in *Semantics and Contextual Expression,* R. Bartsch, J. van Benthem, and P. van Emde Boas, eds., pp. 147–174 (Foris Publications, Dordrecht, The Netherlands).

Perry, J. (1983). "Situations in Action," unpublished ms. of a lecture presented at the annual meeting of the Pacific Division of the American Philosophical Association, March 1983.

Reichenbach, H. (1947). *Elements of Symbolic Logic* (Macmillan Co., New York, New York).

6 Natural language, knowledge representation, and logical form

JAMES F. ALLEN

6.1 Introduction

If current natural language understanding systems reason about the world at all, they generally maintain a strict division between the parsing processes and the representation that supports general reasoning about the world. The parsing processes, which include syntactic analysis, some semantic interpretation, and possibly some discourse processing, I will call *structural* processing, because these processes are primarily concerned with analyzing and determining the linguistic structure of individual sentences. The part of the system that involves representing and reasoning about the world or domain of discourse I will call the *knowledge representation*. The goal of this chapter is to examine why these two forms of processing are separated, to determine the current advantages and limitations of this approach, and to look to the future to attempt to identify the inherent limitations of the approach. I will point out some fundamental problems with the models as they are defined today and suggest some important directions of research in natural language and knowledge representation. In particular, I will argue that one of the crucial issues facing future natural language systems is the development of knowledge representation formalisms that can effectively handle ambiguity.

It has been well recognized since the early days of the field that representing and reasoning about the world are crucial to the natural language understanding task. Before we examine the main issue of the chapter in detail, let us consider some of the issues that have long been identified as demonstrating this idea. Knowledge about the world can be seen to be necessary in almost every aspect of the understanding task. Here we consider lexical ambiguity, determining the appropriate syntactic and semantic structures, identifying the referent of noun phrases, and identifying the intended speech act.

This chapter was greatly improved based on feedback and discussion with Andy Haas, Becky Passonneau, Jeffry Pelletier, and Graeme Hirst, and on feedback from talks on early versions of the chapter given at Rochester, BBN Labs, and AT&T Bell Labs. The work was supported in part by ONR/DARPA research contract no. N00014-82-K-0193 and NSF grant IRI-9003841.

6.1.1   Lexical ambiguity

It is well known that most words in natural language are ambiguous, and this introduces considerable complexity into the understanding task. Some forms of potential ambiguity can be resolved by structural methods: the verb *operate,* for instance, occurs in a transitive form (*He operated the printing press for years*) and an intransitive form (e.g., *The doctor operated on my foot*), and the appropriate word sense can be determined by the syntactic structure of the sentence in which it is used. Other word senses can be identified by exploiting fixed semantic co-occurrence restrictions (i.e., selectional restrictions, as described by Katz and Fodor, 1963). The word *pilot,* for instance, can be a small flame used to start a furnace, a preliminary study, or a person who flies airplanes. But in the sentence *The pilot ate his lunch,* the word appears unambiguously, used in its person sense. This is simply because the verb *eat* requires an animate subject. Selectional restrictions encode such structural restrictions in terms of what are legal combinations of sub-constituents to form new constituents. It is easy to see, however, that such techniques cannot solve all ambiguity resolution problems. Adapting an example from Bar-Hillel (1971), consider the sense of the word *pen* in *I put the pigs in the pen* versus *I put the ink cartridge in the pen.* We must have general knowledge about writing instruments (*pens*) – that they typically contain ink, and that they are not large enough to hold pigs – and about animal compounds (*pens*) – that typically there would be no reason to put ink in one, and that they typically are used to contain animals such as pigs. As we will see in all these motivating examples, the general problem, in this case word-sense ambiguity, cannot be solved without using both structural constraints and general reasoning.

6.1.2   Structural ambiguity

Similar issues arise in dealing with syntactic-structure ambiguity, as in prepositional phrase attachment. There seems to be structural influences that prefer certain attachment assignments. One of the most studied is the preference called minimal attachment, which suggests that prepositional phrases are attached so as to minimize the depth of the final syntactic tree. Therefore, using an example from Schubert, the sentence *I saw the bird with the binoculars* has a preferred reading where binoculars were used to see the bird, rather than being related to the bird in some way. Another preference that has been extensively studied is called *right association,* in which the preferred attachment is to the right-most constituent. Right association would predict the incorrect reading for the above sentence but be correct for the sentence *I saw the bird with the yellow feathers.* Even if we choose a single strategy, or introduce some way to resolve conflicts between these preferences, it still remains that some sentences clearly violate these constraints and the appropriate reading can only be identified by the knowledge representation. So the knowledge representation (KR) seems to have the final say. On the other hand, we know that certain structures seem to yield such strong preferences that a comprehensible parse cannot easily be found even though it exists. These are the so-called "garden path" sentences such as *The horse raced past the barn fell* (Bever, 1970). So the structure of the sentence can have great influence on the interpretation, but so can general world knowledge and reasoning. Thus, a reasonable solution must allow the structural constraints and general reasoning about the world to be used together to identify the appropriate reading.

6.1.3 Reference

Another area concerns determining the referent of noun phrases. Consider pronominal reference as an example. Although there may be strong structural suggestions for determining the referent of a pronoun, structure does not completely determine the issue. Hobbs (1978) and Brennan, Friedman, and Pollard (1987), for instance, develop algorithms based on syntactic structure and simple type restrictions that can correctly identify up to 90% of the antecedents in news articles. But examples that cannot be resolved on structural grounds and require general reasoning are easily found. Consider a variant of an example from Winograd: *I dropped the glass on the table and it broke.* The pronoun *it* appears to refer to the glass, just as it does in *I dropped the table on the glass and it broke.* Determining the correct referent in both of these sentences can only be a result of general knowledge about tables and glasses and which are more likely to break in certain situations. On the other hand, general reasoning cannot account for all cases; otherwise the discourse segment (adapted from Wilks, 1975) *I put the wine on the table. It was brown and round* would not seem anomalous. In this case, as Hirst (1981) pointed out, there is a perfectly good referent for the pronoun, namely the table, but the structure of the sentence seems to prohibit this, leaving us with the anomalous situation of having brown, round wine! Grosz et al. (1983) have explored various structural constraints on pronominal reference that may be able to explain such phenomena. But again, this structural model must interact with general reasoning in order to determine the appropriate interpretation.

6.1.4 Speech acts

Another aspect of language that is highly dependent on general reasoning is recognition of the intended speech act. The sentence *Do you know the time?* for instance, can be intended in different situations as a yes–no question, as a request for the time, as an offer to tell someone the time, or as a reminder that it is late. This seems like a situation in which structural processing may be of little value, and general reasoning dominates. In fact, the model of Perrault and Allen (1980), and most of the speech act work undertaken since, has made this assumption explicitly. The intended speech act is determined solely from the propositional content of the sentence, together with minimal structural information, specifically the syntactic mood of the sentence. Perrault and Allen show how a wide range of interpretations can be derived simply from reasoning about the speaker's beliefs, actions, and intentions in the situation. But there are strong structural indicators of the intended speech act as well. For instance, *Can you pass the salt?* is much more likely a request to pass the salt than *Tell me if you are able to pass the salt.* As another example, any sentence with the adverbial *please* must be taken as some form of request. So speech act interpretation is yet one more phenomenon that depends on both structural constraints and general reasoning.

Given these examples, it has been known for years that a central problem in natural language understanding is how linguistic structure and general reasoning interact in order to produce an understanding of the sentence. But progress on this problem has been slight and the usual approach taken is a combination of avoidance and enumeration. First, the test application is carefully constrained to avoid as many ambiguity problems as possible. For the remaining ambiguity, the structural processing enumerates a set of unambiguous interpretations for the knowledge representation to select from. But even after constraining ambiguity extensively, the enumerate-and-filter model is hard to manage in practice. As a result, current systems depend on being able to heuristically resolve the remaining ambiguity during the parsing process, so that a single unambiguous representation of the sentence is produced as the starting point of general reasoning.

This chapter will examine these issues in detail and conclude that the current methods used will not be extendable to a general solution to the problem. Progress on handling ambiguity will occur only after we re-consider the architecture of natural language systems and make a considerable change in emphasis in our research in knowledge representation.

Before I continue with the main thrust of the chapter, I want to eliminate the following possible source of confusion. Could we not view the *entire* language understanding process as reasoning in some knowledge representation? After all, logic-grammar systems have been used for syntactic and semantic processing for a long time now (e.g., Colmerauer, 1978; Pereira and Warren, 1985). These systems can be viewed as theorem provers in a Horn-clause logic, as in the formal development of PROLOG. So is there any issue here? If we all used such systems, then could there be a uniform representation for parsing and general world reasoning?

At a superficial level, the answer to this may be yes. But that only serves further to hide the problems we want to examine, rather than eliminate them. There are significant differences between a parser built in a Horn-clause formalism, and a knowledge representation for general reasoning about the world. In fact, they are two completely different levels of representation, even if they do share certain syntactic similarities to each other. On the one hand, the terms in a logic grammar denote abstract structures in some theory of syntax. The terms in a general reasoning system, on the other hand, denote objects in the world. Even if we allowed the domain of syntactic objects into the domain of our general representation, we would still have the problem of defining the form of these structures (i.e., traditional syntactic theory) and, more important, defining how these syntactic structures relate to the world they describe. This is the same problem with which we started, so collapsing the two representations has not solved anything.

More important, the types of inference allowed at each level of representation are significantly different. In particular, if we view a parser's operation as an inference process, then the inference rules allowed are highly constrained: they all take certain previous "conclusions" (i.e., subconstituents) and combine them syntactically to produce a larger "conclusion" (i.e., the new constituent defined by the rule). Furthermore, the nature of the underlying syntactic theory constrains the types of composition that are allowed. These are the crucial properties that allow us to build efficient parsers. For instance, the compositional nature of this "inference process" allows us to use techniques such as well-formed substring tables and top-down filtering in order to optimize parsing algorithms.

General reasoning, on the other hand, appears to be unconstrained: there is provably no effective algorithm for determining all possible inferences and there certainly is no convenient structural relationship between a conclusion and its premises. Because of this, there is great concern in the knowledge representation community about the trade-off between the expressive power of the formalism and the computational complexity of the reasoning processes (e.g., Levesque and Brachman, 1984). Even highly restricted forms of reasoning, such as determining whether a set of temporal interval constraints is consistent, can be shown to be NP-hard (Vilain and Kautz, 1986). There is certainly no sort of compositionality constraint on general inference that allows us to guarantee efficient algorithms, although a few subareas (e.g., type subsumption in a tree-structured type hierarchy) can be analyzed in this fashion.

Therefore, it does not help to have a uniform representational language that can encode the different levels of representation needed for language understanding. In fact, although it may be a reasonable implementation technique, for the purposes of this chapter it is much more helpful to assume different representation languages for structural analysis and general reasoning, and thus underline this chapter's issues of concern.

6.2   Two views of knowledge representation

Not only do most systems use separate representations for parsing and knowledge representation, they also often have the parser produce an initial meaning representation, or *logical form,* in a different language from the final knowledge representation. The reasons for this reflect the very different requirements on a representation required by researchers in the natural language community and those in the knowledge representation community. The two main representational concerns in the natural language community are expressive power and the handling of ambiguity. Both of these issues push the formalisms used in natural language systems away from those developed in the knowledge representation community. This section considers these issues in more detail.

In natural language work, the knowledge representation must be expressive enough to conveniently capture the types of information conveyed in language, and it is clear that a representation with the expressive power of the first-order predicate calculus is not sufficient. For instance, many verbs in natural language are more closely related to modal operators than standard first-order predicates – beliefs, wants, possibility, and so on. In addition, there is a need to have predicate-modifying operators. For example, if the sentence *The box is red* has some representation of the form RED(B1), then how would one represent the meaning of the sentence *The box is very red*? It could be that there is another predicate VERY-RED, say, that captures the meaning of this sentence, but this seems to miss some important generalizations. We would, for instance, need an extra predicate of the form VERY-P for every predicate P that can be so modified. A much more satisfying representation would involve a predicate operator VERY, producing a meaning representation of the form VERY(RED)(B1).

In addition, there is significant interest currently in defining compositional semantic interpretation algorithms. In these schemes, the semantic representation of one constituent is a function of the semantic interpretation of its sub-constituents. Compositionality is a highly desirable feature in semantic interpretation, as it allows a close correspondence between semantic interpretation and syntactic parsing, and because of this produces a representation that is cleanly defined and generally more easily extended than the non-compositional approaches. But taking this approach makes requirements on the representational language. Returning to the example above, the meaning of the phrase *very red* should be a simple function of the meaning of the sub-constituent *red*. If the representation contains predicate operators, this is trivial: the meaning of *red* might be the predicate RED, and the meaning of *very red* could be the predicate VERY(RED). Consider the alternative. If RED and VERY-RED are distinct predicates, even though they are inferentially related (i.e., very red things are red), they have no systematic connection between each other. Thus the meaning of the phrase *very red* would have no systematic connection to the meaning of the phrase *red,* making a compositional analysis impossible. Compositionality also requires further extensions to the representation. For example, the standard technique for combining sub-constituent meanings into the constituent meaning requires the use of the lambda-calculus, as well as an ability to distinguish extensional and intensional meanings (e.g., Scha and Stallard, 1988).

Another very important representational issue that is often ignored is nominalization. In natural language almost anything can be nominalized. For example, although *red* above was represented as a predicate, we can also talk about it as an object and assert properties of it, as in *Red is my favorite color*. As above, it could be that we have a predicate RED, and an object for the color red, but this misses the significant generality of this phenomenon. A much better representation would involve the introduction of a nominalization operator that can turn a predicate into an object. Moreover, it appears that arbitrarily complex actions and situations can be referred to in natural language. To handle these phenomena adequately, we need to introduce some situation-producing operator as well (e.g., see Schubert and Hwang, 1989).

So natural language researchers require a rich, highly expressive formal representation language in order to capture adequately the meaning of natural sentences. The issue of the complexity of complete reasoning within the representation does not appear as a central issue.

The other central concern in the natural language (NL) community is the handling of ambiguity. Because enumeration does not seem to be a viable strategy, some method is needed of concisely encoding ambiguity until it reaches the stage when it can be resolved. There are many techniques that can be used, and they are often found in various logical forms. Scha and Stallard (1988), for example, introduce a representation, EFL, that encodes the structural semantics of a sentence. EFL contains a term for every word in the lexicon, which in a sense is an ambiguous encoding of all the possible senses for that word. Allen (1987) uses a logical form representation that allows an enumeration of possible values anywhere in the language where a term may appear as a concise encoding of certain simple forms of disjunction. Many researchers (e.g., Woods, 1975; Schubert and Pelletier, 1982; McCord, 1986; Allen, 1987; Hobbs and Shieber, 1987; Alshawi, 1990) use a representation in which quantifier scoping may be undetermined in the logical form. Many of these representations keep the quantifier directly with the rest of the interpretation of the noun phrase. Thus, rather than the sentence *Every boy loves a dog* being ambiguous between the two meanings, say

$$\forall b \, . \, BOY(b) \supset (\exists d \, . \, DOG(d) \wedge LOVES(b,d))$$
$$\exists d \, . \, DOG(d) \wedge (\forall b \, . \, BOY(b) \supset LOVES(b,d))$$

the sentence has a single, but ambiguous, representation such as this:

$$LOVES(<\forall b \, BOY(b)>,<\exists d \, DOG(d)>).$$

Furthermore, the argument structure of this representation corresponds reasonably closely to the syntactic structure of the sentence itself, making a compositional analysis much simpler. Schubert and Pelletier (1982) and McCord (1986) extend this technique further to include other forms of scoping ambiguity, including the negation operator and various modal and adverbial forms.

The knowledge representation community, on the other hand, views model-theoretic semantics and the computational complexity of the inference processes as the primary issues (e.g., Woods, 1975; Levesque and Brachman, 1984). After an initial period of development of informally defined, procedural representation systems, in the mid-1970s the definition of a formal semantics for representational frameworks became a central issue. With the exception of the identification of default inference strategies (e.g., Reiter, 1980; McCarthy, 1980), many representations were found to be expressively equivalent to the first-order predicate calculus once they were analyzed (e.g., Hayes, 1979). Since that time, virtually all new representations have been introduced with a formal semantics, and attention has turned to defining the inferential power of the reasoning component. The simplest and most common method of defining inferential power is to use a complete inference strategy – one that can infer all the logical consequences of the represented knowledge. Unfortunately, representations with the full power of the first-order predicate calculus (FOPC) cannot have a tractable complete inference procedure, and considerable effort has been made recently to deal with this problem.

The general response to this difficulty is to limit the expressive power of the formalism so that the inference procedure becomes tractable. For instance, Levesque and Brachman (1984) and Patel-Schneider (1986) both suggest representations that allow a tractable complete inference procedure. The KRYPTON system (Brachman et al., 1983) isolates a particular form of representation, the terminological component, that also has provably tractable inference procedures. Unfortunately, these representations lack the expressive power required for natural language semantic processing, which as we discussed above, really requires representations more expressive than FOPC. A possible solution to this dilemma is to retain an expressive language, but define a tractable limited-inference procedure on this representation. Frisch (1987) explores such an approach for a language with the expressive power of FOPC.

Another approach to this problem is the development of hybrid representation systems (e.g., KRYPTON [Brachman et al., 1983]). These systems consist of several specialized reasoning systems, each one with well-defined inferential properties, that are combined together to form a representation more expressive than any of its parts. Of course, there is no free lunch, and the overall representational system either has an intractable inference procedure or is incomplete. It is very easy to combine two tractable systems to form an intractable combined system.

Thus the natural language community and knowledge representation community have very different goals: the NL researchers are interested in expressiveness and handling ambiguity, whereas the KR researchers are interested in devising representations with limited tractable inference procedures. This is unfortunate for both camps: only a few natural language researchers are developing representational systems that involve significant inferential power or can represent complex knowledge about the world, whereas the knowledge representation researchers are developing representations that do not address the issues of concern to one of the largest groups of potential users. Given this situation, it is interesting to examine how current natural language systems deal with this dilemma, and this is the subject of the next section.

6.3   Language and knowledge in existing systems

Surprisingly, many current NL systems do not have any general reasoning component at all, so the issues of concern in this paper are avoided altogether. The typical database query systems such as JANUS (Weischedel, 1989) or TEAM (Grosz et al., 1987), and story understanders such as SCISOR (Jacobs and Rau, 1990) do not use any general reasoning. The processing is based entirely on structural knowledge such as syntax, selectional restrictions, case grammar, and static knowledge such as frames. Because of these constraints, such systems are only feasible to highly specialized, limited-application domains where ambiguity resolution can be reduced to structure-based heuristics.

Although systems that do employ a knowledge representation differ radically from one another, they all draw a sharp division between the parsing (i.e., structural) processes and the general inference processes. I will discuss several specific examples in this section to justify this claim, but will start with a discussion of a hypothetical "generic" system as shown in Figure 6.1. This system has a syntactic grammar and a structural semantic interpretation scheme (for example, based on selectional restrictions and case grammar), and produces a representation that we will call the *logical form*. This logical form is then translated into the knowledge representation language using a combination of simple expression-to-expression mapping rules, some structural discourse models, and some highly constrained inference processes such as enforcing-type constraints. This representation then may be used to initiate inference processes such as plan recognition, script/frame matching, question-answering, or other techniques.

Depending on the actual system, the logical form might already be a valid expression in the knowledge representation, and no translation phase is required, or it might be a separate formalism serving as a bridge between the more expressive linguistic representation and a less expressive knowledge representation that supports inference. Systems also differ on whether syntax plays a dominant role in the parsing process, or whether the parser is driven more by a structural semantics (i.e., selectional restrictions and case grammar). Irrespective of all these variations, every system operates in two major phases – the structural processing is done, a logical form produced (and translated into the knowledge representation if required), and then inference is performed on the literal meaning. Of course, the amount of general reasoning required varies significantly from system to system depending on the task that the system has to perform.

Consider JANUS (Weischedel, 1989), a system that has been aimed primarily at database query applications. The parsing and semantic interpretation processes

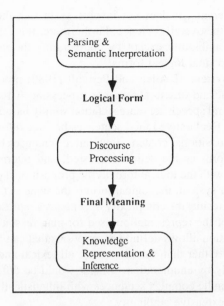

Figure 6.1. A generic natural language understanding system.

derive a formula in an initial representation called EFL, an expressive formalism that concisely encodes word sense ambiguity, and includes many of the features needed to support a compositional Montague-style semantic interpretation. This expression is then translated into an intensional logic meaning representation language, MRL, in which all ambiguity is resolved. This representation is translated into the final representation, be it a limited inference system or a database query language, which then allows for inference and/or retrieval for question answering. No general inference processing by the knowledge representation is involved at any stage of the structural analysis. The semantic interpretation is a structural process closely tied to the parsing process, and the mapping from EFL to MRL uses solely such techniques as static type restrictions to disambiguate the terms. The mapping to the final representation is based entirely on the structural properties of MRL.

The representation in SRI's Core Language Engine (Alshawi, 1990) uses a similar sequence of representations in its analysis. The parser produces a *quasi-logical form* (*QLF*), which is neutral with respect to quantifier scope and certain referential ambiguities. The QLF is then transformed into a *resolved quasi-logical form* (*RQLF*) in which all scoping ambiguity is removed. This is done using structural properties of the sentence and does not involve inference. The final logical form is produced from the RQLF by resolving all the referents for the definite noun phrases. Although this may involve queries to a knowledge representation to obtain possible referents, it does not involve evaluating the plausibility of different readings for the overall sentence. Furthermore, this representation does not encode lexical ambiguity except by enumerating the lexically unambiguous QLFs, RQLFs, and final logical forms.

The speech act recognition system of Allen and Perrault (1980) produces a logical form solely from syntactic and structural semantic processing. This analysis is then transformed into a literal speech act representation simply based on the syntactic mood of the sentence. Declarative mood sentences become *inform* acts with the logical form as the propositional content, imperative sentences become *request* acts with the logical form as the action requested, and interrogative sentences become *question* acts with the logical form as the propositional content of the question. In this particular system, the logical form is the same as the final knowledge representation. As a result, the complexity of sentences representable is restricted by the limitations of the representation used for plan reasoning. To handle reference, the representation allows definite descriptions that can later be resolved during plan reasoning. Other than this, however, all lexical and structural ambiguity is handled solely by enumeration. Thus it would be difficult to extend directly this system to handle complex sentences with linguistically complex semantic phenomena and extensive ambiguity.

Narrative understanding systems such as SAM (Cullingford, 1981) and PAM (Wilensky, 1983) are organized similarly. Parsing is completely separate from the general reasoning mechanism. It produces a logical form directly in the final knowledge representation that serves as the starting point for inference. Any ambiguity has to be resolved during parsing, and thus could not rely on general inference, although some techniques were developed to allow some influence on parsing by the representation. These techniques, for instance, allow the current active script to identify appropriate word senses at the time the word is initially input.

BORIS (Dyer, 1983) presents a much richer model of interaction between the parser and the reasoning component. In fact, BORIS performs all parsing and reasoning simultaneously. As each word is read, various demons are fired that enforce structural constraints (e.g., thematic role analysis using type restrictions), or perform memory search (for reference), or are designed for disambiguation of particular words. Although this system demonstrates integration, it also shows what the limits are for such an organization. In particular, ambiguity for the most part must be ignored as a research issue – only lexical ambiguity that can be resolved through structural constraints or techniques of matching into memory (into scripts, or lists of objects mentioned recently, for instance) can be handled. There is no capability of retaining ambiguity after the sentence is initially parsed, or of allowing general inference to select the most appropriate sense in context. Furthermore, the syntactic theory is very primitive, and linguistically complex sentences with significant structural ambiguity simply cannot be handled.

Small and Reiger (1982) define a decision tree for each word that is used to identify the appropriate sense in context, but again the tests are on structural properties of the words rather than general inferential techniques.

Hirst (1987) has the most extensive examination of ambiguity problems in the computational literature. His system uses selectional restrictions, verb case role restrictions, semantic associations (cf. Quillian, 1967; Hayes, 1977), local referent finding techniques to handle lexical ambiguity and some structural ambiguity such as PP attachment. These techniques use the structure of the KR for finding semantic relationships between word senses. The system also allows limited access to the general reasoning component of the KR to resolve ambiguity. In particular, the SED mechanism allows queries to the knowledge representation to help in certain pre-determined disambiguation questions. These queries, however, must eventually result in an unambiguous representation before the processing is completed. Fawcett and Hirst (1986) generalize this approach to allow unambiguous definite descriptions in the final knowledge representation.

The problem every one of these systems is avoiding is that in order to invoke inference, one must start with some proposition to either add or query the knowledge representation system. Although this can be done in certain pre-anticipated cases, say to find all objects in a database that could match a certain definite description, the lexical ambiguities in the descriptions themselves must be resolved before such queries can be made, because the KR does not support ambiguous expressions. So inference based on the meaning of the entire sentence cannot be used to resolve the ambiguities except by enumeration. As a result, existing systems are restricted to using the static structure of the KR (i.e., its type hierarchy and role restrictions, etc.) to find connections between word senses, or to check if a certain predicate (say derived from a PP) can apply to a certain term (say derived from the constituent to be modified). These techniques are very useful, but they do not bring us any closer to a solution to the real problem – how general reasoning in context can be used to resolve ambiguity.

6.4   Must we explicitly represent ambiguity?

As seen above, current systems are organized on the assumption that almost all ambiguity can be resolved before general reasoning is needed, and that the remaining ambiguity, if any, could be resolved by enumeration. In this section, I argue that this is not a viable long-term strategy. In particular, enumeration is much worse a strategy than one might think. In order to use general reasoning to disambiguate sentences, the choices must be represented in the final knowledge representation so that inference is defined on them. Furthermore, in some cases ambiguity may remain over several sentences in a discourse, or never be resolved. In other words, the ambiguity must be representable in the representation that supports inference.

Before we examine the issues in detail, we must distinguish between ambiguity and lack of specificity. Both are present in language, and different techniques must be used to handle each. Terms are unspecific to the extent that there are other terms that can be more specific than them. An example is the word *horse,* which is unspecific in the sense that there are other terms that are more specific such as *mare, filly, colt,* etc. Terms are ambiguous when they may denote two or more different things. Thus *pilot* is ambiguous because it can refer to a flame, a study, or a person. Various intuitive tests have been developed in the linguistics literature to distinguish these two (e.g., McCawley, 1981). For example, we can say *Jack bought a horse, and Jill did too,* even in the case where Jack bought a mare and Jill bought a colt. On the other hand, we cannot say (except possibly as a joke) *Jack saw a pilot, and Jill did too* where Jack saw a person flying a plane and Jill saw a flame on a furnace. In this chapter, we are solely concerned with representing ambiguity.

If the necessary techniques for resolving a specific ambiguity could be anticipated in advance, and could be performed reasonably efficiently, then the procedures could be incorporated into the structural processing without requiring the general reasoning abilities of the KR. For example, the major form of disambiguation in current systems depends on the use of co-occurrence restrictions first formulated as selectional restrictions by Katz and Fodor (1963). In the final representation, these restrictions correspond to type restrictions on expressions. Current systems either use redundant representations, encoding such knowledge twice – once in the parser (as selectional restrictions), and once in the KR (as type constraints), or they use the KR type restrictions directly to perform the disambiguation. In the latter case, of course, the words need to have been translated into possible KR expressions before these constraints can be tested. In the former case, the translation into the KR can be delayed because of the redundant encoding of the information as selectional restrictions. If such techniques were sufficient to perform all potential disambiguation, then all ambiguity could be resolved procedurally before the final KR meaning was produced.

Unfortunately, as we have already seen, selectional restrictions are not sufficient. On one hand, they encode only semantically possible interpretations and give no indication of what readings are more likely than others. The sentence *The pilot was out* could either describe a situation in which a person is missing, or describe why a furnace was not working. The only way to decide between these interpretations is to see which best fits the context. No technique based solely on the context-independent meanings of the words can choose the appropriate interpretation. Certainly, other techniques such as spreading activation from concepts mentioned in previous utterances may suggest the more likely interpretation, but these predications can be wrong in some cases, so they only play a heuristic role in choosing which interpretations to enumerate first. The final interpretation still ultimately depends on what makes sense in the context, i.e., the decision is made by the knowledge representation. Furthermore, determining this may involve considerable reasoning about causality, and other forms of reasoning such as plan recognition.

As mentioned before, current systems handle such problems by enumeration. In the above example, two representations are produced, one for each reading. But this technique will certainly not generalize as other forms of ambiguity need to be considered simultaneously. In particular, if a sentence is made up of n phrases, each k ways ambiguous, then there would be k^n different readings of the sentence to consider! Language is sufficiently ambiguous to make this a truly formidable number. For example, consider quantifier scoping. This is well known to be a complex problem, where there may be certain structural constraints and preferences on the scope. The final determination of the full scoping, if it can be done at all, can only be made by general reasoning about what interpretation is likely. Hobbs and Shieber (1987) give an example of a sentence with five quantifiers that, even after using sophisticated structural constraints, has 42 different readings due solely to scope ambiguity! If we combined scoping ambiguity with word sense ambiguity, or operator scoping, the number of interpretations grows exponentially.

One promising technique used in systems with incremental semantic interpretation is to invoke the knowledge representation to disambiguate each sub-constituent as it is formed. If this were feasible, then the knowledge representation would only have to consider k interpretations at any one time, and after n calls, would have a single interpretation of the sentence. Although this technique can be used to advantage, the basic problem remains the same. Many decisions cannot be made locally but require the context of the entire sentence. Reconsider the sentence *We put the pigs in the pen.* Calling the knowledge representation to disambiguate the noun phrase, *the pen,* would not select an interpretation as both readings of *the pen* could be appropriate in some sentence. The appropriate sense of *pen* can only be determined at the sentence level, so we are back to the original situation. Quantifier scoping is another example. It must be determined at the sentence level and cannot be done on a sub-constituent by sub-constituent basis.

The other technique that seems promising in avoiding this issue is to use preferences to order the interpretations and to pass only one reading at a time to the knowledge representation, which then accepts the interpretation if it seems sufficiently reasonable. For example, consider PP attachment in a sentence such as *I saw the bird with yellow feathers.* If we assume a preference for right association, the preferred reading will be the one where the bird has the feathers. This would be the interpretation suggested. Because it is reasonable, it would be accepted by the knowledge representation. The other interpretations would never be considered. On the other hand, with the sentence *I saw the bird with the binoculars,* the initial reading would be that the bird was with the binoculars. If this were deemed unreasonable by the knowledge representation and rejected, a second interpretation, that the seeing was done with the binoculars, would be suggested. This is a fine technique as long as the knowledge representation can decide whether to accept or reject an interpretation without seeing the other interpretations to come. But this seems an impossible task. Even in the above example, the phrase *the bird with the binoculars* could have a reasonable reading

in certain contexts: maybe the bird has stolen the binoculars and is flying away
with them in its beak. The point here is not that this is likely, but that it is
possible, and so the interpretation cannot be eliminated on the grounds of violating some constraint. Rather, it is a matter of which reading is more likely. But if
the knowledge representation receives one reading at a time, how can it decide
whether ones to follow would be more likely? Schubert (1986) argues that no
such serial processing strategy can produce a satisfactory solution to this problem, where he defines a serial strategy to be one that uses preferences to suggest
preferred readings in some order, and the first one that is semantically and
pragmatically acceptable is chosen.

But what is the alternative to such approaches? It seems that the only one is to
encode ambiguity within the knowledge representation language. Now this might
seem in one sense simply to be delaying the problem and thus not helping. But
this is not necessarily so. What it allows is the ability to do inference on ambiguous sentences, which then may allow us to infer something that eliminates some
of the potential readings. Furthermore, the ambiguity would have to be encoded
in a way that is not combinatorially explosive, so that options reveal themselves
as a result of inference, rather than inference being used to select from a long list
of options. For example, one encoding of ambiguity that would not help would
be a disjunction of the enumerated possible unambiguous readings!

6.5   Can a logical form save us?

In Section 6.3, we saw that existing systems either artificially limit the amount of
ambiguity and sheer complexity of the input, and parse directly into the knowledge representation, or they use an intermediate logical form level to build a
bridge between the structural processing and the knowledge representation. The
logical form is typically defined to be the context-independent, or literal, meaning of the sentence (e.g., Allen, 1987; Scha, 1983; Moore, 1981). In practice, it
is used in order to resolve the incompatibilities that arise between the needs of
parsing and semantic interpretation and the need to support general inference, as
described in Section 6.2. In this section I examine whether this technique of
introducing an intermediate representation, the logical form, has potential to
resolve the difficult issue of handling ambiguity. Unfortunately, I will conclude
that it does not and that there is no long-term gain from having a logical form
representation as distinct from the knowledge representation, if the logical form
is taken as a literal meaning of the sentence.

This is not to say that separate logical forms are not useful in the short-term.
The division of the structural and reasoning processes allows progress to proceed
in each area without being constrained by the other. For instance, the researcher
building a language system can design a richly expressive logical form language
(e.g., Scha and Stallard, 1988) without worrying about designing a tractable,
complete inference system. Since producing a logical form is a well-defined

ending-point for a research project, the fact that we then lose expressive power by the partial translation into the simpler knowledge representation language in an actual implementation may not be of theoretical concern. Knowledge representation researchers, on the other hand, can examine issues of representation without the requirement of satisfying a demanding user, namely the NL system. Although this may have been a reasonable initial research strategy, the dangers of the approach should be apparent. NL people may design representations that could never be used to support inference about the world, and KR people may design representations that few natural language researchers will find useful. Clearly if general reasoning is ever going to be able to assist to disambiguation, some middle ground is essential.

The principal long-term issue is this: will the approach of using a separate logical form allow us to define a system with significant ambiguity resolution between the parser and the general reasoner, but not require us to represent ambiguity in the knowledge representation? I am going to argue that it is not, and that for our purposes the logical form should be in the same language as the knowledge representation. Depending on one's preference, one can view this as saying we need to generalize knowledge representation languages to the full expressive power found in logical forms, or one can view it as saying we need to define inference processes on the logical form representation. Either way, we end up in the same place. The argument depends on examining the main reasons that a logical form might help us, and showing that if we take ambiguity seriously, none of the reasons are valid in the long term. In particular, the logical form representation is used for the following reasons:

1. to encode semantic ambiguity concisely and to support the disambiguation process;
2. to obtain the expressive power needed, which is not available in current knowledge representations;
3. to support compositional semantic interpretation.

In response to these needs, I will argue the following three points below:

1. the KR must support long-term representation of ambiguity anyway;
2. the KR cannot avoid having full expressive power;
3. compositional semantic interpretation need not be constrained by the final KR language.

If I can establish these points, then there is little advantage to having a logical form that is distinct from the knowledge representation. In fact, a separate representation could only serve to complicate the issues. In effect, all the issues that drove researchers to defining a logical form in the first place must eventually be faced in the knowledge representation itself if ambiguity is to be taken seriously. Given this conclusion, it seems that a central problem for natural language research in the next decade should be the development of representations that are considerably more expressive than the current KR systems. In addition, because such representations are assured of having intractable complete inferential properties, considerable work must be done on defining limited inference systems that do not depend on the limited expressive power of the representation.

Having a logical form that supports ambiguity does not eliminate the need for the knowledge representation to handle ambiguity as well. To see why, consider what would happen if the KR did not represent ambiguity. In order to disambiguate the logical form, it must be closely tied to the final representation. For example, to make an appropriate prepositional phrase attachment decision, we will need to consider a representation of the prepositional phrase and the potentially modified expression to decide if the attachment makes sense or is expected in the situation. But to do this will require inference in the KR, and thus the logical form of the prepositional phrase and of the potentially modified expression must be translated into the KR (resolving any ambiguities) before the decision can be made. If we have to go to all this work each time, it is not clear what role the logical form (LF) plays in the process at all. As another example, determining the referent of the pronoun *it* in the sentence *I dropped the glass on the table and it broke* requires general reasoning about the likelihood of a glass breaking a table in contrast to a table breaking a glass. Again the LF is not useful in this situation. Rather it concerns the actual object classes (i.e., tables and glasses) in the KR, and what knowledge is known about such situations (i.e., dropping things). If there is a logical form for *it broke,* then it must be translated into a KR representation with the *it* remaining ambiguous before the question of resolving the pronoun can be considered.

In other cases, ambiguity may not be resolvable at all at the sentence level, and may extend indefinitely through a discourse. In fact, it is easy to find conversations where a certain sentence is ambiguous, and the conversation continues in an effort to define the appropriate reading through a clarification subdialog. In other cases, an ambiguity may be present that is never resolved. In response to this problem, one might suggest a model in which sentences are not encoded into the KR until they are fully disambiguated by further conversation, but this is untenable. Because no inference could ever be made from such sentences until they were disambiguated, this would prevent the reasoning system from finding the connections between sentences that are necessary to disambiguate the sentences in the first place!

As an example, consider the sentence *Jill is visiting us next Friday.* It may be ambiguous as to whether the speaker meant this coming Friday (say tomorrow), or a week from that date. Now it is not hard to construct reasonable scenarios in which this ambiguity remains for an indefinite period of time. We might not know the correct referent until the day arrives, or we might never resolve it. We can still perform inference based on this sentence, however – and, say, infer that Jill likes us, or that we will be seeing her sometime in the next two weeks – but the reference of *next Friday* remains undetermined. Hirst (1990) suggests the example *John bought a vxzfl,* where *vxzfl* is an unknown word. Even so, this sentence could be stored in the knowledge base and inference could be performed. For example, a reasonable system should be able to answer the question *Did he pay for it?*

Finally, it may be the case that a speaker is intentionally ambiguous or vague in a sentence, and that the hearer recognizes this and draws certain conclusions from it (say that the speaker is being evasive and does not want to reveal some implication of the true meaning). If we are ever going to be able to model this sort of interaction, the KR not only needs to be able to represent ambiguity, but it must be able to represent explicitly that sentences are ambiguous, and that such ambiguity may be intended! This is clearly beyond our present capabilities but remains a very interesting long-term research problem.

6.5.1 Expressive power

I have just argued that the logical form representation does not remove the need to represent ambiguity in the KR, or help in mediating between the parsing processes and the KR reasoning. This section argues that the KR language must be as expressive as any logical form anyway, eliminating the second reason that one might wish to retain a logical form representation. This argument rests on the point that every distinction representable in the logical form may make a difference to some inference process, and so needs to be captured in the knowledge representation.

We have already argued that the logical form must represent modal operators. But the need for such operators does not disappear once the meaning is encoded in the knowledge representation. Propositions involving modal operators for belief, want, and possibility, for instance, are crucial in reasoning about the speaker's intentions and in determining appropriate responses in dialog (e.g., Allen and Perrault, 1980).

The argument given earlier for needing predicate operators in the LF to capture significant generalizations in language applies just as well to the KR, where the same information must be represented. The representation of *very,* for instance, cannot be encoded by some absolute value on some intensity scale – rather its interpretation depends on the property it modifies, and the context in which it is used. As before, determining a precise interpretation depends on general reasoning in context. In addition, it may be that a precise interpretation cannot be derived and exact implications of the term remain vague. In either case, the KR needs some representation of the vague reading of *very,* for which the predicate operator representation seems as direct as any could be.

Nominalizations play an important role in reference processing. They also are useful to capture the meanings of common sentences, such as the relation between *The book is red* and *Red is my favorite color.* Although the KR could represent the property and the nominalization independently, it would lose significant generalizations on the types of inferences that can be made to relate such sentences. In addition, it is not clear how the nominalization of complex situations could be handled in a general way without such an operator. For example, consider the discourse fragment *Everybody in the room saw Jack kiss Mary. It embarrassed them greatly.* The referent of *it* is the situation of everybody seeing the kiss, and this situation needs to be explicitly represented in the discourse model so that the anaphora resolution algorithm works. But, in addition, this information needs to be represented in the KR. What is the object that appears in the assertion about John and Mary being embarrassed – it must be the situation again, represented in the knowledge representation. The system explicitly needs such constructs to be able to answer a question such as *What was embarrassing?* with an answer such as *The fact that everyone saw John and Mary kiss.* The different constructions that appear in language reflect strongly on the structure of the underlying reasoning system. Note also that the pronoun *them* in the above sentence is ambiguous: it could be John and Mary, or everybody in the room. This is another example of an ambiguity that may not ever be resolved. Consider that I have just spent a paragraph talking about an ambiguous sentence without the ambiguity ever creating a problem!

It can also be easily shown that other distinctions such as the generic/specific distinction, or the collective/distributive distinction for plural NPs have great effect on the inferences that can be made about the situations described. Thus these must be represented in the final KR language as well. So the KR must eventually be able to represent all the complexities that arise in language and the logical form is not needed.

6.5.2   *Compositional semantic interpretation*

The final argument for logical form is that even if the knowledge representation were fully expressive and supported ambiguity, a separate logical form might still be needed in order to support compositional semantic interpretation. Although there is no conclusive argument to make here, I find this unlikely.

Before discussing this final argument, however, consider what is meant by compositional semantic interpretation. Compositionality requires that the semantic interpretation can be defined incrementally, where the interpretation of each constituent is a function of the interpretations of its sub-constituents. The strongest form of this is found in Montague-style semantics, where the semantic interpretation of a constituent was derived by applying a function (which was the meaning of the first sub-constituent) to the interpretation of the other sub-constituents. But systems may be compositional and not be of this flavor. Many computational systems, for instance, annotate each syntactic rule with a definition of how the semantic interpretation is to be computed from the interpretation of the sub-constituents (e.g., Schubert and Pelletier, 1982). This allows a much simpler semantic form in most cases, yet retains the full power of the original approach.

Another form of compositionality is based on unification, where the interpretation of a constituent is defined by a set of unification equations showing how to combine the interpretations of the sub-constituents. As the methods of defining the interpretation become more flexible and powerful, the constraints on the form of the representation become less restrictive.

In addition, all the requirements discussed in the last section involved extensions to the KR that brought it into closer correspondence with the constructs present in language. Each one of these additions makes compositional semantics easier. For example, a KR supporting predicate modifier directly mirrors the structural relationships found with adverbials such as *very*. In other cases, the extensions needed to encode ambiguity concisely simplify matters. For instance, a representation that allows unscoped or partially scoped quantifiers requires a mechanism much more general than the simple structural encoding of quantifier scope found in FOPC. With this more general representation, it may be that the interpretation of noun phrases can be encoded locally in the representation in parallel to the syntactic structure. In the following section I briefly discuss one such technique that allows this.

Although it is not possible to give a definitive answer, it appears that there is much to be gained by assuming that there is no separate logical form, at least in its role as a literal meaning representation, and that we should be exploring ways of extending KRs in ways that support compositional semantics.

The final argument for maintaining a separate logical form even if the KR supports ambiguity is that the logical form might simplify further processing by eliminating various syntactic complexities that do not affect general reasoning. But this does not seem possible, as I would claim that virtually every syntactic distinction may have an influence on the reasoning system. Consider speech act disambiguation as an example. Perrault and Allen (1980) showed that certain indirect speech act readings can be obtained by general inference from an initial literal reading of the sentence. But this approach ignores many of the subtleties that appear in general conversation. For example, in many systems, the logical form of the sentences *Can you lift that rock?*, *Are you able to lift that rock?*, and *Tell me whether you can lift that rock?* are identical. Thus if the plan reasoner in the KR can infer an indirect reading for one, it would also be able to do it for the other. Clearly, this is not always desirable. Furthermore, there can be adverbial modifiers that do not affect the logical form in that they make no truth-theoretic contribution to the sentence. The adverbial *please*, for instance, does not affect the truth conditions of the sentence, yet it should restrict the KR from deriving interpretations that are not in the general class of requests (the directive class in the taxonomy of Searle [1975]). Potentially, arbitrary syntactic structures might be used conventionally to have some intentional significance. Therefore the logical form would need to be able to encode these subtleties, or the KR needs to be able to operate directly from information in the syntactic structure. Either way the logical form seems redundant: if it encodes the entire syntactic structure then it hasn't simplified the later processing, and if the reasoning system can access the syntactic form directly then the logical form yields no advantage.

So on one hand each part of the logical form must have a close correspondence to some expression in the KR (for disambiguation), and on the other hand it must encode the syntactic structure of the sentence. It is not clear how designing such a representation would give us an advantage over working directly with the syntactic structure and the KR alone. It is possible, however, that the notion of syntactic structure might be usefully generalized to include certain semantic phenomena, which we might then call a logical form. But this representation is not the meaning of the sentence any longer, it is the structure of the sentence. Schubert and Pelletier (1982) suggest a logical form representation that seems closest to this approach, and the technique appears to be very useful.

6.6   Ambiguity and knowledge representation

Given that we have established that the knowledge representation must be able to support reasoning under ambiguity, what techniques seem promising for allowing this extension? In this section, I explore some possibilities.

There are three requirements for a representation of ambiguity that seem most important:

1.   The KR must distinguish between ambiguity and disjunction;
2.   The KR must support inference over ambiguity; and
3.   The KR must support disambiguation techniques.

These three criteria are discussed in more detail below, and then I will examine some techniques that may prove useful in building such a representation.

6.6.1   Ambiguity and disjunction

There is an important distinction between an ambiguous statement and a corresponding statement that is a disjunction of non-ambiguous statements, although they can be easily confused as they are so closely related. In particular, the logical consequences of an ambiguous formula appear to be the same as the logical consequences of its corresponding unambiguous disjunctive formula. For example, let α be an ambiguous term that could refer to one of the objects a_1, $a_2, \ldots, a_n$. In this case, the logical consequences of the formula p_α would appear to be the same as $p_{a1} \bigvee p_{a2} \bigvee \cdots \bigvee p_{an}$. For example, let α be the ambiguous referent of the NP *the block,* which might be ambiguous between a toy block relevant in the current context (say *a1*) or a city block relevant in the context (say *a2*). Now the sentence *The block is long* would be $Long(\alpha)$ in the ambiguous representation and $Long(a1) \bigvee Long(a2)$ in the unambiguous representation. But if these two formulas were truly equivalent, then the sentences *The block is long* and *Either the toy block is long or the city block is long* would have identical meanings. But there is a big difference. In the former, the speaker knows which block is being talked about, but the hearer does not, whereas in the latter the speaker does not know which block is long either. Although this may seem to be splitting hairs, this distinction could make a large difference to processes such as plan recognition where the speaker's intent must be characterized. We could capture this distinction by introducing a modality to capture the speaker's intended meaning. If we assume such an operator I (which we might take as having a modal S5 structure as a rough start), then the distinction between the two sentences above is the distinction between

$$\exists \beta((\beta=b1) \bigvee (\beta=b2)) \bigwedge I(L(\beta))$$

and

$$I(L(b1) \bigvee L(b2)).$$

This is not to say that a KR must represent ambiguity by using such an operator, but it must be able to make the distinction. Such a distinction could make a significant difference to reasoning systems that perform plan recognition and other reasoning tasks to further interpret the utterance.

6.6.2   Direct inference on ambiguous terms

For the ambiguous representation to be any advantage over a straight enumeration technique, the KR must support inference from ambiguous formulas to produce ambiguous conclusions. For instance, let α be an ambiguous formula with the corresponding disjunctive formula $A1 \bigvee A2 \bigvee \ldots \bigvee An$. If we have an inference rule R that can apply to any disjunct Ai and produce a conclusion Bi, then R should also apply directly to α to produce an ambiguous conclusion β that corresponds to $B1 \bigvee B2 \bigvee \ldots \bigvee Bn$. This property would allow an inference rule to operate on ambiguous sentences to produce an ambiguous conclusion and, in a very real sense, collapse an entire set of inferences corresponding to applying the rule to each unambiguous disjunct. If this can be done successively, we could possibly gain an exponential speedup in processing.

In addition, if the KR supports reasoning over ambiguous assertions, then there is not such a need to resolve completely the ambiguities within a sentence. Rather, some ambiguities might only be resolved "on demand", i.e., if they are needed in order to accomplish some goal of the understander. Ambiguities irrelevant to the goals of the understander might remain unresolved and even unnoticed! Hirst (1990) suggests some ideas along these lines for mixed-depth text understanding.

6.6.3   Disambiguation inference

Finally, the KR must support inferences that serve to disambiguate, or partially disambiguate, formulas. In particular, given an ambiguous formula α and its corresponding disjunctive formula $A1 \bigvee A2 \bigvee \ldots \bigvee An$, if an inference operation R can eliminate some A_i from the disjunct, then the result of applying R to α should be a formula β where the disjunct has been removed. The simplest example involves the resolution rule: Given $A_1 \lor A_2 \lor \ldots \lor A_n$ and $\sim A_i$, the resolution rule concludes $A_1 \lor \ldots \lor A_{i-1} \lor A_{i+1} \lor \ldots A_n$. What we would like is to be able to apply this operation directly to α to yield an ambiguous conclusion β corresponding to $A_1 \lor \ldots \lor A_{i-1} \lor A_{i+1} \lor \ldots \lor A_n$.

Although no current representation systems maintain a distinction between ambiguity and disjunction, some techniques already exist in these systems that are not far from meeting the other criteria for certain classes of ambiguity. I will look at a few of these techniques here.

One technique that can be quite effective for referential ambiguity involves allowing reasoning about equality and inequality. Many implemented knowledge representations impose the restriction that all lexically distinct constants refer to distinct objects, i.e., they support no facility for adding equalities between terms, and hence also avoid the issue of reasoning about distinctness as well. Unfortunately, with such a representation, the NL system must precisely determine the referent of its terms before it is added to the KR. Thus, while the sentence is processed, the NL system must either commit a term, say the noun phrase, *the happy cat,* to refer to an existing constant, say *CAT37,* or the system must create a new constant (say *CAT58*) that is distinct from all other cats in the knowledge representation. A KR that uses equality, however (e.g., RHET, Allen and Miller, 1989; Vilain, 1985), or limited equality reasoning (e.g., Charniak et al., 1985), does not force this problem. A new constant, *CAT58,* may or may not be equal to another constant already in the KR.

A KR with equality can support an approach to ambiguity that meets the inferential properties described above. In particular, certain inferences can be made directly from the representation using the new constant without knowing how it relates to the other cats in the KR. For instance, we could let our ambiguous term α be *CAT58,* and the corresponding disjunction would involve an enumeration over all known cats, e.g., $CAT58 = CAT1 \lor CAT58 = CAT2 \lor \ldots \lor CAT58 = CATn \ldots$ If we later add an equality relation, say $CAT37 = CAT58,$ then we would have disambiguated α. But inference can be performed without having to disambiguate the term. A universal statement such as *All cats have four legs* can be applied to α directly without considering the disjunction. General disambiguating inferences are also possible: say we know *Calico(CAT58),* then an equality between α and a non-calico cat would be inconsistent. Furthermore, if we apply the axiom that all calico cats are necessarily female then any inequality between α and a male cat would be inconsistent. Thus, applying this rule to α would implicitly eliminate all male cats from the enumerated disjunction. Although this technique satisfies the two inferential properties described above, it does not explicitly distinguish between the differing intentions underlying an ambiguous term and its enumerated disjunction. If this distinction is important for a given application, then the representation requires extending. Otherwise, it meets the requirements nicely, for one never needs to construct explicitly the enumerated disjunction.

Such a technique can also greatly simplify the semantic interpretation process because it can eliminate large classes of ambiguity problems that need not be resolved before the consequences of the sentence can be explored in context. All that is required of the semantic interpreter is that it encodes whatever constraints are imposed on the interpretation by the structural properties of the sentences. For instance, if we are given the sentence *The old man saw him,* the NL system may create a new constant, say *M44,* to represent the referent of the NP *the old man,* and another, say *M45,* to represent the referent of the pronoun. We would also add $MAN(M44) \land OLD(M44)$ and $MALE(M45)$ based on the structure of the sentence. In addition, constraints on the use of a non-reflexive pronoun would require us to add the constraint that *M44* does not equal *M45.* Thus the "ambiguity" and the structural constraint are captured simply and directly in this equality-based representation.

Other sources of ambiguity seem amenable to similar techniques, once the representational details have been worked out. For example, consider the collective/distributive distinction, as in the sentence *Two men lifted the piano* – did they lift it together, or did they both do it separately? The ambiguous form of this sentence would entail that the two men were both involved in piano-lifting acts, and consequences could be drawn from this, even though it is not known if they acted together or if there were two separate acts. Alshawi (1990) describes many phenomena along these lines that could be candidates for extensions to the KR.

Another example of this is quantifier scoping. A suggestion that has appeared many times in the literature is to extend the representation to allow unscoped quantifiers such as

$$LOVES(<\forall \ b \ BOY(b)>,<\exists \ d \ DOG(d)>).$$

The set of models that satisfies such a formula is the union of the models that satisfy each of the unambiguous formulas allowed. In other words, such a formula would correspond to the disjunction

$$(\forall \ b \ . \ BOY(b) \supset (\exists \ d \ . \ DOG(d) \land LOVES(b,d))) \lor (\exists \ d \ . \ DOG(d) \land$$
$$(\forall \ b \ . \ BOY(b) \supset LOVES(b,d)))$$

Under reasonable assumptions about the domain, this disjunction is logically equivalent to the formula

$$\forall \ b \ . \ BOY(b) \supset (\exists \ d \ . \ DOG(d) \land LOVES(b,d))$$

Thus all conclusions that can be drawn from this formula should be valid conclusions from the ambiguous formula. But this does not mean that the ambiguous expression can be collapsed to this unambiguous form. A sentence later on could still result in this ambiguous interpretation acquiring the "stronger" interpretation, namely

$$\exists \, d \, . \, DOG(d) \, \wedge \, (\forall \, b \, . \, BOY(b) \supset LOVES(b,d))$$

These are very simple examples, but they show that such techniques for dealing with ambiguous expressions are possible. One other way of enumerating possibilities implicitly is to allow the ambiguous terms into the language as predications and encode the ambiguity using axioms. For example, the ambiguous word *pit* might be represented by introducing three predicates, *PIT*, *FRUIT-PIT*, and *HOLE-IN-GROUND* and the following axioms:

$$\forall \, x \, . \, FRUIT\text{-}PIT(x) \supset PIT(x)$$
$$\forall \, x \, . \, HOLE\text{-}IN\text{-}GROUND(x) \supset PIT(x)$$
$$\forall \, x \, . \, PIT(x) \supset (FRUIT\text{-}PIT(x) \vee HOLE\text{-}IN\text{-}GROUND(x))$$

With this, the word *pit* would initially map into a description involving the predicate *PIT*, and then inference could identify the correct interpretation later if one reading was inconsistent. This could prove to be a powerful technique if systems can be developed that can perform efficient inference over axiom clusters like the above. It is more attractive than enumeration because of its ability to represent more subtle distinctions and interactions, and its ability to leave the ambiguity implicit until some inference process operates on it.

Examining techniques like this is going to be crucial. Not only do such representations allow us to non-combinatorially encode ambiguity, they provide a concise representation to be used as a start for interpretation in context. For instance, some plan recognition technique might be used, starting from this form, that results in selecting an interpretation that best fits the context in terms of what is known about the speaker's beliefs and goals.

Forms involving lexical ambiguity require more complex techniques to be developed. But in certain cases, the ambiguity may be maintained by a generalization of the technique based on equality. For instance, an ambiguous headword in a definite noun phrase might be handled by creating a constant with a disjunctive type. The NP *the report* might refer to a document (say, type *DOC*) and the sound of a gun (say, type *BANG*). We could encode this in the KR by creating a constant *REP89,* say, with the constraint $DOC(REP89) \vee BANG(REP89)$. Again, in integrating the expression into context, or in processing a subsequent sentence, the inappropriate sense might be eliminated, disambiguating the intended meaning. Of course, many knowledge representations do not allow such constraints, and a constant cannot be created without specifying its immediate type. So this is another case where assuming a more general representation can simplify the semantic interpretation. Note that this is an enumeration technique, and therefore it will only be viable if the ambiguity can be successfully localized in the representation and does not interact badly with other forms of ambiguity.

Other forms of lexical ambiguity are harder to handle, and new techniques need to be developed. It is much more difficult to capture verb ambiguity, for instance, because the different senses of the verb might impose different structural interpretations of the sentence. Thus the verb sense ambiguity is not easily localized. It is hoped that situations like this are rare, as the structure of the sentence itself serves as a strong selector of the verb sense. The remaining senses may all involve the same structural analysis of the sentence. It is very important to distinguish the different types of ambiguity that may occur. Certain senses appear to be semantically unrelated to each other, as though it is just chance that the same word can refer to both. In many other cases, the senses are semantically related to each other, and represent variations on some common semantic theme. In these latter cases, a very promising technique is to encode the ambiguity by a generality. In particular, if the representation supports an abstraction hierarchy, and the different semantically related senses all share a reasonable common parent, then we could use the parent type as a generality encoding of the sentence meaning. As before, we may be able to draw conclusions from this representation at the abstract level, and later inference processes might eventually identify the particular interpretation intended. But even if it is never disambiguated, it is still a fine representation of the sentence. Of course, we may lose information. Say we have an abstract type A, with three subtypes, $A1$, $A2$, and $A3$, and a verb that is ambiguous between senses $A2$ and $A3$. If we use A as the meaning of the verb, we have introduced the possibility that some later process might erroneously identify $A1$ as the specific meaning. Note that if the verb sense is never specialized, however, then we cannot get into trouble. But this may be the price we have to pay in order to retain a computationally effective representation. This technique for reducing disjunction in a representation is currently being explored by Etherington et al. (1989).

Other forms of structural ambiguity pose significant problems, although the techniques that I have suggested might be used to advantage. For example, the sentence *The warden reported a fire in the hills* has at least two readings, corresponding to whether the prepositional phrase *in the hills* modifies the act of reporting or the fire itself. One possibility would be a representation where the PP *in the hills* has a uniform interpretation across the potential modifiers, say as a predicate *LOC(X,HILLS)*, for some X, either the reporting act or the fire, then the representation of this sentence might be (where $W13$ is the warden, $F45$ is the fire, and $R67$ is the reporting act):

$$REPORT(W13,F45,R67) \wedge LOC(X,HILLS) \wedge (X = F45 \vee X = R67)$$

One final technique for ambiguity could involve localized enumeration. If the rest of the interpretation of the sentence is independent of the particular interpretation of a term, that term could be represented by a simple enumeration of its possible interpretations. Completely independent sets of choices do not significantly affect the number of possible interpretations that need to be explicitly constructed. For example, consider a two-place predicate P with the first term ambiguous between A, B, and C, and the second ambiguous between D and E.

We might write this as $P(\{A,B,C\},\{D,E\})$, where curly brackets indicate an enumerated set of choices. Although there are six possible unambiguous formulas characterized by this term, if the two argument positions are independent of each other, we will never need to enumerate them. Rather, each locally enumerated set can remain until some process reduces its membership to a single term. If the argument positions are not independent, however, we may need to enumerate the cross-product of unambiguous interpretations in order to capture the interactions. For example, if the interactions were such that only four interpretations were possible, we would have to resort to listing explicitly these four alternatives rather than using the single representation. Reasoning systems based on constraint satisfaction (e.g., Waltz, 1975; Allen, 1983) often assume such independence properties. Allen, for example, gives an algorithm for reasoning about temporal intervals that uses all three-way constraints between times, but not higher-level interactions (say interactions between four intervals). Because such higher-level interactions are possible, his algorithm is incomplete, but still performs well in typical everyday situations. To the extent that similar techniques can be developed for disambiguation, local enumeration can be a useful encoding strategy.

6.7   Concluding remarks

Although I have spent most of my time discussing problems with existing approaches, I hope the ideas in the previous section suggest important areas of work in knowledge representation and semantic interpretation. Given the nature of this chapter, I can only come to very broad, vague, conclusions. The central points are that if we are to handle natural language in general, we must take ambiguity seriously, and that we cannot avoid needing knowledge representations that can encode such ambiguities effectively. Furthermore, expressively limited knowledge representations are not going to be of use for natural language systems. As a result, substantial work needs to be done in defining highly expressive representations that have well-understood inferential power. Because complete inference systems for such representations will be intractable, we need more research into ways of defining the inferential power of representations that are not based on completeness properties.

References

Allen, J. (1983). "Maintaining knowledge about temporal intervals", *Comm. of the ACM*, *26*, 11, 832–843 (reprinted in Brachman and Levesque, 1985).
Allen, J. F. (1978). *Natural Language Understanding*, Benjamin/Cummings Pub Co.
Allen, J. and Miller, B. (1989). *The RHET User's Manual*, Technical report 238, Dept. of Computer Science, Univ. of Rochester.
Allen, J. and Perrault, C. R. (1980). Analyzing intention in utterances, *Artificial Intelligence*, *15*, 3, 143–178.

Alshawi, H. (1990). "Resolving quasi logical forms", *Computational Linguistics, 16,* 3.

Bar-Hillel, Y. (1971). "Some reflections on the present outlook for high-quality machine translation", in W. P. Lehmann and R. Stachowitz (eds.), *Feasibility Studies on Fully Automatic High Quality Translation,* Technical Report RADC-TR-71-295, Linguistics Research Center, Univ. of Texas at Austin.

Bates, M., Moser, M. G., and Stallard, D. (1986). "The IRUS transportable natural language database interface", in Kershberg, L. (ed.), *Expert Database Systems,* Menlo Park, CA: Benjamin/Cummings Pub. Co.

Bever, T. (1970). "The cognitive basis for linguistic structures", in Hayes, J. (ed.) *Cognition and the Development of Language,* John Wiley, 279–362.

Brachman, R., Fikes, R., and Levesque, H. (1983). A Functional Approach to Knowledge Representation, IEEE Computer 16:10, pp. 67–73.

Brachman, R. and Levesque, H. (eds.) (1985). *Readings in Knowledge Representation,* Morgan-Kaufman.

Brennan, S., Friedman, M., and Pollard, C. (1987). "A centering approach to pronouns", *Proc. of the 25th ACL,* Stanford, CA.

Charniak, E., Gavin, M., and Hendler, J. (1985). *The Frail/NASL Reference Manual,* Technical report CS-83-06, Dept. of Computer Science, Brown University.

Colmerauer, A. (1978). "Metamorphosis Grammars", in L. Bloc (ed.), *Natural Language Communication with Computers,* Berlin: Springer-Verlag.

Cullingford, R. (1981). "SAM", in *Inside Computer Understanding,* Lawrence Erlbaum Associates.

Dyer, M. (1983). *In-depth Understanding,* MIT Press.

Etherington, D., Borgida, A., Brachman, R., and Kautz, H. (1989). "Vivid knowledge and tractable reasoning: preliminary report", *IJCAI-89,* Detroit.

Fawcett, B. and Hirst, G. (1986). "The detection and representation of ambiguities of intension and description", *Proc. of the 24th ACL,* New York.

Frisch, A. (1987). "Inference without chaining", *Proc. IJCAI-87,* Morgan Kaufmann, 515–519.

Grosz, B. J., Appelt, D., Martin, P., and Pereira, F. (1987). "TEAM: An experiment in the design of transportable natural-language interfaces", *Artificial Intelligence, 32,* 2, 173–244.

Grosz, B., Joshi, A., and Weinstein, S. (1983). "Providing a unified account of definite noun phrases in discourse", *Proc. of the Association for Computational Linguistics,* 44–50.

Grosz, B., Sparcek Jones, K., and Webber, B. (eds.). (1986). *Readings in Natural Language Processing,* Morgan Kaufmann.

Hayes, P. J. (1979). "The logic of frames", in Metzing (ed.), *Frame Conceptions and Text Understanding,* de Gruyter.

Hayes, P. (1977). *Some Association-based Techniques for Lexical Disambiguation,* Doctoral Dissertation, Dept. of Mathematics, Ecole Polytechnique federale de Lausanne.

Hirst, G. (1981). *Anaphora in Natural Language Understanding,* Springer-Verlag.

Hirst, G. (1987). *Semantic Interpretation and the Resolution of Ambiguity,* Cambridge University Press.

Hirst, G. (1990). "Mixed-depth representations for natural language text", *Proc. of the AAAI Symposium on Text-based Intelligent Systems.*

Hobbs, J. (1978). "Resolving pronoun references", *Lingua, 44* (reprinted in Grosz et al., 1986).

Hobbs, J. and Shieber, S. (1987). "An algorithm for generating quantifier scopings", *Computational Linguistics, 13.*

Jacobs, P. S. and Rau, L. F. (1990). "SCISOR: A System for Extracting Information from On-line News", *Comm. of the ACM, 33,* 11:88–97.

Katz, J. and Fodor, J. (1963). "The structure of a semantic theory", *Language, 39,* 2:170–210.

Levesque, H. and Brachman, R. (1984). "A Fundamental Tradeoff in Knowledge Representation and Reasoning", in *Proc. of CSCSI-84* (reprinted in Brachman and Levesque, 1985).

McCarthy, J. (1980). "Circumscription: A form of non-monotonic reasoning", *Artificial Intelligence, 13,* 27–39.

McCawley, J. D. (1981). *Everything That Linguists Have Always Wanted to Know about Logic,* U. Chicago Press.

McCord, M. (1986). "Focalizers, the scoping problem, and semantic interpretation", in D. H. Warren and M. van Canegham (eds.), *Logic Programming and its Applications,* Norwood, NJ: Ablex.

Moore, R. C. (1981). "Problems in Logical Form", *Proceedings of the ACL,* 117–124.

Patel-Schneider, P. (1986). "A four-valued semantics for frame-based description languages", *Proc. of the AAAI-86.* Morgan Kaufmann.

Pereira, F. and Warren, D. (1985). "Definite clause grammars for language analysis", *Artificial Intelligence, 25,* 3:301–322.

Perrault, C. R. and Allen, J. (1980). "A plan-based analysis of indirect speech acts", *American Journal of Computational Linguistics, 6,* 167–182.

Quillian, M. R. (1967). "Word concepts: A theory and simulation of some basic semantic capabilities", *Behavioral Science, 12* (reprinted in Brachman and Levesque, 1985).

Reiter, Ray. (1980). "A logic for default reasoning", *Artificial Intelligence, 13,* 81–132.

Ringle, M. (ed.). (1982). *Strategies for Natural Language Processing,* Lawrence Erlbaum Associates.

Scha, R. (1983). *Logical Foundations for Question Answering,* Philips Research Labs, Eindhoven, The Netherlands.

Scha, R. and Stallard, D. (1988). "Multi-level plurals and distributivity", in *Proc. of the 26th ACL.*

Schubert, L. K. (1986). "Are there preference tradeoffs in attachment decisions?" *Proceedings of the AAAI,* 601–605.

Schubert, L. and Hwang, C. H. (1989). "An episodic knowledge representation for narrative texts", *Proc. of the First International Conference on Knowledge Representation,* Morgan Kaufmann.

Schubert, L. and Pelletier, J. (1982). "From English to logic: context-free computation of conventional logical translation", *Computational Linguistics, 8* (reprinted in Grosz et al., 1986).

Searle, J. R. (1975). "A taxonomy of illocutionary acts", in K. Gunderson (ed.), *Language, Mind and Knowledge,* Univ. of Minnesota Press.

Small, S. and Rieger, C. (1982). "Parsing and comprehending with word experts", in Lehnert, W. and Ringle, M., (eds.) *Strategies for Natural Language Processing,* Lawrence Erlbaum Associates, 1982.

Vilain, M. (1985). "The restriction language architecture of a hybrid representation system", *Proc. IJCAI-85,* Morgan Kaufmann, 547–554.

Vilain, M. and Kautz, H. (1986). "Constraint propagation algorithms for temporal reasoning", *Proc. of the AAAI,* 377–382.

Waltz, D. (1975). "Understanding line drawings of scenes with shadows", in P. Winston (ed.), *The Psychology of Human Vision,* McGraw-Hill.

Weischedel, R. (1989). "A hybrid approach to representation in the JANUS natural language processor", *Proc. of the 27th Meeting of the ACL,* 193–202.

Wilensky, R. (1983). *Planning and Understanding,* Addison-Wesley.
Wilks, Y. (1975). "An intelligent analyzer and understander of English", *Artificial Intelligence, 6,* 264–274.
Woods, W. A. (1975). "What's in a link?", in D. Bobrow and A. Collins (eds.), *Representation and Understanding,* Academic Press.

PART IV

Discourse

7　Getting and keeping the center of attention

REBECCA J. PASSONNEAU

7.1　Introduction

The present work investigates the contrastive discourse functions of a definite and a demonstrative pronoun in similar contexts of use. It therefore provides an opportunity to examine the separate contributions to attentional state (Grosz and Sidner, 1986) of two linguistic features – definiteness and demonstrativity – independently of pronominalization *per se*. The two pronouns, *it* and *that*, have clearly contrastive contexts of use, explained here in terms of distinct pragmatic functions. Certain uses of *it* are claimed to perform a distinctive cohesive function, namely, to establish a *local center* (that modifies rather than replaces the notion of a center). The crucial distinction between a local center and the Cb (backward-looking center) of the centering framework (cf. Sidner, 1983; Grosz et al., 1983; Grosz et al., 1986; Kameyama, 1986) is that there is only a single potential local center rather than an ordered set of Cfs (forward-looking centers). The local center is argued to constitute a reference point in the model of the speech situation in a manner analogous to 1st and 2nd person pronouns. In contrast, a deictic function is posited for apparently anaphoric uses of *that* whereby the attentional status of a discourse entity is changed, or a new discourse entity is constructed based on non-referential constituents of the linguistic structure. Because it is impossible to observe attentional processes directly, I present an empirical method for investigating discourse coherence relations. I analyze statistically significant distributional models in terms of three types of transitions

Thanks are due to many people. My introduction to the use of multivariate contingency tables as a technique for looking at interactional events came from Starkey Duncan and his students, especially Harty Mokros. The inspiration to look at cohesive relations in ordinary dialogue came from my former professors Michael Silverstein and David McNeill, and fellow participants in the Sloan Foundation Workshop on Deixis and Anaphora, not least of whom was Elena Levy. While reinterpreting the data in a computational framework I profited from discussions with and the helpful encouragement of Candy Sidner, Megumi Kameyama, James Allen, Elena Levy, and Bonnie Webber.

The initial phase of this work was supported by Sloan Foundation Grant 1-5680-22-4898, while the author was a graduate student at the University of Chicago. Initial reinterpretation of the data with respect to the centering framework was carried out at Unisys and partially supported by DARPA Contract N000014-85-C-1002 (Passonneau, 1989). The chapter in its current form was completed at Columbia University under the support of DARPA grant N000039-84-C-0165 and NSF grant IRT-84-51438.

in the cognitive states of conversational participants: expected transitions, unexpected transitions, and transitions with no relevant effect.

7.2   Pronouns: a heterogeneous category

Pronouns are semantically inexplicit referring expressions whose referents are resolved in complex, context-dependent ways. I have compared a pair of semantically and syntactically similar pronouns on the hypothesis that the subtle pragmatic differences in their contexts of occurrence should be attributed to the critical semantic difference between them, the presence or absence of the feature of demonstrativity. By looking at contexts in which the two pronouns *it* and *that* have superficially similar functions, I have found new evidence about the relationship between pronouns and their contexts of occurrence. The evidence indicates that in addition to the lexical distinction between distinct types of pronouns, the inter-utterance configuration in which a pronoun and its antecedent occurs also contributes to distinct means for establishing and maintaining discourse reference. I posit distinct pragmatic functions for the two pronouns based on their contrastive contexts of use, and also posit distinct functions for the same pronoun, based on contrasts between one context of use and another.

Apart from the semantic property of demonstrativity, referential tokens of *it* and *that* are similar enough to be mutually replaceable in many of their contexts of occurrence, as will be demonstrated shortly (Section 7.2.2). *It* has generally been classified as having a primarily anaphoric function, and *that* a deictic one. Anaphora and deixis are variously described in a large body of linguistic and philosophical literature that will not be reviewed here.[1] But simply put, an anaphor acquires its reference by virtue of a previously occurring referential expression whose referential value it shares, or to which it is inferentially related. The referent must have been added to the context prior to the anaphoric pronoun in order for the speaker to take for granted that the hearer will be able to identify it. Referents for such pronouns are represented in a component of the discourse model that McCawley (1979) refers to as the *contextual domain*. He defines contextual domain as *the set of objects that have been [mutually] identified up to that point in the discourse*. Further, McCawley takes the contextual domain to be hierarchically structured in a manner that anticipates the hierarchically structured focus spaces of Grosz and Sidner's discourse model.

In contrast with anaphoric pronouns, the reference of a deictic pronoun depends on an ostensive relation to some object in the non-linguistic context (cf. Kaplan, 1989). The actual object of demonstration may be directly or indirectly related to the referent. One may look at a disordered room (the object of demonstration, or *demonstratum*) and say *That's the biggest mess we've ever made*, referring (directly) to the state of the room, or *That was a great party*, referring (indirectly) to the cause of the disorder.

---

[1]Cf. ([Passonneau] Schiffman, 1984) for a discussion of these terms as they relate to *it* and *that*.

The apparent parallel of the functional contrast between anaphora and deixis with the morpho-semantic contrast between *it* and *that* is belied by the fact that the demonstrative pronoun often occurs in purely textual contexts in which there is no non-linguistic context within which to point, but where there is a linguistic antecedent, as illustrated in this excerpt from a recent book about Mozart (Robbins Landon, 1988, p. 35):

(1)   Being much more of a pragmatist than is generally realized, Mozart was quick to shift his emphasis as circumstances required. If public concerts were now scarce, why not *concentrate on music for private concerts*? Towards the middle of 1791, *that* is what he proceeded to do.

Note that *it* can occur with the same types of antecedents as *that:*

(2)   Mozart decided to *concentrate on music for private concerts*. *It* seemed like a good thing to do at the time, and *it* would please his wife.

Rather than begin from the theoretical contrast between anaphora and deixis in attempting to understand the functional contrast between examples like (1) and (2), I report on the results of an empirical study in which I compared tokens of *it* and *that* having linguistic antecedents. I account for the observed differences in terms of the presumed attentional status of the referents of the two types of pronouns, building on the centering framework found in the computational literature on discourse reference. Comparing definite and demonstrative pronouns in contexts where each has a linguistic antecedent provides an arena for investigating two distinct kinds of pronominalization, thus separating the issue of pronominalization *per se* from that of whether there are distinct means for managing attentional processes, corresponding in some degree to the theoretical distinction between anaphora and deixis.

In the next subsection (Section 7.2.1), I briefly review Grosz and Sidner's (1986) model of discourse structure with particular reference to their construct of attentional state. Then I review (Section 7.2.2) the major linguistic differences between *it* and *that,* and illustrate through examples that despite these differences, the two pronouns seem to have a similar cohesive function in apparently anaphoric contexts. In Section 7.3 I present a general method for abstracting significant contextual features from naturalistic data, and demonstrate its use in identifying other linguistic choices that are correlated with the lexical choice between *it* and *that*. I argue that contingency tables that correlate one set of cohesive choices with another can be interpreted as state-transition models of attentional state. In Section 7.4 and Section 7.5, I account for the distinct distributions of *it* and *that,* respectively, in terms of functional contrasts between the two pronouns.

Grosz and Sidner posit a local focusing mechanism they refer to as centering. In Section 7.4, I first review the centering model and propose an alternative approach to analyzing attentional state based on empirically established coherence relations across utterances. I then present evidence that one function of *it* is to establish what I refer to as a local center from among the entities within the current focus space, and that the demonstrative typically does not serve this function. *Local center* extends rather than replaces the notion of a center. The crucial distinction between a local center and the Cb of the centering framework is that there is only a single potential local center rather than an ordered set of Cfs. The local center is argued to constitute a reference point in the model of the speech situation in a manner analogous to 1st and 2nd person pronouns. In contrast, I posit deictic functions for the apparently anaphoric uses of *that*. I present evidence for three functions of the demonstrative in local coherence contexts. The demonstrative can signal a change in local center status, or it can indicate that an entity within the current focus space should not be regarded as a candidate local center even though it is referred to by a pronoun. Or finally, it can trigger a process by which a new discourse entity is constructed from non-referential constituents of the linguistic structure.

7.2.1   Background on attentional state

The question of how pronouns are selected and interpreted directly addresses the broader issue of the relationship between language use and the organization of conversational participants' attentional processes in actual communicative situations. Given a pronoun that is used referentially, its reference is resolved to a large degree on the basis of the participants' understanding of the current context of use, rather than on the descriptive content of the referring expression itself. By definition, pronouns have very little syntactic or semantic content. Syntactically, a pronoun is a single-word phrase; it generally excludes any pre- or post-modification:

(3)   *the big it
       *clever she
       *they working for the Daily News

Semantically, pronouns encode such grammaticalized semantic features as number, person, gender and so on (Givon, 1976), but little, if any, other semantic content.

I assume the basic components of the model of discourse structure proposed by Grosz and Sidner (1986), which has the three distinct components of attentional state, segmental structure, and intentional structure. Although there are no hard and fast criteria for assigning segment boundaries within a discourse, evidence suggests that segmental divisions have processing consequences along several dimensions. The same word has been shown to occur with distinct prosodic features depending on whether it functions to mark a discourse segment boundary or to contribute to the propositional level of an utterance (Hirschberg and Litman, 1987). Contrastive choices of referring expressions and of verb form have been shown to correlate with episode boundaries in narrative (Marslen-Wilson et al., 1982; Levy, 1984). Early work by Grosz on task-oriented dialogues indicated that when a pronoun occurs long after its nearest antecedent expression, the apparent remoteness of the two co-specifying expressions can be reanalyzed as proximity within the same focus space, where the focus spaces (Grosz, 1977) defined by the discourse parallel the task structure. Grosz and Sidner's more recent formulation of segmental structure as essentially a projection of intentional structure (1986) is more general because it is independent of discourse genre. A segment is characterized as a unit of discourse exhibiting a single communicative purpose. Segments can be hierarchically related to one another, reflecting hierarchical relations in intentional structure.

Grosz and Sidner define attentional state as "an abstraction of the focus of attention of the discourse participants [that] summarizes information from previous utterances crucial for processing subsequent ones." Attentional state has a hierarchical structure paralleling the segmental structure of the discourse. Each focus space in the current attentional state corresponds to a discourse segment that is currently in focus. Each focus space contains, among other things, representations of the discourse entities that have been mentioned within the corresponding discourse segment. The primary function of the representation of focused discourse entities is to provide referents for anaphoric expressions, including definite (but not demonstrative) pronouns.

Recent work by Webber (1991) on uses of demonstrative pronouns where discourse segments are the demonstrata has provided another use for representing focused discourse segments. She argues that only segments that are currently in focus can be demonstrated. Thus, the current attentional state serves to represent segments that are currently available for supporting what she refers to as discourse deixis. However, neither Webber (1991) nor Grosz and Sidner (1986) attempt to model the distinction between anaphoric and demonstrative reference in cases where the pronoun has an explicit linguistic antecedent.

The on-line choices that conversational participants make are extremely rapid ones, and the complex contextual factors that condition those choices change very rapidly. Despite the difficulties of confronting a rich, uncontrolled context as opposed to a selectively constructed one, I believe it is particularly useful to examine actual interactive conversational data as a means of understanding changes in attentional state. The processes by which we as conversational participants select and interpret anaphoric or demonstrative pronouns are patently outside our conscious control. As soon as one brings conscious awareness to the process of selecting and interpreting pronouns, one has altered the process that normally takes place in actual conversational interaction. Also, conversational interaction is a shared activity, and the discourse phenomena that constrain pronoun selection and interpretation are mutually supported by multiple participants. By examining data from actual conversational interaction, one can be sure to have a situation in which there is a jointly established and maintained attentional state, complete with actual intentions, that is reflected in the linguistic structure of the interaction. The analytic method presented here allows one to abstract significant factors from such naturalistic, interactional data, and to investigate how the current attentional state is actively maintained or altered.

7.2.2   *Comparison of the linguistic properties of* it *and* that

The motivation for comparing the uses of *it* and *that* is to determine what differences in the attentional status of their referents correlate with the distinct linguistic properties of the two pronouns. The major linguistic differences between the two pronouns *it* and *that* can be summarized as follows:

1. *it* is prosodically reducible, and more restricted in its stress possibilities, than *that;*
2. *it* is syntactically a true pronoun whereas *that* is more properly a prenominal modifier functioning as a phrasal head;
3. *it* is semantically a pronoun whereas *that* has some of the properties of a full referring expression;
4. *it* and *that* have the same values of a number of grammatical features, including person and number, but *that* has the additional semantic feature of demonstrativity.

Please note that although I claim that *that* is not a true pronoun, for the sake of convenience I still refer to the relevant usage of *that* as pronominal.

Prosodic differences. The vowel of *it* can be pronounced either as the short front vowel of words like *hit, kit,* and so on, or as the reduced mid-vowel (schwa) found in most unstressed syllables of spoken English. The vowel of *that* cannot be reduced. Lexical stress placement is irrelevant to both *it* and *that,* since they are both monosyllabic, but in addition to the vowel reduction difference there is a phrasal stress, or pitch accent difference (cf. e.g., Beckman, unpublished manuscript, on pitch accent in English). The demonstrative can take various pitch accents, whereas *it* typically cannot, except in special cases, such as in metalinguistic reference to the lexical item itself: *the pronoun I'm studying is 'it'*. In sum, *it* has a reducible vowel whereas *that* does not; *it* is more restricted with respect to pitch accent.

Syntactic differences. Both *it* and *that* can occur where full noun phrases (NPs) occur, and can have explicit linguistic antecedents that introduce the referent of the pronoun:

(4)   I have *a new dress* to wear to Marcia's party.
   a.   I bought *it* last week.
   b.   I bought *that* last week.

But there are several morpho-syntactic facts differentiating *it* and *that* that put the former in the class of pronouns and the latter in the class of determiners. The demonstrative but not the definite pronoun can occur as a determiner (*that/*it book*). The demonstrative pronoun shares with other prenominal modifiers acting as head – such as quantifiers – certain properties that distinguish it from true pronouns. Thus, unlike a true pronoun, *that* does not have a possessive form:

(5) a.   The car is new but *its* engine is old.
    b.   *The car is new but *thats* engine is old.

nor a reflexive form:

(6) a.   The cassette player shuts *itself* off.
    b.   *The cassette player shuts *thatself* off.

On the other hand, the demonstrative – like quantifiers that can become NP heads and unlike *it* – is not absolutely prevented from occurring with certain post-nominal modifiers, e.g., relative clauses:

(7) a.   *All* who want cake should clear their plates.
    b.   *That* which I see before me is a dagger.
    c.   **It* which I see before me is a dagger.

The morpho-syntactic differences between *it* and *that* illustrated in examples (5)–(7) provide grounds for the claim that they are categorially distinct. A true pronoun is a phrasal word that can be viewed as syntactically reduced in the sense that a minimal syntactic unit – a word – occurs in the place of a syntactically more structured one – a phrase. Although the demonstrative seems to function as a single-word phrase, it neither allows the morphological reflexes of a true pronoun, nor absolutely excludes post-modification within the phrase.

Semantic differences: referentiality. It can function referentially or as an expletive (non-referential) expression. The demonstrative cannot occur in the expletive contexts that *it* can occur in, e.g.:

(8) a.   *It*'s raining.
    b.   **That*'s raining.
(9) a.   *It*'s difficult to please everyone.
    b.   **That*'s difficult to please everyone.

The definite pronoun, but not the demonstrative, can occur in contexts in which it corefers with a c-commanding NP:[2]

(10) a.   I prefer the table with a drawer in *it*.
     b.   *I prefer the table with a drawer in *that*.

Thus non-referential contexts exclude *that* but allow *it*.[3]

---

[2]I am using the term c-command purely descriptively to identify a class of contexts, not to imply anything about the syntactic properties of those contexts. This class of examples was brought to my attention by Jerry Sadock.

[3]Demonstrative pronouns occur in what Ball has referred to as *th*-clefts, as in *That was in 1962 that Peter met Betsy,* which she once argued to be non-referential uses (Ball, 1979). If these are indeed non-referential, they constitute an exception. However, Ball has recently suggested that there may be grounds for considering these to be referential after all (personal communication).

Semantic differences: demonstrativity. Both pronouns have the same values of the features of number, animacy, and person – singular, non-animate, and third person – where these features are applicable. Number and animacy are sometimes inapplicable, as in cases similar to the excerpt about Mozart, where the antecedent is a type of constituent that cannot express number or animacy (as in 1 above; cf. Channon, 1980). The principal difference in semantic content between the two pronouns, however, is that the feature of demonstrativity, typically construed as having deictic force, is associated only with *that*.

In order to illustrate *it* and *that* in contexts where they have antecedents,[4] I present some excerpts from several interview dialogues I recorded for the purpose of data collection.[5] For each token of *it* or *that* I've also included the alternate form in parentheses in order to illustrate the acceptability of the pronoun substitutions.[6]

(11)   C: so [you plan to] work for a while, save some money, travel –

        S: save *some money* and then blow *it* (*that*) off

(12)   C: what does *notoriety* mean to you

        C: where does *that* (*it*) put you

(13)   S: I didn't really want *to* [*unfilled pause*] *teach people,*

        S: *that* (*it*) wasn't the main focus

(14)   the drawback is *that I'm on call 24 hours a day*

        S: but *it* (*that*) also means I get different periods of time off

(15)   S: I don't think *each situation is inherently different from the other,*

        S: at least, *that*(*?it*)'s not the way I look at it

Various syntactic types are found as the antecedent expressions in these examples, including simple noun phrases (e.g., 11), infinitival phrases (e.g., 13), and embedded clauses with or without a *that* complementizer (e.g., 14 and 15). In each case (with the possible exception of 15), the non-occurring pronoun can be substituted for the occurring one without altering the acceptability or the truth conditions of the utterances. However, there is a subtle and as yet inexplicable pragmatic difference between the altered and unaltered texts. The hypothesis that even in these contexts the two pronouns have distinct functions is supported by,

---

[4]I use the term antecedent in a neutral sense to refer to the antecedent of an anaphoric expression or to a consitutent serving as the object of demonstration of a demonstrative one.

[5]The interviews were career-counseling sessions that took place at the University of Chicago. In these examples, C denotes the counselor and S denotes the student.

[6]In each example, the relevant pronoun token and its phrasal antecedent are italicized.

but not directly explained by, their distinct linguistic properties. The data presented in Section 7.3 will demonstrate that the apparently anaphoric contexts for the two pronouns are distributionally very distinct. As noted, the results will be accounted for in Section 7.4 and Section 7.5 by positing distinct pragmatic functions pertaining to the attentional status of their referents. It is perhaps these functional differences that underlie the subtle differences between the alternative texts presented above.

7.3   An observational study of on-line local coherence phenomena

7.3.1   Goal of study

The data in this section were originally gathered as part of a larger investigation conducted independently of the centering framework.[7] However, the data from the original study that pertain specifically to the apparently anaphoric uses of *it* and *that* lend themselves to an examination of the roles of *it* and *that* in centering. The data presented here, drawn from a corpus of naturally occurring dialogues, include all the tokens of *it* and *that* in the corpus that had an explicit linguistic antecedent. I examined numerous linguistic features of the local context consisting of each pronoun/antecedent pair. Thus the data can be used to partly test three hypotheses: (1) that the centering framework makes reliable predictions about the behavior of speakers in actual, on-line, dialogic interaction, (2) that *it* is a more likely choice than *that* for realizing the center, and (3) that *that* has a deictic function that conflicts with centering, even in apparently anaphoric contexts. In the next subsection (Section 7.3.2), I present the results of a statistical analysis of the distributional data. The results show markedly distinct patterns of usage for *it* and *that*. (The statistical tool used here, the χ^2 statistic, is explained in the appendix.) In Section 7.3.3, I argue that the distributional tables of conversational data can be interpreted as state transition models of changes in attentional state.

7.3.2   Results

The principal tool of the methodology presented here is a statistical test of the *goodness of fit* of a particular classification of observations with respect to a set of criteria upon which the classification is presumably dependent, or contingent. In short, I present hypotheses about lexical choice as contingency tables and use the χ^2 *goodness of fit* test to quantitatively assess the hypotheses. I refer readers unfamiliar with this tool to the appendix.

[7]The earlier study investigated a larger variety of discourse functions of *it* and *that*, including discourse deixis ([Passonneau] Schiffman, 1984, 1985). Additionally, I tested and ultimately rejected several hypotheses regarding the effects of the distance between an anaphoric or deictic pronoun and its antecedent, where distance was construed in various ways ([Passonneau] Schiffman, 1985).

Table 7.1. *A two-way distribution of the data, showing absolute frequency, expected frequency, and χ-squares for each cell (individual cells are numbered for convenient reference)*

Grammatical role and form of ant. (N_1)	Subsequent pronoun (N_2)			
	Subject		Non-subject	
	it	*that*	*it*	*that*
Cell no.	(1)	(2)	(3)	(4)
	147	31	39	19
PRO-SUBJ	96.0	48.7	48.7	42.4
	27.1	**6.4**	1.9	**12.9**
Cell no.	(5)	(6)	(7)	(8)
	37	21	34	14
PRO-NonSUBJ	43.1	21.9	21.9	19.1
	.9	.0	**6.7**	1.3
Cell no.	(9)	(10)	(11)	(12)
	18	6	11	10
NP-SUBJ	18.3	9.3	9.3	8.1
	.0	1.1	.3	.1
Cell no.	(13)	(14)	(15)	(16)
	43	33	36	45
NP-NonSUBJ	63.9	32.4	32.4	28.2
	6.8	.0	.4	**10.0**
Cell no.	(17)	(18)	(19)	(20)
	8	5	1	1
NonNP-SUBJ	6.1	3.1	3.1	2.7
	.6	1.2	1.4	1.1
Cell no.	(21)	(22)	(23)	(24)
	23	44	19	33
NonNP-NonSUBJ	48.4	24.6	24.6	21.4
	13.3	**15.3**	1.3	**6.3**
Table χ-Square				116.3
Degrees of Freedom				15
Probability				0.00001

Table 7.1 presents the two-dimensional table that best predicts the lexical choice between *it* and *that,* given the contextual features that were examined.[8] The row headings represent the categories pertaining to the antecedent expression (N_1): the grammatical role of the antecedent, and the syntactic form of the antecedent. The relevant two values of grammatical role were found to be subject (SUBJ) and non-subject (nonSUBJ). The three values for antecedent form

---

[8]Roughly a dozen features were analyzed; cf. Schiffman (1985), esp. chapter 2.

consist of pronoun (PRO),[9] full noun phrase (NP), and non-noun phrase constituents (NonNP). The cross-classification of these two variables (2X3) gives the six rows shown in the table. Noun phrases headed by lexical or derived nouns and with the syntactic structure of true noun phrases (determiners, prepositional phrase modifiers, etc.) were classified as NPs. Non-noun phrase constituents included other phrases that can fill a grammatical role, such as gerundive and infinitival phrases, *that*-clauses, and so on.[10] The relevant characteristics of the pronoun are represented in the column headings. They include the grammatical role (also SUBJ versus nonSUBJ) and lexical choice of the subsequent pronoun. Thus, each data point in Table 7.1 represents a succession of two communicative events: an expression of N_1 of a particular form with a particular grammatical role, followed by a co-specifying pronoun N_2 of a particular lexical choice and grammatical role. The χ^2 for the table is very high (116.3, with 15 degrees of freedom), giving the extremely low probability of .001% for the observed distribution.[11] Thus the χ^2 confirms the predictive force of the data classification. The individual cells of the table indicate the absolute frequency, the expected frequency (assuming the null hypothesis; cf. the appendix), and the cell χ^2, with the latter in boldface type in cells where the χ^2 is significantly high. Also, the twenty-four cells of the table are numbered (in italics) for ease of cross-reference.

Finding a statistical correlation between dependent and independent variables (columns and rows) confirms the predictive power of the distribution. However, a predictive model does not necessarily translate directly into an explanatory one.[12] Explanatory power comes from positing a plausible relationship between the independent and dependent variables, such as one of cause-and-effect. Here, the independent and dependent variables pertain equally to surface structure choices in local coherence contexts. As opposed to a causal model, finding an explanatory model for these data consists in positing abstract attentional states that can plausibly account for the various configurations of linguistic choices represented in the statistical model. The next section outlines how to interpret Table 7.1 as a set of attentional state transitions.

7.3.3   Analysis

As noted above, each cell of Table 7.1 represents a transition from a particular initial state (N_1) to a particular final state (N_2). The statistics in each cell indicate

---

[9]The pronoun antecedent was *it* 64% of the time, *that* 34% of the time, and *this* 2%.

[10]For an account of how these variables were determined to best fit the data, cf. (Passonneau) Schiffman (1984a,b, 1985) and Passonneau (1989).

[11]Passonneau (1989), I incorrectly reported this table to have only 7 degrees of freedom and a probability of only .1%.

[12]The classic example of a valid statistical correlation with no explanatory force is the discovery of a correlation between increased soft drink consumption and increased incidence of polio. This correlation was later shown to result from a direct link of each with a third factor; both increase in the summer months (Freedman et al., 1978).

	N₁		N₂
1.	Pro-Subj	⊢	IT-Subj
2.		⊣	THAT-Subj
3.			IT-NonSubj
4.		⊣	THAT-NonSubj
5.	Pro-NonSubj		IT-Subj
6.			THAT-Subj
7.		⊢	IT-NonSubj
8.			THAT-NonSubj
9.	NP-Subj		IT-Subj
10.			THAT-Subj
11.			IT-NonSubj
12.			THAT-NonSubj
13.	NP-NonSubj	⊣	IT-Subj
14.			THAT-Subj
15.			IT-NonSubj
16.		⊢	THAT-NonSubj
17.	NonNP-Subj		IT-Subj
18.			THAT-Subj
19.			IT-NonSubj
20.			THAT-NonSubj
21.	NonNP-NonSubj	⊣	IT-Subj
22.		⊢	THAT-Subj
23.			IT-NonSubj
24.		⊢	THAT-NonSubj

KEY	
N₁	antecedent expression
N₂	subsequent pronoun
⊢	enhanced transition
⊣	suppressed transition
	neutral transition

Figure 7.1. Schematic representation of local coherence relations as a set of state transitions.

the likelihood of the transition. Thus, cell 1 represents the state transition from an antecedent PRO-SUBJ to a co-specifying *it*-SUBJ. The observed frequency of 147 is higher than the expected frequency of 96.0 (cf. appendix), so much so that it contributes a cell χ^2 of 27.1, or nearly a quarter of the χ^2 for the whole table. There are nine significant cells, as indicated by the boldface cell χ^2s. The significance results either from a much higher or a much lower frequency than predicted by the null hypothesis, which is that the row and column variables *do not* co-vary. Therefore there are three possible types of state transition: a likely, or enhanced transition, an unlikely or suppressed transition, or a chance transition (non-significant). The three transition types in Table 7.1 are represented graphically in Figure 7.1, with the symbol ⊢ representing enhanced transitions, ⊣ representing suppressed transitions, and chance transitions represented by the absence of a symbol. Note that each cell from Table 7.1 is represented in Figure 7.1 with the line numbers of the state transition contexts matching the cell numbers of the table. Note also that the nine significant cells of Table 7.1 appear as the five enhanced contexts (⊢) and four suppressed contexts (⊣) of Figure 7.1.

Every cohesive choice made by a conversational participant has a dual nature (Isard, 1975). First, it is constrained by the prior context with which it has a cohesive link. But it also immediately becomes part of, and thus increments the context. It affects the cohesiveness of the emergent discourse, perhaps maintaining the existing attentional state, perhaps changing it. Due to the dual nature of every linguistic choice, each state transition, represented quantitatively in Table 7.1 and schematically in Figure 7.1, simultaneously represents two hypotheses, one pertaining to the constraints of the prior context on the target pronoun, one pertaining to the manner in which the target pronoun increments the context.

> *Hypothesis 1:* The form and grammatical role of the antecedent – N_1 – reflects the current attentional status of its referent, and thereby establishes expectations regarding the form and grammatical role of a subsequent co-specifying expression N_2.
>
> *Hypothesis 2:* The subsequent referring expression – N_2 – increments the context either by conforming to the expectations, in which case the current attentional status of the referent is actively maintained; or by defeating the expectations, in which case the current attentional status of the referent is changed.

As previously noted, there are three possible outcomes for every cell in Table 7.1 representing three distinct types of state transition. Each reflects a different outcome regarding the hypotheses.

1. A low cell χ^2:
   This outcome refutes the hypotheses that there are any expectations triggered by the form and grammatical role of N_1, and that the form and grammatical role of N_2 reflect some outcome regarding these expectations.

2. A high cell χ^2 with a positive deviation, i.e., the observed frequency is much higher than predicted by the null hypothesis:
   This outcome indicates that the form and grammatical role of N_1 establish expectations regarding N_2, and that the subsequent referring expression (N_2) confirms these expectations. As a consequence, it can be assumed that a particular attentional status of the referent is signaled by the features of the local context, and is maintained as is from N_1 to N_2.

3. A high cell χ^2 with a negative deviation, i.e., the observed frequency is much lower than predicted by the null hypothesis:
   This outcome indicates that the form and grammatical role of N_1 establish expectations regarding N_2, and that the subsequent referring expression (N_2) defeats these expectations. A particular attentional status of the referent is signaled by the features of the local context, and is changed from N_1 to N_2.

In the following two sections, I discuss the specific cohesive effects consequent upon the lexical choice of *it* (Section 7.4) or *that* (Section 7.5) in the significant state transitions of Figure 7.1.

7.4   Discussion I: Implications for the centering model

Computational models of focus and attention have been successful in demonstrating that pragmatic phenomena can and need to be implemented if natural language systems are to deal with ordinary language input and output. Pragmatic phenomena, by definition, are not directly encoded in linguistic structure, and they are context-dependent. Since context is both transitory and very rich, pragmatic theories must be carefully formulated so as to be testable, and then tested against various kinds of observational and experimental data.[13] Additionally, they need to be firmly grounded in linguistic theory if they are to handle a significant range of phenomena within and across languages in an efficient and compelling fashion. In this section I examine the data presented in Section 7.3 with the goal of formulating an approach to local coherence phenomena that has greater explanatory power than the centering model can provide. The two means toward this end are to formulate operational definitions of local coherence phenomena, and to explain them in terms of other independently motivated theoretical constructs.

The first step in arriving at a revised view of the centering model is to determine exactly what claims are currently made, which claims can be tested, and what range of phenomena is brought within its scope (cf. Section 7.4.1). When weighing the pronoun data against the specific claims of the centering model, one must keep in mind the earlier discussion of how to evaluate the data as evidence for attentional processes. The data are evaluated in Section 7.4.2 with respect to three issues: delimiting the relevant utterance context, specifying the relevant surface linguistic features of those contexts, and grounding the observations in terms of independently motivated processes. As a result of this evaluation, I posit a new attentional construct, referred to here as local center, that is similar to but more narrowly defined than the backward-looking center (Cb) of the centering framework (Grosz et al., 1983; Kameyama, 1987). In the following sections, I summarize the new operationally defined construct of a *local center* and I present an account for why there are two distinct surface realizations of local center. Finally, I ground the notion of a local center in the distinct theoretical notion of an *indexical*.

7.4.1   Review of centering model

The centering model is not a fully elaborated predictive model, but is rather a proposal for how to start constructing one. Centering is a processing mechanism

---

[13]Cf. the review chapters in the dissertations (Hudson-D'Zmura, 1988) and (Nelson, 1987) for discussions of experimental literature on discourse coherence.

originally posited by Joshi and Weinstein (1981), and in more detail by Grosz, Joshi, and Weinstein (1983). One goal of Grosz et al. was to explain the default reasoning processes by which definite pronouns are produced and understood. Positing such a default mechanism explains the preference for interpreting the pronouns in the sentences in (16) below according to the subscripting shown in (16a) over that in (16b):

(16) Marjorie$_i$ drove slowly past her mother$_k$.
  a. She$_i$ waved at her$_k$.
  b. She$_k$ waved at her$_i$.
(17) Marjorie$_i$ saw her mother$_k$ yesterday.
  a. She$_i$ looked fine to her$_k$.
  b. She$_k$ looked fine to her$_i$.

The semantic contexts in (16) do not predispose a particular interpretation of the pronouns in the (a) and (b) sentences. In contrast, the relation of the 'see' and 'look' events in (17) predisposes an interpretation in which the perceiver and perceived participants of both events remain the same (interpretation 17b) (Fillmore, 1971; Kameyama, 1986). Centering has been proposed as a processing mechanism to account for the preference for the interpretation in (16a), where attentional rather than semantic considerations constrain pronoun interpretation. An intuitive characterization of the center is that it is the single entity that an individual utterance most centrally concerns. If this entity has already been made attentionally prominent by the prior context, it can subsequently be referred to by a pronoun. As illustrated in (16), other pronouns can occur within the same sentence, and can refer to entities other than the center.

Centering simplifies an earlier model proposed by Sidner (1981) that included two types of focus – discourse focus and actor focus – to account for certain kinds of sentences with more than one definite pronoun. This earlier proposal failed to account for cases where only the discourse focus was pronominalized, in case a sentence mentioned both foci. Grosz et al. (1983) simplified the model of local focusing constraints by using a single type of local focus – *Backward-Looking Center (Cb)* – and were able to provide an account that was compatible with a broader range of data. In one sense, the predictive power of the emerging model of local focus was thereby strengthened. Their claim that other entities can be referred to pronominally within the same sentence as long as the Cb (the center) is pronominalized is very specific, and empirically useful to the degree that one has a means for identifying the center. As we will see in the following section, however, there is a lack of objective criteria for identifying the center. Either 'Marjorie' or 'her mother' could be the center of (17), depending on the preceding context.[14] In other ways, the predictive power of the centering model is relatively weak. It makes only relative predictions about the form of referring

[14]Following the conventions used in Grosz et al. (1983), I use italic typeface for an expression qua linguistic object, and single quotes for the entity that the expression refers to.

expression for entities other than the current center. For example, it predicts that, given an entity that is the Cb of an utterance U, if this entity is also the highest ranking Cf within the utterance and is expressed as a pronoun, then other Cfs in U can also be expressed by pronouns. The centering framework treats pro-nominalization as a more homogeneous phenomenon than is warranted, as if the same constraints – but more weakly enforced – influence the occurrence of all pronouns. As we will see, it is also somewhat ambivalent regarding the bound-aries of the segment that centering pertains to.

Centering model: definitions

The centering mechanism pertains to *local,* as opposed to *global,* coherence relations (Grosz et al., 1983; Grosz and Sidner, 1986). The local context consists of two utterances in the same discourse segment that are objectively or virtually adjacent, depending on whether the segment is interrupted by intervening mate-rial.[15] Although the notion of a center is not restricted to constraints on pro-nominal usage, that will be the major focus here. Of special concern is the *center rule,* a proposal regarding constraints on the production and interpretation of definite pronouns within a local discourse context.

Because centering pertains to a cohesive link between two utterances in a discourse, it provides indirect evidence about the local segmental structure of that discourse. As noted in Grosz et al. (1983), local coherence relations pertain to the individual subconstituents, or segments, of a discourse, which can include two (or more) contiguous utterances; equally, *two utterances that are not con-tiguous [can be] members of the same subconstituent* (Grosz and Sidner, 1986). Given a linear sequence of utterances in a discourse (U_n, U_{n+1}, . . . , U_{n+k}), if an utterance U_n and an utterance U_{n+2} comprise a single centering context, then they are presumed to be *virtually adjacent* within a single discourse segment that is temporarily interrupted by the intervening utterance U_{n+1}. Henceforth, when I talk about two utterances being adjacent, I will mean adjacent within their segment.

Every utterance is said to have a unique *backward-looking center (Cb)* – generally referred to as *the center* of a sentence – and an ordered set of *forward-looking centers (Cfs)* (Grosz et al., 1983).[16] The Cb provides a cohesive link between the current utterance and the prior discourse, whereas the Cfs are the referents of expressions in the utterance that are potential points of cohesive linkage to subsequent discourse. Thus in one sense, the utterance is the relevant context. But given the prototypical case of a Cb of one utterance that is the same as the Cb or one of the Cfs of the preceding utterance, the relevant context

---

[15]In Grosz et al. (1983), the terms sentence and utterance are used interchangeably. I will follow linguistic usage by distinguishing between a sentence – a syntactically characterized unit abstracted away from any particular context – and an utterance, which may or may not be a complete sentence, but which is viewed as occurring in a particular context. Cf. Kameyama (1987).

[16]Kameyama (1987) differs from Grosz et al. (1983) in viewing the Cb as optional.

becomes the pair of utterances that are thereby cohesively linked. When I later introduce the notion of a local center, I will show that it pertains only to an utterance pair, not to an individual utterance. I later argue (Section 7.5.1) that the relevant domain for local centering is no larger than an utterance pair.

By definition, a center is a conceptual object rather than a linguistic one. That is, a discourse entity in the evolving model can be a center, but linguistic expressions that refer to those entities are not centers. Further, a center may be *realized by* a linguistic expression N in a given utterance U, or alternatively, the center may be implicit in the utterance rather than overtly expressed. Center realization may involve any of a number of semantic relationships between linguistic expressions and conceptual objects, including but not restricted to the relation: *N denotes c* (cf. Grosz et al., 1983).

The nature of the conceptual relation between the center of an utterance and the linguistic structure of that utterance is purposely left open so as to accommodate a number of distinct syntactic, semantic, and pragmatic phenomena within the single rubric of local coherence relations. However, a consequence of this open-endedness is that it is impossible to determine for any particular utterance how to identify unequivocally the unique Cb that it is asserted to have. In other words, attempts at data collection and analysis are hindered by the inability to make use of the initial assumption that every utterance indeed has a Cb.

Centering model: claims and observations

Although unequivocal identification of the center (Cb) of an utterance is impossible, observable effects on surface form are proposed with respect to the distribution of definite pronouns. There are two major claims. The first takes the form of a general principle, or default rule, regarding pronominalization (Grosz et al., 1983). The second claim adds another dimension – grammatical role – to the linguistic cues that establish the current center (Kameyama 1986, 1987).

The centering rule states a relationship between continuation of the same discourse entity as center (Cb) in two adjacent utterances and the form of the expression that realizes the center (Cb):

If the center of the current [utterance] is the same as the center of the previous [utterance], a definite pronoun should be used (Grosz et al., 1983).

Thus the center rule pertains to the form of expression that realizes the Cb in a context of center *continuation*.[17]

Figure 7.2 schematically represents the type of context in which the centering rule applies. Assume that U_1 and U_2 are adjacent utterances, that Cb_1 and Cb_2 are their respective centers, and that N_1 and N_2 are referring expressions that realize Cb_1 and Cb_2. The centering rule says that if Cb_1 and Cb_2 are the same

---

[17]Center continuation, as defined in Grosz et al. (1986), refers to cases where the same entity is the center (Cb) of two adjacent utterances; this contrasts with center retention, where the center of U_n is one of the forward-looking centers (Cfs) of U_{n+1}, but is not the Cb.

```
                          KEY
       Uᵢ    An utterance, where i indicates
             linear position in its discourse segment

       Nᵢ    A linguistic expression in Uᵢ

       ↑     A relation of center (Cb) realization

      Cbᵢ    The backward-looking center of Uᵢ;
             a local attentional status that a discourse
             entity (e.g., Cᵢ) can be assigned
```

$$\boxed{Cb_1}\ (=C_i)$$
$$\uparrow$$
$$U_1: \quad \ldots\ldots \quad N_1 \quad\quad \ldots\ldots$$

$$\boxed{Cb_2}\ (=C_i)$$
$$\uparrow$$
$$U_2: \quad \ldots\ldots \quad N_2 \quad\quad \ldots\ldots$$

Figure 7.2. Schematic representations of centering context.

entity (e.g., C_i), then N_2 is likely to be a pronoun. It makes no predictions about the form of expressions in U_2 if Cb_1 and Cb_2 are not the same entity, or about the form of N_1. It also makes no predictions about the likelihood of Cb_2 being the same as Cb_1 if U_2 contains a pronoun, since other factors may presumably lead to the occurrence of a pronoun in U_2 besides the centering rule (cf. discussion pertaining to example 16 above).

Kameyama addresses what other linguistic factors contribute to signaling the current center, both within and across languages. On the basis of her analysis of Japanese and English data she claims that the relevant pronominal expressions vary from language to language, but tend to be those with less phonetic content. For Japanese, this pertains to zero pronominals, and for English, it pertains to unstressed rather than stressed definite pronouns (Kameyama, 1986). She also claims that pronominal expressions for realizing the same center in two successive utterances must obey what she terms the property sharing constraint:[18]

Two *unstressed* definite pronouns that retain the same center in adjacent utterances should share one of the following properties, in order of preference: preferably, both should share

[18]Cf. Brennan et al. (1987) for a slightly different proposal that treats grammatical role status as a side-effect of Cf ranking, rather than as an independent dimension.

the grammatical role of subject (SUBJ), or alternatively, both should be non-subjects (nonSUBJ).

In Kameyama's terminology, sharing of SUBJ grammatical role constitutes canonical Cb-retention; sharing of nonSUBJ grammatical role constitutes non-canonical Cb-retention.[19] Note that the center rule as stated applies to all center continuation contexts, whereas the property sharing constraint applies only to the subset of center continuation contexts where the centers of a pair of adjacent utterances are both realized by pronouns.

Kameyama has attempted to delimit more precisely the relevant class of pronouns as well as the separate contributions of pronominalization and grammatical role to the realization of the center. However, this initial extension needs further development if theories of the attentional mechanisms that constrain local coherence phenomena are to account for the rich variety of contexts in which pronouns and other cohesive devices occur. A preponderance of the examples that have been investigated are restricted to animate rather than non-animate pronouns, and to singular rather than plural pronouns, whereas other linguistic factors, such as demonstrativity or prosody, are ignored. Because I examined pronoun distributions in naturally occurring dialogues, my data provide evidence about actual attentional processes – that are to some degree out of awareness – in a way that constructed examples cannot. By focusing on non-animate pronouns, and by including demonstrative pronouns, the present study has been able to clarify Kameyama's property sharing constraint. As she implicitly predicts, property sharing applies to *it* but not *that*. Also, the non-canonical context is shown to interact with the occurrence of 1st and 2nd person pronouns in the same utterance pair.

Do all sentences have a center?

The definition of center relies on the highly subjective notion that there is an entity of most central concern in every utterance, and assumes that the attentional status of this entity always constrains pronoun usage. Local coherence relations are not yet well enough understood to generate a fully comprehensive algorithm for finding the center of an utterance. In fact, centering is not a mechanism pertaining to an utterance alone, but rather to an utterance in a particular context of occurrence. For a sentence such as *Max saw Rosa*, 'Max' is said to be the center in (18) and 'Rosa' is said to be the center in (19):[20]

(18)
    a.   Who did Max see yesterday?
    b.   Max saw Rosa.   (Cb = 'Max')

---

[19]What Kameyama refers to here as Cb retention is termed center continuation in Grosz et al. (1986), as noted above in n. 17.

[20]These two examples are taken from Grosz et al. (1983). Cf. n. 14 *in re* typographical conventions.

(19)
  a.   Did anyone see Rosa yesterday?
  b.   Max saw Rosa.   (Cb = 'Rosa')

Note that if (19b) had been the utterance *Max did,* 'Rosa' would presumably still be the center of the utterance, thus illustrating the partial independence of the pragmatic notion of center from surface linguistic form.

Like various other concepts that have been proposed in attempts to account for discourse constraints on definite referring expressions, such as topic (as in the topic/focus distinction), givenness (as in the given/new distinction), and so on, the notion of center becomes more elusive as one considers a broader range of examples and possible contexts. For example, in (19b), how do we know 'Rosa' is of more concern than 'Max', and what consequences should the presumption that 'Rosa' is the center have on subsequent discourse? Example (20) is an excerpt from the interview data that can be used to illustrate several such questions about the nature of centering.[21]

(20) S_0: I don't have *the mental capacity*
         C_0:

         S_1: *to handle uh what I would like to teach*
         C_1:

         S_2: which'd be philosophy (or) history at U of C
         C_2:   (hm)   [uh huh]

         S_3: uh with that level students um
         C_3:

         S_4: maybe with time and experience I'll gain $\boxed{it}$
         C_4:

         S_5: but I don't have $\boxed{it}$ now
         C_5:   uh huh

The pair of utterances S_4 and S_5 contain co-specifying instances of the pronoun *it,* both of which are direct objects. The full referring expression that introduces the conceptual entity being referred to occurs in the utterance spanning S_0 through S_1: the italicized noun phrase *the mental capacity to handle uh what I would like to teach.* In both S_4 and S_5, the grammatical subject of the clause is a 1st person pronoun.

It is not obvious that all the utterances in (20) have centers. What is the center of the long utterance spanning S_0–S_3? Is it the entity that is evoked by the NP *the*

---

[21]In all examples taken from the career-counseling interviews, S stands for the student and C for the counselor. Pairs of co-subscripted lines (e.g., C_1 and S_1) co-occur in time. The use of parentheses around expressions in contemporaneous lines, e.g., *or* and *hm* in S_2 and C_2, indicates coarticulation by the two participants. Note that the transcripts include repetitions.

mental capacity . . . ? The fact that this entity is later re-evoked by a pronoun in S_4 suggests so. But perhaps this is not a fair question because we do not have here the utterance that preceded S_0. On the other hand, if we can't determine the center without the prior utterance, why is the center said to be a property of an utterance? The utterance pair S_4 and S_5 contains two co-specifying pronouns. Is the entity evoked by these pronouns the center? If so, when does it become the center? Is it the center when it is first introduced, i.e., in the utterance spanning S_0–S_3? If so, then why does the utterance pair S_4 and S_5 seem more cohesive than the pair S_0–S_3 and S_4? Is there a context in (20) for which we can confidently identify the center? The utterance pair S_4 and S_5 looks promising because it contains two co-specifying pronouns in the same grammatical role, thus conforming not only to the center rule, but also to Kameyama's property sharing constraint. On what basis can we say that the entity of most central concern at either S_4 or S_5 is the referent of the two italicized tokens of *it*, as opposed to the referent of the subject pronoun *I* – the speaker herself? In fact, the centering literature never addresses the issue of 1st and 2nd person pronouns; centering is implicitly concerned with 3rd person reference. Questions arise as to how the attentional status of 1st and 2nd person pronouns differs from 3rd person pronouns, and what happens when both types of pronouns occur in the same utterance or the same local context.

These are some of the numerous problematic questions about identifying the Cb of an utterance, questions that I do not attempt to answer directly. I believe a more promising approach to investigating local coherence phenomena is to work from operational definitions of presumed attentional constructs in order to construct predictive models. The ultimate goal is for the operational definitions to account eventually for the processing strategies that conversational participants actually use in producing and interpreting their contributions to interactive discourse.

Although we cannot definitively identify the center of any utterance, we can assume that because all of the contexts depicted in Figure 7.1 involve an explicit cohesive tie between adjacent utterances, then a significant portion of them should (theoretically) exemplify centering. All the contexts conform to the schematic representation of Figure 7.2, insofar as any of the relevant referents are centers. All of the contexts involve two successive linguistic expressions (N_1 and N_2) evoking the same conceptual object (C_i), where the second expression is often a definite pronoun. Also, the two expressions N_1 and N_2 occur in objectively adjacent utterances roughly two-thirds of the time,[22] in the same utterance about a sixth of the time,[23] and in contexts where at least one utterance intervened between those containing the pronoun and its antecedent roughly one-sixth

---

[22]Because the speakers in the interview data use far more sentence coordination than is typically found in prose, an utterance was operationally defined as an independent clause, possibly introduced by one of the conjunctions *and, or,* or *but*.

[23]In these cases, the pronoun and its antecedent were generally in distinct tensed clauses.

of the time. As shown elsewhere, this distance measure had no effect on the lexical choice between *it* and *that* ([Passonneau] Schiffman, 1985). Although the cohesive relation linking N_1 and N_2 does not always involve two literally adjacent utterances, it is extremely likely that the two non-adjacent contexts (remote utterances; same utterance) are virtually equivalent to the adjacent one. In the cases where there were intervening utterances, the intervening material was often apparently part of a distinct discourse segment, making it possible to see U_2 as a continuation of the segment containing U_1. In the case where the successive clauses containing N_1 and N_2 were in the same sentence, the syntactic linkage between the two clauses was often relatively loose, e.g., via subordinating conjunctions. The centering literature explicitly allows for the former case (Grosz et al., 1983, 1986) as noted above, but to my knowledge does not discuss the issue of coordinated or loosely subordinated clauses. However, the cohesive relations between such clauses have been argued to be similar to those between independent clauses (Silverstein, 1987; Foley and Van Valin, 1984).

To establish incontestable criteria for *virtual adjacency* would require a separate investigation. However, people apparently arrive at a rough consensus when asked to segment a discourse (Grosz and Sidner, 1986), thus I believe that my assumption of virtual adjacency could be corroborated. In any case, since the objective distance between N_1 and N_2 had absolutely no statistical effect on the distributions represented in Table 7.1, it is safe to assume that N_1 and N_2 were utterances adjacent in their segment in all cases.

Given that all the contexts in Figure 7.1 conform to the prototypical context for the original centering rule – keeping in mind the qualification that there is no way to determine definitively whether the entity referred to in each inter-clausal context is the Cb of its utterance – then all of the state transitions should be equally likely unless the two pronouns do not function equivalently. As shown by the extremely significant χ^2 of Table 7.1, the state transitions are definitively not equally likely. The factors that most clearly differentiate among the contexts – the grammatical roles of N_1 and N_2, and the form of the antecedent expression N_1 – contribute to a complex interrelation among surface form, the paired grammatical roles of N_1 and N_2, and the lexical choice of N_2 that suggests quite distinct coherence functions for the two pronouns.

7.4.2   Local center

The centering model reviewed in the preceding section acknowledges the multiple dependencies of linguistic factors and local attentional state on processing referring expressions. However, as noted, many aspects of the model are not verifiable. By comparing the distributions of *it* and *that,* I identify contexts that definitively select for the definite pronoun. My analysis of these contexts leads to an operational definition of a theoretical construct referred to here as *local center.* I use a distinct term to emphasize that the definition of local center is narrower than that of center, while acknowledging the similarity of assumptions regarding attentional state.

Establishment of a default referent

Occurrence of *it* is enhanced in precisely two of the twenty-four contexts in Table 7.1: the contexts represented in cells 1 and 7. The two contexts selecting for *it* are where N_1 is a pronoun and both N_1 and N_2 are SUBJ (cell 1) or both nonSUBJ (cell 7). The two properties characterizing these contexts are: pronominalization of both N_1 and N_2, and sharing of the same grammatical role property (both SUBJ or both nonSUBJ). The context with the highest significance – where N_1 is a pronominal subject – is also where *that* turns out to be most significantly suppressed (cf. contexts 2 and 4). In the discussion below, I will describe how surface form and grammatical role each contribute to maintaining a referent in a particular attentional state.

Of the two pronouns, *it* is the minimal form along the several dimensions reviewed in Section 7.2.1, and is thereby expected to add the least new information, and to be the more cohesive pronoun. Consequently, the context in which *it* is most enhanced is taken as the baseline context for understanding the distinct contributions to local cohesion of surface form and grammatical role. The underlying attentional state that these surface choices are assumed to be a reflection of will be referred to as the establishment of a local center (LC). Given the strong statistical significance of the LC contexts, they presumably serve some communicative function. In the discussion that follows, we will see that the local center bears a strong resemblance to proposed realizations of the backward-looking center (Cb). But unlike the Cb, LC is defined only in terms of the observed distributional pattern, and its communicative function is a matter of investigation rather than stipulation. The individual features of the contexts where *it* is enhanced are assumed to contribute separately to local centering, in the sense that they do not necessarily co-occur, but it will be seen that their co-presence strengthens the relevant attentional state. The fact that *that* is suppressed where these features co-occur,[24] and that where these features do not occur *that* is sometimes enhanced and *it* is suppressed or unaffected, are also taken as supporting evidence that the local center context represents a distinctive pragmatic function.

Surface form of the antecedent. The data include all the cases in the transcripts where, given a pair of co-specifying phrases N_1 and N_2, N_2 is *it* or *that*. The centering rule says nothing about the effect of the form of N_1 on the likelihood that N_2 will be a definite pronoun. It does predict that if the same entity continues to be maintained as the Cb in subsequent utterances, expressions realizing that entity will be pronouns. The data demonstrate a very strong effect of the form of

---

[24]Elsewhere I have argued that the entities in Kameyama's canonical center retention context are in an attentional state that makes them relatively inaccessible to demonstrative reference (Passonneau, 1989).

N_1 in line with this prediction. The two cases of enhanced transitions where N_1 is a pronoun both favor the choice of *it*. When N_1 is not a pronoun, a transition to *it* is never enhanced, but is in fact sometimes suppressed, as in contexts 13 and 21 of Table 7.1 and Figure 7.1. Because no context where N_1 is not a pronoun leads to an enhanced transition to *it*, no contexts other than 1 and 7 contribute to local centering.

It is notable that no context where N_1 is a full noun phrase favors *it* as the choice for N_2. In fact, if N_1 is a full noun phrase and is moreover not the subject of its clause, then *it* is suppressed (context 13) and *that* is enhanced (context 16); this is exactly the opposite of the pattern observed for cases where N_1 is a pronoun. Unfortunately, the data provided here do not include cases where N_2 is not a pronoun. As a consequence, we do not have the opportunity to compare the likelihood for N_2 to be a co-specifying pronoun as opposed to a co-specifying full referring expression. Lacking this data, and having no evidence in the current data to assume that the attentional status of referents in contexts where N_1 is a full NP resembles that of local center, these cases are excluded from the local center context on the basis of the contrast between the full NP contexts and the local center context.

The centering literature does not mention cases of co-specifying phrases where the antecedent phrase is neither a pronoun nor a full noun phrase, but is instead a clause-like argument (nonNP). This case, represented by contexts 17–24 in Table 7.1 and Figure 7.1, comprises yet a third class where the form of N_1 affects pronominalization patterns. It is distributionally distinct from the cases where N_1 is a pronoun, because transition to *it* is never enhanced whereas transition to *that* is enhanced in two contexts (22 and 24). It is also distinct from the cases where N_1 is a true noun phrase. For example, noun phrases often occur as the subjects of their clauses in cases where the subsequent utterance contains a co-specifying pronoun, but nonNPs much less so.[25] In Section 7.5, other differences between NP and nonNP antecedents are discussed.

There are two possibilities regarding the attentional status of entities in the two classes of contexts where N_1 is not a pronoun. One possibility is that the relevant entities have a totally distinct attentional status from that associated with the local center. Another possibility is that the means for signaling the attentional status of local center, given the use of a full expression at N_1, are distinct from the means used when N_1 is a pronoun. Given the distributional evidence of features selecting for *it*, I propose that one component of the operational definition for local center is to exclude overtly non-pronominal constituents from realizing the local center; both relevant referring expressions must be definite pronouns, and in particular, N_1 must be unstressed and non-demonstrative.[26]

---

[25]By computing the row totals for NP-Subjects shown in Table 7.1, and dividing by the sum of the row totals for NP-Subjects and NP-NonSubjects, we find that 22% of NPs in the relevant cohesive context were subjects of their clauses. But nonNPs were subjects of their clauses at only half that rate, 11% of the time. For the sake of completeness, note that antecedent pronouns were subjects more often than they were non-subjects, at a ratio of 3 to 1.

[26]Recall that in most cases, N_1 was *it;* cf. n. 9.

Grammatical role. According to Kameyama's property-sharing constraint, if two unstressed, definite pronouns retain the same Cb in adjacent utterances, both should be subjects or both should be non-subjects, corresponding to canonical and non-canonical Cb-retention, respectively (Kameyama, 1986). Transition to *it* was enhanced in both contexts conforming to the property-sharing constraint (contexts 1 and 7). In context 1, where both expressions were grammatical subjects, there was far more significant enhancement. Table 7.1 shows that the cell representing the canonical context (cell 1) has a much higher cell χ^2 (27.1), and is therefore much more significant, than the cell representing the non-canonical Cb-retention context (cell 7; cell $\chi^2 = 6.7$). On the other hand, the lower cell χ^2 of 6.7 is still much higher than in the non-significant cells, where it ranges from .0 to 1.9. The positive deviation from expected frequency is what tells us that the cells represent enhancement. The data thus support the two hypotheses embodied in the property-sharing constraint that sharing of the same subject role status by two successive referring expressions – both subject or both non-subject – contributes to greater cohesiveness, and that sharing of subject role has the more cohesive effect. Following Kameyama, I will use the terms canonical and non-canonical to refer to these two local center contexts. The evidence also indicates that lack of property sharing inhibits local centering. This leads to a stronger characterization of the local center because it allows us to make bi-directional claims, thus supporting generation or understanding.[27]

Other surface features. As pointed out in Section 7.3, many other classifications of grammatical role and antecedent type, as well as other multi-valued variables and configurations of contexts were examined, with the conclusion that the most significant factors affecting lexical choice of *it* and *that* were those represented in Table 7.1. There was no evidence for the hypothesis that there is a gradient of contexts that increasingly favor *it*. This indicates that individual tokens of *it* either participate in local centering or not and that other tokens of *it* bear other kinds of coherence relations to the prior context that cannot be scaled according to a gradient of more to less typical of local center establishment.

Local center establishment. The data support the conclusions that the most cohesive context is the local center context, that there is a preferred realization of local center, and that lexical choice of *that* conflicts with the context in which the form of N_1 anticipates the preferred, or canonical local center.[28] These findings

---

[27]Kameyama (1987) asserts the need for bi-directional constraints, but doesn't explicitly discuss the difference in applying her constraints for generation versus understanding. Her examples only pertain to understanding.

[28]Note: the data presented here pertain to the formal choices correlating with two co-specifying expressions. Complementary data shows that two expressions are very likely to co-specify given the formal features corresponding to local center contexts (Passonneau, 1991).

are summarized in the following local center establishment (LCE) rule. The rule has two parts, pertaining to understanding ($\mathcal{A}$) and generation ($\mathcal{B}$).

Local center establishment rule.

$\mathcal{A}$: Recognizing a local center
Two utterances U_1 and U_2 that are adjacent in their segment establish an entity $\mathcal{E}$ as a local center only if U_1 contains a third person, singular, non-demonstrative pronoun N_1 referring to $\mathcal{E}$, U_2 contains a co-specifying third person, singular, non-demonstrative pronoun N_2, and N_1 and N_2 are both subjects or both non-subjects, in that order of preference.

$\mathcal{B}$: Generating a local center
Precondition: To establish an entity $\mathcal{E}$ as a local center, $\mathcal{E}$ must be in the current focus space, and it must be possible to refer to it with a singular, third person, non-animate pronoun.

To establish $\mathcal{E}$ as a local center in a pair of adjacent utterances U_1 and U_2, use an expression of type N to refer to $\mathcal{E}$ in both utterances where each token, N_1 and N_2, is a third person, singular, non-demonstrative pronoun. Both should be subjects or both non-subjects, in that order of preference.

A context conforming the local center establishment (LCE) rule establishes an entity $\mathcal{E}$ as a local center, which thereby becomes the default referent for an immediately following local center context, as in (21):

(21)

C_1: well *public relations* is basically representing people

C_2: ideas   things in a very positive way to others
S_2:   uhhuh

C_3 and $\boxed{it's}$ doing it in a written form

C_4: $\boxed{it's}$ doing it in a crowd control (laugh) form
S_4:   (laugh)   yeah

C_4: $\boxed{it's}$ doing it in a verbal form
S_5:   uhhuh

(Cf. utterances S_4 and S_5 in example 20 for an illustration of a non-canonical local center.) The very next local context, or overlapping utterance pair, starts at the current U_2, which is then the initial utterance of the next utterance pair. As exemplified in (21), once a local center is established, it is often maintained. (Contexts maintaining a LC beyond the initial utterance pair are discussed in Section 7.5.1.)

The conversational data demonstrate that participants can presume that they and other participants will adhere to the LCE rule.[29] This presumption has conse-

---

[29]Reliability measures are not explicitly discussed here, but cf. (Passonneau) Schiffman (1985) for evidence that all the participants in the interview data and all the distinct interviews adhered equally to the effects presented in Table 7.1.

quences on the form and the interpretation of utterance U_2. If an utterance conforms to the requirements imposed by the LCE rule on the initial utterance of a pair, this creates strong expectations that a local center is to be established. It is easy to see how such expectations on the part of the hearer would influence the hearer's interpretation of N_2. But the presumption of conformity to the LCE rule presumably affects the actual form of N_2 as well. It is presumably the case that when uttering U_1, the speaker has already selected an entity to be the local center for the utterance pair that U_1 initiates. But the speaker might have a change of mind before completing utterance U_2. It is through the speaker's commitment or lack of commitment to the local center throughout the utterance pair that the form of U_1 has consequences on the form of U_2.

It is also possible that the current hearer might become the speaker at U_2. In my previous analyses of the interview data, speaker alternation was examined as a possible conditioning factor for lexical choice ([Passonneau] Schiffman, 1985). Although there was often a change of speaker from the antecedent expression to the target pronoun, this factor was found to have absolutely no effect on lexical choice. This indicates that speakers cooperatively conform to the local center establishment rule. Thus if the speaker at U_2 is different from the speaker at U_1, the new speaker's decisions about whether and how to re-mention the entity % are guided by the LCE rule. Like the center rule, the LCE rule is a pragmatic one and can be violated to good communicative effect, as demonstrated by the fact that although certain contexts are suppressed, they still occur (e.g., cf. discussion of 23–25 in Section 7.5.2). However, as noted in Section 7.3, violations alter the presumed attentional status whereas adherence to the rule maintains it.

Non-canonical local center

Since there are two inter-utterance configurations that select for *it*, both are assumed to reflect a common attentional mechanism. In this and the following subsections, we examine this assumption further. Here we look at why there should be two ways to realize a local center. In the next subsection, we consider the relative processing efficiency of local center contexts.

The non-canonical local center contexts can be seen to exhibit the interaction of two distinct pragmatic effects. The question that naturally suggests itself about the non-canonical context is, given that N_1 and N_2 are not the subjects of their clauses, what kinds of constituents do occur as the subjects? In this data, the subjects in the non-canonical contexts were most often 1st or 2nd person pronouns.[30] After that, there was a very small heterogeneous category. These data conform to a proposal made by Givon (1976) and others (Li, 1976) that preferred

---

[30]The two next most likely possibilities were that the subject was an animate full referring phrase, or a non-referential (expletive) expression, e.g., existential *there;* in this study, the category subject always refers to a surface grammatical function.

subjects are animate rather than inanimate, definite rather than indefinite, full expressions rather than pronominal, and 1st or 2nd person rather than 3rd person. The interview dialogues examined here are intentionally biased toward the discussion of non-animate entities, e.g., college courses, degree requirements, career options, résumés, and so on. For every matrix clause utterance, there can be only one subject. But if a non-animate entity and an animate one are mentioned within a single utterance, Givon's subject hierarchy predicts that the latter will more often occur as the subject. My conclusion is that the non-canonical local center context involves an interaction between two separate organizing forces: the local center status of the referent – that in this data is necessarily a non-animate entity – and the attentional prominence of animate entities, in particular the speaker and hearer themselves.

Given two conceptually distinct classes of entity that can be referred to with distinct types of pronouns in the same sentence – e.g., animate and non-animate pronouns – there is a potential for competition as to which entity will be expressed as the subject. Given that the subject role has both an intra-clausal function, with respect to argument structure, and an inter-clausal function, with respect to attentional status, there will be various forces shaping the competition for subject role. The non-canonical LCE context illustrates that if the subject role is pre-empted by a distinct pragmatic phenomenon, it is still possible for the attentional status of the local center to be realized by another inter-clausal configuration: sharing of non-subjecthood by co-specifying pronouns in adjacent utterances. Thus an essential aspect of the grammatical role dimension is that it must be shared by N_1 and N_2. On these grounds, the data can be viewed in yet more abstract terms such that there is only one context that favors lexical choice of *it*. The non-canonical local center context is in fact a variant of the first, where the pragmatic motive for the alternation arises from the occasional conflict with 1st and 2nd person pronoun subjects within the same utterance pair.

Indexical basis of local center

The motivation for distinguishing the local center from other kinds of centering is that the data reviewed here strongly support this interpretation. But there are other reasons for the plausibility of such a construct, given the general properties of indexical expressions. I will argue that the LCE rule is a mechanism for creating a pure index, albeit one that is pragmatically realized rather than grammatically realized, and therefore not obligatory. Doing so alters the processing demands of a pronoun that typically functions anaphorically into one that requires no search or inference. In order to provide a basis for this argument, I first review the notion of indexicality.

Peirce's tripartite classification of signs – icons, indices, and symbols – has had a long influence in semantics (Peirce, 1931–1935; Buchler, 1955). For Peirce, an index was a sign that signified by virtue of a *dynamical connection*

both with the individual object [or denotatum], on the one hand, and with the
senses of the person for whom it serves as a sign; [it represents] a junction
between two portions of experience (Buchler, 1955). In other words, the defining
property of an indexical expression is that the expression and some phenomenon
in the world must co-occur, of which the expression becomes an index. Peirce's
concept of an indexical sign persists in formal semantics, for example, in the
notion of a coordinate in a model (cf. Kaplan, 1989; Bennett, 1978). Expressions
whose reference depends on circumstances of the co-occurring speech situations,
such as 1st and 2nd person pronouns, tense, demonstrative pronouns, and so on,
are all indexical expressions. First and 2nd person pronouns, which refer to the
current speaker and addressee, cannot be anaphoric. Their referents, in contrast
to anaphoric pronouns, are non-arbitrary, fixed components of the non-linguistic
context. As a consequence, there is no need to add them to the contextual domain
in order to insure successful reference.

Jakobson (1971) discusses another important distinction between 1st and 2nd
person pronouns versus 3rd person pronouns. Because the conversational roles of
speaker and addressee change during the course of a speech situation, the referents of the pronouns *I* and *you* correspondingly *shift* as the conversational roles
shift. The referents of 3rd person pronouns, whether established linguistically or
non-linguistically, do not shift along with corresponding shifts of components of
the speech situation. Rather, they refer now to one thing, now to another, as a
consequence of the fact that conversational participants mutually attend to and
talk about a succession of different entities. Following Kaplan (1989), I will use
the term *pure index* to mean an expression that indexes a unique, non-arbitrary,
non-linguistic component of the speech situation, e.g., the 1st person pronoun *I*.
The demonstrative pronoun, whose defining characteristic is that it demonstrates
an object or phenomenon in the non-linguistic context, is also indexical. However, the demonstrative is not a pure index because its referent is not completely
determined by the context.

Finding the referent of a pure index depends only on the fact of a speech
situation taking place. Its referent is a necessary component of the ongoing
speech situation. Thus, the process of interpreting a pure index requires no search
or inference, but depends only on the manner in which the speech situation is
currently construed. The denotatum of a pure index can be viewed as a contextual
parameter – e.g., *current speaker* – that must have a particular referential value
whenever an utterance occurs. The pragmatic interpretation is the current value
of the relevant parameter, and shifts as the crucial components of the speech
situation shift. I assume that a non-linguistic processing mechanism insures that
the current value of the parameter is updated whenever necessary.

In many ways, a pronoun referring to a local center is like a pure index. At the
beginning of a discourse there is no local center, because the LCE rule depends
minimally on an utterance pair. The first time there can be a local center is for the
utterance pair $< U_2, U_3 >$, assuming that the relevant entity is introduced by a

full referring expression (or a deictic pronoun) in U_1. For any pair of utterances where the LCE rule has applied, there will be a discourse entity that is by default indexed to the use of subsequent referring expressions with the right lexico-grammatical properties. For such a pair, there exists one of the preconditions of an index, i.e., the local center has been established as a transient parameter of the speech situation analogous to the permanent parameter *current speaker*. The processing mechanism for interpreting subsequent expressions conforming to the LCE rule is thus analogous, although not identical, to the process for pure indices. The difference is that the local center is only a candidate referent, and after the current value of the local center is accessed, it can be rejected if it is not semantically coherent in the local context.[31]

There are three key differences between a pure index and a local center. First, the denotata of pure indices are non-accidental properties of the speech situation, and therefore inherent at all times in every speech situation, whereas the local center must be established for a particular context, and then maintained. Second, the former are directly encoded in the grammar whereas the latter are realized through non-conscious conventions of use. Third, the latter represents a default mechanism only, and can be overridden.

7.5   Discussion II: Coherence functions of the demonstrative pronoun

The hypothesis that the demonstrative pronoun contrasts with *it* even in apparently anaphoric contexts is borne out by the very distinct distributional facts represented in the data reviewed above. Here I will develop and evaluate the more specific hypothesis that the demonstrative pronoun exhibits a variety of pragmatic functions corresponding to distinct dimensions of contrast with the local center. I will propose that using a demonstrative pronoun in an apparently anaphoric context indicates two things: that a referent for the pronoun can be located somewhere in the current context, and that the relevant contextual location is distinct from that for referents of the definite pronoun. As a preliminary step in developing this hypothesis, I will first consider the general range of possibilities for referring expressions other than those that participate in local centering.

I presume local centering to be a cognitively and formally distinct coherence phenomenon in which an entity already in the local focus space serves as a default referent in a manner analogous to the symbolic function of 1st and 2nd person pronouns. If the pragmatic function of local centering is strictly to constrain the interpretation of pronouns within a local utterance context, then pronouns that do not contribute to local centering may yet pertain to the process by which entities in the local focus space become candidate local centers. It is

---

[31]As noted in Passonneau (1991), in roughly 10% of contexts that looked like LC contexts, the two relevant pronouns did not co-specify.

possible that the referents of all pronouns – or even all referring expressions – within a local segment, have a certain likelihood for becoming local centers. This likelihood may be predicted in some fashion resembling the proposals for ordering the Cfs of an utterance found in the centering framework (cf. Sidner, 1983; Brennan et al., 1987; Kameyama, 1987). However, as noted above, I have as yet found no evidence of such an ordering.

Another possibility is that local centering not only constrains the interpretation of pronouns, but also indicates the longer-term relevance of locally centered entities in a larger discourse segment, or in the discourse as a whole. The conviction that there is a relationship between local coherence phenomena and discourse relevance may in fact motivate the assertion in the centering literature that the Cb of an utterance is the entity of most concern. For present purposes, it does not matter precisely how the notion of longer-term relevance is construed, merely that we assume that this is another pragmatic function, perhaps even a side effect, of local centering. In this case, entities that are not currently local centers can fall into two classes. One class would consist of those entities that are not currently local centers, but have or will have an overtly signaled longer-term relevance either as a consequence of having been local centers or by being candidate local centers. I will review one class of uses of the demonstrative pronoun where its function seems to pertain to accessing candidate or former local centers. In other words, the demonstrative seems to be used to make a transition toward or out of a local centering context (Section 7.5.1).

The other logical possibility is for there to be a class of entities that have been mentioned in the local context, but which, perhaps because they are merely transitory vehicles for making assertions about more relevant entities, do not have the requisite longer-term relevance associated with past, present, and future local centers. Given the possibility that such a class of entities can exist at any particular time, and that the class membership will certainly change over time, it is entirely reasonable to suppose that any such entity may need to be mentioned more than once. It is also reasonable to suppose that such entities can be referred to in such a way that the absence of longer-term relevance is overtly signaled in order to distinguish such entities from past, present, and future local centers. I will refer to this function as *non-center retention* and provide examples supporting the hypothesis that certain uses of *that* perform this function (cf. Section 7.5.2).

The final function proposed for the demonstrative pronoun is also the most distinct from local centering, both in terms of its statistical significance as reflected in the data in Section 7.3, and in terms of its theoretical consequences. A precondition for local centering is that there be an entity in the local focus space that can be assigned the local center status. Thus the final possible function for the demonstrative pertains to cases where the referent does not exist as an entity in the local focus space at all, prior to the use of the cohesive device itself. Here the pragmatic effect of the demonstrative is to bring a new entity into the local focus space. In Section 7.5.3 I will argue that demonstrative pronouns whose antecedents are nonNPs trigger the creation of new discourse entities in a manner analogous to that proposed for demonstrative pronouns whose antecedents are discourse segments, as described by Webber (1991).

7.5.1   The role of the demonstrative in bracketing cohesive chains

So far, the cohesive contexts examined here have consisted of utterance pairs. In the original investigation from which the data are drawn, only one larger type of context was examined, and referred to as a *cohesive chain*. A cohesive chain is a succession of utterance pairs in which every utterance contains a co-specifying pronoun token.[32] Here I will briefly describe the contextual features affecting lexical choice of pronoun within this more global context.[33] The data illustrate a contrast between the role of the demonstrative when it introduces or terminates a cohesive chain, versus when it occurs within a cohesive chain.

There were 101 cohesive chains in the interview data ranging in length from 2 successive utterances to 13. For any pronoun token within a chain, lexical choice and grammatical role depended only on characteristics of the prior pronoun token in the preceding utterance. No new effects were found. Factors arising from properties unique to cohesive chains such as the length of the chain, absolute position of a token within a chain, whether the initial pronoun token in the chain had an antecedent, and if so, the syntactic form of this initial antecedent, all had no effect on the behavior of pronouns within chains (cf. discussion in Passonneau, 1989; [Passonneau] Schiffman, 1985). The absence of any effects of properties peculiar to cohesive chains suggests that they should be viewed in terms of the local contexts for which we have already found significant characteristics. We have seen that the form and grammatical role of a referring expression depends upon the form and grammatical role of a co-specifying expression in the preceding utterance, if there is one, and conversely, that it constrains the form and grammatical role of a co-specifying expression in the subsequent utterance, if there is one. The local center establishment rule specifies the nature of these bi-directional effects when the referring expressions are pronouns. Because the successive utterance pairs in a cohesive chain are potentially local center contexts, the LCE rule should predict the behavior of pronouns within chains. To a large degree, this is the case.

The LCE rule makes the following predictions regarding cohesive chains. First, it predicts that there should be a strong effect of *relative* position of a pronoun in a cohesive chain. By definition, all the pronouns in cohesive chains have a pronominal antecedent except for the initial pronoun. Consequently, the LCE rule makes no predictions about the lexical choice or grammatical role of the initial

---

[32]The term seems to have appeared in the philosophical and linguistic literature at about the same time, e.g., in works by K. Donnellan, C. Chastain, M. Halliday, and D. Zubin.

[33]Cf. Passonneau (1989), and especially, chapter 6 of (Passonneau) Schiffman (1985).

Table 7.2. *Relative position in cohesive chains:*
effects on lexical choice

Chain position	Lexical choice		Row totals
	it	*that*	
First	85	86	171
	113.9	57.1	
	7.3	14.6	
Mid	134	30	164
	109.2	54.8	
	5.6	11.2	
Last	118	53	171
	113.9	57.1	
	.1	.3	
Column totals	337	169	506
Table χ-Square			39.1
Degrees of freedom			2
Probability			0.00001

pronoun in a cohesive chain. Instead, we should expect a relatively equal distribution of *it* and *that* in initial position because if the initial pronoun has an antecedent, it must be an NP or a nonNP. In addition, the cohesive chain data include many cases where the initial pronoun had no antecedent. Within a cohesive chain, each pronoun token plays a dual role, both as the subsequent referring expression in the second utterance of a pair, and as the antecedent referring expression for a following utterance conforming to the LCE rule. The LCE rule predicts that within chains, most tokens should be *it,* and that the grammatical role status of the initial token should be maintained throughout the chain. The last position in a chain, like the initial position, is distinctive. It is the only token not followed by a co-specifying pronoun. That is, the last utterance in a cohesive chain is the first point where the local center context is necessarily not maintained. Thus, the last pronoun token should deviate from the LCE context, either in its form or its grammatical role. That is, the demonstrative should occur more often in the final position, and the transition to the final position should less often maintain the same grammatical role status. Unfortunately, given the current format of the data, it was not possible to test directly the effects of grammatical role. However, the effects of relative position are just as expected, as shown in Table 7.2.

Chain position encodes relative position, and discriminates among three contexts: the initial pronoun of a chain (First), pronouns within a chain (Mid), and the last pronoun (Last). Table 7.2 depicts the cohesive chain data, showing the expected effects of chain position.[34] First, note that chain position is strongly

---

[34]Each cell of the table gives the observed frequency, the expected frequency, and the cell χ^2, in that order.

Table 7.3. *Local centering within chains*

Grammatical role and form of ant. (N_1)	Subsequent pronoun (N_2)			
	it-GR_i	*that*-GR_i	*it*-GR_k	*that*-GR_k
it-GR_i	73	18	32	11
	65.4	24.5	29.4	14.7
	.9	1.7	.2	.9
that-GR_i	7	12	4	7
	14.6	5.5	6.6	3.3
	4.0	7.7	1.0	4.1
Table χ-Square				20.5
Degrees of Freedom				3
Probability				.017%

correlated with lexical choice ($p = .001\%$). Secondly, the relative distribution of the two pronouns varies with position in the predicted manner. As shown, the two pronouns occur equally often in First position, which is statistically significant, relative to the overall distribution; *it* occurs significantly infrequently (cell $\chi^2 = 7.3$) and *that* occurs significantly frequently (cell $\chi^2 = 14.6$). Also as expected, *it* occurs significantly frequently (cell $\chi^2 = 5.6$) and *that* occurs significantly infrequently (cell $\chi^2 = 11.2$) in Mid position. Finally, it is particularly interesting that in Last position, the frequencies of *it* and *that* are quite close to the expected frequencies. In Last position, the likelihood of an *it* or a *that* is dependent only on their relative distribution in the chain data set as a whole.[35] That is, as soon as the LCE context is necessarily not maintained, the lexical choice of pronoun becomes a chance event, rather than constrained by the properties of the prior context or the current attentional status of the referent.

The data in their current form do not make it possible to determine the precise degree to which pronouns in Mid position conform to the LCE rule, or to account for the cases that deviate from the LCE rule. Answering such questions depends on being able to evaluate progression throughout a chain, and to compare such progressions across cohesive chains.[36] It is only possible in the current data set to examine the relationship between antecedent/pronoun pairs. Table 7.3 presents the results of examining each type of antecedent/pronoun sequence for all the Mid pronouns, and demonstrates an interesting result about the occurrence of demonstratives within chains. The two row headings represent the two cases where the antecedent (N_1) is either *it* or *that,* with the symbol GR_i to indicate that it has a particular grammatical role status (SUBJ or nonSUBJ). The column headings represent the four cases where the subsequent pronoun (N_2) is:

[35]Cf. column totals for *it* ($N = 337$) and *that* ($N = 169$).
[36]The data is currently being recoded to permit this type of analysis.

1. a token of *it* that **matches** the grammatical role status of the antecedent (GR_i),
2. a token of *that* that **matches** the grammatical role status of the antecedent (GR_i),
3. a token of *it* that **does not match** the grammatical role status of the antecedent (GR_k),
4. a token of *that* that **does not match** the grammatical role status of the antecedent (GR_k).

Thus the first cell of the table represents the canonical and non-canonical LCE contexts: both N_1 and N_2 are *it,* and both have the same grammatical role status. None of the cases where the antecedent is *it* is significant. Because most of the Mid pronouns are *it* anyway, it is not significant that 73 out of 164, or 45%, of all the Mid pronouns conform to the LCE context. What is highly significant is that there are an unexpectedly frequent number of cases where the demonstrative is followed by another token of the demonstrative. The demonstrative is rare in cohesive chains, but when it occurs, it tends to recur right away. Thus, whatever attentional status is signaled by the demonstrative within cohesive chains tends to persist at least across consecutive utterance pairs. Actual inspection of these contexts indicates that the utterances within cohesive chains that contain consecutive occurrences of *that* are often verbatim or near-verbatim repetitions, as in 22.

(22) C_0: ya know if you can't teach don't do it

C_1: some people do it because they also do research here yeah
S_1:   they have to   yeah

C_2: $\boxed{that's}$ a real problem
S_2:   uhhuh

C_3: $\boxed{that's}$ a real problem

The cohesive chain data indicate that the demonstrative pronoun rarely occurs within cohesive chains, but can occur initially or finally in a cohesive chain. These are the two contexts in a cohesive chain that are most likely to deviate from local centering, and the increased likelihood of the demonstrative in just these two contexts is compatible with the view that an entity can be more easily accessed by the demonstrative if it is about to be established as a local center, or if it is a former local center, and much less so if it is a local center. In the majority of mid-chain contexts, the LCE context is preserved, but it is not known what factors correlate with deviation from the LCE context within a chain. It is shown, however, that once the demonstrative has occurred within a cohesive chain, it is likely to occur in the very next position within the chain.

7.5.2   Non-local center retention

By definition, the referent of a full noun phrase is not a local center at the time of the full noun phrase specification. There are two significant contexts where N_1 is a full NP (contexts 13 and 16), and they exemplify complementary patterns of significance. If N_1 is an NP-nonSUBJ, then transition to *it*-SUBJ is suppressed (context 13) and transition to *that*-nonSUBJ is enhanced (context 16).[37] This pattern suggests that the NP-nonSUBJ configuration signals an attentional status for the referent that conflicts with local centering because subsequent reference by an expression that would initiate the LCE context is inhibited. Furthermore, this type of antecedent conflicts with the LCE rule on two counts: N_1 is not a pronoun and N_1 is not a subject. This suggests that the function of the demonstrative in context 16 is to maintain reference to an entity that is not a current, former, or imminent local center. This function is referred to as non-local center retention. The pragmatic effect of the non-local center retention context would be to establish a cohesive relation between two utterances that marks the relevant entity as not having the global relevance that a local center has.[38]

Contexts where the antecedent is NP-nonSUBJ are distinctive not only because lexical choice of *that* is enhanced, but also because *it* is suppressed. The suppression of the transition from NP-nonSUBJ to *it*-SUBJ (context 13) conflicts with many persons' intuitions.[39] For many people, examples such as those in (23)–(25), exemplifying context 13, are naively expected to be quite frequent.

(23)   S: I'd always liked *history* (pause) um *it* seemed like a

        S: like a good jumping off point for everything else uh languages

        S: philosophy art religion

(24)   C: I know people who have uh who have been successful doctors

        C: who haven't enjoyed *the emergency room* –

        C: *it*'s not the kind of work they want to do.

(25)   C: I had *a bad upper respiratory infection* and she she told

        C: me what to take and and she was right and *it* went away.

These excerpts illustrate how natural the suppressed transition appears. Why would the transition to *it*-SUBJ be suppressed? When N_2 is an *it*-nonSUBJ, transition to *it*-SUBJ is not suppressed (context 15). When N_1 is a NP-SUBJ

---

[37]Subsequent research has shown that the givenness of the antecedent correlates with lexical choice between *it* and *that* when the antecedent is a NP (Passonneau, 1991).

[38]This hypothesis has been substantiated; cf. Passonneau (1991).

[39]Wlodek Zadrozny, Candy Sidner, and others have expressed surprise at the infrequency of this context, thus bringing its significance more to my attention.

instead of an NP-nonSUBJ, transition to *it*-SUBJ is not suppressed. I conclude that the combination of factors that N_1 is neither a pronoun nor a subject marks the entity being referred to as an unlikely candidate for local center status. Enhanced transitions are interpreted here as contexts in which the attentional status of the entity is maintained. Context 16, in which N_2 is the demonstrative rather than *it*, and is not a subject, signals an entity as an unlikely candidate for local center status throughout the utterance pair (cf. Passonneau, 1991). The communicative effect of violating this expectation, i.e., producing the unexpected transition to *it*-SUBJ at N_2, would be to cause a shift in the attentional status of the entity. Context 13 may thus exemplify a mechanism for transforming an entity that is expected not to be a local center into one that is expected to be a local center.

7.5.3 Establishing new discourse entities

In the previous two sections, I proposed hypotheses to account for the demonstrative in contexts where the entity it refers to is not a local center, and therefore more accessible to the demonstrative than a local center is. In one case, the entity is a former or potential local center; in the other, the entity is not a candidate local center. However, the most provocative results pertaining to the demonstrative concern contexts where its referent is not a discourse entity until the demonstrative reference itself has been resolved. Here, the functions of the demonstrative are first to access a semantic object that is not currently an entity within the mutually established local focus space, and second to increment the local focus space with this new referent.

The type of antecedent that most enhances the occurrence of *that* is also the only type of antecedent that suppresses the occurrence of *it*. In contexts 21–24, N_1 is a nonNP-nonSUBJ. Transition to *it*-SUBJ is suppressed, as shown in context 21, and both transitions to *that*-SUBJ (context 22) and *that*-nonSUBJ (context 24) are enhanced. I will argue that the latter two contexts exemplify intra-textual deixis, which is analogous to the cases of discourse deixis studied by Webber (1991). Webber defines discourse deixis to be deictic reference in which a discourse segment is the object of demonstration. She characterizes deixis as a relation between a deictic expression, some region in the context containing the ostensive object, or *demonstratum*, and the actual referent. Her primary concern is to identify constraints on which segments can serve as the demonstrata for discourse deixis (Webber, 1991). She provides a useful framework for looking at the relationship between a deictic expression, a discourse segment serving as a demonstratum, and the referent of the deictic expression, in which she makes use of Nunberg's notion of a referring function (1979). I follow Webber in relying on the distinction between the referent and the demonstratum in looking at cases where the demonstrata consist of nonNP constituents. I refer to these cases as intra-textual deixis because the deictic reference involves referents related to the denotations of sentence-internal constituents rather than to discourse segments.

In previous work, I pointed out that the critical feature of the antecedent type that favors the lexical choice of *that* is syntactic, namely, the distinction between true noun phrase syntax and other types of constituents ([Passonneau] Schiffman, 1984b). Contexts where N_1 is an NP whose head is a derived nominalization (such as *the careful choice of one's words*) pattern like those where the head is a lexical noun.[40] There are a number of differences between nonNPs and canonical NPs (full noun phrases with a lexical or derived head) that have consequences on the status of their semantic interpretation.

Referential NPs have both a denotation and a referent. In contrast, nonNPs must have a denotation but do not necessarily evoke a discourse entity, or referent, into the discourse model. Questions as to the denotation and reference of sentences, NPs, and various other kinds of sentence internal constituents are too complex to be reviewed thoroughly here (cf. Barwise and Perry, 1983). However, I offer two sorts of reasons for distinguishing the referential properties of NPs from nonNPs. The first has to do with linguistic differences between NPs and nonNPs, the second with the pragmatic problem of identifying referents for nonNPs.

Unlike NPs, nonNPs cannot be marked for definiteness: **a/the carefully choosing one's words* versus *a/the careful choice of words*. Definiteness is one of the means for indicating whether a referent is presupposed to be uniquely identifiable within the current context (cf. McCawley, 1979). Although the relationship between definiteness and presuppositions of existence and identifiability is not absolute, the inapplicability of the grammatical feature of definiteness to nonNP constituents perhaps reflects the irrelevance of the question of what they presuppose. Thus a difference between the interpretation of the two types of phrases *carefully choosing one's words* and *a/the careful choice of words* would have to do with whether there is a discourse entity in the contextual domain (cf. Section 7.2, discussion of McCawley, 1979) either prior to or as a consequence of the occurrence of the phrase. An indefinite NP often involves a presupposition that the referent is not yet part of the current context, whereas a definite NP often presupposes that it is. In contrast, the interpretation of a gerundive phrase, or other nonNP constituent, involves neither presuppositions of existence nor of identifiability.

In addition to a referential difference, there is also a difference in denotation between NPs and nonNPs. The denotations of NPs and nonNPs can be very similar, thus the NP *the careful choice of one's words* and the nonNP *carefully choosing one's words* both denote a 'choose' relation between an unspecified person and 'words' chosen by that person. But despite this similarity, there are reasons to view the denotations of NPs and nonNPs as categorically distinct. For example, all of the nonNP constituent types under consideration here permit

---

[40]Mixed nominals, such as *the careful choosing of one's words,* occurred too rarely to have a discriminating effect on contexts favoring *it* or *that.*

alternations in the expression of a verbal category such as tense, perfect or progressive (e.g., *to choose/be choosing one's words; choosing/having chosen one's words*), whereas NPs never do (**the careful have been choice of one's words*). Thus, the denotations of nonNPs, but not of NPs, must include a specification of the temporal properties associated with tense and aspect. Also, NPs express number and permit count determiners but nonNPs do not (*three choices of words* versus **three choosings one's words*). Thomason, for example, uses the latter type of evidence to argue that NPs whose heads are derived nominals refer to individuated events but that gerundive phrases do not refer to events (Thomason, 1985).

Because NPs are both referentially and semantically distinct from nonNPs, the cohesive relations between a token of *it* and an NP antecedent, versus between a token of *that* and a nonNP antecedent, are necessarily different. In addition, the relation of *that* to its antecedent is inherently more vague than in the anaphoric relation. Contrast the uses of *it* and *that* in the following example. The token of *it* in (26) C_4 unambiguously refers to the *one* book called *Sweaty Palms,* previously identified in C_2.

(26) C_1: there are some books that we have that talk about interviewing

     C_2: um *one's* called Sweaty Palms

     C_3: which I think is a great title (laugh)

     C_4: um but *it* talks very interestingly about *how to go about interviewing*

     C_5: and that's *that*'s going to be important for you now

     C_6: but *it*'s important all your life

The referent of *that* in C_5 is much harder to pin down. Determining the referent depends first on determining what is being demonstrated, which itself is problematic given that the demonstratum can be located in any number of places, including the physical surroundings or the discourse model. In this case, where the demonstratum is provided by the prior linguistic context, there are no a priori means for determining which constituent is the demonstratum. For example, it is *interviewing,* or *how to go about interviewing?*

Webber notes that deictic reference is inherently ambiguous:

[The] ambiguity as to which segment interpretation a deictic pronoun is referring to seems very similar to the ambiguity associated with the use of deixis for pointing within a shared physical context. Both Quine and Miller have observed in this regard that all pointing is ambiguous: the intended demonstratum of a pointing gesture can be any of the infinite number of points *intersected* by the gesture or any of the structures encompassing those points. (Webber, 1991)

Webber argues persuasively that deictic reference involving discourse segments is restricted to open segments on the right frontier, but that *there is still an ambiguity as to which segment* might be referred to, due to the recursive nature of discourse segmentation. Because an open segment on the right frontier may contain within it an embedded open segment that is also on the right frontier, a token of the demonstrative whose demonstratum is a discourse segment can be ambiguous between a more inclusive segment and a less inclusive one (Webber, 1991). The ambiguity can be eliminated if the context in which the deictic expression occurs clearly selects one of the possible readings. This phenomenon pertaining to deictic reference to segments is replicated in the cases where *that* has a nonNP antecedent, thus in C_5 of (26), the demonstratum of the demonstrative pronoun could be *interviewing,* or the more inclusive expression *go about interviewing,* or the more inclusive one yet *how to go about interviewing.*

The inherent vagueness of demonstrative reference involving a nonNP antecedent is dramatically illustrated in (27). Assume for an utterance pair U_1 and U_2 that U_2 is initiated with a demonstrative pronoun and that the demonstratum of the pronoun is a nonNP constituent of U_1, possibly the entire sentence. Given this assumption, there are numerous possible demonstrata that are more or less inclusive subconstituents of U_1. Example (27) shows only some of the many possible constituents that could serve as demonstrata for inter-textual deixis. In each case, the referent of the demonstrative pronoun is further constrained by the semantic properties of the sentence containing the demonstrative. Thus both the semantic properties of the deictic pronoun and the semantic context in which it occurs constrain the possible referents.

(27) U_1: I see that Carol insists on sewing her dresses from non-synthetic fabric.

U_{2a}: *That*'s an example of how observant I am.
[I see that Carol insists on sewing her dresses from non-synthetic fabric]

U_{2b}: *That*'s because she's allergic to synthetics.
[Carol insists on sewing her dresses from non-synthetic fabric]

U_{2c}: When she's feeling assertive, *that*'s what Roberta does too.
[insists on sewing her dresses from non-synthetic fabric]

U_{2d}: *That*'s one of Carol's favorite activities.
[sewing her dresses from non-synthetic fabric]

U_{2e}: *That*'s the only kind of fabric she's not allergic to.
[non-synthetic fabric]

The alternative second utterances in (27) demonstrate that many different internal constituents of the utterance U_1 can serve as the denotatum of a subsequent demonstrative pronoun. In each variant of U_2 (U_{2a}–U_{2e}), the intended demonstratum appears in italics after the utterance containing the demonstrative pronoun. In the abstract, the referent is either part of the context by virtue of the occurrence of the nonNP antecedent, or by virtue of the occurrence of the subsequent co-specifying demonstrative pronoun. If the former is the case, then all the referents illustrated in U_{2a}–U_{2d} must be part of the context as soon as U_1 occurs. Because in principle any constituent can be deictically referenced, this would mean that every constituent introduces a discourse entity into the contextual domain. However, this move would conflict with the theoretical motivation for the contextual domain, which is to indicate which entities are currently available for anaphoric reference. Some contexts allow either anaphoric reference or intratextual deixis, as was illustrated in (11)–(15). However, the constraints on the two kinds of reference are clearly distinct, as shown below.

The examples in (28)–(31) show that entities introduced by referential NPs in U_1 are still available for pronominal reference in U_3.

(28) U_1: I see that Carol$_i$ insists on sewing her dresses$_k$ from non-synthetic fabric.

     U_{2a}: *That*'s an example of how observant I am.

     U_{2b}: I like sewing too.

     U_3: She$_i$ should try the new rayon challis, though.

(29) U_1: I see that Carol$_i$ insists on sewing her dresses$_k$ from non-synthetic fabric.

     U_{2a}: *That*'s an example of how observant I am.

     U_{2b}: I like sewing too.

     U_3: They$_k$ always turn out beautifully.

(30) U_1: I see that Carol$_i$ insists on sewing her dresses$_k$ from non-synthetic fabric.

     U_2: *That*'s an example of how observant I am.

     U_3: **That*'s because she's allergic to synthetics.

(31) U_1: I see that Carol$_i$ insists on sewing her dresses$_k$ from non-synthetic fabric.

     U_2: She$_i$ should try the new rayon challis, though.

     U_3: **That*'s because she's allergic to synthetics.

U_1 introduces the referring expressions *Carol* and *her dresses*. Examples (28) and (29) show that the referents of *Carol* and *her dresses* are still available for anaphoric reference in U_3 even though they are not mentioned in U_2. This is the case whether the intervening utterance contains a reference to something introduced in U_1, as in the examples U_{2a}, or not, as in the examples U_{2b}. The examples U_{2a} illustrate demonstrative reference involving the nonNP antecedent, *that Carol insisted on sewing her dresses from non-synthetic fabric*. In contrast to the examples of anaphoric reference in (28) and (29), the *that*-clause cannot function as the antecedent, or demonstratum, of *that* after an intervening sentence, as illustrated by (30) and (31).

The preceding arguments suggest that nonNP constituents do not introduce entities into the discourse context. The demonstrative does not access a pre-existing discourse entity, but rather, plays a role in adding a new discourse entity to the context.[41] The enhanced transition arcs illustrated in contexts 22 and 24 are interpreted as other enhanced arcs have been interpreted. They indicate that the attentional status associated with the antecedent expression (nonNP) is maintained by the speaker's lexical choice of (*that*). This status is that the context contains a temporary semantic representation that can serve as an object of demonstration in intra-textual deixis, but no discourse entity. However, after the demonstrative has been fully interpreted, its referent is added to the contextual domain; thus the demonstrative also alters the prior attentional state.

7.6   Conclusions: Attentional state, linguistic representations, and discourse models

The contributions of the present work are both methodological and theoretical. I have illustrated the application of a methodology for interpreting and collecting naturalistic data that is particularly well-suited to investigating on-line choices of conversational participants. The distributions of objectively verifiable surface linguistic features in a corpus of naturally occurring dialogues, among a number of different conversational participants, were first encoded and then analyzed. The observed distributions were statistically evaluated in order to identify significant co-occurrence patterns. I have argued that contingency tables representing successive sets of linguistic choices in local coherence contexts can be directly interpreted as state transitions. In these tables, where each cell corresponds to a type of state transition, the presence or lack of statistical significance in individual cells translates directly into communicatively significant versus non-significant combinations of linguistic choices. For significant state transitions, a particular initial state creates expectations regarding what final states will occur. Where the observed frequency is high, the final state is expected to occur; where it is low, the final state is expected not to occur. An actual instance of one of these state transitions either confirms or defeats the conversational participants' expectations, thereby acquiring communicative significance. Assuming the initial state

---

[41]Note that my position on intra-textual deixis differs from Webber's position on discourse deixis, which is that the demonstrative referring function accesses a pre-existing discourse entity (Webber, 1991).

to correspond to some abstract attentional state, a state transition that confirms conversational participants' expectations is interpreted as maintaining the attentional state. A state transition that defeats conversational participants' expectations is interpreted as altering the attentional state. A state transition with no relevant expectations is interpreted as a context where the relevant attentional state does not exist, or does not inhere in the combinations of features that were investigated.

In the analysis and interpretation of pronominal usage, my initial concern has been with establishing the most likely or canonical pragmatic functions of two semantically contrastive pronouns. Thus most of the discussion has focused on interpreting the contexts in which a particular pronominal choice maintains the current attentional status of its referent. In future work I will investigate the two other classes of contexts in which the choice of referring expression changes the attentional status of its referent, or makes no contribution to its attentional status.

I have tested and amplified the centering framework and have proposed how the distributional differences between *it* and *that* in contexts where there is a linguistic antecedent can be accounted for in terms of distinct cohesive functions. The data support the hypothesis embodied in the centering framework that conversational participants make use of default processes for resolving pronominal reference, and also clearly demonstrate that *it* plays a role in this default process whereas *that* has distinct functions even in apparently similar contexts. By investigating actual on-line linguistic choices, I have clarified the dimensions of linguistic variation that contribute to this default mechanism and have summarized the results in an operational definition of local centering. I have demonstrated that the grammatical role and surface form of both the antecedent and subsequent pronoun contribute to local centering.

A local center is a distinguished attentional status of a discourse entity within a local context consisting of adjacent utterances. It is distinct from the Cb of the centering framework in that there is only a single potential local center, rather than an ordered set of Cfs. Like Kameyama's property-sharing constraint, the rule for local center establishment has a canonical and a non-canonical form. By investigating the non-canonical contexts, I have shown that there is an interaction between local centering and a competing pragmatic effect in which 1st and 2nd person pronouns pre-empt the subject grammatical role within the local context consisting of both utterances, thereby demoting the local center to non-subject grammatical roles. Therefore I have provided an account of a cognitively distinct coherence phenomenon and have motivated the range of surface configurations that realize this phenomenon.

By comparing the properties of local centers with the symbolic properties of 1st and 2nd person pronouns, I have also shown that the two referring functions are quite similar, differing primarily in that the former is pragmatically realized whereas the latter is grammatically encoded. The cognitive mechanism for local centering is thereby accounted for in terms of a more general cognitive process pertaining to pure indexicals like 1st and 2nd person pronouns. The process of finding a referent for referring expressions that are pure indexicals depends on a fixed set of parameters in terms of which conversational participants construe the speech situation. The referent of the indexical expression is simply the current value of the relevant parameter. The cognitive mechanism for finding the local center presumably involves an automatic retrieval of the current value of the local center, and a compatibility check against the local semantic context. In contrast, resolving the referents of other sorts of referring expressions, such as full referring phrases or demonstrative pronouns, is a non-automatic process requiring reasoning and search within the current local focus space.

The nature of the pragmatic function of demonstrative pronouns in apparently anaphoric contexts has long been a puzzle. I have provided an explanation for certain uses of the demonstrative where there is a linguistic antecedent, based on object contrasts between the contexts in which *that* tends to occur and those in which *it* tends to occur. The demonstrative has differing functions, depending on the form of the antecedent, thereby reinforcing the view that the form of a referring expression is a significant indicator of the current attentional status of the referent. The demonstrative does not play a role in local center establishment, but does play a role in anticipating or terminating a cohesive chain. Thus a local center is not typically accessible to a demonstrative pronoun, but a candidate or former local center is. No positive results were found pertaining to entities introduced by full noun phrases in subject grammatical role, but the typical use of the demonstrative to co-specify with a full NP antecedent in non-subject grammatical role suggests that alongside local centering, there exists an alternative cohesive relation, referred to here as non-local-center retention. It is assumed that in addition to providing an efficient mechanism for re-mentioning focused entities, definite pronouns and other cohesive devices may also indirectly indicate whether the referent is only locally relevant, or both locally and globally relevant. I proposed that the coherence context in which the antecedent expression is an NP-nonSUBJ and the target pronoun is the demonstrative mark the entity as a non-candidate local center while permitting the entity to be referred to via a cohesive expression. Finally, I have argued that the demonstrative plays a role in adding new entities to the local focus space when the antecedent is itself not a referring expression. I have asserted that in these cases, the referent is added to the context by virtue of a referring function that is non-automatic, but dependent on reasoning. It remains to future work to specify exactly how this reasoning process is constrained.

Because local center establishment depends on a pair of utterances that are adjacent in the current segment, all utterances within a segment except the initial and final utterances play a dual role, both terminating a local coherence context and initiating the next local coherence context. Consequently, persistence or change in the status of local center takes place in successive, overlapping utterance pairs. Cohesive chains of pronouns illustrate that a local center, once established, can be maintained throughout a more or less long sequence of utterances. By this means, the local center establishment rule is presumed to contribute to discourse segmentation, and thereby to the global context.

Hopefully the methodology presented here proves itself to some degree in the plausibility and merit of the theoretical claims. But, as in any speculative work, the results include far more new questions than definitive answers. The present work demonstrates that pronominalization is a heterogeneous phenomenon: not all tokens of *it* represent local center establishment, nor do all coherence contexts have the same pragmatic effects (local center establishment versus non-local center retention). Of the several distinct uses of *it* and *that* manifested in my data, I have focused my efforts on explaining the canonical cases. Many of the hypotheses I have proposed need further confirmation and development, for example, in regard to the relationship between local coherence relations and the global context. Also, the contexts in which a target expression was suppressed or played no significant role need to be explained, perhaps by looking at larger contexts, or perhaps by looking at new sets of linguistic factors in the local context, such as prosodic cues. I believe such questions are answerable, and will lead us to increasingly explicit models of discourse structure.

7.7   Appendix: Distributional analysis

In this study, there are two classes of observation – the occurrence of *it* and the occurrence of *that*. Let us assume for the moment a case in which the conditioning criterion is the presence of an antecedent, and that the criterion has two values: *lacks* (−) *antecedent,* and *has* (+) *antecedent.* Arranging the set of observations in a table where the classes of observation define the columns of the table (one column each for tokens of *it* and *that*), and the conditioning criteria define the rows (e.g., one row for +*antecedent,* another row for −*antecedent*), yields a 2 × 2 contingency table with four cells, as in Table 7.4. The table as a whole represents the population of observations in which *it* or *that* occur (N = 100). A χ^2 for the table can provide a measure of the degree to which the classification (lexical choice of *it* or *that*) is contingent upon the conditioning criteria (presence or absence of an antecedent).[42]

The crucial question at which a contingency table is directed is whether the distribution across the classes always has the same probability, i.e., is *independent* of the sampling criteria. If there is no correlation between the classification (dependent variable) and the sampling criteria (independent variable), then the frequency within each cell of the table should fall within a range predicted by chance, as described below. This is called the null hypothesis.

The row and column totals of a contingency table provide a method for estimating a chance distribution of the population in all four cells of the sample

---

[42]The data for this table were fabricated so as to provide simple ratios of row and column totals.

Table 7.4. *Sample contingency table*

	it	that	Row totals
+ Antecedent	34	26	60
− Antecedent	16	24	40
Column totals	50	50	
Table total			100

contingency table, and thus for testing the deviation of the actual cell counts (observed frequency: f) from the number predicted by the null hypothesis (expected frequency: F). Refuting the null hypothesis confirms that the independent variable is statistically correlated with, or is a good predictor of, the dependent variable.

The expected frequencies are predicted from the row and column totals of a contingency table as follows. In Table 7.4 we see that the total sample size of *it* and *that* is 100 ($N = 100$), and the ratio of *it* to *that* is 1:1, as given by the ratio of column totals. Overall, 60% of the pronouns have antecedents and 40% do not, as given by the ratio of row totals to table total. The null hypothesis predicts that the probability of occurrence of *it* versus *that* is independent of the probability that a pronoun will have an antecedent. If many samples of pronouns are tested, then the mean percentages of pronouns across samples should eventually approximate the probabilities for the population as a whole. Letting P_C represent the probability that a particular class of observation will occur (e.g., *it*), P_C is estimated by: (Column total for that class, e.g., *it*)/N, or in this case, by $50/100$. Analogously, letting P_R be the probability that a particular value of the independent variable will hold (e.g., +*antecedent*), then P_R is estimated by (Row total for that value, e.g., +*antecedent*)/N, or in this case, by $60/100$. The expected frequency of each cell of the contingency table is then given by the formula:

$$P_R \times P_C \times N.$$

By applying this formula, we find the expected distribution, given the null hypothesis, that is shown in Table 7.5.

The χ^2 statistic is a test of the null hypothesis because it gives a quantitative measure of the discrepancies between observed frequencies (f) and expected frequencies (F) – e.g., between Tables 7.4 and 7.5 – as a single sum:[43]

$$\chi^2 = \Sigma(f - F)^2/F.$$

The χ^2 is always evaluated relative to the degrees of freedom in the distribution, in this case, the number of contrasts in the row (R-1) times the number of

---

[43]Note that what is being summed are the χ^2s of the individual cells of the contingency table, each cell χ^2 given by $(f - F)^2/F$.

Table 7.5. *Expected distribution,*
assuming the null hypothesis

	it	that	Row totals
+ Antecedent	30	30	60
− Antecedent	20	20	40
Column totals	50	50	
Table total			100

contrasts in the column (C-1).[44] Most elementary statistics texts provide probability tables for χ^2s for a large range of degrees of freedom. A statistical correlation is generally assumed for probabilities less than 5%, and unquestionably if the probability is less than 1%.

References

Ball, C. N. (1979). *Th*-clefts. In *Penn Linguistics Colloquium,* pages 57–69, Philadelphia.

Barwise, J. and Perry, J. (1983). *Situations and Attitudes.* MIT Press, Cambridge, MA.

Beckman, M. (1991). Notes on prosody, Ms.

Bennett, M. (1978). Demonstratives and indexicals in Montague grammar. *Synthèse,* 39:1–80.

Brennan, S. E., Friedman, M. W., and Pollard, C. J. (1987). A centering approach to pronouns. In *Proceedings of the 25th Annual Meeting of the Association for Computational Linguistics,* pages 155–162, Stanford, CA.

Buchler, J. (1955). *Philosophical Writings of Peirce.* Dover Publications, Inc., New York.

Channon, R. (1980). Anaphoric *that:* A friend in need. In *Pronouns and Anaphora: Papers from the Parasession of the Chicago Linguistic Society,* pages 98–109, Chicago.

Fillmore, C. J. (1971). Santa Cruz lectures on deixis. Technical report, Indiana University Linguistics Club, Bloomington, IN.

Foley, W. A. and Van Valin Jr., R. D. (1984). *Functional Syntax and Universal Grammar.* Cambridge University Press, Cambridge.

Freedman, D., Pisani, R., and Purves, R. (1978). *Statistics.* W. W. Norton & Company, New York.

Givon, T. (1976). Topic, pronoun, and grammatical agreement. In C. N. Li, editor, *Subject and Topic,* pages 149–188. Academic Press, New York.

Grosz, B. J. (1977). *The Representation and Use of Focus in Dialogue Understanding.* Ph.D. thesis, University of California, Berkeley.

Grosz, B. J., Joshi, A. K., and Weinstein, S. (1983). Providing a unified account of definite noun phrases in discourse. In *Proceedings of the 21st ACL,* pages 44–50.

[44]In a 2 × 2 table, there is one degree of freedom. An intuitive explanation of this notion is that if the row and column totals are known, then knowing the value of any one cell determines the values of the three other cells.

Grosz, B. J., Joshi, A. K., and Weinstein, S. (1986). Towards a computational theory of discourse interpretation, Ms.

Grosz, B. J. and Sidner, C. L. (1986). Attention, intentions and the structure of discourse. *Computational Linguistics, 12*:175–204.

Hirschberg, J. and Litman, D. (1987). Now let's talk about *now:* Identifying cue phrases intonationally. In *Proceedings of the 25th Annual Meeting of the ACL*.

Hudson-D'Zmura, S. B. (1988). *The Structure of Discourse and Anaphor Resolution: The Discourse Center and the Roles of Nouns and Pronouns*. Ph.D. thesis, University of Rochester.

Isard, S. (1975). Changing the context. In E. L. Keenan, editor, *Formal Semantics of Natural Language*, pages 287–296. Cambridge University Press, Cambridge.

Jakobson, R. (1971). Shifters, verbal categories and the Russian verb. In *Selected Writings of Roman Jakobson*, pages 130–147. Mouton, The Hague [1957].

Joshi, A. and Weinstein, S. (1981). Control of inference: Role of some aspects of discourse structure – centering. In *Proceedings of the International Joint Conference on Artificial Intelligence*, pages 385–387, Vancouver, B.C.

Kameyama, M. (1986). A property-sharing constraint in centering. In *Proceedings of the 24th Annual Meeting of the ACL*, pages 200–206.

Kameyama, M. (1987). Computing Japanese discourse: Grammatical disambiguation with centering constraints. In *Proceedings of University of Manchester Institute of Science and Technology: Workshop on Computing Japanese*.

Kaplan, D. (1989). Demonstratives. In J. Almog, J. Perry, and H. Wettstein, editors, *Themes from Kaplan*, pages 481–566. Oxford University Press, New York, [1977].

Landon, H. C. Robbins (1988). *Mozart's Last Year*. Schirmer Books, New York.

Levy, E. (1984). *Communicating Thematic Structure in Narrative Discourse: The Use of Referring Terms and Gestures*. Ph.D thesis, University of Chicago.

Li, C. N. (1976). *Subject and Topic*. Academic Press, New York.

Marslen-Wilson, W., Levy, E., and Tyler, L. K. (1982). Producing interpretable discourse: The establishment and maintenance of reference. In R. J. Jarvella and W. Klein, editors, *Speech, Place and Action*, pages 339–378. John Wiley and Sons Ltd., New York.

McCawley, J. D. (1979). Presupposition and discourse structure. In *Syntax and Semantics, Vol 11: Presupposition*, pages 371–403. Academic Press, Inc., New York.

Nelson, E. (1987). *Effects on Memory of Discourse Coherence in Encoding*. Ph.D thesis, University of Chicago.

Nunberg, G. (1979). The non-uniqueness of semantic solutions: Polysemy. *Linguistics and Philosophy*, pages 143–184.

Passonneau, R. J. (1989). Getting at discourse referents. In *Proceedings of the 27th Annual Meeting of the ACL*, pages 51–59.

Passonneau, R. J. (1991). Some facts about centers, indexicals and demonstratives. In *Proceedings of the 29th Annual Meeting of the ACL*, pages 63–70.

Peirce, C. S. (1931–1935). In C. Hartshorne and P. Weiss, editors, *Collected Papers of Charles Sanders Peirce*. Harvard University Press, Cambridge, MA.

(Passonneau) Schiffman, R. J. (1984a). Categories of discourse deixis, 1984. Presented at the 29th Annual Conference of the International Linguistics Association.

(Passonneau) Schiffman, R. J. (1984b). The two nominal anaphors *it* and *that*. In *Proceedings of the 20th Regional Meeting of the Chicago Linguistic Society*, pages 322–357.

(Passonneau) Schiffman, R. J. (1985). *Discourse Constraints on IT and THAT: A Study of Language Use in Career-Counseling Interviews*. Ph.D thesis, University of Chicago.

Sidner, C. L. (1981). Focusing for the interpretation of pronouns. *American Journal of Computational Linguistics,* 7:51–59.

Sidner, C. L. (1983). Focusing in the comprehension of definite anaphora. In M. Brady and R. C. Berwick, editors, *Computational Models of Discourse,* pages 267–330. The MIT Press, Cambridge, MA.

Silverstein, M. (1987). Cognitive implications of a referential hierarchy. In Maya Hickmann, editor, *Social and Functional Approaches to Language and Thought,* pages 125–163. Academic Press, Orlando, FL.

Thomason, R. H. (1985). Some issues concerning the interpretation of derived and gerundive nominals. *Linguistics and Philosophy,* 8:73–80.

Webber, B. L. (1991). Structure and ostension in the interpretation of discourse deixis. Technical Report MS-CIS-90-58, LINC LAB 183, University of Pennsylvania Computer and Information Science Department. (Also in *Language and Cognitive Processes,* 6(2):107–135.)

8 Surface structure, intonation, and discourse meaning

MARK STEEDMAN

8.1 Introduction

The structural units of phrasal intonation are frequently orthogonal to the syntactic constituent boundaries that are recognized by traditional grammar and embodied in most current theories of syntax. As a result, much recent work on the relation of intonation to discourse context and information structure has either eschewed syntax entirely (cf. Bolinger, 1972; Cutler and Isard, 1980; Gussenhoven, 1983; Brown and Yule, 1983), or has supplemented traditional syntax with entirely non-syntactic string-related principles (cf. Cooper and Paccia-Cooper, 1980). Recently, Selkirk (1984) and others have postulated an autonomous level of "intonational structure" for spoken language, distinct from syntactic structure. Structures at this level are plausibly claimed to be related to discourse-related notions, such as "focus". However, the involvement of two apparently uncoupled levels of structure in Natural Language grammar appears to complicate the path from speech to interpretation unreasonably, and thereby to threaten the feasibility of computational speech recognition and speech synthesis.

In Steedman (1991a), I argue that the notion of intonational structure formalized by Pierrehumbert, Selkirk, and others, can be subsumed under a rather different notion of syntactic surface structure, which emerges from the "Combinatory Categorial" theory of grammar (Steedman, 1987, 1990). This theory engenders surface structure constituents corresponding directly to phonological phrase structure. Moreover, the grammar assigns to these constituents interpretations that directly correspond to what is here called "information structure" – that is, the aspects of discourse-meaning that have variously been termed "topic" and "comment", "theme" and "rheme", "given" and "new" information, and/or "presupposition" and "focus".

The consequent simplification of the path from speech to higher level modules including syntax, semantics, and discourse pragmatics, seems likely to facilitate a number of applications in spoken language understanding. On the analysis side, it can be expected to facilitate the use of such high-level modules to "filter" the ambiguities that unavoidably arise from low-level word recognition. On the synthesis side, it can be expected to similarly facilitate the production of intona-

The research was supported in part by NSF grants nos. IRI-90-18513 and IRI-91-17110, DARPA grant no. N00014-90-J-1863, and ARO grant no. DAAL03-89-C0031.

tion contours that are more appropriate to discourse context than the default intonations characteristic of current "text-to-speech" packages. This chapter considers these further implications for speech processing.

8.2   The combinatory grammar of intonation

8.2.1   The problem

One quite normal prosody (b, below) for an answer to the question (a) intuitively imposes the intonational structure indicated by the brackets (stress, marked in this case by raised pitch, is indicated by capitals):

(1)   a. I know that Alice likes velvet. But what does MAry prefer?
       b. (MA-ry prefers) (CORduroy).

Such a grouping is orthogonal to the traditional syntactic structure of the sentence.

This phenomenon is a property of grammar, and should not be confused with the disruptions caused by hesitation and other performance disfluencies. Intonational structure remains strongly constrained by meaning. For example, contours imposing bracketings like the following are not allowed:

(2)   #(Three cats)(in ten prefer corduroy)

Halliday (1967) observed that this constraint, which Selkirk (1984) has called the "Sense Unit Condition", seems to follow from the *function* of phrasal intonation, which is to convey what will here be called "information structure" – that is, distinctions of focus, presupposition, and propositional attitude toward entities in the discourse model. These discourse entities are more diverse than mere noun phrase or propositional referents, but they do not include such non-concepts as "in ten prefer corduroy".

Among the categories that they *do* include are what Wilson and Sperber and E. Prince (1986) have termed "open propositions". One way of introducing an open proposition into the discourse context is by asking a Wh-question. For example, the question in (1), *What does Mary prefer?* introduces an open proposition. As Jackendoff (1972) pointed out, it is natural to think of this open proposition as a functional *abstraction,* and to express it as follows, using the notation of the λ-calculus:

(3) $\lambda x \, [(prefer' \; x) \; mary']$

(Primes indicate semantic interpretations whose detailed nature is of no direct concern here.) When this function or concept is supplied with an argument *corduroy'*, it *reduces* to give a proposition, with the same function argument relations as the canonical sentence.

(4) $(prefer' \; corduroy') \; mary'$

It is the presence of the above open proposition rather than some other that makes the intonation contour in (1)b felicitous. (That is not to say that its presence uniquely *determines* this response, nor that its explicit mention is necessary for interpreting the response.)

These observations have led linguists such as Selkirk to postulate a level of "intonational structure", independent of syntactic structure and related to information structure. The involvement of two apparently uncoupled levels of structure in natural language grammar appears to complicate the path from speech to interpretation unreasonably, and thereby to threaten a number of computational applications in speech recognition and speech synthesis.

It is therefore interesting to observe that all natural languages include syntactic constructions whose semantics are also reminiscent of functional abstraction. The most obvious and tractable class are Wh-constructions themselves, in which some of the same fragments that can be delineated by a single intonation contour appear as the residue of the subordinate clause. Another and much more problematic class of fragments results from coordinate constructions. It is striking that the residues of wh-movement and conjunction reduction are also subject to something like a "sense unit condition". For example, strings like "in ten prefer corduroy" are as resistant to coordination as they are to being intonational phrases.[1]

(5)   *Three cats in twenty like velvet, and in ten prefer corduroy.

Because coordinate constructions constitute another major source of complexity for theories of natural language grammar, and also offer serious obstacles to computational applications, the earlier papers in this area suggest that this conspiracy between syntax and prosody should be interpreted as evidence for a unified notion of structure that is somewhat different from traditional surface constituency, based on Combinatory Grammar.

8.2.2   Combinatory grammars

Combinatory Categorical Grammar (CCG, Steedman, 1987) is an extension of Categorial Grammar (CG). Elements like verbs are associated with a syntactic "category" that identifies them as *functions,* and specifies the type and directionality of their arguments and the type of their result. We use a notation in which a rightward-combining functor over a domain β into a range α are written α/β, whereas the corresponding leftward-combining functor is written $\alpha\backslash\beta$. α and β may themselves be function categories. For example, a transitive verb is a function from (object) noun phrases (NPs) into predicates – that is, into functions from (subject) NPs into S:

---

[1] I do not claim that such coordinations are absolutely excluded, just that if they are allowed at all then: (a) extremely strong and unusual contexts are required, and (b) that such contexts will tend to support (2) as well.

(6)   *prefers* := *(S\NP)/NP* : *prefer'*

Such categories can be regarded as encoding the semantic type of their translation, which in the notation used here is identified by the expression to the right of
the colon. Such functions can combine with arguments of the appropriate type
and position by functional application:

(7)   Mary   prefers   corduroy
       ———   ————   ————
       NP   *(S\NP)/NP*   *NP*
               ————————————————>
                       S\NP
               ————————————<
                       S

The syntactic types are identical to semantic types, apart from the addition of
directional information. The derivation can therefore also be regarded as building
a compositional interpretation, (*prefer' corduroy'*) *mary'*, and of course such a
"pure" categorial grammar is context free.

Coordination might be included in CG via the following rule, allowing constituents of like type to conjoin to yield a single constituent of the same type:

(8) $X \; conj \; X \Rightarrow X$

(9)   I   loathe   and   detest   velvet
       —   ————   ———   ————   ————
       NP   *(S\NP)/NP*   *conj*   *(S\NP)/NP*   *NP*
               ————————————————————&
                       (S\NP)/NP

(The rest of the derivation is omitted, being the same as in (7).) In order to allow
coordination of contiguous strings that do not constitute constituents, CCG gener-
alizes the grammar to allow certain operations on functions related to Curry's
combinators (1958). For example, functions may nondeterministically *compose,*
as well as apply, under the following rule:

(10)   *Forward Composition:* (>B)
        $X/Y : F \quad Y/Z : G \Rightarrow X/Z : \lambda x \, F(Gx)$

The most important single property of combinatory rules like this is that they
have an invariant semantics. This one composes the interpretations of the functions to which it applies, as is apparent from the right-hand side of the rule.[2]
Thus sentences like *I suggested, and would prefer, corduroy* can be accepted, via
the following composition of two verbs (indexed as *B*, following Curry's nomen-
clature) to yield a composite of the same category as a transitive verb. Crucially,

---

[2]The rule uses the notation of the λ-calculus in the semantics for clarity. This should not obscure the
fact that it is functional composition itself that is the primitive, not the λ operator.

composition also yields the appropriate interpretation for the composite verb *would prefer:*

(11)   . . . suggested   and   would   prefer . . .

$$\frac{\overline{(S\backslash NP)/NP}\quad \overline{conj}\quad \frac{\overline{(S\backslash NP)/VP}\quad \overline{VP/NP}}{(S\backslash NP)/NP}>B}{(S\backslash NP)/NP}\&$$

Combinatory grammars also include type-raising rules, which turn arguments into functions over functions-over-such-arguments. These rules allow arguments to compose, and thereby take part in coordinations like *I dislike, and Mary prefers, corduroy.* They too have an invariant compositional semantics that ensures that the result has an appropriate interpretation. For example, the following rule allows the conjuncts to form as below (again, the remainder of the derivation is omitted):

(12)   *Subject Type-raising:* (>T)
$$NP:y \Rightarrow S/(S\backslash NP):\lambda F\ Fy$$

(13)   I   dislike   and   Mary   prefers   . . .

$$\frac{\frac{\overline{NP}}{S/(S\backslash NP)}>T\quad \overline{(S\backslash NP)/NP}\quad \overline{conj}\quad \frac{\overline{NP}}{S/(S\backslash NP)}>T\quad \overline{(S\backslash NP)/NP}}{\frac{S/NP}{S/NP}>B\qquad \frac{S/NP}{S/NP}>B}\&$$

This apparatus has been applied to a wide variety of coordination phenomena, including "left node raising" (Dowty, 1988), "backward gapping" in Germanic languages, including verb-raising constructions (Steedman, 1985a), and gapping, (Steedman, 1990a). For example, the following analysis is proposed by Dowty (1988) for the first of these:

(14)

give	Mary	corduroy	and	Harry	velvet
$(VP/NP)/NP$	$(VP/NP)\backslash((VP/NP)/NP)$ <T	$VP\backslash(VP/NP)$ <T	*conj*	$(VP/NP)\backslash((VP/NP)/NP)$ <T	$VP\backslash(VP/NP)$ <T
	$VP\backslash((VP/NP)/NP)$	<B		$VP\backslash((VP/NP)/NP)$	<B
			$VP\backslash((VP/NP)/NP)$	<&>	
	VP				

The important feature of this analysis is that it uses "backward" rules of type-raising $<$T and composition $<$B that are the exact mirror-image of the two "forward" versions introduced as examples (10) and (12). It is therefore a prediction of the theory that such a construction can exist in English, and its inclusion in the grammar requires no additional mechanism whatsoever. The earlier papers on this work show that no *other* non-constituent coordinations of dative-accusative NP sequences are allowed in any language with the English verb categories, given the assumptions of CCG. Thus the following are ruled out in principle, rather than by stipulation:

(15) a. *Harry velvet and give Mary corduroy
      b. *give corduroy Mary and velvet Harry

A number of related well-known cross-linguistic generalizations concerning the dependency of so-called "gapping" upon lexical word order are also captured (see Dowty, 1988, and Steedman, 1985a, 1990a).

8.2.3 *Intonation, parsing, and context*

Examples like the above show that combinatory grammars embody a view of surface structure according to which strings like *Mary prefers* are constituents. It follows, according to this view, that they must also be possible constituents of non-coordinate sentences like *Mary prefers corduroy,* as in the following derivation:

(16)   Mary   prefers   corduroy
      ————   ————   ————
        NP   (S\NP)/NP   NP
      ————>T
       S/(S\NP)
                  ——————————>B
                    S/NP
                          ——————————>
                              S

An entirely unconstrained combinatory grammar would in fact allow any bracketing on a sentence, although the grammars we actually write for configurational languages like English are heavily constrained by local conditions. (An example might be a condition on the composition rule that is tacitly assumed below, forbidding the variable Y in the composition rule to be instantiated as NP, thus excluding constituents like *[ate the]$_{VP/N}$.) It nevertheless follows that, for each semantically distinct analysis of a sentence, the involvement of the combinatory operation of functional composition engenders an equivalence class of derivations, which impose different constituent structures but are guaranteed to yield identical interpretations. In more complex sentences than the above, there will be many semantically equivalent derivations for each distinct interpretation.

Such additional non-determinism in grammar, over and above the non-determinism that is usually recognized, creates obvious problems for the parser, and has on occasion been referred to as "spurious" ambiguity. This term is very misleading. Whether or not the present theory is correct, the non-determinism is *there,* in the competence grammar of coordinate constructions, and any parser that actually covers this range of constructions will have to deal with it. It is only the comparative neglect of these constructions by the parsing community that has led them to ignore this perfectly genuine source of non-determinism. Papers by Pareschi et al., 1987; Steedman, 1991b; Vijay-Shankar and Weir, 1990; and Wittenburg, 1987, discuss the complexity of this problem in the worst case. However, in Crain et al. (1985) it is suggested that the evaluation of partial, incomplete, interpretations with respect to a discourse model including a representation of discourse information plays a crucial role. These possibilities will be explored further below.

However the parsing problem is resolved, the interest of such non-standard structures for present purposes should be obvious. The claim is simply that the non-standard surface structures that are induced by the combinatory grammar to explain coordination in English subsume the intonational structures that are postulated by Pierrehumbert et al. to explain the possible intonation contours for sentences of English. The claim is that in spoken utterances, intonation helps to determine *which* of the many possible bracketings permitted by the combinatory syntax of English is intended, and that the interpretations of the constituents that arise from these derivations, far from being "spurious", are related to distinctions of discourse focus among the concepts and open propositions that the speaker has in mind.

The proof of this claim lies in showing that the rules of combinatory grammar can be made sensitive to intonation contour, which limit their application in spoken discourse. We must also show that the major constituents of intonated utterances like (1)b, under the analyses that are permitted by any given intonation, correspond to the information structure of the context to which the intonation is appropriate, as in (a) in the example (1) with which the proposal begins. This demonstration will be quite simple, once we have established the following notation for intonation contours.

We will use a notation that is based on the theory of Pierrehumbert (1980), as modified in more recent work by Selkirk (1984), Beckman and Pierrehumbert (1986), Pierrehumbert and Beckman (1989), and Pierrehumbert and Hirschberg (1987), and as explicated in the chapter by Pierrehumbert in the present volume. The theory proposed below is in fact compatible with any of the standard descriptive accounts of phrasal intonation. However, a crucial feature of Pierrehumbert's theory for present purposes is that it distinguishes two subcomponents of the prosodic phrase, the *pitch accent* and the *boundary*.[3] The first of these tones or tone-sequences coincides with the perceived major stress or stresses of the prosodic phrase, whereas the second marks the right-hand boundary of the phrase. These two components are essentially invariant, and all other parts of the intonational tune are interpolated. Pierrehumbert's theory thus captures in a very natural way the intuition that the same tune can be spread over longer or shorter strings, in order to mark the corresponding constituents for the particular distinction of focus and propositional attitude that the melody denotes. It will help the exposition to augment Pierrehumbert's notation with explicit prosodic phrase boundaries, using brackets. These do not change her theory in any way: all the information is implicit in the original notation.

Consider for example the prosody of the sentence *Mary prefers corduroy* in the following pair of discourse settings, which are adapted from Jackendoff (1972, pp. 260):

(17) Q: Well, what about the CORduroy? Who prefers THAT?
      A: (MARy)   (prefers Corduroy).
          H* L   L+H* LH%

(18) Q: Well, what about MARy? What does SHE prefer?
      A: (MARy   prefers)   (CORduroy).
          L+H*   LH%   H* LL%

In these contexts, the main stressed syllables on both *Mary* and *corduroy* receive a pitch accent, but a different one. In the former example, (17), there is a prosodic phrase on *Mary* made up of the pitch accent that Pierrehumbert calls H*, immediately followed by an L boundary. There is another prosodic phrase having the pitch accent called L+H* on *corduroy,* preceded by null or interpolated tone on the word *prefers,* and immediately followed by a boundary that is written LH%. (I base these annotations on Pierrehumbert and Hirschberg's [1987, ex. 33] discussion of a similar example.)[4] In the second example (18) above, the two tunes are reversed: this time the tune with pitch accent L+H* and boundary LH% is spread across a prosodic phrase *Mary prefers,* while the other tune with pitch accent H* and boundary LL% is carried by the prosodic phrase *corduroy* (again starting with an interpolated or null tone).[5]

The meaning that these tunes convey is intuitively very obvious. As Pierre-

---

[3]For the purposes of this chapter, the distinction between the intonational phrase proper, and what Pierrehumbert and her colleagues call the "intermediate" phrase will be largely suppressed. However, these categories differ in respect of boundary tone-sequences – see the chapter by Pierrehumbert in the present volume – and the distinction is implicit below.

[4]We continue for the moment to gloss over Pierrehumbert's distinction between "intermediate" and "intonational" phrases.

[5]The reason for notating the latter boundary as LL%, rather than L, reflects the distinction between intonational and intermediate phrases.

humbert and Hirschberg point out, the latter tune seems to be used to mark some or all of that part of the sentence expressing information that the speaker believes to be *novel to the hearer*. In traditional terms, it marks the "comment" – more precisely, what Halliday called the "rheme". In contrast, the L+H* LH% tune seems to be used to mark some or all of that part of the sentence that expresses information that in traditional terms is the "topic" – in Halliday's terms, the "theme".[6] For present purposes, a theme can be thought of as conveying *what the speaker assumes to be the subject of mutual interest,* and this particular tune marks a theme as *novel to the conversation as a whole,* and as standing in a contrastive relation to the previous theme. (If the theme is not novel in this sense, it receives *no* tone in Pierrehumbert's terms, and may even be left out altogether.)[7] Thus in (18), the L+H* LH% phrase including this accent is spread across the phrase *Mary prefers.*[8] Similarly, in (17), the same tune is confined to the object of the open proposition *prefers corduroy,* because the intonation of the original question indicates that preferring corduroy *as opposed to some other stuff* is the new topic or theme.[9]

8.2.4   Combinatory prosody

The L+H* LH% intonational melody in example (18) belongs to a phrase *Mary prefers . . .* that corresponds under the combinatory theory of grammar to a grammatical constituent, complete with a translation equivalent to the open proposition $\lambda x[(prefer'\ x)\ mary']$. The combinatory theory thus offers a way to derive such intonational phrases, using only the independently motivated rules of combinatory grammar, entirely under the control of appropriate intonation contours like L+H* LH%.[10]

One extremely simple way to do this is the following. We interpret the two pitch accents as functions over boundaries, of the following types:

(19)   L+H* := *Theme/Bh*
          H*   := *Rheme/Bl*
          H*   := *rheme/Bl*

---

[6]The concepts of theme and rheme are distantly related to Grosz et al.'s (1983) concepts of "backward looking center" and "forward looking center".

[7]Here I depart slightly from Halliday's definition. The present proposal also follows Lyons (1977) in rejecting Halliday's claim that the theme must necessarily be sentence-initial.

[8]An alternative prosody, in which the contrastive tune is confined to *Mary,* seems equally coherent, and may be the one intended by Jackendoff. I believe that this alternative is informationally distinct, and arises from an ambiguity as to whether the topic of this discourse is *Mary* or *What Mary prefers.* It too is accepted by the rules below.

[9]Note that the position of the pitch accent in the phrase has to do with a further dimension of information structure within both theme and rheme, which it is tempting to call "focus" but safer to call "emphasis". I ignore this dimension here.

[10]This section is a simplified summary of the fuller accounts presented in Steedman (1991a,b).

that is, as functions over boundary tones into the two major informational types, the Hallidean "Theme" and "Rheme". The Rheme is further distinguished as *Rheme* or *rheme*, according to the type of its boundary, a distinction which reflects its status as an intonational or intermediate phrase. The reader may wonder at this point why we do not replace the category *Theme* by a functional category, say *Utterance/Rheme*, corresponding to its semantic type. The answer is that we do not want this category to combine with anything but a *complete* rheme. In particular, it must not combine with a function into the category *Rheme* by functional composition. Accordingly we give it a non-functional category, and supply the following special purpose prosodic combinatory rules:[11]

(20)   *Theme Rheme* $\Rightarrow$ *Utterance*
         rheme Theme $\Rightarrow$ *Utterance*

We next define the various boundary tones as arguments to these functions, as follows:

(21)   LH% := *Bh*
         LL% := *Bl*
         L   := *bl*

Finally, we accomplish the effect of interpolation of other parts of the tune by assigning the following polymorphic category to all elements bearing no tone specification, which we will represent as the tone $\varnothing$:

(22) $\varnothing := X/X$

Syntactic combination can then be made subject to the following simple restriction:

(23)   *The Prosodic Constituent Condition:* Combination of two syntactic categories via a syntactic combinatory rule is only allowed if their prosodic categories can *also* combine.

(The prosodic and syntactic combinatory rules need not be the same.)

This principle has the sole effect of excluding certain derivations for spoken utterances that would be allowed for the equivalent written sentences. For example, consider the derivations that it permits for example (18) above. The rule of forward composition is allowed to apply to the words *Mary* and *ate*, because the prosodic categories can combine (by functional application):

---

[11]This pair of rules is a rather crude simplification for the sake of brevity of the account in Steedman 1991a as revised in 1991b.

(24)

Mary	prefers	. . .
L+H*	LH%	

$$NP : mary'$$
$$Theme/Bh$$

$$(S\backslash NP)/NP : prefer'$$
$$Bh$$

---------------->T

$$S/(S\backslash NP) : \lambda P[P\ mary']$$
$$Theme/Bh$$

--->B

$$S/NP : \lambda X[(prefer'\ X)\ mary']$$
$$Theme$$

The category X/X of the null tone allows intonational phrasal tunes like L+H* LH% tune to spread across any sequence that forms a grammatical constituent according to the combinatory grammar. For example, if the reply to the same question *What does Mary prefer?* is *MARY says she prefers CORduroy,* then the tune will typically be spread over *Mary says she prefers . . .* as in the following (incomplete) derivation, in which much of the syntactic and semantic detail has been omitted in the interest of brevity:

(25)

Mary	says	she	prefers	. . .
L+H*			LH%	

------------>T --------- ------------>T ---------

$$S/(S\backslash NP)$$ $$(S\backslash NP)/S$$ $$S/(S\backslash NP)$$ $$(S\backslash NP)/NP$$
$$Theme/Bh$$ $$X/X$$ $$X/X$$ $$Bh$$

------------------------------>B

$$Theme/Bh$$

--->B

$$Theme/Bh$$

--->B

$$Theme$$

The rest of the derivation of (18) is completed as follows, using the first rule in example (20):

(26)

Mary	prefers	corduroy	
L+H*	LH%	H*	LL%

$$NP : mary'$$
$$Theme/Bh$$

$$(S\backslash NP)/NP : prefer'$$
$$Bh$$

$$NP : corduroy'$$
$$Rheme$$

---------------->T

$$S/(S\backslash N)P) : \lambda P[P\ mary']$$
$$Theme/Bh$$

----------------------------------->B

$S/NP : \lambda X[(prefer' \ X) \ mary']$
Theme

$$\underline{\hspace{8cm}} >$$

$S: prefer' \ corduroy' \ mary'$
Utterance

The division of the utterance into an open proposition constituting the theme and an argument constituting the rheme is appropriate to the context established in (18). Moreover, the theory permits no *other* derivation for this intonation contour. Of course, repeated application of the composition rule, as in (25), would allow the L+H* LH% contour to spread further, as in (*MARY says she prefers*)(*CORduroy*.

In contrast, the parallel derivation is forbidden by the prosodic constituent condition for the alternative intonation contour on (17). Instead, the following derivation, excluded for the previous example, is now allowed:

(27)

Mary	prefers	corduroy
H* L		L+H* LH%

$NP : mary'$	$(S \backslash NP)/NP : prefer'$	$NP : corduroy'$
Rheme	X/X	*Theme*

$\underline{\hspace{3cm}} > T$ $\underline{\hspace{6cm}} >$

$S/(S \backslash NP):$
$\lambda P[P \ mary']$
Theme

$S \backslash NP : prefer' \ corduroy'$
Theme

$$\underline{\hspace{9cm}} >$$

$S: prefer' \ corduroy' \ mary'$
Utterance

No other analysis is allowed for (27). Again, the derivation divides the sentence into new and given information consistent with the context given in the example. The effect of the derivation is to annotate the entire predicate as an L+H* LH%. It is emphasized that this does *not* mean that the *tone* is spread, but that the whole constituent is marked for the corresponding discourse function – roughly, as contrastive given, or theme. The finer grain information that it is the object that is contrasted, whereas the verb is given, resides in the tree itself. Similarly, the fact that boundary sequences are associated with words at the lowest level of the derivation does not mean that they are *part of* the word, or specified in the lexicon, nor that the word is the entity that they are a boundary *of*. It is prosodic phrases that they bound, and these also are defined by the tree.

All the other possibilities for combining these two contours in a simple sentence are shown elsewhere (Steedman, 1991) to yield similarly unique and contextually appropriate interpretations.

Sentences like the above, including marked theme and rheme expressed as two distinct intonational/intermediate phrases are by that token unambiguous as to their information structure. However, sentences like the following, which in Pierrehumbert's terms bear a single intonational phrase, are much more ambiguous as to the division that they convey between theme and rheme:

(28)   (I read a book about CORduroy)
                    H* LL%

Such a sentence is notoriously ambiguous as to the open proposition it presupposes, for it seems equally appropriate as a response to any of the following questions:

(29)   a. What did you read a book about?
        b. What did you read?
        c. What did you do?

Such questions could in suitably contrastive contexts give rise to themes marked by the L+H* LH% tune, bracketing the sentence as follows:

(30)   a. (I read a book about)(CORduroy)
        b. (I read)(a book about CORduroy)
        c. (I)(read a book about CORduroy)

It seems that we shall miss a generalization concerning the relation of intonation to discourse information unless we extend Pierrehumbert's theory very slightly, to allow prosodic constituents resembling *null* intermediate phrases, without pitch accents, expressing unmarked themes. Because the boundaries of such intermediate phrases are not explicitly marked, we shall immediately allow all of the above analyses for (28). Such a modification to the theory can be introduced by the following rule, which non-deterministically allows constituents bearing the null tone to become a theme:

(31) $X/X \Rightarrow Theme$

The rule is non-deterministic, so it correctly continues to allow a further analysis of the entire sentence as a single Intonational Phrase conveying the Rheme. Such an utterance is the appropriate response to yet another open-proposition establishing question, *What happened?*

The following observation is worth noting at this point, with respect to the parsing problem for CCG (see the section below). The above rule introduces non-determinism into the intonational grammar, just when it looked as though intonation acted to eliminate non-determinism from the syntax. However, the null tone is used precisely when the theme is entirely mutually known, and established in the context. It follows that this nondeterminism *only arises when the hearer can be assumed to be able to resolve it on the basis of discourse context*. This observation is in line with the results of Altmann and Steedman (1988), which suggest that the resolution of non-determinism by reference to discourse context is an important factor in human parsing for both written and spoken language, a matter to which we return in the second part of the chapter.

With the generalization implicit in the above rule, we are now in a position to make the following claim:

(32)   The structures demanded by the theory of intonation and its relation to contextual information are the same as the surface syntactic structures permitted by the combinatory grammar.

Because constructions like relativization and coordination are more limited in the derivations they require, often forcing composition, rather than permitting it, a number of corollaries follow, such as the following:

(33)   Anything that can coordinate can be an intonational constituent, and *vice versa.*

and

(34)   Anything that can be the residue of relativization can be an intonational constituent.

These claims are discussed further in Steedman (1991b).

8.3   Applications to speech processing

Under the present theory, the pathway between the speech wave and the sort of logical form that can be used to interrogate a database is as in Figure 8.1. Such an architecture is considerably simpler than the one that is implicit in the standard theories. Phonetic form now maps via the rules of combinatory grammar directly onto a surface structure, whose highest level constituents correspond to intonational constituents, annotated as to their discourse function. Surface structure is therefore identical to intonational structure. It also subsumes information structure, since the translations of those surface constituents correspond to the entities and open propositions that constitute the topic or theme (if any) and the comment or rheme. These in turn reduce via functional application to yield canonical function-argument structure, or "logical form".[12] There are a number of obvious potential advantages for the automatic synthesis and recognition of spoken language in such a theory, and perhaps it is not too early to speculate a little on how they might be realized.

8.3.1   Intonation and the analysis of spoken language

The most important potential application for the theory lies in the area of speech recognition. Whereas in the past parsing and phonological processing have tend-

---

[12]This term is used loosely. We have said nothing here about how questions of quantifier scope are to be handled, and we assume that they are derived from this representation at a deeper level still.

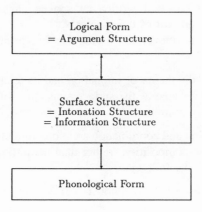

Figure 8.1. Architecture of a CCG-based prosody.

ed to deliver conflicting phrase-structural analyses, and have had to be pursued independently, they now are seen to be in concert. The theory therefore offers the possibility that simply structured modular processors that use both sources of information at once will one day be more easily devised. That is not of course to say that intonational cues remove all local structural ambiguity. Nor is it to underestimate the other huge problems that must be solved before this potential can be realized. But such an architecture may reasonably be expected to simplify the problem of resolving local structural ambiguity in both domains, for the following reason.

First, why is practical speech recognition hard? There seem to be two reasons. One is that the discrete segmental or word-level representations that provide the input to processes of comprehension are realized in the speech wave as the result of a highly non-linear physical system in the form of the vocal tract and its muscular control. This system has many of the computational characteristics of a "relaxation" process of the kind discussed by (for example) Hinton (1984), in which a number of autonomous but interacting parallel motor processes combine by an interactive approximating procedure to achieve a cooperative result. (In Hinton's paper, this kind of algorithm is used to control reaching by a jointed robot.) In the speech domain, this sort of system, in which the articulators act in concert to produce the segments, the result is the phenomenon of "coarticulation", which causes the realization of any given ideal segment to depend upon the neighboring segments in very complex ways. It is very hard to invert the process, and to work backward from the resulting speech-wave to the underlying abstract segments that are relevant to higher levels of analysis.

For this reason, the problem of automatically recognizing such intonational cues as pitch accents and boundary tones should not be underestimated. The acoustic realization in the fundamental frequency F_0 of the intonational tunes discussed above is entirely dependent upon the rest of the phonology – that is, upon the phonemes and words that bear the tune. In particular: the realization of boundary tones and pitch accents is heavily dependent on segmental effects, so that the former can be confounded with the latter. Moreover F_0 itself may be locally undefined, due to non-linearities and chaotic effects in the vocal tract.[13] (For example, the realization of the tune H* LL% on the two words "TitiCAca" and "CineRAma" is dramatically different.) It therefore seems most unlikely that intonational contour can be identified in isolation from word recognition. The converse also applies: intonation contour affects the acoustic realization of words, particularly with respect to timing. It is therefore likely that the benefits of combining intonational recognition and word recognition will eventually be mutual, and will extend the benefits that already accrue to stochastic techniques for word recognition (cf. Jelinek, 1976; Lee, 1989, 1990). As Pierrehumbert has pointed out, part of their success stems from the way in which Hidden Markov Models represent a combination of prosodic and segmental information.

However, such techniques alone may well not be enough to support practical general purpose speech recognition, because of a second source of difficulty in speech recognition. Acoustic information seems to be exceedingly under-specified with respect to the segments. As a result, the output of phonetic- or word-recognition processes is genuinely ambiguous, and characterized by numerous acoustically plausible but spurious alternative candidates. This is probably not just an artifact of the current speech recognition algorithms. It is very likely that the best we shall be able to do with low-level analysis alone on the waveform corresponding to a phrase like "recognize speech", even taking account of coarticulation with intonation, will be to produce a table of candidates that might be orthographically represented as follows. (The example is made up, and is adapted from Henry Thompson. But I think it is a fair representation):

(35) wreck# a# nice# beach
      recognize # speech
      wreck# on# ice# beach
      wreck# an# eyes# peach
      recondite's # beach
      recondite # speech
      reckon# nice# speech
      . . .

– and these are only the candidates that constitute lexical words.

Such massive ambiguity is likely to swamp completely higher-level processing unless it can be rapidly eliminated. It seems likely that the way that this is done is by "filtering" the low-level candidates on the grounds of coherence at higher

---

[13]Although smoothing algorithms go some way toward mitigating the latter effects, they are not completely effective.

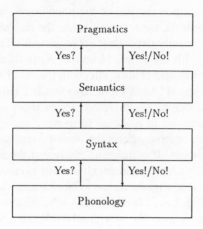

Figure 8.2. Architecture of a weakly interactive processor.

levels of analysis, such as syntactic and semantic levels. This is the mechanism of "weak" or selective interaction between modules proposed in Crain and Steedman (1985) and Altmann and Steedman (1988), according to which the higher level is confined to sending "interrupts" to lower-level processes, causing them to be abandoned or suspended, but cannot otherwise affect the autonomy of the lower level. They and Fodor (1983) contrast such models with the "strong" interaction, which compromises modularity by allowing higher levels to direct the inner workings of the lower, affecting the actual analyses that get proposed in the first place.

Thus one might expect that syntactic well-formedness could be used to select among the word candidates, in much the same way that we assumed above that the lexicon would be used to reject incoherent strings of phonemes. However, inspection of the example suggests that syntax alone may not be much help, for all of the above word strings are syntactically coherent. (The example is artificial, but it is typical in this respect.) It is only at the level of semantics that many of them can be ruled out, and only at the level of pragmatics that in a context like the present discussion all but one can be excluded as incoherent.

However, non-determinism at low levels of analysis must be eliminated quickly, or it will swamp the processor at that level. It follows that we would like to begin this filtering process as early as possible, and therefore need to "cascade" processors at the different levels, so that the filtering process can begin while the analysis is still in progress. Because we have noted that syntax alone is not going to do much for us, we need semantics and pragmatics to kick in at an early stage, too. The resultant architecture can be viewed as in Figure 8.2.

Since the late 1970s, in work by such researchers as Carroll et al. (1978), Marslen-Wilson et al. (1978), Tanenhaus (1978), and Swinney (1979), an increasing number of studies have shown that some such architecture is in fact at work, and in Altmann and Steedman (1988) and Crain and Steedman (1985), it is suggested that the weak interaction bears the major responsibility for resolving nondeterminism in syntactic processing. However, for such a mechanism to work, all levels must be *monotonically* related – that is, rules must be essentially declarative and unordered, if partial information at a low level is to be usable at a higher level.

The present theory has all of the requisite properties. Not only is syntactic structure closely related to the structure of the speech signal, and therefore easier to use to "filter" the ambiguities arising from lexical recognition, but more important, the constituents that arise under this analysis are also semantically interpreted. These interpretations have been shown above to be directly related to the concepts, referents, and themes that have been established in the context of discourse, say as the result of a question. These discourse entities are in turn directly reducible to the structures involved in knowledge representation and inference. The direct path from speech to these higher levels of analysis offered by the present theory should therefore make it possible to use more effectively the much more powerful resources of semantics and domain-specific knowledge, including knowledge of the discourse, to filter low-level ambiguities, using larger grammars of a more expressive class than is currently possible. Although vast improvements in purely bottom-up word recognition can be expected to continue, such filtering is likely to remain crucial to successful speech processing by machine, and appears to be characteristic of all levels of human processing, for both spoken and written language.

However, to realize the potential of the present theory for the domain of analysis requires a considerable further amount of basic research into significant extensions of available techniques at many levels other than syntax, including the phonological level and the level of Knowledge Representation, related to pragmatics. It will be a long project.

8.3.2   Discourse-model-driven synthesis of intonation

A more immediate return can be expected from the present theory in the form of significant improvements in both acceptability and intelligibility over the fixed or default intonation contours that are assigned by text-to-speech programs like MITalk and its commercial offspring (Allen et al., 1987). One of the main shortcomings of current text-to-speech synthesis programs is their inability to vary intonation contour dependent upon context. Although considerable ingenuity has been devoted to minimizing the undesirable effects, via algorithms with some degree of sensitivity to syntax, and the generation of general-purpose default intonations, this shortcoming is really an inevitable concomitant of the text-to-speech task itself. In fact, a truly general solution to the problem of assigning intonation to unconstrained text is nothing less than a solution to the entire problem of understanding written Natural Language. We therefore propose the more circumscribed goal of generating intonation from a known discourse model in a constrained and well-understood domain, such as inventory management, or travel planning.[14]

The inability to vary intonation appropriately affects more than the mere aesthetic qualities of synthetic speech. On occasion, it affects intelligibility as well. Consider the following example, from an inventory management task:

Example. The context is as follows: *A storekeeper carries a number of items including Widgets and Wodgets. The storekeeper and his customer are aware that Widgets and Wodgets are two different kinds of advanced pencil sharpener, and that the 286 and 386 processors are both suitable for use in such devices. The latter is of course a faster processor, but it will emerge that the customer is unaware of this fact.* The following conversation ensues:[15]

(36)   Q1: Do you carry PENCIL sharpeners?
                         L*   LH%
         A1: We carry WIDgets, and WODgets.
                  H*   H   H* LL%

For storekeepers to be asked to answer questions about the stock that they carry is expected by both parties, so both utterances have an unmarked theme $\lambda X \ carry'$ $X \ storekeeper'$, signaled by null tone on the relevant substring. The question includes a marked rheme, concerning pencil sharpeners. The response also includes a marked rheme, concerning specific varieties of this device. The dialogue continues:

(37)   Q2: Which pencil sharpener has a THREE-eight-six PROcessor?
                  H*   H*   LH%   H*   H* LL%
         A2: WODGets have a THREE-eight-six PROcessor
                  H*   L   L+H*   L+H* LH%
         Q3: WHAT PROcessor do WIDgets have?
                  H*   H* LH%   H*   LL%
         A3: WIDGets have a TWO-eight-six processor.
                  L+H*   LH% H*   LL%

[14]The proposal to drive intonation from context or the model is of course not a new one. Work in the area includes an early study by Young and Fallside (1979) and more recent studies by Houghton, Isard, and Pearson (cf. Houghton, 1986; Houghton and Isard, 1987; Houghton and Pearson, 1988; Isard and Pearson, 1988), and by Davis and Hirschberg (cf. [1988]) on synthesis of intonation in context, and by Yoshimara Sagisaka (1990), although the representations of information structure and its relation to syntax that these authors use are quite different from those we propose. The work of 'tHart et al. at IPO ('tHart and Cohen, 1973; 'tHart and Collier, 1975; Terken, 1984) and that implicit in the MITalk algorithm itself (O'Shaughnessy, 1977; Allen et al., 1987) do not make explicit reference to information structure, and are more indirectly relevant.

[15]Once again, we use Pierrehumbert's notation to make the tune explicit. However, the contours we have in mind should be obvious from the context alone and the use of capitals to indicate stress.

The two responses A2 and A3 are almost identical, as far as lexical items and traditional surface structure go. However, the context has changed in between, and the intonation should change accordingly, if the sentence is to be easily understood. In the first case, answer A2, the theme, which might be written $\lambda X[(have'386')X]$, has been established by the previous Wh-question Q2. This theme is in contrast to the previous one (which concerned varieties of pencil sharpeners), and is therefore intonationally marked.[16] (Only a part of the theme was emphasized in Q2, so the same is true in A3.) However, the next Wh-question Q3 establishes a new theme, roughly, $\lambda X[(have'X)widget']$. Because it is again different than the previous theme, it is again marked with the tune L+H* LH%.[17]

It is important to observe that comprehension would be seriously impeded if the two intonational tunes were exchanged.

The dialogue continues with the following exchange (recall that Wodgets are the device with the faster processor):[18]

(38)   Q4: Are WODgets FASter than Widgets?
    H*   H*   LH%
  A4: The three-eight-SIX machine is ALways faster.
      L+H* LH% H*   LL%

The expression "the three-eight-six machine" refers to the Wodget, because of contextually available information. Accordingly, it is marked as such by the L+H* LH% tune, and the predicate is marked as rheme. The answer therefore amounts to a positive answer to the question. It simultaneously conveys the *reason* for the answer. (To expect that a question-answering program for a real database could exhibit such cooperative and conversationally adept responses is not unreasonable – see papers in Joshi et al., 1981, and Appelt, 1985 – although it may go beyond the capability of the system we shall develop for present purposes.)

Contrast the above continuation with the following, in which a similarly cooperative response is negative:

(39)   Q4': Are WIDgets FASter than Wodgets?
    H*   H*   LH%
  A4': The three-eight-SIX machine is always FASter
      H*   L   L+H* LH%

The expression *the three-eight-six machine* refers again to Wodgets, but this time

---

[16]An unmarked theme bearing the null tone seems equally appropriate. However, it is as easy (and much safer) for the generator to err on the side of over-specificity.

[17]Again, an unmarked theme with null tone would be a possible (but less cooperative) alternative. However, the position of the pitch-accent would remain unchanged.

[18]The example is adapted to the present domain from a related example discussed by Pierrehumbert and Hirschberg (1987).

it does *not* correspond to the theme established by Q4′. Accordingly, an H* pitch accent is used to mark it as part of the rheme, *not* part of the theme established by Q4′. Note that A4 and A4′ are identical strings, but that exchanging their intonation contours would again result in both cases in infelicity, caused by the failure of the presupposition that Widgets are a three-eight-six-based machine. In this case, any given default intonation, say one having an unmarked theme and final H*LL%, will force one of the two readings, and will therefore mislead the hearer.

How might such a system be brought into being? The analysis of spoken language is, as we have seen, a problem in it own right, to which we briefly return below. But within the present framework one can readily imagine a query system that processes either written or spoken language concerning some simple and widely studied domain, such as the "inventory management" domain illustrated above, the "travel agent" domain that has been studied in a number of recent projects, or the "route-finding" domain used by Davis and Hirschberg (1988), to yield analyses of the present kind, related to the information structure of the query. Such domains are quite adequate to motivate the distinctions of information structure that are of interest here, and could readily be extended to include aspects of the "intelligent user-manual" paradigm, as in the last example. Quite modest extensions to incorporate open propositions as individuals in the model would provide opportunities to use intonation contours whose discourse function is the correction of misconceptions, without enlarging the knowledge representation problem unduly.

Analyzing queries. Such a query system would parse and interpret the questions according to a combinatory grammar, to produce interpretations including a representation of information structure, including distinctions of theme, rheme, and focus, associated with interpretations such as open propositions and arguments, as well as a traditional function-argument structure. For example, the parser might deliver something like the following analysis for question Q3 above, *What processor do Widgets have?*:[19]

(40)   Function/Argument-Structure $= \lambda X[(processor'X)\&((have'X)widget')]$
        Theme $= S/(S/NP): \lambda Pred[\lambda X[(processor'X)\&(Pred\ X)]]$
        Rheme $= S/NP: \lambda X[((have'X)widget')]$

Such a representation could be used in two ways. First, it could be used to update a discourse model by establishing the corresponding discourse entities in the model. Second, it could be used to derive an answer to the question, the function-argument structure being used to interrogate a simple relational

---

[19]The example is based on the output of a prototype parser written in Prolog using a simplified Montague-style semantics. Interpretations again appear to the right of syntactic categories, separated by a colon. Again the use of the lambda calculus is a notational convenience. The system itself uses a different unification-based representation for categories and their interpretations, following Steedman (1990), and uses combinators as applicative primitives.

database of facts to yield an answer, perhaps looking something like the following:

(41)   Function/Argument-Structure = (*processor'*386')&((*have'*386')
         widget')

The discourse representation and this answer to the database query could then be used to generate entirely from scratch a representation of a response, including a representation of its information structure, the latter including all distinctions of theme and focus that are relevant to specifying its intonation contour, as follows.

Generating responses. It seems reasonable to assume initially (no doubt oversimplifying with respect to real human generators of utterances) that the discourse representation and the query between them deterministically specify the response, and that no backtracking or replanning of the utterance of the complex kinds discussed by McDonald (1983) will be involved. In particular, it seems reasonable initially to assume that *the Rheme of the original question determines the Theme of the answer,* so that some structure such as the following can be used as the input to a generator:

(42)   utterance(theme(S/NP: $\lambda X[((have'X)widget')]$), rheme (NP:386'))

This structure will then be used to determine by rule a complete specification of the phonological form of the corresponding string, including all details of pitch and timing, in a form suitable for input to the speech synthesizer itself.

The question of whether entities like *widget* and *386processor* should be expressed in the form of NPs like "Widgets" and "the 386 processor", or as pronouns, or as more complex NPs, is of course also determined by discourse context. The much fuller discourse representations envisaged in the present system could also be exploited to make these finer "tactical" decisions as well (Thompson, 1977; McDonald, 1983; Dale, 1989). Promising candidates for attention in this regard are cleft constructions, ellipses, and the coordinate constructions, all of which provided the original motivation for combinatory grammars (see Section 8.2.2 above), and all of which are strongly constrained by discourse information and by intonation. They would be required for examples like the following, in the inventory management domain:

(43)   Q: Do Widgets have a 386 processor?

         A: It is Wodgets that have a 386 processor.

(44)   Q: Do both pencil sharpeners include a serial port?

         A: Widgets do, and Wodgets do not, include a RS232 interface.

(45)   Q: What processor do Widgets and Wodgets have?

         A: Widgets have a 286 processor, and Wodgets, a 386 processor.

A further promising area for investigation lies in the interaction of intonation with "focusing operators" like *only* and *even,* and with semantic notions of scope, as evinced in examples like the following (cf. Rooth, 1985; von Stechow, 1989):

(46)   Q: Do all pencil sharpeners have a serial port?

A: Only Widgets have a serial port.

The rules for specifying phonological form, including pitch and timing, remain to be specified within the CCG framework, and are a subject for further research. One set of techniques that could be used in at least a preliminary application, and which fall short of full synthesis-by-rule, are to be found in the literature of Concatenative text-to-speech Synthesis using Linear Projective Coding, and other techniques (cf. Olive and Nakatani, 1974; Fallside and Young, 1978; Markel and Gray, 1976; Rabiner and Schafer, 1976; Allen, 1976; Hamon et al., 1989; Charpentier and Moulines, 1989).

References

Allen, Jonathan. (1976). 'Short-term Spectral Analysis, Synthesis, and Modification by Discrete Fourier Transform', *Proceedings of the International Conference on Acoustics, Speech, and Signal Processing,* 25, pp. 235–238.

Allen, Jonathan, Sharon Hunnicutt, and Dennis Klatt. (1987). *From Text to Speech: the MITalk System,* Cambridge University Press.

Altmann, Gerry and Mark Steedman. (1988). 'Interaction with Context During Human Sentence Processing', *Cognition,* 30, 191–238.

Anderson, M., J. Pierrehumbert, M. Liberman. (1984). 'Synthesis by Rule of English Intonation Patterns,' *Proceedings of the International Conference on Acoustics, Speech, and Signal Processing, 1984.*

Appelt, Doug. (1985). 'Planning English Referring Expressions', *Artificial Intelligence,* 26, 1–33.

Beckman, Mary and Janet Pierrehumbert. (1986). 'Intonational Structure in Japanese and English', *Phonology Yearbook,* 3, 255–310.

Bolinger, Dwight. (1972). 'Accent is Predictable (If You're a Mind Reader)', *Language,* 48, 633–644.

Brown, Gillian and George Yule. (1983). *Discourse Analysis,* Cambridge University Press.

Carroll, J. and Tom Bever. (1978). 'The Perception of Relations', in William J. M. Levelt and Giovanni Flores d'Arcais (eds.), *Studies in the Perception of Language,* Wiley, New York, NY.

Charpentier, F. and E. Moulines. (1989). 'Pitch-synchronous Waveform Processing Techniques for Text-to-speech Synthesis Using Diphones,' Proceedings EUROSPEECH89, vol. 2, pp. 13–19.

Chomsky, Noam. (1970). 'Deep Structure, Surface Structure, and Semantic Interpretation', in D. Steinberg and L. Jakobovits, *Semantics,* Cambridge University Press, 1971, 183–216.

Cooper, William and Julia Paccia-Cooper. (1980). *Syntax and Speech,* Harvard University Press, Cambridge, MA.

Crain, Stephen and Mark Steedman. (1985). 'On Not Being Led up the Garden Path: The Use of Context by the Psychological Parser', in D. Dowty, L. Kartunnen, and A. Zwicky, (eds.), *Natural Language Parsing: Psychological, Computational and Theoretical Perspectives*, ACL Studies in Natural Language Processing, Cambridge University Press, 320–358.

Curry, Haskell and Robert Feys. (1958). *Combinatory Logic*, North Holland, Amsterdam.

Cutler, Anne, and Stephen Isard. (1980). 'The Production of Prosody', in Brian Butterworth, (ed.), *Language Production, Vol. 1*, New York, Wiley, 246–269.

Dale, Robert. (1989). 'Cooking up Referring Expressions', *Proceedings of the 27th Annual Conference of the ACL*, Vancouver, 68–75.

Davis, James and Julia Hirschberg. (1988). 'Assigning Intonational Features in Synthesised Spoken Directions', *Proceedings of the 26th Annual Conference of the ACL*, Buffalo, 187–193.

Dowty, David. (1988). 'Type Raising, Functional Composition, and Non-constituent Coordination,' in Richard T. Oehrle, E. Bach, and D. Wheeler, (eds.), *Categorial Grammars and Natural Language Structures*, Reidel, Dordrecht, 153–198.

Fallside, Frank and S. J. Young. (1978). 'Speech Output from a Computer-controlled Water-supply Network', *Proc. IEEE*, 125, 157–161.

Fodor, Gerry. (1983). *The Modularity of Mind*, MIT Press, Cambridge, MA.

Grosz, Barbara, Aravind Joshi, and Scott Weinstein. (1983). 'Providing a Unified Account of Definite Noun Phrases in Discourse', *Proceedings of the 21st Annual Conference of the ACL*, Cambridge, MA, 44–50.

Gussenhoven, Carlos. (1983). *On the Grammar and Semantics of Sentence Accent*, Dordrecht, Foris.

Halliday, Michael. (1967). *Intonation and Grammar in British English*, Mouton, The Hague.

Hamon, C. et al. (1989). 'A Diphone Synthesis System Based on Time-domain Prosodic Modifications of Speech,' ICASSP89, 238–241.

't Hart, J. and A. Cohen. (1973). 'Intonation by Rule: a Perceptual Quest', *Journal of Phonetics*, 1, 309–327.

't Hart, J. and R. Collier. (1975). 'Integrating Different Levels of Phonetic Analysis,' *Journal of Phonetics*, 3, 235–255.

Hinton, Geoffrey. (1984). 'Parallel Computation for Controlling an Arm', *Journal of Motor Behaviour*, 16, 171–194.

Houghton, George. (1986). *The Production of Language in Dialogue: a Computational Model*, unpublished Ph.D. dissertation, University of Sussex.

Houghton, George and Stephen Isard. (1987). 'Why to Speak, What to Say, and How to Say It', in P. Morris (ed.), *Modelling Cognition*, Wiley.

Houghton, George and M. Pearson. (1988). 'The Production of Spoken Dialogue,' in M. Zock and G. Sabah (eds.), *Advances in Natural Language Generation: An Interdisciplinary Perspective, Vol. 1*, Pinter Publishers, London.

Isard, Stephen and M. Pearson. (1988). 'A Repertoire of British English Intonation Contours for Synthetic Speech', *Proceedings of Speech '88, 7th FASE Symposium, Edinburgh, 1988*, pp. 1233–1240.

Jackendoff, Ray. (1972). *Semantic Interpretation in Generative Grammar*, MIT Press, Cambridge, MA.

Jelinek, Fred. (1976). 'Continuous Speech Recognition by Continuous Methods', *Proceedings of Institute of Electrical and Electronic Engineers*, 64, 532–556.

Joshi, Aravind, Bonnie Lynn Webber, and Ivan Sag (Eds.). (1981). *Elements of Discourse Understanding*, Cambridge University Press.

Lee, Kai-Fu. (1989). *Automatic Speech Recognition*, Kluwer, Dordrecht.

Lee, Kai-Fu. (1990). 'Context-dependent Phonetic Hidden Markov Models for Continuous Speech Recognition', *IEEE Transactions on Acoustics Speech and Signal Processing*.

Liberman, Mark and J. Pierrehumbert. (1984). 'Intonational Invariance under Changes in Pitch Range and Length', in M. Aranoff and R. Oehrle, (eds.), *Language Sound Structure: Studies in Phonology Presented to Morris Halle*, MIT Press, Cambridge, MA.

Lyons, John. (1977). *Semantics, Vol. II*, Cambridge University Press.

McDonald, David. (1983). 'Description-directed Control', *Computers and Mathematics*, 9, 111–130.

Markel, John, and Augustine Gray. (1976). *Linear Prediction of Speech*, Springer-Verlag, Berlin.

Marslen-Wilson, William, Lorraine K. Tyler, and Mark Seidenberg. (1978). 'The Semantic Control of Sentence Segmentation', in William J. M. Levelt and Giovanni Flores d'Arcais (eds.), *Studies in the Perception of Language*, Wiley, New York, NY.

Moens, Marc, and M. Steedman. (1987). 'Temporal Ontology and Temporal Reference', *Journal of Computational Linguistics*, 14, 15–28.

Olive, J. P. and L. Nakatani. (1974). 'Rule Synthesis by Word-concatenation: a First Step', *Journal of the Acoustical Society of America*, 55, 660–666.

O'Shaughnessy, D. (1977). 'Fundamental Frequency by Rule for a Text-to-Speech System', *Proceedings of the International Conference on Acoustics, Speech, and Signal Processing*, IEEE Cat. No. 77CH1197-3 ASSP, New York, IEEE, 568–570.

Pareschi, Remo, and Mark Steedman. (1987). 'A lazy way to chart parse with categorial grammars,' *Proceedings of the 25th Annual Conference of the ACL*, Stanford, CA, 81–88.

Pierrehumbert, Janet. (1980). *The Phonology and Phonetics of English Intonation*, Ph.D. dissertation, MIT. (Dist. by Indiana University Linguistics Club, Bloomington, IN.)

Pierrehumbert, Janet and Mary Beckman. (1989). *Japanese Tone Structure*, MIT Press, Cambridge, MA.

Pierrehumbert, Janet and Julia Hirschberg. (1987). 'The Meaning of Intonational Contours in the Interpretation of Discourse', ms., Bell Labs.

Pereira, Fernando and Martha Pollack. (1990). 'Incremental Interpretation', ms., AT&T Bell Labs, Murray Hill, NJ/SRI International, Menlo Park, CA.

Prince, Ellen F. (1986). 'On the Syntactic Marking of Presupposed Open Propositions'. *Papers from the Parasession on Pragmatics and Grammatical Theory at the 22nd Regional Meeting of the Chicago Linguistic Society*, 208–222.

Rabiner, L. and R. Schafer. (1976). 'Digital Techniques for Computer Voice Response: Implementations and Applications', *Proceedings of Institute of Electrical and Electronic Engineers*, 64, 416–433.

Rooth, Mats. (1985). *Association with Focus*, unpublished Ph.D. dissertation, University of Massachusetts, Amherst.

Sagisaka, Yoshinori. (1990). 'On the Prediction of Global F0 Shape for Japanese Text-to-Speech', ICASSP 90, pp. 325–328.

Selkirk, Elisabeth. (1984). *Phonology and Syntax*, MIT Press, Cambridge MA.

von Stechow, Arnim. (1989). 'Focussing and Backgrounding Operators', Fachgruppe Sprachwissenschaft der Universität Konstanz, Arbeitspapier Nr. 6.

Steedman, Mark. (1985a). 'Dependency and Coordination in the Grammar of Dutch and English', *Language*, 61:523–568.

Steedman, Mark. (1987). 'Combinatory Grammars and Parasitic Gaps'. *Natural Language & Linguistic Theory*,' 5, 403–439.

Steedman, Mark. (1990). 'Gapping as Constituent Coordination', *Linguistics & Philosophy*, 13, 207–263.

Steedman, Mark. (1991a). 'Structure and Intonation', *Language*, 67, 260–296.

Steedman, Mark. (1991b). 'Syntax, Intonation, and Focus', in E. Klein and F. Veltmann (eds.), *Natural Language and Speech*, Springer-Verlag, Berlin, 21–38.

Swinney, David. (1979). 'Lexical Access during Sentence Comprehension: (Re)consideration of Context Effects', *Journal of Verbal Learning and Verbal Behaviour*, 18, 645–660.

Tanenhaus, Michael. (1978). *Sentence Context and Sentence Perception*, Ph.D. thesis, Columbia University.

Terken, Jacques. (1984). 'The Distribution of Accents in Instructions as a Function of Discourse Structure', *Language and Speech*, 27, 269–289.

Thompson, Henry. (1977). 'Strategy and Tactics in Language Production', *Proceedings of the 13th Annual Conference of the Chicago Linguistics Society*, Chicago IL.

Vijay-Shankar, K. and David Weir. (1990). 'Polynomial Time Parsing of Combinatory Categorial Grammars', *Proceedings of the 28th Annual Conference of the ACL*, Pittsburgh.

Wittenburg, Kent. (1987). 'Predictive Combinators: a Method for Efficient Processing of Combinatory Grammars', *Proceedings of the 25th Annual Conference of the ACL*, Stanford, CA, 73–80.

Young, S. and F. Fallside. (1979). 'Speech Synthesis from Concept: a Method for Speech Output from Information Systems', *Journal of the Acoustical Society of America*, 66, 685–695.

PART V

Spoken language systems

9 Prosody, intonation, and speech technology

JANET PIERREHUMBERT

9.1 Introduction

The purpose of this chapter is to explore the implications of some facts about prosody and intonation for efforts to create more general and higher quality speech technology. It will emphasize parallels between speech synthesis and speech recognition, because I believe that the challenges presented in these two areas exhibit strong similarities and that the best progress will be made by working on both together.

In the area of synthesis, there are now text-to-speech systems that are useful in many practical applications, especially ones in which the users are experienced and motivated. In order to have more general and higher quality synthesis technology it will be desirable (1) to improve the phonetic quality of synthetic speech to the point where it is as easily comprehended as natural speech and where it is fully acceptable to naive or unmotivated listeners, (2) to use expressive variation appropriately to convey the structure and relative importance of information in complex materials, and (3) to model the speech of people of different ages, sexes, and dialects in order to support applications requiring use of multiple voices.

Engineers working on recognition have a long-standing goal of building systems that can handle large-vocabulary continuous speech. To be useful, such systems must be either speaker-independent or speaker-dependent; if speaker-dependent, engineers must be trained using a sample of speech that can feasibly be collected and analyzed. Present systems exhibit a strong trade-off between degree of speaker independence on the one hand and the size of the vocabulary and branching factor in the grammar on the other. As the vocabulary size increases, the extent of the acoustic differences between words decreases, on the average, and it becomes more likely that productions of different words by different speakers will be confused with each other. Similarly, the more words that are grammatically possible at any particular point in the sentence, the greater the risk of confusion. Even speaker-dependent systems are far from the desired level of generality. In addition, systems will need a vastly enhanced ability to recover and manipulate semantic and pragmatic information. In understanding

I would like to thank Alex Waibel and Stephen Levinson for stimulating discussions concerning the capabilities of HMM recognizers.

the speech of other people, we make many leaps of inference, as in the following examples:

1. I'm parked on 52nd St. (I == my car)
2. Can you tell me who is authorized to sign a PO? [= Please tell me . . .]

It is widely acknowledged that systems that cannot make such inferences will strike users as maddeningly literal-minded in all but the simplest exchanges.

In view of these goals, I would like to highlight two strategic problems presented by prosody and intonation as they function in speech. The first is the challenge that the allophonic effects of prosody and intonation present for training procedures. These are the procedures whereby a representative sample of utterances is collected and analyzed in order to construct a statistically optimal model of all the utterances that a speech system will handle. The second is the problem of formalizing what prosody and intonation mean. It is clear that human listeners can use prosody and intonation to make inferences about a speaker's goals and attitudes, and can use these inferences to make their own conversational contributions appropriate and useful. Machines will not be able to do this until a more explicit theory of the meaning of prosody and intonation is discovered.

Section 9.2 discusses training procedures in relation to both synthesis and recognition. It will summarize the present state of theory in the representation of prosody and intonation, and provide examples of allophonic effects that would pose a problem for present training procedures. Section 9.3 will turn to the issue of intonational and prosodic meaning.

9.2   Prosody, intonation, and allophony

9.2.1   Training procedures and why they are an issue

The success of Hidden Markov Models (HMMs) in speech recognition demonstrates the power of effective training procedures. HMMs use a transition network (or a hierarchy of such networks) to describe the utterances they can recognize. An introduction to the method is provided in Rabiner and Juang (1986). Jelinek (1985) discusses how it has been applied in a 5,000-word vocabulary recognition system at IBM. Levinson (1985) develops the mathematical relationship between HMMs, template matching, and stochastic parsing.

As Levinson points out, some linguistic regularities, such as coarticulation across word boundaries, are systematically omitted by HMMs. Nonetheless, HMMs outperform systems that are based on attempts to implement linguistic theory without using a statistical training method. This fact indicates the power of statistical training. However, the property of HMMs that makes them easy to train – the assumption that transitional probabilities are statistically independent – also limits their ability to capture generalizations. Consider what happens in the vicinity of a single node in the network – for the sake of concreteness, let us say that this node is a spectral section representing the noise burst for /t/. The network can have a single such node if what can follow the burst does not depend on how it was reached. If there is such a dependence, then the network must have more than one /t/ burst node, and must segregate from each other the sequences of transitions that exhibit the dependence.

In fact, however, these dependencies are the norm. The theory of prosodic representation in phonology, as sketched in Section 9.2.2, is based on the finding that different levels of grouping each control both aspects of phonological well-formedness and details of pronunciation. For example, we find effects of syllable structure, word structure, and intonational phrasing. HMMs implicitly model the objective consequences of syllable and word structure by constructing a separate model for each word, as pointed out in Levinson (1985). This is one reason for their success. However, effects that encompass more than one word are not modeled. Any statistically important effects that are not effectively modeled can be expected to degrade the overall performance. Although the tremendous redundancy of some domains (e.g., connected digit recognition) can make this loss of information affordable, systems handling large vocabulary continuous speech will need to exploit the available information as effectively as possible. Furthermore, the implicit treatment of word level prosodic effects does not lead to the same efficiency in representation and training that a more explicit treatment might make possible. For example, a human listener who observed a velar fricative in the word "foggy" would be able to infer that other words with an intervocalic /g/ in a falling stress environment could also be pronounced with a fricative. An HMM system would need to acquire this information for each word separately. For large-scale systems, the ability to make relevant generalizations across the possible variants of different words may prove crucial to efficient training.

It is not widely recognized that training is also a central issue for progress in speech synthesis by rule. The text-to-speech systems we now have reached commercial potential only after many years of work by speech scientists, and companies like AT&T, DEC, and Infovox all have large development teams devoted to improving their speech synthesis and incorporating it into applications. Of course building a system for the first voice is the hardest, and the creation of comparable systems for additional speakers, dialects, or languages is considerably expedited by the lessons learned in developing the first, and by the feasibility of adapting a considerable portion of the software. This fact has indeed been demonstrated both by the multiple voices available for the DEC synthesizer, and by the rule compilers described in Hertz (1982) and Granstrom and Carlson (1986). The Granstrom and Carlson compiler has supported the relatively rapid development of commercial synthesis systems for many languages. Nonetheless, a considerable amount of work in descriptive phonetics is involved in the creation of each new synthetic voice, even at the current state-of-the-art level of quality. The work will be considerably greater as we aim for fully fluent and natural quality. This is the case because voices, dialects, and languages differ from each other in every aspect of the sound structure, not in just some particular such area as the phoneme inventory or the pattern of coarticulation between adjacent phonemes.

Let us consider some examples. As Fourakis and Port (1986) have shown, the detailed timing of the nasal-fricative transition in words like "tense" differs according to dialect; for American speakers the velum closes before the release of the tongue, but not for South Africans. American speakers ordinarily flap the /t/ in words like "butter", but others aspirate. Words such as "aluminum" and "elementary" have different phoneme sequences and stress patterns in British and American speech. The Received Pronunciation, Anglo–Irish, and Scots dialects of English differ in their phrasal intonation (Bolinger, 1989). In Pierrehumbert and Talkin (in press), one subject used a generally breathy voice following the main stress of an utterance, whereas the other used a creaky voice. This difference in overall voice quality in turn had ramifications for the segmental allophony. Pitch range and voice quality are used conventionally by speakers as markers of social identity; Finnish men favor a gravelly voice quality and Russian women in positions of authority use a much higher pitch range than their American counterparts.

Building speech synthesizers that incorporate such differences amounts to creating a comprehensive quantitative model of the sound structure for each voice. This is something that phoneticians have not yet accomplished even once; Klatt's model of his own voice, as incorporated in his synthesis rules, may be considered the most complete such model to date. To achieve this goal, an alternative must be found to carrying out innumerable phonetics experiments, each involving innumerable measurements. In short, it will be necessary to find some way of acquiring quantitative descriptions semiautomatically. This will mean finding ways to use a large sample of speech to set the parameters of a general phonetic and phonological model. Let us now give some idea of what such a model looks like.

9.2.2   Sound structure and its phonetic correlates

A traditional view of sound structure contrasts speech segments with suprasegmentals. The string of segments arises from a sequence of local paradigmatic distinctions (for example, the contrast between "pat" and "bat" or between "pat" and "pad"), is taken to be phonetically expressed in properties of the speech spectrum. All nonlocal distinctions, whether syntagmatic or paradigmatic, are grouped together as suprasegmentals. For example, suprasegmentals are taken to include both stress (which is a syntagmatic feature since it describes the relative strength of syllables) and the paradigmatic distinction between rising and falling phrasal melodies. The phonetic domain of the suprasegmentals is taken to be fundamental frequency (f0), amplitude, and duration.

Although this view is implemented in current text-to-speech systems and underlies proposals for the use of prosody and intonation in speech recognition (Lea, 1980; Waibel, 1988), it is not supported by the results of research in linguistic phonetics. On the one hand, effects of segment type on f0, amplitude, and duration are both substantial and well established (see Lehiste, 1970; Steele, 1985; Silverman, 1987; and literature reviews in these works). On the other hand, prosody and intonation have large effects on the speech spectrum. The effects of syllable structure (the smallest unit of prosodic structure) are particularly well accepted. Randolph (1989) shows position within the syllable to be a stronger statistical predictor of stop allophony than the local phonemic context. In addition, experiments have demonstrated various spectral effects of stress, phrasing, and intonation pattern (Harris, 1978; Monsen, Engebretson, and Vemula 1978; Gobl, 1988; Pierrehumbert, 1990; Pierrehumbert and Talkin [in press]).

Therefore, the view of sound structure that will be adopted here does not contrast segments with suprasegmentals. Instead, it draws a contrast between content and structure. Content, which is taken to cover all paradigmatic distinctions whether local or nonlocal, is phonetically expressed in terms of relative positions along dimensions of articulatory control, and therefore in the corresponding acoustic parameters. Structure covers the grouping and strength of elements of the content. It has an indirect phonetic expression, by influencing the extent and timing of articulatory gestures, and consequently by helping to determine which particular values of acoustic parameters realize each paradigmatic distinction in each particular case.

As an example of "content", consider the contrast between /p/ and /b/. It involves a contrast in laryngeal articulation. Phonetic parameters reflecting this contrast include the spectrum during the stop gap and right after the release, the duration of the voiceless region following the release, and the f0 when the voicing begins. Similarly, the intonational contrast between Low and High tone (L and H) (which is found, among other places, in the difference between a terminal declarative and one with a continuation rise) also involves a contrast in laryngeal articulation. The laryngeal articulation is reflected not only in f0 but also in the source spectrum, and therefore in the speech spectrum.

Intonational phrasing is an example of "structure". That is, an intonation phrase specifies that certain words are grouped together, and that one of these words is the strongest prosodically. The intonation phrase does not in and of itself specify any part of the content. Rather, it provides opportunities to make choices of content. For each intonation phrase, the speaker selects not only the words, but also a phrasal melody. The phonetic manifestations of the various elements of the content depend on their position with respect to the intonational phrasing. It

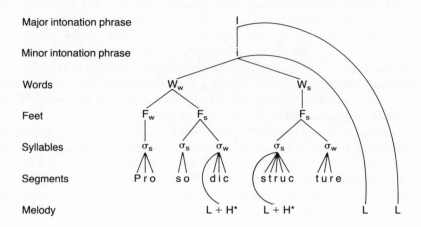

Figure 9.1. A phonological representation for the phrase "Prosodic structure".

is well known that syllables are being lengthened before intonation phrase boundaries. Phrasing affects the actual f0 values achieved for L and H tones; H tones marking phrase boundaries are subject to a different scaling rule than phrase medial H tones (Pierrehumbert, 1980). Pierrehumbert and Talkin (in press) also report that intonational phrasing affects the voice onset time for stops, even when there is no pause at the phrase boundary.

Figure 9.1 illustrates how content and structure are represented in a modern phonological framework. Details of the representational scheme are taken from Pierrehumbert and Beckman (1988). The figure shows the representation for the phrase "Prosodic structure", produced with a particular declarative melody that is often used to present information in a contrastive light. Two streams of content are produced simultaneously: the segments arising from the word choice and the tones comprising the melody. These two streams are coordinated by their links to a hierarchical structure with well-defined levels: the syllable, the foot, the word, and minor phrase, and the major phrase. Many phonological theories advocate more levels, such as a subsyllabic unit of the "mora" (Hyman, 1985; McCarthy and Prince, 1990) or a level of the "Phonological phrase" above the word but below the minor phrase (Selkirk, 1984), but the exact number of levels will not be important here. Each node at a given level dominates one or more nodes of the next lower level; one node within each grouping is singled out as the strongest or most prominent one. For example, each foot begins with a strong syllable. The strongest foot in the word is the one containing the main stress of the word. The timing of the tones with respect to the phoneme string follows from which syllables they are linked to.

The phonetic expression of any particular element of the content depends on what it is, what the neighboring content is, and its relation to the prosodic structure. All levels of prosodic structure, even the highest, are demonstrated experimentally to play a part in controlling details of pronunciation. The discussion here will concentrate on effects of prosodic structure that are both nonlocal and gradient, because these present a strategic problem for future training methods. I view this problem as the central one, because present technology has a certain level of success in handling effects that are gradient but local, or nonlocal but qualitative. Local gradient effects are presently handled by encoding detailed phonetic properties in detailed whole-word models. This method performs well for systems of small to moderate vocabulary size, although it has a poor ability to represent or infer generalizations across words, as discussed above. It also neglects local effects that cross word boundaries. Hierarchically organized networks can handle the type of nonlocal qualitative constraints that arise from, e.g., sentence grammar; see discussion in Jelinek (1985) and Levinson (1985). In this approach, the nodes of one network each represent networks at a lower level. One network may represent possible sentences by specifying which words can follow each other; the word nodes are then expanded into detailed acoustic networks in which each node is a spectral section. Although it has not yet been done, nothing in principle prevents the same approach from being applied to prosodic trees.

However, there is at present no obvious method of combining these two approaches (detailed acoustic models and network layering) to handle nonlocal gradient effects. Hierarchical organization of networks is intrinsically qualitative. On the other hand, whole-phrase templates (that is, statistically adequate acoustic representatives of all possible phrases the system might encounter) would be prohibitively large and numerous for anything but extremely limited systems. Even a system that recognizes telephone numbers will be built on the assumption that telephone numbers can be decomposed down to the word level. Using separate templates for all intonation phrases in telephone numbers (that is, all possible sequences of three to four digits) would mean recording and processing a statistically significant sample of each of more than 10,000 items, and then evaluating these as unrelated alternative candidates during recognition. Such an approach would be out of the question for a domain of moderate complexity, permitting, say, phrases of one to five words constructed over a vocabulary of 1,000 items.

At the same time, it is clear that a general treatment of nonlocal gradient effects would subsume local or qualitative effects as subcases. An approach that handles nonlocal dependencies can view local dependencies as particularly small nonlocal dependencies. Similarly, qualitative effects can be viewed as instances of gradient effects that are restricted to just a few values.

9.2.3   Some nonlocal effects of prosody and intonation

In this section, we discuss three examples in which prosody and intonation affect the pronunciation of speech segments. In the examples, the structure of the whole phrase determines how some particular portion of it is pronounced.

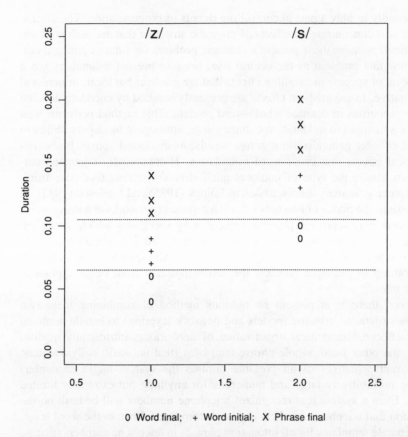

Figure 9.2. Durations of /s/ and /z/ in an illustrative set of utterances from one speaker. The phonemes are found word-initially, word-finally (but not phrase-finally), and phrase-finally.

The first example is based on a small data set that was collected for illustrative purposes. In the data set, produced by a single speaker, the phonemes /s/ and /z/ occurred word-initially, word-finally (but not phrase-finally), and phrase-finally. Figure 9.2 shows the durations of the /s/s and /z/s, with different plotting characters used for the different prosodic contexts. As is evident in the figure, there is a substantial overlap between the /s/ durations and /z/ durations when prosodic position is ignored. However, in each individual position, the /z/s are shorter than the /s/s. This is a typical illustration of the concept of "relational invariance" discussed in Fant (1987). Phonetic properties of phonemes are much better separated statistically when context (including both neighboring content and prosodic position) is taken into account than when it is ignored. Even when context drastically shifts the phonetic realizations of both members of a contrasting pair, the paradigmatic contrast between the two is still usually expressed.

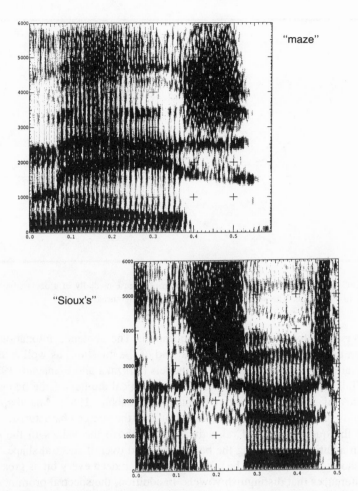

Figure 9.3. Spectrograms for /s/ in "Sioux's" versus phrase-final /z/ in "maze".

A critical phonetician might question whether the duration measurements in Figure 9.2 give a misleading impression by ignoring differences in the spectrum of /s/ and /z/. Figure 9.3, comparing phrase-final /z/ in "maze" with word-initial /s/ in "Sioux's", indicates that spectral characteristics for the two phonemes overlap statistically just as durations do. In particular, in these particular utterances, both fricatives have exactly two pitch periods of voicing, because the /z/ is typically devoiced phrase-finally.

The second example concerns the effects of intonation on vowel spectra. Figure 9.4 displays LPC spectral sections for the schwa in "tuba", spoken by a single speaker in a single recording session, in the middle of a declarative

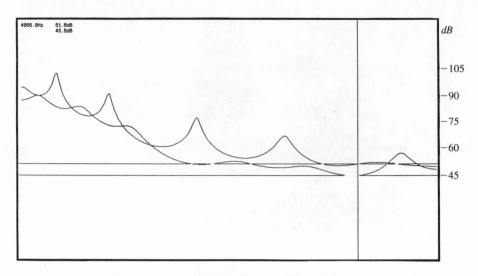

Figure 9.4. LPC spectra for the schwa in "tuba", occurring phrase-medially in a declarative and phrase-finally in a question. The same speaker produced both utterances.

sentence versus at the end of a yes/no question. The sentence intonation is related to an extremely high f0 value at the end of the question, as well as to a soft and breathy voice quality. Laryngeal models (Ishizaka and Flanagan, 1972; Titze and Talkin, 1979) in combination with analytical studies of the acoustic consequences of source variation (Ananthapadmanabha, 1982; Ananthapad-manabha and Fant, 1982) lead to the prediction that the source characteristics at the end of the question should raise the formats above the values in the de-clarative, in addition to affecting the bandwidths and overall spectral shape. As the figure shows, this effect can be quite substantial, indeed every bit as great as formant differences that distinguish vowels. In addition, the spectral prominence of the fundamental in the high breathy voice creates the potential for confusing it with a formant.

The pronunciation of /h/ in continuous speech provides a third example. The data given here are drawn from Pierrehumbert and Talkin (in press). Their experi-mental materials varied the position of /h/ relative to the word prosody (e.g., "hawkweed" vs. "Omaha"), and also the position of the target words relative to the phrasal prosody. In (3), the target word "hawkweed" has the main stress of the sentence, whereas in (4) it follow the main stress that is on the state name because of the constrastive stress.

3.   Is it Oklahoma hawkweed?

4.   It's Alabama hawkweed, not Oklahoma hawkweed.

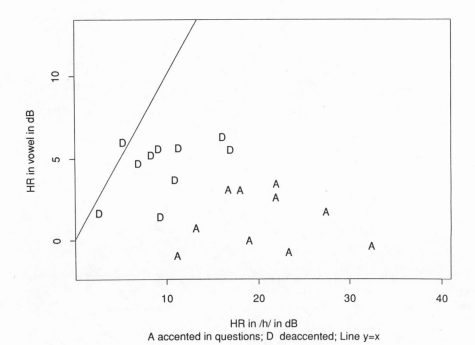

Figure 9.5. HR in "hawkweed" and "hogfarmer," subject DT. Harmonic ratio in /h/ plotted against harmonic ratio in the following vowel, for word-initial /h/. Plotting characters contrast the cases where the target word is accented in a question and where it is deaccented following a focused word.

Note that both (3) and (4) have low tones at the target location. This was an important aspect of the experimental design. By keeping the fundamental frequency below one-third of the first formant value, it was possible to obtain some indications of the source characteristics (or characteristics of the glottal waveform) without inverse filtering, a problematic procedure for breathy sounds.

The measure whose behavior is plotted in Figures 9.5 and 9.6 is the harmonic ratio, defined as the difference on dB between the energy at the fundamental and the energy at the next harmonic. This is an index of the degree of vocal fold spreading, and is expected to be greater for more /h/-like sounds and less for more vocalic sounds. In the figures, the harmonic ratio during /h/ is plotted against the ratio during the following vowel. A diagonal line in each figure represents y = x, or the case in which the vowel and the /h/ have the same value and are accordingly neutralized as seen through this measure. The degree of contrast between the /h/ and the vowel can therefore be related to the perpendicular distance from this line. A line perpendicular to the y = x diagonal is also drawn for reference.

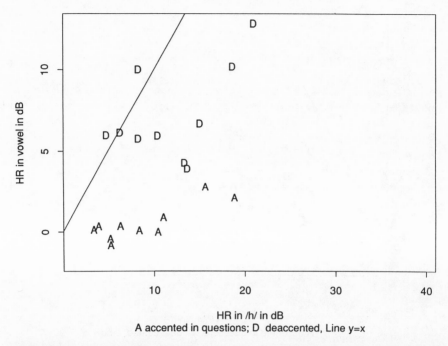

Figure 9.6. HR in "tomahawk" and "Omaha," subject DT. Harmonic ratio in /h/ plotted against harmonic ratio in the following vowel, for word-medial /h/ beginning a syllable without main word stress. Plotting characters contrast the cases where the target word is accented in a question and where it is deaccented following a focused word.

Figure 9.5 shows the outcome for stressed word-initial /h/ ("hawkweed" and "hogfarmer"), contrasting the cases where the word is accented in a question such as (3) and the cases where it is deaccented following a focus, such as (4). The sentence prosody has a major effect on the degree of contrast between the /h/ and the following vowel, with the accented tokens showing the consequences of stronger articulation, especially of the /h/.

Figure 9.6 shows the outcome for word-medial /h/ when it begins a syllable with subordinate stress or no stress ("tomahawk" and "Omaha"). Again, a contrast is found between accented and deaccented words. However, here the main effect of accent is to shift production of both the /h/ and the vowel in a more vocalic direction (toward the lower left corner of the graph), without a substantial effect on the degree of contrast between the /h/ and the vowel.

The comparison of Figures 9.5 and 9.6 shows that word and sentence prosody interact to determine how /h/ is pronounced. The combined data also have a nontrivial amount of overlap, in the range of 0 to 10 dB, between HR values for /h/ and those for vowels. However, the /h/s and the vowels are well distinguished from each other in context, as indicated by the fact that only a few data points fall on or above the y = x line.

The phoneme /h/ was chosen for study by Pierrehumbert and Talkin (in press) because characterizing its source was a relatively tractable problem, in comparison to phonemes that have an oral constriction as well as a distinctive laryngeal articulation. However, both the phonetics literature and informal observation indicate that prosodic structure has both widespread and large influences on source characteristics. For voiceless stops, the alternation between aspirated and glottalized variants under the control of syllable structure and stress is well known. The quantitative extent of such effects depends on the phrasal prosody; for example, Pierrehumbert and Talkin also report that the voice onset time for /t/ (in "tomahawk") is approximately doubled at an intonation phrase boundary even in the absence of a pause. Voiced stops range phonetically from voiceless unaspirated stops to voiced fricatives, with /d/ even having a sonorant allophone, the flap. Similarly, the weak-voiced fricatives can be produced as stops in a strong position and as sonorants in a weak one. Many speakers have an overall shift in voice quality after the main stress, with some adopting a breather quality and others a creaky one. In addition, in utterance final position we find a reduction in subglottal pressure and a tendency toward devoicing.

9.2.4   Consequences for speech technology

The examples discussed in Section 9.2.3 indicate that it is impossible to recognize the speech segments without recognizing the prosody and intonation. It is also impossible to recognize the prosody and intonation without recognizing the segments. For example, what counts as long /z/ would count as a short /s/. Thus a judgment about whether a particular fricative region was in phrase-final position (and had accordingly undergone phrase-final lengthening) would depend on what phoneme that region was taken to represent.

This situation causes some speech engineers to throw up their hands, asking "Which comes first, the chicken or the egg?" This sense of being at an impasse has its source in the assumption that speech processing must recover some aspect of the representation first, or bottom-up. A considerable effort has been put into analysis schemes that attempt to carry out bottom-up classification robustly; that is, without falling into the confusions or errors that can readily arise from the statistical overlap of phonemes taken out of context.

Note that there is no impasse as far as the human mind is concerned; it apparently recognizes the phonemes and the prosody together. Furthermore, in other areas we actually have a technology for knitting together local information into a coherent overall structure, and that is parsing. One forte, indeed a raison d'être, of parsing technology is its ability to handle nonlocal dependencies. For example, sentence (5) is ill-formed as it stands, but well-formed in the larger context in (6), and any serious proposal about sentence parsing provides a mechanism for dealing with this dependency.

5.   *You put in the basket.
6.   The pie that you put in the basket was delicious.

What we need to do for speech, then, is to develop parsers that can handle the observed nonlocal dependencies. The relevance of parsing technology to sound structure has already been established by Church's work on parsing syllable structure from a fine phonetic transcription, as discussed in Church (1983) and (1987). This important demonstration has been recently followed up by Randolph (1989), whose syllable parser takes as input a manually defined collection of predicates on the speech signal. The parsers we need would work from parameterizations of the speech signal that are automatically computable, rather than manually specified. They need to handle all levels of prosodic structure, as they interact with each other, instead of only the lowest level. In addition, they need to be trainable; that is, we need methods using a transcribed corpus to set the statistical parameters of a general grammar.

9.3   Prosody, intonation, and meaning

The example of a phonological representation given in Figure 9.2 above showed two streams of content, the phonemes and the intonation pattern. This section describes what intonation is like and how it relates to sentence prosody. It sketches what kind of information intonation and sentence prosody convey. The sketch will give an idea of what theoretical problems must be solved before a computationally tractable formal treatment becomes available.

9.3.1   The English intonation system

English has a large variety of different intonation patterns. The same words can be produced with many different patterns, with different semantic and pragmatic meanings. Figure 9.7 shows f0 contours for a few different renditions of the phrase "another orange". The patterns are labeled according to the transcription system developed in Pierrehumbert (1980) and modified in Beckman and Pierrehumbert (1986). The patterns are made up of pitch accents (which align with stressed syllables) and boundary tones, which mark phrasal edges regardless of stress. The pitch accents can consist of one or two tones, and the diacritic * is used to mark the tones that fall on the stress; in a bitonal accent the unstarred tone falls in the immediate vicinity of the starred tone, either on the same syllable or on a nearby one. A stressed syllable will lack a pitch accent if it belongs to a word that is not prominent in the phrase (for example, because it contains given information), but each phrase must have at least one pitch accent somewhere. Boundary tones are assigned for two levels of phrasing, which coincide in the

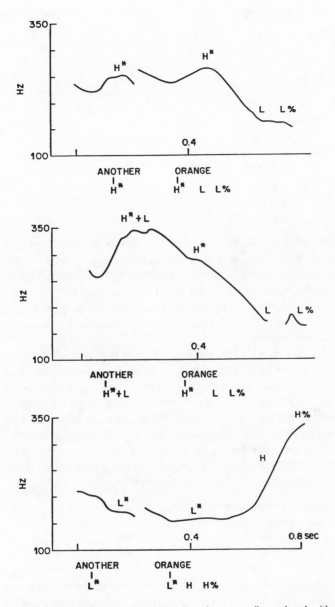

Figure 9.7. F0 contours for the phrase "another orange", produced with a variety of intonation patterns. Transcriptions are according to the system developed in Pierrehumbert (1980) and Beckman and Pierrehumbert (1986).

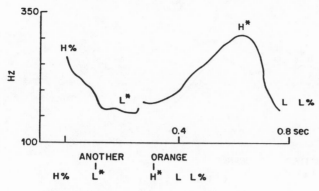

Figure 9.7. *(cont.)*

very simple materials in the figure. The diacritic % marks the boundary tone for the stronger phrase boundary (the intonation phrase boundary).

As the figure indicates, the pitch accents in a phrase can differ from each other. Furthermore, most of the possible combinations of pitch accents and boundary tones are attested. A compositional treatment of intonational meaning developed in Pierrehumbert and Hirschberg (1990) relates these different choices to different elements of pragmatic meaning.

It is important to distinguish what the intonation pattern is from where it goes. The same pattern can be aligned with the words in different ways, depending on the phrasing and on the phrasal stress as influenced by focus. Figure 9.8 shows the H* L H% pattern (a declarative intonation with a continuation rise) assigned to the same text in two different ways. In the first, the main stress falls on "vitamins"; in the second it falls on "Legumes". This is a difference in sentence prosody – the grouping and prominence of words in the sentence – but not a difference in intonation. The second version might arise in a dialogue that establishes the later words in the sentence as given information, e.g.,

7. Tell me some good sources of vitamins.
8. LEGUMES are a good source of vitamins.

9.3.2 Focus

Figure 9.8 brought out the phonological distinction between what the intonation pattern is and where it goes. This phonological distinction goes along with a distinction in the type of meaning conveyed. This section discusses meaning differences related to differences in the location of pitch accents. Discussion of what intonation patterns proper mean will follow in Section 9.3.3.

In the linguistics literature, words like "LEGUMES" in example 7 are described as focused. These elements are marked with pitch accents and other

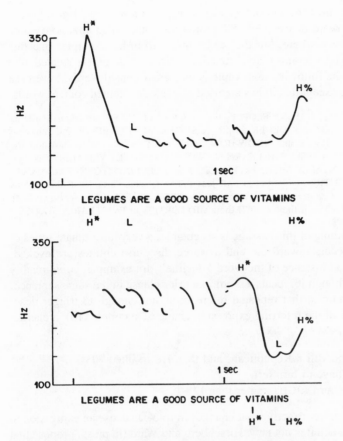

Figure 9.8. F0 contours for a declarative pattern with a continuation rise, produced on a sentence with the main phrase stress in two different places. Stress on "legumes" would be appropriate if previous context had already introduced the rest of the information in the sentence.

phonetic manifestations of emphasis, such as long and fully produced stressed vowels. In the natural language processing literature "focus" is used in a different sense. Discourse entities are taken to be in focus if they belong to a set of entities that have been (directly or indirectly) evoked in the discourse, and that are presumed to be salient for the conversational participants. (See Grosz and Sidner, 1986.) Because the words for already salient discourse entities are often (though not necessarily) deaccented, these two differing usages can lead to confusion. I will use "focus" in the sense it is used in linguistics.

Focus has a conspicuous relationship to the distinction between old and new information, with new information tending to receive focus. A heuristic developed by Silverman for assigning pitch accents in a text-to-speech system brings out this relationship while revealing its limitations. The system maintained a buffer of the forty most recent content words (modulo affix stripping). Content words on the list were deaccented. Silverman also states that function words were deaccented everywhere, but the reader infers from his examples that this rule was restricted to monosyllabic function words, with others treated like content words. In the following text, capitals indicate accented words, lowercase deaccented words, except that italics are used to mark deaccented content words.

9.   In the MINDS of MANY PEOPLE, the EFFECTS of AGING are REGARDED as NEGATIVE. At BEST, OLDER people are SEEN as MORE CAREFUL and as having *more* EXPERIENCE and KNOW-HOW, but RESISTANT to CRITICISM and IN-STRUCTION, and SLOW to LEARN. At WORST, ANYONE OVER THIRTY is seen as LESS MENTALLY ABLE, less HEALTHY, and DECLINING GENERALLY. CUR-RENT SCIENTIFIC OPINION is FAR less PESSIMISTIC. IT is TRUE that TESTS SHOW a *decline* in *mental ability* as *people* GROW *older,* but this *decline* is NOT SIGNIFICANT until they REACH their MID FORTIES or EVEN EARLY SIXTIES.

Although the beginning of this passage is acceptable, a very unfortunate series of deaccentuations occurs toward the end as more discourse entities are evoked. Note that the second instance of the word "decline", for example, could readily be accented even though it repeats a word in a prior clause in the same sentence. Many examples indicate that repeated reference is not enough to trigger deac-centing, if the role of the referring expression changes. Example (10), a classic, is due to Lakoff (1971).

10.   John called Bill a Republican, and then HE insulted HIM.
11.   Now we have to turn left.
      – No, we turn RIGHT rather than LEFT.

However, it is unclear exactly what changes in role can cause an expression to be accented even when it is not new. Hirschberg and Ward (in press) propose that the pronouns in (10) are accented because they appear with new case features; although Bill is already mentioned in the discourse, he is new as an AGENT. This suggestion appears to be a step in the right direction, because it takes focus not to apply to words per se, but rather to words as they function in sentences and discourses. However, Hirschberg and Ward have not empirically evaluated or even proposed a treatment of all cases of accent on previously mentioned words. In addition, a formal theory is needed for cases in which words not previously mentioned are deaccented because they are sufficiently inferable.

Focus also contributes to meaning by affecting the scope of adverbs, as in the following examples analyzed in Rooth (1985).

12.   a. I only said that Carl likes HERRINGS.
      b. I only said that CARL likes herrings.
13.   a. A u usually follows a Q.
      versus
      b. A U usually follows a q.

(12a) is false if I said that Carl likes some other type of fish; (12b) is false if I said that someone else likes herring. Although (13b) is true, (13a) is false because most u's follow some other letter than q. Rooth develops a technical treatment of such phenomena within the framework of Montague semantics. However, this treatment does not handle the phenomena sketched in (9) through (11), and a comprehensive formal treatment of focus is still not available. Filling this need will be an important step toward the creation of computer programs that either provide or understand prosody.

9.3.3 *Information conveyed by tunes*

Listeners infer from the intonation pattern information about the speaker's attitude, his goals in making his utterance, and the type of speech act he intends to perform. For example, Sag and Liberman (1975) discuss cases in which intonation can fairly reliably serve to suggest that a syntactic yes/no question is really an indirect request.

However, further investigation has shown that the basic meanings of intonation patterns cannot be taken to be speaker attitudes or types of speech acts. In different contexts, the same pattern can be associated with different attitudes or speech acts and likewise different patterns can be associated with the same attitudes or speech acts. Therefore, this information must be inferred from basic meanings as they interact with context. The general character of the basic meanings for intonation patterns is brought out by two highly important case studies.

Ladd (1978) investigated the so called "vocative" pattern, which has an f0 peak on the stressed syllable and then falls to a mid value, sustained to the end of the utterance. This pattern is transcribed H*+ L H L% in Pierrehumbert's notation, and is often used for calling out to someone, e.g.,

14. Christopher! Your lunch!

Ladd shows that this pattern is not really a vocative. It cannot be used for calling out in a true emergency; it can be used on sentences other than vocatives. One example he discusses is

15. Watch out for the crevasse!

Mountain climbers warning of a possible emergency would hardly use the H*+L H L% pattern on this sentence; however, it might be used by the abominable snow mother giving her child a reminder as he departs for school. Ladd suggests that the basic or general meaning of the contour is to mark information that should be in some way expected or known.

Two studies by Ward and Hirschberg (1985, 1988) analyzed superficially diverse uses of the rise-fall-rise, or L*+H L H% contour. This pattern is commonly used to convey either uncertainty or incredulity, as in the second and third turns of the following conversation, respectively:

16.   Did you take out the garbage?
      Sort of.
      Sort of!

The first study, dealing only with the "uncertainty" reading of the contour, proposes that the contour is appropriate when a scale of alternatives is available (because of the preceding material in the discourse or the utterance that carries the contour itself). The contour conveys uncertainty with respect to the scale. This uncertainty could be about whether the value of the accented item on the scale is appropriate, about whether the scale is the particular scale that is appropriate, or about whether a scale is appropriate at all. The second study unifies the "uncertainty" and "incredulity" readings by proposing that the contour conveys lack of speaker commitment with respect to the scale. It also demonstrates experimentally using LPC hybridization that the same melody is actually used in both cases.

This work provides strong evidence that different melodies do not directly convey truth, speaker attitude, or emotion. A person might use the contour on information that is true if some aspect of the social situation makes him uncertain about asserting it. On the other hand, on the "incredulous" reading, he could use it to mark information that he wishes to imply to be false. The first "sort of" in (16) is polite and even timid; the second, which uses the very same melody, is angry and assertive. Thus deductions about matters such as truth, anger, politeness, or assertiveness are made from the basic meaning of the contour and from all other information in the context, including the meaning of the words, the voice quality, and the relationship between the speakers.

Following up this approach in their compositional pragmatics for tune meanings, Pierrehumbert and Hirschberg (1990) claim that pitch accents in general convey information about how the accented item is related to the mutual beliefs being built up during the course of a conversation. Meanings for all six pitch accents are proposed. For example, the L* marks information whose status is in doubt:

17.   Your name is Mark Liberman?
           L* H   H%

It can also suggest that the information is already known; compare (18b) ("For your information . . . ") with (18c) ("As you should already be aware . . . ")

18.   a. Let's order the Chateaubriand for two.
      b. I don't eat beef.
             H* L H%
      c. I don't eat beef.
             L* L H%

The L* is also used on information that is extrapropositional. One example is

The L* is also used on information that is extrapropositional. One example is the use of L* on "now" when used as a discourse marker. In Litman and Hirschberg's (1990) study of tapes from a radio talk show, they found that L* was much more common on instances of the word "now" used to mark organization of the discourse than it was on instances of the same word used as a temporal adverb. Postposed vocatives provide a second example of L* on extrapropositional information, according to the analysis in Beckman and Pierrehumbert (1986).

19.   Your lunch is ready, Sam.
      L* L H%

We see from these examples that intonation conveys pragmatic information that has a central function in successful dialogue and is poorly marked in ordinary text. Because of this, analysis of intonation has the potential for playing an important part in systems that engage in dialogue with people. Any effective use of intonation for this purpose, however, will require substantial progress in circumscribing and formalizing the pragmatic deductions that human listeners perform with such virtuosity.

9.3.4   Will f0 assist word recognition?

Researchers who have little experience with intonation sometimes hope that, if fully exploited, it could resolve ambiguities that are presently found to be problematic. However, the sketch in Section 9.3.3 makes it clear that f0 cannot be expected to substantially assist word recognition in unrestricted running speech. This is the case because the melody is not provided by the lexical choice, but rather functions as a separate simultaneous channel of information.

In order to appreciate this point, consider the phonological reasons for a syllable to exhibit a high f0 value.

It is stressed and has a H* pitch accent.
It is in the domain of a H boundary tone.
It is in between two H tones.

Reasons for it to exhibit a low f0 value are:

It is stressed and has a L* pitch accent.
It is in the domain of a L boundary tone.
It is in between two L tones.

That is, any f0 value is phonologically compatible with any stress pattern, and the primary determinant of f0 is the phrasal melody rather than any aspect of the word.

In view of this situation, the probability distributions for f0 in relation to stress presented in Waibel (1988) should not be unsurprising. They show that the f0 values for unstressed syllables are not in general very different than those for stressed syllables. F0 might provide useful information about stress in extremely restricted domains that effectively constrain the intonation patterns used.

9.4   Conclusion

This chapter has discussed two areas in which our present scientific understanding of prosody and intonation has ramifications for the future of speech technology. First, we considered the problems posed by the prosodic and intonational control of allophony, emphasizing the nonlocal long distance dependencies that pose the most serious challenges. The lesson from these examples is that future technology will need to integrate the representational insights of modern phonology with the effective training procedures now available only for HMMs. Second, we laid out some types of pragmatic information that are conveyed by intonation. Because this pragmatic information is both central to effective dialogue and poorly marked in text, intonation has the potential for playing an important role in interactive systems. However, considerable progress in formalizing pragmatic inference will be necessary to make this possible.

In the discussion of these two cases, speech recognition and speech synthesis have been treated together. From a strategic point of view, these fields face many of the same problems. Coordinating work more tightly in these areas would help assist progress in speech technology in general.

References

Ananthapadmanabha. (1982). "Truncation and Superposition," STL-QPSR 2-3/1982, 1–17, Royal Institute of Technology, Stockholm.

Ananthapadmanabha and G. Fant. (1982). "Calculation of True Glottal Flow and its Components," *Speech Communication,* 1, 167–184.

Beckman, M., and J. Pierrehumbert. (1986). "Intonational Structure in Japanese and English," *Phonology Yearbook 3,* 255–310.

Bolinger, D. (1989). *Intonation and its Uses.* Stanford University Press.

Church, K. (1983). *Phrase-structure Parsing: A Method for Taking Advantage of Allophonic Constraints.* Ph.D. Dissertation, MIT. Distributed by Indiana University Linguistics Club, Bloomington.

Church, K. (1987). "Phonological Parsing and Lexical Retrieval." In U. Frauenfelder and L. Tyler, Eds., *Spoken Word Recognition* (a Cognition Special Issue), MIT Press, Cambridge. 53–70.

Fant, G. (1987). "Interactive Phenomena in Speech Production," *Proc. of 11th International Congress of Phonetic Sciences.*

Fourakis, M. S. and R. Port. (1986). "Stop Epenthesis in English," *J. of Phonetics,* 14, 197–221.

Gobl, C. (1988). "Voice Source Dynamics in Connected Speech," STL-QPSR 1/1988, Royal Institute of Technology, Stockholm, 123–159.

Granstrom and Carlson. (1986). *Linguistic Processing in the KTH Multi-lingual Text-to-Speech System*, International Conference on Acoustics, Speech, and Signal Processing. 45(1)1–4.

Grosz, B. and C. Sidner. (1986). "The Structures of Discourse Structure," *Computational Linguistics*, 12(3).

Harris, K. (1978). "Vowel Duration and its Underlying Physiological Mechanisms," *Language and Speech*, 21(4), 354–361.

Hertz, S. (1982). "From Text to Speech with SRS," *J. Acoust. Soc. Am.*, 72(4), 1155–1170.

Hirschberg, J. and G. Ward. (in press). *Accent and Bound Anaphora*.

Hyman, L. (1985). *A Theory of Phonological Weight*. Foris Publications, Dordrecht.

Ishizaka, K. and J. L. Flanagan. (1972). "Synthesis of Voiced Sounds from a Two-mass Model of the Vocal Cords," *Bell Syst. Tech. Jour.*, 51, 1233–1268.

Jelinek, F. (1985). "The Development of an Experimental Discrete Dictation Recognizer." *Proceedings of the IEEE*, 73(11), 1616–1625.

Ladd, D. R. (1978). "Stylized Intonation," *Language*, 54, 517–540.

Lakoff, G. (1971). "Presupposition and Well-formedness." In *Semantics: An Interdisciplinary Reader in Philosophy, Linguistics and Psychology*, 329–340. Cambridge Univ. Press.

Lea, W. A. (1980). "Prosodic Aids to Speech Recognition." In W. A. Lea, ed., *Trends in Speech Recognition*. Prentice-Hall, Englewood Cliffs.

Lehiste, I. (1970). *Suprasegmentals*. MIT Press.

Levinson, S. (1985). "Structural Methods in Automatic Speech Recognition." *Proceedings of the IEEE*, 73(11), 1625–1646.

Litman, D. and J. Hirschberg (1990). "Disambiguation Cue Phrases in Text and Speech." *Proceedings of COLING 90*, Helsinki.

McCarthy, J. and A. Prince. (1990). "Foot and Word in Prosodic Morphology: The Arabic Broken Plural," *Natural Language and Linguistic Theory*, 8, 209–238.

Monsen, R. B., A. M. Engebretson and N. R. Vemula. (1978). "Indirect Assessment of the Contribution of Subglottal Air Pressure and Vocal-fold Tension to Changes of Fundamental Frequency in English," *J. Acoust. Soc. Am.*, 64, 65–80.

Pierrehumbert, J. (1980). *The Phonology and Phonetics of English Intonation*, MIT Ph.D. dissertation. Available from Indiana University Linguistics Club, Bloomington, Indiana.

Pierrehumbert, J. (1990). "A preliminary study of consequences of intonation for the voice source." In *Quarterly Progress and Status Report, Speech Transmission Laboratory*, Royal Institute of Technology, Stockholm.

Pierrehumbert, J. and M. Beckman. (1988). *Japanese Tone Structure, Linguistic Inquiry Monograph Series 15*, MIT Press, Cambridge.

Pierrehumbert, J. and J. Hirschberg. (1990). "The Meaning of Intonation Contours in the Interpretation of Discourse." In Cohen, Morgan, and Pollack, eds., *Intentions in Communication*. SDF Benchmark Series in Computational Linguistics, MIT Press, Cambridge.

Pierrehumbert, J. and D. Talkin. (in press). "Lenition of /h/ and glottal stop," in Ladd and Doherty (eds.), *Papers in Laboratory Phonology II*, Cambridge University Press, Cambridge.

Rabiner, L. and B. H. Juang. (1986). "An Introduction to Hidden Markov Models." *IEEE ASSP Magazine* (1) 4–16.

Randolph, M. (1989). *Syllable-based Constraints on Properties of English Sounds*. Ph.D. dissertation, MIT.

Rooth, M. (1985). *Association with Focus*. Ph.D. dissertation, U. Mass., Amherst.

Sag, I. and M. Liberman. (1975). "The Intonational Disambiguation of Indirect Speech Acts." *Papers from the Eleventh Regional Meeting of the Chicago Linguistic Society*, Chicago Linguistic Society, University of Chicago. 487–497.

Selkirk, E. O. (1984). *Phonology and Syntax: The Relation Between Sound and Structure*. MIT Press, Cambridge.

Silverman, K. (1987). *The Structure and Processing of Fundamental Frequency Contours*. Ph.D. dissertation, Cambridge University.

Steele, S. (1985). *Vowel Intrinsic Fundamental Frequency in Prosodic Context*. Ph.D. dissertation, University of Texas at Dallas.

Titze, I. R., and D. T. Talkin. (1979). "A Theoretical Study of the Effects of Various Laryngeal Configurations on the Acoustics of Phonation," *J. Acoust. Soc. Am.*, 66, 60–74.

Waibel, A. (1988). *Prosody and Speech Recognition*. Pitman, London.

Ward, G. and J. Hirschberg. (1985). "Implicating Uncertainty; The Pragmatics of Fall-Rise Intonation," *Language* 61, 747–776.

Ward, G. and J. Hirschberg. (1988). "Intonation and Propositional Attitude; the Pragmatics of the L*+H L H%." *Proceedings of the 5th Eastern States Conference on Linguistics*, 512–522.

PART VI

Conclusion

10   The future of computational linguistics

MADELEINE BATES AND RALPH M. WEISCHEDEL

10.1   Introduction

One of the most delightful features of a small symposium is that it allows for
protracted discussions in which many people participate. Ample time for discussion was built into the symposium schedule throughout, but we allocated a
special two-hour slot to challenge ourselves to identify the most significant
problems capable of being solved in a five- to ten-year period. That they be
solvable in that time frame challenges us beyond what we can see, but not
beyond what we can reasonably extrapolate. That their solution be significant
takes the discussion beyond questions of purely academic interest.

Furthermore, at the suggestion of one of the government representatives, we
asked what applications should drive research (much as the application of natural
language interfaces to database drove research in the 1970s and 1980s).

All attendees, including representatives of various governmental agencies,
participated in this discussion. To keep our thoughts large, we construed natural
language processing (NLP) as broadly as possible, freely including such areas as
lexicography and spoken language processing.

To direct the discussion without focusing it too tightly, we set forth the following questions:

1. What are the most critical areas for the next seven (plus or minus two)
    years of natural language processing? ("Critical" is taken to mean that
    which will produce the greatest impact in the technology.)
2. What resources are needed (such as people, training, and corpora) to
    accomplish the goals involved in that work?
3. What organization is needed (e.g., coordinated efforts, international
    participation) to accomplish those goals?
4. What application areas and markets should open up in response to
    progress toward those goals?

The first question is addressed in Section 10.2 below. Questions 2 and 3 are
combined in Section 3, and the final question is covered in Section 10.4.

283

10.2   Critical areas for work in NLP

Because the meeting was conducted as a brainstorming session, the reader should not interpret any of the suggestions as representing a unanimous view, or even a majority view. The following suggestions are presented in the order in which they were originally proposed:

1. Grammars. Most important are grammars that cover a broad range of language as measured by corpora of collected texts, not just a broad set of examples. These grammars should specifically facilitate the integration of speech and discourse. The group felt a strong need for broad coverage grammars in constrained formalisms that could be shared among organizations.

2. Automatic methods to derive models of syntax, semantics, and probabilities; self-adapting systems. Many domains have either idiosyncratic subgrammars or idiosyncratic lexical entities (such as part numbers consisting of two letters and three digits). In order to obtain useful systems, it will be necessary to move strongly away from hand-crafted knowledge bases such as grammars and semantic rules. Automatic methods of inferring knowledge bases (or of adapting previously existing knowledge bases) will have a large payoff for both theoretical and practical work. Methods that work with smaller, rather than larger, bodies of original data are to be preferred, but very little is currently known about the amount of data that will be required for various automatic methods to work effectively.

3. Knowledge representation of sound structure. This would be useful in incorporating prosodic information into the understanding process. For further information on this topic, see the chapter by Janet Pierrehumbert in this volume.

4. Integration of speech and natural language. Many participants felt that the development of practical speech interfaces is essential for the eventual success of NLP in the marketplace. Others felt that speech alone would not necessarily bring about either financial or technical success. Nonetheless, speech is an important part of language use and will certainly continue to be an important field of research.

5. Methods for combining analytic and stochastic knowledge. Both theoretical linguistics and computational linguistics have tended to focus on symbol manipulation mechanisms. Although there is no mathematical reason for these mechanisms to be devoid of statistical models, they almost invariably have been. Surely, some linguistic phenomena are rare whereas others are common. Even grammaticality and ungrammaticality are relative, not absolute. An appropriate hybrid of stochastic and knowledge-based techniques is likely to be more powerful than either alone.

6. Ecological study of language. This is the study of what people actually say in diverse contexts. For example, a mother unconsciously uses different vocabulary, syntax, and probably other linguistic attributes when talking to a one-year-old child than she does when talking with a six-year-old child; a person giving orders uses different language than a person requesting information; a person trying to clarify a misunderstanding with another person will probably use different language than a person trying to clarify a similar misunderstanding with a machine. Very little is known about how to characterize these language differences, or about how to use those differences in building language understanding systems.

7. Methodology. Until quite recently, normal research technique revolved around in-depth study of some examples, and the development of an account of those examples with no analysis of how frequently or real those examples were compared to any other set. Rather than placing such heavy reliance on intuition, of late there has been a strong movement toward the analysis of corpora, that is, language that is collected in real or at least realistic settings. This is clearly a major step forward for the field, and it should be encouraged. One outcome of this process is that there is increased emphasis on the empirical evaluation of systems for NL processing using large corpora and knowledge bases.

8. Intention in discourse. By understanding more about how intention is conveyed in human discourse, we may make it possible for computers to infer better the intentions of their users, thus making the computer systems more helpful and the users more satisfied.

9. Measuring utility of NL systems. This is an attempt to focus on the ultimate users of systems that involve NL processing, to determine just exactly what benefit they derive from the system's NL capabilities. In some areas this is fairly clear (processing N messages per day X% faster by machine than by humans will save $Y per year, and will change the error rate by Z%), but in others, such as NL interfaces to databases, it is much harder to express and to quantify.

10. Ways to evaluate accurately and meaningfully the effectiveness of NL systems. This is clearly related to the previous point, but it is not identical. There are aspects of NL systems that developers need to quantify and evaluate whether or not they directly map into perceived benefits by the users. Evaluation should become an integral part of every NL system development, whether it is to be a product or a research demonstration system.

11. Knowledge representation for NLP. This may be considered an old topic, because it has been around virtually since the beginning of NL processing, but participants felt that a particular area that promises high payoff in the near future is the study of representation and reasoning about events.

12. Dialogue phenomena. Large bodies of text exhibit discourse structure, but conversations between two (or more) parties exhibit dialogue structure and phenomena that are quite different from what occurs in text. Clarification sub-dialogues abound. Fragments of language are produced frequently. Interruptions are common. New subjects are introduced in a variety of ways. Will computer systems have to be as facile as humans in order to carry on spoken dialogues? Probably not, but right now we do not know how much computer systems will have to be able to do, or even how to characterize it.

13. Interaction phenomena for the human-computer interface. Many people feel that trying to manipulate language of the sort that people produce for one another is not only too hard, but also unnecessary. People will almost certainly modify their use of language when they are faced with a much less than human machine, but we know very little of what form this new interaction will take.

14. Tools for coping with and analyzing large amounts of data. Examples might include tools for corpus collection, corpus analysis and sharing, lexicon development, and evaluation. As more and more groups are working with larger and larger amounts of data, the need for good software tools becomes acute, and the potential for cross-fertilization of research work becomes enormous.

15. Partial understanding. How can one represent information that is only partially understood? What effect does this have on other components of a fully integrated system, such as reasoning, or the user interface? Under what circumstances is partial understanding sufficient? When and how should it be clarified?

This listing is very different from what would have been produced by a similar group a decade ago, yet there are some interesting similarities as well. The desire for grammars with broader coverage, for knowledge representation to support the reasoning that is an integral part of language understanding, for the inclusion of speech, and for systems capable of handling dialogues in a theoretically based way has been with us for much longer than a single decade.

But the widespread emphasis on dealing with large amounts of data is quite new, as are the pushes toward evaluation and partial understanding, the inclusion of techniques from other disciplines (such as the way probabilities are used in speech processing), and the desire to collect data.

10.3   Resources and organizations needed

Several efforts are already underway to facilitate the availability of linguistic data. A Consortium for Lexical Research has been started at New Mexico State University under the auspices of the Association for Computational Linguistics. It will serve as a repository for lexical resources, including both data and software.

The Data Collection Initiative of the Association for Computational Linguistics will distribute material at cost (that is, at the cost of the media used for distribution). The raw text corpora in this collection are not proprietary, nor are the tools that are being built to operate on them, but perhaps some of the databases, complement structures, etc., may be proprietary.

Sue Atkins reported that Oxford University Press, SRI, the University of Oxford, the British Library, the University of Lancaster, and the University of Cambridge are supporting this consortium, which will build a British National Corpus, and, in addition, build a database (and ultimately a machine-readable dictionary). The consortium is trying to get government matching funds for the project.

In Japan, the Electronic Dictionary Research Project (EDR) is a multi-year, joint government/industry project to collect large corpora, labeling them morphologically, syntactically, and semantically.

The following additional needs were expressed:

1. Collections of spoken language, containing both the speech and the transcribed language

There are several corpora of spoken language data that are being collected under the DARPA spoken language systems program. These corpora are available from the National Institute of Standards and Technology (NIST). Anyone interested in learning more about these corpora should contact either David Pallett, NIST, Technology Building Room A-216, Gaithersburg, MD 20899, email at dave@ssi.ncsl.nist.gov., or Mark Liberman at the Linguistic Data Consortium, 215–898–0464, ldc@cis.upenn.edu.

2. Correct, complete, well-represented pronunciations in a machine-readable dictionary

The problems involved in defining such a dictionary are great, starting with the fact that speech and natural language people have different ideas of what constitutes a word.

3. A morphological analyzer for English and other languages

This should be a standard that all can use.

4. A formalism for input to a speech synthesizer

This should permit the transfer of more than lexical information; it should allow, for example, the constituent structure of the sentence to be represented, so the synthesizer can use this information for intonation.

10.4   Markets and applications

The question addressed was "What markets will be available in a 5-year time frame?" That is, what applied technology will be ready to transfer to product development within that time?

The initial suggestions put forth, in the order they were proposed, are:

1. Document checking. This should incorporate grammar and style checking that is as accurate and as easy to use as today's spelling checkers.

2. Data extraction from text. This assumes that the kind of information to be extracted from free text can be specified quite tightly, e.g., sufficient to be added to a relational database.

3. Speech production. This means a next-generation language and speech synthesizer that is capable of starting with a meaning representation (not a word or phoneme string), producing a word string, and then synthesizing speech whose quality is better than the current widely used DECTALK synthesizer from Digital Equipment Corporation. It is also important that this technology be easily ported to new domains.

4. Language generation. This could be used for summaries, report generation (e.g., generate a paragraph of text from a structured database, such as the summary of a medical or financial record of a patient/client from the last twenty-four-hour period), explanation, status monitoring, etc.

5. Languages other than English. In this area, improved machine assisted translation is possible. In addition, there is a need for automating non-translation tasks involving a second language, or the combination of a first and second language.

6. Over-the-telephone information services. This may or may not involve speech recognition or understanding. It may involve language generation.

7. Information retrieval. This is particularly needed for bodies of free text, as in tax law documents. Both the input and output of the IR system may have to deal with virtually unconstrained language.

8. Help/advisor systems. One example of this is over-the-phone help systems, which could be used for home appliance diagnosis and repair, simple income tax reporting questions, local directions, etc. These systems may involve an expert system, and may use both images and speech in their output.

9. Spoken language systems. If achievable, it will result in automatic dictation systems, voice control of devices, and highly interactive systems that are very cost effective because of the savings in human labor, and a world very different from what we are accustomed to!

After considerable discussion, it was decided that items 1, 3, and 4 could probably get private funding because of the potential for short-term return on investment.

On the other hand, problems 2, 5, and 7, although representing an enormous need, also require significant technical advances, and thus are less likely to attract private funding, and therefore a higher priority for government funding.

Author index

Allen, J., 245, 246n14, 250
Allen, J. F., 148, 152, 156, 160, 163, 165, 168, 172
Alshawi, H., 101, 103, 152, 155, 169
Altmann, G., 240, 244, 245
Amsler, R. A., 53, 93, 101, 117
Ananthapadmanabha, 266
Appelt, D., 247
Apresjan, Ju. D., 50n4, 51
Atkins, B. T., 38, 39, 43, 52, 53, 76n, 77, 78, 79, 81, 84, 86, 88, 92, 94, 100, 101, 120, 128
Ayuso, D., 14

Ball, C. N., 185
Bar-Hillel, Y., 147
Barwise, J., 135n1, 136, 216
Bates, M., 4, 31
Beckman, M., 184, 234, 262, 270, 271, 277
Bennett, M., 207
Bever, T., 148
Binot, J.-L., 13
Blake, E. G., 104
Boguraev, B. K., 13, 53, 76, 77, 94, 101, 102, 103, 104, 105, 109, 112, 113, 120, 128, 130
Boisen, S., 31
Bolinger, D., 228, 260
Brachman, R., 150, 153
Brennan, S. E., 148, 196n18, 209
Bresnan, J., 79, 90
Briscoe, T., 53, 76, 77, 101, 103, 120, 122, 128
Brown, G., 228
Buchler, J., 206, 207
Byrd, R. J., 53, 54, 57, 93, 108, 124, 126

Calzolari, N., 53, 101, 103
Carbonell, J. G., 26
Carlson, R., 259
Carroll, J., 244
Carter, R. J., 79, 82, 94
Channon, R., 186
Charniak, E., 168
Charpentier, F., 250

Chodorow, M. S., 13, 53, 93, 117
Chomsky, N., 89
Church, K. C., 94, 128, 270
Clark, H. H., 14
Cohen, A., 246n14
Collier, R., 246n14
Colmerauer, A., 149
Cooper, W., 228
Crain, S., 234, 244, 245
Crowther, W., 11, 13
Cruse, D. A., 42, 50, 51
Cullingford, R., 156
Curry, H., 231
Cutler, A., 228

Dale, R., 249
Davidson, D., 135, 136
Davis, J., 246n14, 248
Dowty, D., 232, 233
Dyer, M., 156

Eastman, C. M., 25
Engebretson, A. M., 261
Erteschik, N., 85n6
Etherington, D., 171
Evans, R., 120

Fallside, F., 246, 250
Fant, G., 264, 266
Fawcett, B., 157
Fellbaum, C., 82
Fillmore, C. J., 43, 50n4, 79, 84, 193
Finin, T. W., 14
Flanagan, J. L., 266
Fodor, J., 147, 158, 244
Foley, W. A., 79, 200
Fontenelle, T., 118
Fourakis, M. S., 260
Fox, E. A., 93
Freedman, D., 189n12
Friedman, M., 148
Frisch, A., 153
Fromkin, V. A., 25, 27

Garside, R., 128
Gazdar, G., 120

289

Subject index

absolute ill-formedness, 27
accented expressions, 272–7
acyclic data flow graphs, 17
adjacencies, 203–5
adverbs: and event sentences, 137–9; "fact" versus "manner" use of, 137–9; and focus, 274–5; relationships in sentences, 135–44
ambiguity: in current natural language systems, 156–7; and direct inference, 167; in discourse segments, 218, 243–5; and disjunction, 166–7; equality reasoning, 168–9; general reasoning approaches, 157–60; and intonation, 234, 243–5; in knowledge representation, 147–72; lexical aspects, 147; in machine-readable dictionaries, 126; requirements for representation of, 166–72; in syntax and structure, 147–8
anaphoric expressions: in discourse, 219–20; interpretation problem, 14; and pronouns, 180–1, 219–20
annotations, 15, 30
antecedent/pronoun sequence, 212–15, 222–5
argument-taking properties, 80, 82, 89–90
articulation, 260
attentional state, 179–225; centering model, 192–220; context effects, discourse, 208–23; and discourse structure, 179–225; and grammar, 203; and pronoun demonstrativity, 179–225; and surface form of referent, 201–3
augmented transmission network, 5–6
automatic methods, 100–2, 284; *see also* computational lexicography

backward-looking center, 179, 182, 192, 236*n*6
bilingual dictionaries, 94
bootstrapping, 11
BORIS system, 156
bottom-up classification, 269
boundary tones, 235, 242–3; and pragmatic meaning, 270–2
"bridges," 14

CASES system, 16, 22
CASREP, 31
center continuation, 195–7
center rule, 194–7
centering model (*see also* local center); definition, 194–5; discourse study, 187–220; pronoun interpretation, 179–225; review of, 192–200
"coarticulation," 242–3, 258
Cobuild Corpus, 40*n*2, 43, 95, 126*n*6, 127
cohesive chain data, 212–13, 222
collective/distributive distinction, 169
Collins Cobuild English Language Dictionary: ambiguity in communication component, 43–50; comparative word meanings, 39–73; homonymy versus polysemy, 39–43
Collins English Dictionary: ambiguity in communication component, 43–50; comparative word meanings, 37–73; homonymy versus polysemy, 39–43; verbs of sound, 93
Collins-Robert English-French Dictionary, 94, 124
combinatory grammars, 228–41
Common Facts Data Base, 13
compaction schemes, 109
complete inference strategy, 153
complete sentences, 24–9
compositional approaches: and logical form, 164–6; semantic interpretation, 151–2
computational lexicography, 99–130; and distributed lexical knowledge, 113–17; future of, 283–8; 'one-off' programs, 103–4; path specifications, 114–17; semantics in, 117–30; theory, 120–30
Consortium for Lexical Research, 286
constraint satisfaction, 172
context: and attentional state, discourse, 179–225; intonation effect, 233–6, 263–9; modeling of, 7; in speech segment pronunciation, 263–9
contour, 275–6
conversational data, *see* discourse
Core Language Engine, 155

292